What does it mean when the press reports that the European Union (EU) has taken action over the Balkans, in world trade, or in climate negotiations? The EU is undoubtedly a major actor in world affairs. When most major global issues are reported the European Union is increasingly in evidence. In some respects, it is as much a force in global politics as the United States of America. This book is a systematic study of the development and contemporary operation of the EU and its external policy.

Covering an impressive range of topics, *The European Union as a Global Actor* is the first text to challenge orthodox accounts of the EU in International Relations and European Studies. The book examines the entirety of the EU's external relations – whilst avoiding the use of the nation state as a template; and theorizes the nature of actors in contemporary world systems and the way they are constructed. Up to date, the book analyses recent global affairs such as Amsterdam Treaty changes, the EU's role in climate change negotiations, the process of Eastward enlargement and *Agenda 2000*.

Charlotte Bretherton and John Vogler's radical approach provides the most sustained analysis of the EU in global politics, filling a gap in existing literature for all those involved in European Studies, Politics and International Relations.

Charlotte Bretherton is Senior Lecturer in International Relations and European Studies at Liverpool John Moores University. She is the principal editor of *Global Politics: An Introduction*. **John Vogler** is Professor of International Relations at Liverpool John Moores University; his publications include *The Environment and International Relations* (with Mark Imber) also published by Routledge.

The European Union as a Global Actor

Charlotte Bretherton and John Vogler

London and New York

First published 1999
by Routledge
11 New Fetter Lane, London EC4P 4EE

Simultaneously published in the USA and Canada
by Routledge
29 West 35th Street, New York, NY 10001

Reprinted 2000, 2002

Routledge is an imprint of the Taylor & Francis Group

© 1999 Charlotte Bretherton and John Vogler

Typeset in Sabon by RefineCatch Limited, Bungay, Suffolk
Printed and bound in Great Britain by
Biddles Ltd, Guildford and King's Lynn

British Library Cataloguing in Publication Data
A catalogue record for this book is available from the British Library,

Library of Congress Cataloging in Publication Data
Bretherton, Charlotte.
    The European Union as a global actor / Charlotte Bretherton and
John Vogler.
        p.   cm.
    Includes bibliographical references and index.
    1. European Union countries – Foreign relations.   I. Vogler, John.
II. Title.
D1060.B735   1999
327.4–dc21   98–31537
                       CIP

ISBN 0–415–15052–3 (hbk)
ISBN 0–415–15053–1 (pbk)

Contents

Tables

Figures

Abbreviations

AASM	Associated African States and Madagascar
ACP	African, Caribbean and Pacific Group
ALA	Asian and Latin American countries
AMCHAM	American Chamber of Commerce
AMU	Arab Maghreb Union
AOSIS	Alliance of Small Island States
APEC	Asia-Pacific Economic Conference
ASEAN	Association of South East Asian Nations
ASEM	Asia-Europe (Summit) meetings
CAP	Common Agricultural Policy of the EC
CCAMLR	Convention on the Conservation of Antarctic Marine Living Resources
CCP	Common Commercial Policy of the EC
CCT	Common Customs Tariff of the EC
CEEC	Central and East European Countries
CEFTA	Central European Free Trade Area
CFC	Chlorofluorocarbon
CFSP	Common Foreign and Security Policy (Pillar II of the Treaty on European Union)
CIMIC	Civil–military cooperation specialists
CIS	Commonwealth of Independent States (of the former Soviet Union)
CJTF	Combined Joint Task Force
CMEA	Council for Mutual Economic Assistance (also known as Comecon)
CoP	Conference of the Parties
COREPER	Committee of Permanent Representatives (to the EC)
CSCE	Conference on Security and Cooperation in Europe (now OSCE)
CSD	Commission for Sustainable Development
DAC	Development Assistance Countries (of the OECD)
DG	Directorate-General (of the European Commission)
DTI	Department of Trade and Industry (of the UK government)

EAGGF	European Agricultural Guidance and Guarantee Fund
EAPC	Euro–Atlantic Partnership Council
EBRD	European Bank for Reconstruction and Development
EC	European Community
ECHO	European Community Humanitarian Office
ECJ	European Court of Justice
ECOFIN	Economic and Financial Affairs Council
ECOSOC	Economic and Social Council of the United Nations
ECSC	European Coal and Steel Community
ECU	European Currency Unit
EDC	European Defence Community
EDF	European Development Fund
EEA	European Economic Area
EEC	European Economic Community
EFTA	European Free Trade Association
EIB	European Investment Bank
EMU	Economic and Monetary Union
EP	European Parliament
EPC	European Political Cooperation
ERDF	European Regional Development Fund
ERTA	European Road Transport Agreement
ESDI	European Security and Defence Identity (within NATO)
EU	European Union
FAO	Food and Agricultural Organization of the United Nations
FAWEU	Forces answerable to the Western European Union
FCCC	Framework Convention on Climate Change
FCO	Foreign and Commonwealth Office
FDI	Foreign Direct Investment
FTA	Free Trade Area
GAC	General Affairs Council
GATT	General Agreement on Tariffs and Trade
GATS	General Agreement on Trade in Services
GDP	Gross Domestic Product
GMP	Global Mediterranean Policy (of the EC)
GSP	Generalized System of Preferences
HDI	Human Development Index (of United Nations Development Programme)
IFOR	Implementation Force (NATO-led deployment in Bosnia)
ICJ	International Court of Justice (the World Court)
IGC	Intergovernmental Conference
IGO	Intergovernmental Organization
IMF	International Monetary Fund
INC	Intergovernmental Negotiating Committee
INF	Intermediate Nuclear Forces
IPCC	Intergovernmental Panel on Climate Change

IPPC	Integrated Pollution and Prevention Control
IR	International Relations
ITO	International Trade Organization
JHA	Justice and Home Affairs (Pillar III of European Union)
JUSCANZ	Japan, the United States, Canada, Australia and New Zealand
KEDO	Korean Peninsula Energy Development Organization
LDC	Less Developed Countries
LLDC	Least Developed Countries
LRTAP	Long Range Transboundary Air Pollution Convention
MAI	Multilateral Agreement on Investment
MEDA	Mediterranean Assistance programme of the EC
Mercosur	Mercado de Sur (Southern cone common market)
MFA	Multifibre Agreement
MFN	Most Favoured Nation
MNC	Mediterranean Non-member Countries (of the EU)
NACC	North Atlantic Cooperation Council
NAFTA	North American Free Trade Agreement
NATO	North Atlantic Treaty Organization
NGDO	Non-Governmental Development Organization
NGO	Non-Governmental Organization
NIC	Newly Industrializing Countries
NIEO	New International Economic Order
NIP	National Indicative Programme
NIS	New Independent States (of the former Soviet Union)
NTA	New Transatlantic Agenda (US–EU)
NTB	Non-Tariff Barrier
OA	Official Aid (to CEEC and NIS undergoing transition)
ODA	Official Development Assistance
OECD	Organization for Economic Cooperation and Development
OPEC	Organization of Petroleum Exporting Countries
OSCE	Organization for Cooperation and Security in Europe
PfP	Partnership for Peace
Phare	Poland–Hungary: Aid for Reconstruction of the Economy (subsequently extended to other countries)
PIC	Prior Informed Consent
PoCo	Political Committee
QMV	Qualified majority voting (in EU Council of Ministers)
REIO	Regional Economic Integration Organization
SACEUR	Supreme Allied Commander Europe
SADC	South African Development Community
SEA	Single European Act
SEM	Single European Market
SFOR	Stabilization Force (NATO-led replacement for IFOR)

SMAP	Short and Medium Term Priority Environmental Action Programme (of the Euro–Mediterranean Partnership)
Stabex	System for the Stabilization of Export Earnings (in Lomé)
Sysmin	System for the Promotion of Mineral Production and Exports (in Lomé)
Tacis	Technical Assistance to the Commonwealth of Independent States
TEC	Treaty establishing the European Community (Treaty of Rome)
TEU	Treaty on European Union (Treaty of Maastricht)
TNC	Transnational Business Corporation
TOA	Treaty of Amsterdam
TRIMS	Trade Related Investment Measures
TRIPS	Trade Related Intellectual Property Measures
TRNC	Turkish Republic of Northern Cyprus
UNCED	United Nations Conference on Environment and Development, Rio, 1992
UNCHE	United Nations Conference on the Human Environment, Stockholm, 1972
UNCTAD	United Nations Conference on Trade and Development
UNGASS	United Nations General Assembly Special Session
UNDP	United Nations Development Programme
UNEP	United Nations Environment Programme
UNGA	United Nations General Assembly
UNPROFOR	United Nations Protection Force (in ex-Yugoslavia)
USTR	United States Trade Representative
VER	Voluntary Export Restraint
WEU	Western European Union
WTO	World Trade Organization

Acknowledgements

We gratefully acknowledge the generosity of the many external Mission staff and NGO representatives who spared time to talk with us, and whose insights have proved invaluable. We are deeply indebted, also, to the officials we interviewed at the European Commission and the General Secretariat of the Council of Ministers, the UK Foreign Office and the Department of the Environment.

AUTHORS' NOTE

Since entry into force of the Treaty on European Union (in November 1993) many commentators now refer exclusively to the European Union – thus making matters simpler for all concerned. Unfortunately, however, the bifurcation of the actor into the European Community (EC) and the European Union (EU) has considerable significance for our discussion of actorness in external policy, as will become evident. Because of this the title EC continues to be employed when referring specifically to the pre-Maastricht period and in circumstances where it is necessary to emphasize that the policy area under discussion falls within Community competence.

Introduction

Some time ago, when discussing our different research interests, we were struck by the extent to which the external activities of the European Community/Union[1] (EC/EU) impinged upon our areas of concern (global environment, development policy). This, we believed, raised two issues. First, that the cumulative impact of its external activities might suggest that the European Union was a significant actor in the global political system. And, second, that International Relations scholars, in focusing excessively upon the Union's efforts to construct a common foreign policy, were failing to capture its broader significance.

We were therefore concerned to establish the extent to which the European entity could function as an effective, capable actor across the range of its external activities. In the contemporary international system, and especially after the ending of the Cold War, the substance of international politics has broadened well beyond the traditional concerns of the Realist school. The broader context of our study of the European Union is provided by contemporary theoretical debates within the discipline of International Relations (IR). Ideas about actorness have always had a determining effect on the content of the discipline. The characteristics of the European Union have central significance for conceptualization of actorness in the contemporary global system. As John Ruggie (1993:140) has put it, the EU may be 'the first truly postmodern international political form'.

A related debate concerns the extent to which actors have volition. In our view actorness cannot be understood entirely through study of the behaviour of the entity in question. To a significant extent, actorness is constructed through the interplay of internal political factors and the perceptions and expectations of outsiders. We therefore decided, at the outset, that particular attention should be paid to the perceptions and expectations of third parties who interact closely with the EC/EU. To this end a programme of interviews was undertaken, between January 1996 and July 1997, with third country diplomats and representatives of non-governmental organizations. The exercise proved highly productive. In addition to providing fascinating detail about the conduct of our actor and its interlocutors, it produced insights concerning the manner in which perceptions and expectations interact in the construction of shared understandings. We are nevertheless aware that the insights we gained reflected the view from Brussels – where, inevitably, the EU's presence loomed large.[2] Material from our interviews can be found in each of the chapters which follow.

In order effectively to assess actorness in the various areas of EU external activity, it quickly became evident that, in addition to the broad conceptualization we had envisaged, attention must also be devoted to the legal bases and day-to-day practices of external policy. Our alarm at having to develop this 'Euro anorak' dimension to our work was hardly assuaged on discovering Hedley Bull's (1983:151) dismissal of such efforts – 'Nothing is more stifling to the discussion of European affairs'. Nevertheless, we persisted. In each of the policy areas studied we attempt to link a broad conceptualization of the EU's roles, and significance, as a global actor with empirical studies focusing upon the formulation, implementation and effectiveness of external policy. Here Chapter 2, which discusses the EC's central roles as a trade and economic actor, bears a heavy burden; in that it also establishes the basic legal and behavioural criteria which underlie externally oriented action more generally. These matters are further elaborated in Chapter 3, which discusses the role of the EU in the new global environmental diplomacy. Here, Member States have been unwilling to countenance the extensive Community competence that has long existed in the trade area. Instead the EC and Member States share participation in international environmental negotiations and agreements. This highlights the very significant tensions between the Commission and Member State governments which frequently diminish the coherence and effectiveness of action by the EU.

While we must necessarily pay attention to the procedures involved in formulating external policy, there is little discussion of the vexed question of the 'nature of the beast'. Contemporarily there is a sense that this is a tired issue; and that the EU of the late 1990s can simply be assumed to be a form of polity, its policies subject to analysis and evaluation in the same way as a 'domestic' political system.[3] This approach, which utilizes the methodology of Comparative Politics and, *inter alia*, the concepts of policy network analysis, provides an analytical framework which is sufficiently flexible to encompass the multiple sites and levels of formal and informal EU policy processes. However, when applied to external policy, this approach suffers from two major shortcomings.

First, successful application of Comparative Politics methodologies in the EC/EU context has tended to reflect the level of institutionalization of policy processes and interactions (Risse-Kappen 1996:61). This varies considerably according to issue area; but is a particular problem in relation to external policy. Here, there are significant differences in levels of institutionalization between issue areas where exclusive Community competence pertains, and where Comparative Politics methodologies might prove fruitful; areas where competence for external policy is shared between the Community and the Member States; and areas which fall under the aegis of the

Union. Matters are further complicated by the fact that issue areas subject to a particular set of rules are not coterminus with policy domains. Thus, even in matters of external trade, where Community competence is most firmly entrenched, there are anomalous or contested issue areas.

A further problem associated with utilization of a policy analysis perspective is that such an approach, when applied to external policy, introduces the temptation implicitly to treat the EU as a state – or, in all probability, as a would-be, partially formed or incompetent state. We have attempted to avoid reference to the state as comparator; and, also, to avoid locating the EU on a continuum – between intergovernmentalism and supranationalism, or between international organization and federal state. In treating the EU as *sui generis*, however, there is an obligation to offer a brief explication of its evolution and contemporary nature. Since there are numerous, excellent sources of such information, we focus below on matters of particular relevance to an understanding of EU actorness in external policy.

EVOLUTION OF THE EC/EU AS AN EXTERNAL POLICY ACTOR

Since its creation in 1958 the European Community has evolved considerably. It has extended both its membership and the scope of its policy competence; and in the process has changed its character in important ways. These processes of widening and deepening, and the institutional changes which have accompanied them, have impacted in different, and sometimes inconsistent, ways upon the capacity of the EC/EU to act externally. The tensions between widening and deepening remain very much a current issue.

The early phases of community building in Europe took place in the aftermath of the Second World War, at a time when Cold War tensions were increasingly evident. Thus European policy elites faced two major challenges – the need to reconstruct their economies and societies; and the need to ensure a stable and secure external environment in which the processes of reconstruction might prosper. In 1949 this latter concern was largely met through the creation of the North Atlantic Treaty Organization (NATO), which effectively linked United States military capabilities to the defence of Western Europe. Nevertheless, the need to secure peaceful relations between the states of Western Europe remained, as did aspirations to create a strong, united (Western) Europe capable of playing an important role in the post-war world.

To this end, two 'community-building' proposals were launched in the early 1950s. The European Coal and Steel Community (ECSC), established in 1952, aimed to initiate a process of economic integration, sector by sector, which would gradually reconfigure the political landscape of Europe. An immediate practical concern at the centre of this project was to inextricably link the future industrial production (including arms manufacture) of

France and Germany. Alongside the ECSC proposals, ambitious plans were launched for a European Defence Community (EDC). This essentially federalist proposal envisaged a fully integrated European army under supranational control. The defeat of this proposal, after more than two years of debate, was a major setback for federalist aspirations. It ensured that the traditional subject matter of International Relations – foreign and security policy and defence – were excluded from the formal policy agenda of the European Community. They have remained so.

The European Community, established in 1958, was an exclusively civilian body. The Treaty of Rome made no mention of foreign or security policy; nor, indeed, of defence. Responsibility for 'external economic relations', however, was entrusted to the Community. This flowed directly from the aspiration to create a common internal market, which necessitated formation of a customs union and levying a Common Customs Tariff (CCT). In consequence the EC was accorded responsibility for formulation and implementation of external trade policy – a responsibility which was to include external representation and negotiation by the Commission (on behalf of the Member States) in matters of international trade. A further sphere of external activity accorded to the Community by the Rome Treaty was the creation of association agreements with third countries, 'involving reciprocal rights and obligations, common action and special procedures' (Treaty establishing the European Community (TEC), Art.238 [310]).[4] This penultimate and somewhat Delphic provision of the TEC formed the basis for the construction of a vast network of differentiated and multi-faceted agreements between the EC and countries and regional organizations in all parts of the world.

Thus, while 'political' external policy (the traditional 'high politics' concerns of foreign and security policy) formally remained the exclusive responsibility of Member States, the significance of the Community's 'external economic relations' grew over time and inevitably impinged, in practice, upon 'political' relations. Despite attempts from the late 1960s incrementally to increase Member State cooperation on foreign policy matters, however, the distinction between political and economic relations has been maintained and institutionalized. Indeed, when the label 'political' is applied to aspects of external policy it continues to symbolize that, in this area, the commitment of Member State governments to common policies is weak and, in particular, that they are reluctant to countenance too close involvement of the Community/Commission. ('Sensitive' is another much used euphemism for such matters.)

There have been incremental, yet inconclusive, attempts to give overall political direction to external policy – which we refer to below and discuss in detail in Chapter 6. However these have been located outside the EC framework. Our more pressing concern is to explain the significant growth of the *Community's* external activities since 1958. Essentially we see this growth as reflecting a range of internal and external factors, which have combined to create understandings about the external roles which the EC can and should be expected to play. These fall broadly into three categories, which we discuss briefly below and which are reflected in our treatment of each of the policy areas examined subsequently.

- **Presence** – conceptualizes the relationship between internal development of the EC and external expectations.
- **Opportunity** – encapsulates factors in the external environment which enable or constrain actorness.
- **Capability** – refers to the capacity to respond effectively to external expectations and opportunities.

Presence and the construction of actorness

It is our contention, broadly following Allen and Smith (1990), that the Community's growing presence in international affairs has been of great significance. By presence we refer, essentially, to the ability to exert influence; to shape the perceptions and expectations of others. Presence does not connote purposive external action, rather it is a consequence of internal policies and processes.

Various aspects of the Community's evolution, in terms both of deepening and widening, have contributed to its international presence. The significant but largely unintended external impacts of the Common Agricultural Policy (CAP) and of the Single Market programme are discussed in Chapter 2. In both these policy areas, enlargement added to the EC's presence. In the case of the CAP, for example, the mechanisms by which agricultural policy has been managed, and its success in stimulating domestic agricultural production, has impacted significantly on world markets for temperate agricultural products; and has prompted political reactions from third parties to which the EC has been obliged to respond. The accession of Greece, Spain and Portugal in the 1980s greatly increased the quantity of Mediterranean products affected by the CAP. This impacted negatively upon the export potential of the Maghreb countries,[5] triggering a reaction which, in combination with other factors, led the EC to construct a new relationship with non-member Mediterranean countries. Thus, here, the EC's presence initiated a process through which actorness was constructed.

The impact of the Single Market has been of even greater significance. In particular it has had a magnet effect, in attracting foreign investment and in stimulating demands, from a wide range of third countries, for privileged access. Thus the notion of the Commission as 'gatekeeper of the Single Market' is developed in Chapter 2. Here, again, increased presence prompted reactions to which the EC was ultimately obliged to respond actively. One of the most important effects of the Single Market was the initiation of a process which led to the creation of the European Economic Area (EEA), and ultimately the accession of three new members – Austria, Finland and

Sweden – in 1995. This enlargement further increased the size and attractiveness of the Single Market, and hence the EC's presence in the international economy.

Today the EU is faced with major issues of deepening and widening which potentially impact, in significant ways, upon its presence and upon the capacity to act. Accession negotiations are under way with five Central and East European countries and Cyprus, and the EU is also involved in intense pre-accession relationships with further applicants. At the same time preparations for Economic and Monetary Union (EMU) and a single currency are almost complete. Enlargement will potentially enhance the presence of the EU, not least through expansion of the Single Market into areas where consumer demand is likely to be vibrant. However, enlargement will also increase the heterogeneity of the Union and place further strains upon policy processes which are inadequate to meet current needs. Here the failure, at Amsterdam in June 1997, to introduce the institutional reforms necessary to accommodate additional members augurs ill for the ability of current Member States to reach agreement on crucial matters. Economic and Monetary Union and the single currency will greatly increase the economic presence of the Union. Nevertheless here, again, inability or unwillingness to participate, on the part of some Member States, serves to emphasize the internal divisions affecting the Union. This could influence third party expectations of the performance of the Euro and hence undermine its contribution to the Union's presence.

The relationship between presence, external reaction and EC/EU policy response in the construction of actorness is inevitably complex and uncertain. It is reflected differently, and to varying degrees, in each of the policy areas and regions we discuss. Thus, while the EC's presence is experienced globally, it impacts with particular intensity in circumstances where third party expectations are focused primarily upon the EC. Differentiated relationships between presence and actorness are particularly evident in Chapter 5, where we compare the EC's relations with its Southern and Eastern peripheries; and Chapter 7, where approaches to security issues are discussed.

The EC's presence has undoubtedly increased as a consequence of the expansion of its size and policy scope. Nevertheless internal factors, associated with the legitimacy and efficacy of the EC's policy processes, have tended to influence third party perceptions, and hence expectations, of the EC's ability to act. Legitimacy has increasingly been an issue in recent years. In the case of Economic and Monetary Union, for example, public elite dissensus and evident lack of popular support have combined to raise doubts about the viability of the project. An enduring issue, and perhaps a more pressing problem for third parties, has been the efficacy of the decision making processes. Here, again, elements of deepening and widening have combined – to create arrangements whose complexity and obscurity both impinge upon the Community's domestic legitimacy and generate confusion among third parties. This diminishes the presence of the Community, in that it is perceived to be internally divided and, potentially, incoherent and ineffective in its actions. We deal further with this matter in our discussion of capability – which impinges, equally, upon the ability to respond to external opportunity.

Opportunity: the external environment of ideas and events

The external environment since the early 1980s is our particular concern. From this time, changes in perceptions of the international system and its operation have interacted with changes in the ideological climate, and with unfolding events – to produce an environment which has been particularly conducive to increased Community involvement in external policy.

From the mid 1970s the international system was increasingly perceived in terms of its (primarily economic) interdependence. In circumstances where the ability of states to govern effectively was deemed to be in question, the EC, a partially integrated regional policy system, appeared well placed to act on behalf of its members in the management of interdependence. Subsequently notions of interdependence have largely been supplanted by theses about globalization. Here the individual state is depicted as relatively impotent in the face of non-territorial economic actors operating in a system of globalized production and exchange relationships. More than ever before, the strong economic focus of globalization rhetorics, and the emphasis upon the inadequacy of the state to regulate the activities of globally oriented economic actors, appears to present opportunities for the EU to act externally on behalf of its members. Thus, it is argued 'the EU represents an unparalleled test of how government and politics can do more than simply react as other spheres of activity go global' (Leonard 1997:19). We discuss, in Chapter 3, the construction of an EC/EU role in just such an area – global environmental politics.

The rhetoric of globalization is closely linked to the prevailing ideological climate which, from the early 1980s, has increasingly been influenced by neoliberal ideas. While by no means uncontested internally, the reconceptualization, in neoliberal thought, of the relationship between states and markets – to prioritize the economic over the political – has resonated with a policy orientation already embedded at the Community level. This has been reflected internally, in the Single Market programme, and externally in the EC's trade relations and market opening strategies; particularly in the imposition of a range of market reform and other conditionalities in the 'third generation' association agreements of the 1990s (see Figure 2.2 and Chapters 4 and 5).

Theses of globalization and neoliberal ideological orientations have interacted with, and been greatly encouraged by, the series of events which have particular significance for the construction of the contemporary external roles of the EC/EU – that is the peaceful revolutions in Central and Eastern

Europe in 1989 and the dissolution of the Soviet Union in 1991 – which constituted the definitive ending of the Cold War. These events impacted upon the EC in a number of ways.

Most fundamentally, the end of the Cold War brought into question what had appeared to be the more or less fixed boundaries of the European project, thus challenging the appropriation of the concept 'European' by Community Europe. This was manifested in the removal of impediments to membership of the West European neutral countries, in particular Finland, and in the chorus of demands to 'return to Europe' emanating from Central and East European countries. More broadly, the ending of bipolar tensions has provided opportunities for the EC to develop 'external economic relations' with regions previously considered within the sphere of superpower influence – developing links with Cuba, for example, to the intense irritation of the US government.

The end of the Cold War also provided scope for the politicization of the EC's external relations. The collapse of state socialism contributed significantly to the dominance of neoliberal ideas; and this has been increasingly reflected in Western policies towards non-Western countries, including those of the EC/EU. Thus emphasis on observance of individual rights and freedoms, upon democratic principles and 'good governance' features routinely in agreements concluded between the Community and third parties. Beyond the rhetoric, the economic weight of the EC is increasingly employed to cajole or threaten, and indeed, to punish. The preferred EC approach, however, is through the construction of networks of influence, where the Community's own models of cooperation, 'partnership' and regional integration are heavily promoted. Indeed, the EC claims, as a regional organization, to be 'a natural supporter of regional cooperation initiatives' (ACP-EC 1997:23). Thus, in the post-Cold War period, the EC/EU has increasingly become an actor with an agenda.

The final area where the ending of the Cold War presents opportunities for actorness falls, at least in part, outside EC policy competence. The Soviet Union's (and subsequently Russia's) diminished ability to exert control, or even influence, over its former empire generated fears of political instability in countries close to the EC's borders. The Community response, here, has been to adapt its traditional concepts of partnership and cooperation. However, the outbreak of armed conflict in former Yugoslavia, in 1991, provided an 'opportunity' which the EC was ill prepared to meet.

Concerns about potential security risks on the borders of the Community, in circumstances where a continued US military presence in Europe was in question, were very evident in the early 1990s. They combined with a desire to exploit the new opportunities for a politicized external policy, to produce demands that the EC's capacity to respond to external opportunities, and external challenges, be re-examined.

Capability: the EC/EU policy environment

In Chapter 1 we discuss five fundamental requirements for actorness in international politics – commitment to shared values and principles; the ability to formulate coherent policies; the capacity to undertake international negotiation; access to policy instruments and the legitimacy of decision processes. Here we focus specifically upon those characteristics of the EC/EU policy system which impinge directly upon the ability to formulate policy.

The institutional complexity of the EU is largely a function of its evolution over time. In essence the decision making procedures constructed to meet the needs of six Member States across a relatively limited range of policy areas have been the subject of incremental reform rather than fundamental reformulation. Below we briefly outline those aspects of EC/EU evolution which are most pertinent to external policy.

The 1987 Single European Act (SEA), in amending the Rome Treaty, included a number of provisions having relevance for external policy. Most importantly, it provided Treaty status for a system of foreign policy cooperation, known as European Political Cooperation (EPC), which had evolved between Member State governments since 1970. However, as EPC was not incorporated into the Community, it remained an intergovernmental process between 'High Contracting Parties', and its newly established Secretariat was staffed by seconded Member State officials. Effectively the SEA institutionalized the division between political and economic elements of external policy. A further provision of the SEA which is noteworthy here is that ratification of Treaties and formal agreements with third parties was among new powers accorded to the European Parliament (EP). Since the EP has, at best, an advisory role in relation to most areas of external policy, the SEA provisions enabled it to become more proactive in supervising the terms of, and parties to, international agreements. Examples of the use of the EP's increased ability to influence external policy include delay or suspension of agreements to protest the human rights records of Morocco and Turkey, amongst others; addition of measures to support democratization to the financial assistance programmes for Central and Eastern European countries; and insistence that issues of gender equality be included on the agenda of accession negotiations. Nevertheless, while greater consideration must now be given to the views of the EP, the central relationship in terms of external policy remains that between the Council (representing the Member States) and the Commission.[6]

The 1993 Treaty on European Union is of great significance for our discussion of external policy. Its provisions were formulated during the course of a year long Intergovernmental Conference (IGC) which took place at a time, 1990–1, when the new opportunities and challenges provided by the end of the Cold War were very apparent. In recognition of this the Treaty on European Union (TEU) created the European Union, which was both founded upon and supplementary to the European Community. The Union was accorded a number of explicit and overarching political objectives, including –

> to assert its identity on the international scene, in particular through the implementation of a common foreign and security policy including the eventual framing of a common defence policy, which might in time lead to a common defence;
>
> (Art.B [2])

Thus it was intended that the Union would provide overall political direction, through a strengthened common foreign policy, for external policy generally. Among the objectives of Union foreign policy were the consolidation of democracy, respect for the rule of law and fundamental rights and freedoms. These principles were repeated in a revision to the TEC which provided specifically for an EC policy on development cooperation and have subsequently been incorporated in all agreements concluded by the EC. The TEU established principles for the guidance of policy, and aspirations for the acquisition of policy instruments in the sphere of defence. It did not, however, provide adequate mechanisms for formulating coherent policies; nor for effectively connecting the political aspirations of the EU to the economic weight of the EC.

The TEU created a new structure comprising three Pillars. However the Greek temple analogy which informs this appellation is far from appropriate, since the strength of the Pillars is noticeably unbalanced. Pillar I comprises the European Community,[7] and is by far the most substantial of the three Pillars. All the major internal policy areas which establish the EC's presence fall within Pillar I. Moreover, the Community's external responsibilities include trade, aspects of environmental policy and most areas of 'cooperation' and 'association' with third parties. Of great significance is the fact that the Community enjoys legal personality and can enter into formal agreements with third parties. The Union, which does not have legal personality, is unable to do so. Essentially, this reflects differing levels of Member State commitment to common policies in the issue areas encompassed by the Pillars. The differences in decision making procedures between the Pillars similarly reflect Member State sensitivities in relation to Pillar II and III policy areas.

Policy in Pillar I is formulated according to the Community method. Here the Commission has sole right of initiative, although the Council of Ministers ultimately decides upon the fate of measures proposed. An important role is played by the Committee of (Member State) Permanent Representatives to the EC (COREPER), and the numerous Pillar I Working Groups, comprising national officials and experts, which report to COREPER. Policy dossiers are discussed in the Working Groups and channelled to the Council via COREPER, whose recommendations are regularly adopted. The Council itself discusses only the more controversial items.[8] Council decisions, in Pillar I, are frequently taken by Qualified Majority. Thus, in external policy areas within Community competence, there is not an automatic Member State right of veto. Nevertheless Member States can (and occasionally do) block decisions on the grounds of 'national interest'.[9]

In Pillar I policy areas the role of the Commission is significant. Its structural position within the institutional framework of the Community has facilitated, indeed necessitated, the evolution of a leadership or 'policy entrepreneur' role (Cram 1994; Nugent 1995; Laffan 1997). Consequently the Commission has developed the capacity to respond to opportunities for action, and even to create such opportunities. Thus –

> The Commission, acting as a 'purposeful opportunist' has employed a variety of techniques aimed at expanding the scope of [Community] competence, and the extent of its own scope for action.
>
> (Cram 1994:199)

These comments apply equally to external and internal policy. Since external opportunities do not themselves create actorness, the Commission's role as 'purposeful opportunist' is central to understanding how the EC's expanded external policy role was constructed. The Commission's role in external relations has suffered a number of setbacks in recent years, however. Policy coordination has become increasingly difficult due to the fragmentation of the Commission's external relations effort (see Figure 1.1). This reflects both the increased size of the Commission itself and the additional burdens placed upon it by the TEU. However it is hoped that in the new Commission from 2000 this problem will be overcome. Perhaps of greater long-term significance is the challenge to the Commission's 'leadership' role provided by accordance (in the TEU) of an overarching role to the Union. Implicitly, this emphasizes the Commission's role in policy management. In the past the Commission has had inadequate resources, and scant enthusiasm, for its policy management tasks (Laffan 1997). Contemporarily, however, efforts are being made to overcome its 'management deficit' – indeed 'Sound Efficient Management' has been adopted as the theme for the latter half of the Santer Presidency (Interview, Commission DGIB, February 1998).[10] This indicates a pragmatic response to the new structures, and changing policy climate, following entry into force of the TEU.

Pillars II (Common Foreign and Security Policy (CFSP)) and III (Justice and Home Affairs (JHA)) are 'intergovernmental' in character – that is policy formulation takes place outside the Community framework, within the context of the Council of Ministers and its various Pillar II Working Groups, almost exclusively on the basis of unanimity. The operation of Pillar II is described in some detail in Chapter 6. In recognition of the Community's access to economic instruments, the Commission is 'fully associated' with policy making but, in marked contrast with Pillar I, has no special right of policy initiation. Here the Commission does not exercise a 'policy entrepreneur' role. Although the Commission and Member State governments may make policy proposals, policy initiation tends to fall to the Presidency. However policy implementation almost invariably involves major input from the Commission. Since the Commission does not regard itself as the servant of the Council, this arrangement is a source of considerable cross-Pillar tension, which causes numerous difficulties, some of them resulting in extreme pettiness. For example, the Council, in the context of CFSP, has a predilection for appointing Special Envoys, but has no means of providing for their expenses. In the ensuing delay, it has been known for Special Envoys to purchase flight tickets at their own expense (Interview, Council Secretariat DGE, July 1997). The Treaty of Amsterdam attempts to address these and other problems associated with the operation of CFSP (see Chapter 6).

In addition to regular, minor irritations, the structural tensions between the Pillars have serious implications for the implementation of external policy. Among these are problems of external representation and participation in international negotiations, which are particularly acute in areas where policy competence is unclear, or is shared between the Community and the Union. Environmental negotiations are the most evident example, here, although 'new issues' in trade policy are also problematic (see Chapters 2 and 3). Ultimately, the bicephalous nature of the EC/EU serves both to impede formulation of coherent policy/negotiating positions and to inhibit perceptions, and expectations, of actorness on the part of third parties.

In addition to reinforcing the division between political and economic aspects of external policy, the TEU, through making provision for Member State opt-outs from important areas of policy, introduced new notions of 'flexibility' into debates about the future of the EU. Subsequent discussion of various forms of differentiated integration – from multi-speed Europe to Europe *à la carte* – reinforce perceptions of a divided, incoherent policy actor. New opt-outs provided by the Amsterdam Treaty in the field of Justice and Home Affairs, together with explicit provision for flexibility in other policy areas, serve further to reinforce this perception. So too, does the failure, at Amsterdam, to agree the institutional reforms needed to accommodate the further enlargement of the Union for which negotiations have already begun.

ORGANIZATION OF THE BOOK

The interaction of presence, opportunity and capability in creating EU actorness is examined in each of the following chapters. Chapter 1, in particular, focuses upon these matters. It proceeds from a survey of approaches to actorness in the International Relations literature to an examination of the social construction of the EU's various external roles – through the interaction of external expectations and internal capability.

In order to provide maximum scope for exploring the continuities and discontinuities between actorness in different issue areas, the subsequent chapters are organized 'horizontally' according to policy area – an approach which departs from the more traditional focus upon the EU's bilateral relations with third countries or regions. However Chapter 5, in discussing relations with the 'near abroad', more closely resembles the traditional, 'vertical' approach. Nevertheless here, too, a horizontal focus to the chapter is provided through examination of EC/EU association and accession strategies.

We begin by discussing the relatively well established Community policy areas of trade, environment and development cooperation. Subsequently the areas of foreign and security policy and defence are examined. Here there is an aspiration, in principle, to develop common policies at the Union level – but in practice Member State political commitment frequently proves inadequate to permit such development. In considering the potential contribution of the EC/EU to European security and stability more broadly conceived, Chapter 7 moves beyond traditional approaches to security and defence matters to discuss the implications of the EU's presence as an 'island of peace'. Finally, Chapter 8 considers fundamental issues of identity – exploring both the relationship between identity and legitimacy which underpins actor capability; and the problematic development of an EU collective identity, which contributes, potentially, to perceptions of the EU's significance as a global actor – and hence to the social construction of actorness.

1   Actors and actorness in global politics
Locating the European Union

In its 1997 publication, *Agenda 2000: For a stronger and wider Europe*, the European Commission proposes a range of ambitious, global roles for the European Union –

> The Union must increase its influence in world affairs, promote values such as peace and security, democracy and human rights, provide aid for the least developed countries, defend its social model and establish its presence on the world markets ... prevent major damage to the environment and ensure sustainable growth with an optimum use of world resources. Collective action by the European Union is an ever increasing necessity if these interests are to be defended, if full advantage is to be taken of the benefits of globalization and if the constraints it imposes are to be faced successfully. Europe's partners ... expect it to carry out fully its responsibilities.
>
> (Commission 1997a:27)

Despite the hyperbole, the Commission's statement introduces a number of themes which are central to the book. First, it expresses certainty that the EU is a global actor of increasing significance in a range of policy areas. The principal aim of our study is to examine the extent to which this claim is justified. Second, it places particular emphasis upon external factors – the expectations of third parties and the opportunities and constraints associated with the broader external environment. These matters, again, are central to our concerns.

Understanding the extent to which the EU is an actor in the global system necessarily involves us in a wider debate in International Relations. This debate has fundamental significance for the study of the international system because it defines the characteristics of its constituent units. The primary question is, therefore, how do we recognize the actors in the system: are they merely states, or can other entities also fall within the category of actor? In the light of the very extensive changes to which the international system has been subject, and assertions about the declining relevance of the nation state, there is an important, related question as to how actorness is constructed and reconstructed over time. Finally, although we may observe a multi-actor system, not all of its constituents will have equal weight and significance. We must, therefore, be concerned with questions of relative effectiveness and the measurement of actor capability. We cannot infer actorness merely from the internal characteristics of a political unit, however; we must also consider the patterns of constraint and opportunity associated with the political and economic structures within which the EU is located. This leads us to consider issues of structure and agency; and thus to focus upon the external as well as the internal determinants of EU external policy.

Our discussion begins with a brief examination of the relatively formal approach to actorness in international law. Subsequently, treatments of actorness in the International Relations literature are reviewed, and an assessment made of behavioural and structural approaches to analysis. Finally, we consider the roles available to the EU and the resources potentially available for the fulfilment of these roles.

ACTORNESS IN INTERNATIONAL LAW

A formal answer to the question 'How do we recognize an actor?' is provided by public international law. This, by definition, focuses upon the interstate system, and has developed its own formal concept of actorness in terms of the notion of legal personality. As Coplin (1965:146) argued, international law has too often been treated exclusively as a system of restraints upon state activity, rather than as 'a quasi-authoritative system of communicating the assumptions of the state system to policy-makers'. Foremost amongst these assumptions, since the Treaty of Westphalia in 1648 formally inaugurated the modern state system, has been the notion of the sovereign territorial state as the subject of international law, and associated recognition doctrines. Only states could make treaties, join international organizations and be held to account by other states. Legal actorness confers a right to participate, but also to be held responsible by other actors, and to incur obligations.

Whereas for several hundred years there may have been a reasonable correspondence between the legal framework and the political realities of international life, by the mid twentieth century the 'Westphalian assumptions' were under challenge. The first formal recognition of this came with the 1948 International Court of Justice (ICJ) decision on the legal status of the United Nations, in the context of the organization's right to present a claim for damages in respect of the assassination of its mediator in Palestine, Count Folke Bernadotte. The Court established that the UN had international legal status, but that this was not equivalent to that of a state –

By applying the well-known principle of the 'specificity' of corporate persona, the UN and by extension all international organizations are recognized as having the necessary and sufficient capacity to exercise the functions which have been devolved to them by their charters. If IGOs [Intergovernmental Organizations] are in fact governed by international law, distinct from the members which constitute them, they do not enjoy the whole range of competencies which are accorded by law to states.

(Merle 1987:293–4)

On this basis the European Community has achieved legal personality, although its formal status is that of an intergovernmental organization and it is entitled to act only in areas of legally established competence. The process of attaining legally sanctioned actorness might be described in terms of 'structuration' (a concept which we elaborate below), in that there is an ongoing dialectic between the assertion of rights by bodies such as the EC and the understandings which inform the responses of other members of the system and the courts. This process is evident from the manner in which the EC came to be accepted as the successor to the Member States as a party to certain international agreements. Under the General Agreement on Tariffs and Trade (GATT) it was informally accepted as a player representing the contracting parties. It only became a party in its own right, alongside the Member States, with the creation of the World Trade Organization (WTO) in 1994 (Macleod, Hendry and Hyett 1996:235–6). In other areas where a common policy applies, such as international fisheries agreements, the EC is a direct successor to the Member States.

A similar dynamic can also be seen to operate in reverse, in that there is a tension between external demands that the EU should play an active role in the international system and reluctance on the part of Member State governments to accord competence to the EC in areas considered sensitive domestically. Competence is the EC term for 'powers', and can be defined as –

the authority to undertake negotiations, conclude binding agreements, and adopt implementation measures. Where competence is exclusive it belongs solely to the Community to the exclusion of the Member States. Where it is concurrent either the Community or the Member States may act but not simultaneously.

(Macrory and Hession 1996:183)

Disputes relating to the extent of competence are evident, to a greater or lesser degree, in all the policy areas we discuss. A prominent, recent example can be found in controversy over accordance of legal personality to the European Union. The Treaty on European Union (TEU), which entered into force in November 1993, established the Union as an overarching framework which would facilitate partial integration of foreign and security policy, immigration policy and aspects of internal state security. As a consequence of the political sensitivity of these policy areas the TEU did not accord legal personality to the Union. Hence the Union, unlike the Community, cannot conclude international agreements. Not surprisingly this has proved a source of confusion to third parties and an impediment to action by the Union in pursuit of its objectives. The framers of the Treaty of Amsterdam (TOA) sought to rectify this anomaly; however the wording eventually agreed accords the Union legal personality 'in all but name' – an excellent example of the dynamic process by which legal status is acquired.[1]

The international legal structure itself has been subject to continuous alteration and, as Young (1972:127) notes, the currently entrenched ideas about statehood are misleading –

> they actually reflect quite recent developments in the longer flow of history and a good case can be made for the argument that they never described the realities of world politics very accurately. Over the bulk of recorded history man has organized himself for political purposes on bases other than those now subsumed by the concepts 'state' and 'nation-state'.

There is also no necessary correspondence between the achievement of legal personality and actorness in behavioural terms. Weak states may have full legal status but are insignificant as actors, while bodies such as the European Union can fulfil important functions without possessing legal personality. Thus, while it is necessary to have an understanding of actorness as ascribed by international law, it is hardly sufficient. Nonetheless, the law continues to have significance in so far as it shapes expectations and defines the limits of acceptable behaviour.

ACTORS AND ACTORNESS IN INTERNATIONAL RELATIONS

In conventional International Relations the answer to the question 'How do we recognize an actor?' is essentially the same as that given by the lawyers: states. The question of actorness has always been a fundamental one for students of International Relations, even if the concept itself has not been subject to the kind of scrutiny that its significance would seem to merit. It is fundamental because the term actor is used as a synonym for the units that constitute political systems on the largest scale. Actors, here, are akin to the players in a theatre – the *dramatis personae*. The attribution of actorness in this sense will determine what is studied.

The classical, or Realist, approach is state centric, leading to a focus on the international (really interstate) political system. Other actors, such as intergovernmental organizations and transnational business corporations (TNCs), may be admitted but their functions are seen as essentially subordinate to those of states. While, in some respects, this approach resembles that of international law, it departs from it in significant ways. Thus Realism provides an essentially political analysis in which power differentials between states are a central focus. Ultimately, the actors of interest to Realists are powerful states. This is explicit in discussions of polarity and international structure.

A more pluralist approach which specifies a range of significant units, and in which non-state actors are not necessarily always subordinated to states, will give rise to the conception of a 'mixed actor system' (Young 1972). It is then appropriate to speak of the world political system and, when sub-state and transnational actors are emphasized, in line with shifts towards a global organization of economic activities, to refer to a global political system (McGrew *et al.* 1992; Bretherton and Ponton 1996). An example of an extreme disaggregation of world politics into a myriad of individual and social actors, where states exist merely as barriers to interaction, is to be found in the concept of 'world society' developed by John Burton (1972) and his followers. More recently James Rosenau (1990) has sought to accommodate the interests and activities of a range of social actors, from individual citizens to social movements; and to assess their impact upon world politics.

The relative inclusiveness of these approaches reflects, to a considerable extent, the evolution of world politics since 1945. Notions of a mixed actor system were developed in the early 1970s at a time when Realist state centric analyses, with their focus upon 'superpower' relations, appeared inadequate to conceptualize a world greatly complicated by the emergence of what Keohane and Nye (1977) describe as complex interdependence. Moreover, during this post-Vietnam period, when United States economic and even military predominance appeared to be in question, policy makers within the European Community began actively seeking to enhance the external policy capabilities of the EC, in particular through a system of foreign policy coordination, known as European Political Cooperation (EPC), initiated in 1970. For scholars in the fields of International Relations and Foreign Policy analysis, this aspect of the EC's external activity has subsequently been the primary focus of investigation. In principle, at least, the EC's emerging external role could be accommodated in a mixed actor system.

The abrupt ending of the Cold War posed a major challenge to International Relations scholars and, indeed, to practitioners. In relation to the EC, the re-emergence of armed conflict in Europe in the early 1990s, and fears of widespread political instability in Eastern Europe, suggested a significant role as a regional security actor – in addition to its established role as a global economic actor. In relation to IR scholarship, the post-Cold War environment has generated a range of approaches which examine and seek to explain the overlapping and, in part, contradictory processes of globalization, regionalization and fragmentation characteristic of contemporary world politics. In principle, again, such approaches could accommodate the EC/EU.

In practice, however, attempts in the IR literature to categorize the actors in world politics have not been notably successful in accommodating the EC. Thus, for example, the scheme developed by Keohane and Nye (1973: 380) discusses governmental, intergovernmental and non-governmental actors, sub-divided by level of central control to produce six types of actor. The EC is not specifically discussed but, according to this typology, would fall within the intergovernmental category, an outcome which accords with the approach of international law but which, as we shall see, fails to capture the EC's multi-dimensional nature. Rosenau (1990:119) develops a highly complicated scheme to show the potential actors in world politics. This involves 'Micro actors': citizens, officials and leaders, private actors; and 'Macro actors': states, transnational organizations, leaderless publics, social movements.² While its overall inclusiveness is admirable, it is far from clear where the EU *as a whole* might fit into this scheme.

These attempts at categorization exemplify the difficulties encountered in accommodating the complex entity which is the EU. Not only do they suggest that assessments of the EU's actorness will vary according to the perspective of the assessor, which is to be expected, they also alert us to the fact that, in any categorization exercise, the EC/EU is likely to be disaggregated; it will, in effect, appear as several actors. It is possible to avoid this outcome – for example through attributing actorness explicitly to the European Commission, an approach utilized by Hocking and Smith in discussing 'the new variety of international actors' (1990:75). This approach captures an element of the present reality, in that the Commission acts on behalf of the European Community, which, as we have seen, enjoys the legal personality necessary for formal participation in interstate relations. However this would prevent us from assessing the overall impact of the EC/EU – which is our central purpose. This brings us back to the problem of assessing actorness and, since legal criteria are inadequate, we turn to examination of behavioural criteria.

Behavioural criteria of actorness

The attribution of actorness does more than simply designate the units of a system. It implies an entity that exhibits a degree of autonomy from its external environment, and indeed from its internal constituents, and which is capable of volition or purpose. Hence a minimal behavioural definition of an actor would be an entity that is capable of formulating purposes and making decisions, and thus engaging in some form of purposive action.

Behavioural tests of actorness raise some important questions which must concern all social scientists. In the strictest sense only individuals may be regarded as having the capacity to act, and attributes of purpose and will are difficult to transfer to collectivities, still less to 'legal personalities'. Most

International Relations scholars have, however, been quite happy to regard states as 'behaving' and have been notably uninhibited in using this form of words. This is, of course, reification, or the transformation of an abstraction into a concrete object – in this case with characteristics usually associated with individuals.

Useful, here, is recent sociological thought which seeks, explicitly, to avoid reification. Through use of the concept of 'emergence', it is posited that social or organizational actors, such as families or government departments, can exist alongside individuals; provided that the social group or organization in question is capable, in principle, of formulating purposes and acting upon decisions. In consequence organizational actors are 'capable of engaging in actions that are not reducible to the actions of human individuals' (Sibeon 1997:35). In the case of 'international actors such as the European Union', however, actorness is likely to be 'an *intermittent* status that does not apply in all circumstances' (*ibid*:57, original emphasis). For Sibeon, however, the state is not capable of actorness – indeed it is considered to be 'an entity that in no circumstances is an actor' (*ibid*).

Sibeon's conclusion that the EU can, in some circumstances, be an actor, but that the state cannot, may appear to the International Relations scholar as a perverse inversion of accepted truth. Certainly it contrasts sharply with Hedley Bull's contention, from the Realist perspective, that the European Community 'is not an actor in international affairs, and does not seem likely to become one'. For Bull the only actors worthy of consideration, when discussing the EC, are 'nation-states of Western Europe' (Bull 1983:151). Nevertheless Sibeon, from his standpoint as a social theorist seeking to construct a 'non-reified sociology', provides an 'inside' perspective not typically adopted by IR theorists (Sibeon 1997:34). While productive in suggesting alternative ways of conceptualizing actorness, in practice Sibeon's distinction between the EU and a state, both legal entities with associated organizational and decision making capacities, is difficult to sustain if both are viewed externally – and when it is borne in mind that legal statehood confers a legitimate right to act upon particular organizations, cabinets or individuals which do pass Sibeon's actorness test and whose actions (and speech acts) would be meaningless outside this context. However Sibeon's focus is primarily on the domestic political system and, while we have found it useful to draw upon his ideas, there is a need to examine approaches to actorness deriving explicitly from the IR literature.

The concept of autonomy has been accorded central importance in IR approaches to actorness. An early formulation, by Hopkins and Mansbach, proposes as the principal behavioural test of actorness 'the ability to behave in ways that have consequences in international politics and cannot be predicted entirely by reference to other actors or authorities' (1973:36). Moreover Hopkins and Mansbach propose four tasks which are potentially performed by actors in the international system: physical protection, economic development and regulation, residual public interest tasks and provision of group status. Actors must be involved in one or more of these tasks, and the extent of involvement can vary over time. Implicit, here, is the state as comparator; clearly there is a potential to become more 'statelike' as an increasing range of tasks is performed over time.

In a study which includes consideration of intergovernmental organizations (IGOs) and the EC as actors, Merle also emphasizes the importance of autonomy. He argues that, to be autonomous, international actors must be capable of playing 'a specific role independent of their constituent members' (Merle 1987:296). In consequence, Merle dismisses the EC as an actor on the grounds that the decision making procedures of the Council of Ministers were, at that time, subject to unanimity. While this seems to be a somewhat arbitrary judgement, which misses the more subtle aspects of decision making in the complex policy environment of the EC, we must assume that the subsequent introduction of qualified majority voting (QMV) means that, for Merle, the EC has become a (disaggregated) actor in those areas where QMV applies.

This issue is also addressed in an earlier study of 'the new international actors' whose conclusions differed somewhat from those of Merle. Thus Cosgrove and Twitchett (1970:12) identified 'degree of autonomous decision-making power' as the first of three 'mutually interdependent tests' of actorness. In common with Merle they discuss the (then operating) unanimity principle in the Council. However they do not see this as necessarily impeding actorness; rather they conclude that an 'international secretariat' such as the European Commission can, and does, acquire autonomous decision making capacity through a variety of informal as well as formal processes (*ibid*:13). This is an important insight. However the processes by which the Commission acquires autonomy, on behalf of the Community, are by no means automatic – rather they are the subject of a dynamic interinstitutional tension. This is exemplified, in each of the policy areas we discuss, by the vigilance of some Member State governments in relation to informal, and indeed formal, extensions of Community competence. Moreover application of the 'autonomy test' becomes greatly complicated when applied to the contemporary EU – with its 15 Member States, three Pillars (two of which are intergovernmental) and 29 'main' decision making procedures, 11 of which require Member State unanimity.[3]

Clearly the issue of autonomy remains central to discussion of EU actorness. So, too, do Cosgrove and Twitchett's further, related tests of actorness – the ability to perform 'significant and continuing functions having an impact on inter-state relations' and the importance accorded to the would-be international actor both by its members and by third parties (1970:12). Achievement of actorness, according to Cosgrove and Twitchett, requires that all three of the above criteria must be met 'in some degree for most of the time' (*ibid*) – a formula which allowed them to conclude, even in the late 1960s, that the EC was 'a viable international actor' (1970:49).

We return, later, to discuss behavioural criteria of actorness in relation to the contemporary EU. In particular, we address the issue of actor capability, which both contributes to and overlaps with autonomy. Defined by Gunnar Sjöstedt (1977:16) as the 'capacity to behave actively and deliberately in relation to other actors in the international system', actor capability is regarded by Sjöstedt as a function of internal resources. As already indicated, however, we consider an exclusive focus on internal factors – and, indeed on behavioural criteria generally – to be inadequate in assessing actorness. In consequence, before examining the internal factors which contribute to (or inhibit) EU actorness, we question the extent to which its external activities are the product of purposive action, or agency; or are shaped or constrained by structural factors.

Structural/constructivist approaches to actorness

Explanations of social phenomena which rely upon action or agency clearly make up one side of the agency/structure debate that has long been evident in most of the social sciences. In International Relations a version of this debate was expounded over 30 years ago by J.D. Singer (1961) in his 'level of analysis problem'. Singer contrasted systems level analyses with what he referred to as the 'nation-as-actor focus'. He concluded that, in explanatory as opposed to descriptive terms, 'there seems little doubt that the sub-systemic or actor orientation is considerably more fruitful'. By 1961 the assumption of what came to be known as 'subsystem dominance', and a strong predilection for analysis and explanation based upon nation state actors and the variations between them, was strongly entrenched. Referring to a survey of the texts, Sondermann wrote 'almost without exception, the analysis is mainly "actor orientated"' (Sondermann 1961:11).

While the 1970s saw the scope of International Relations broaden to admit 'new' international actors, the predominant approaches to analysis continued to privilege the state, as we have seen; moreover they remained primarily focused on behaviour. Nevertheless the field of IR has seen the development, or application, of a number of structural and, more recently constructivist, perspectives which have relevance to EU actorness. To a greater or lesser extent these perspectives conceive of actors, or the units of a system, as subordinate to the operating rules and embedded practices – that is to the structure – of the system itself. There are considerable differences between these perspectives, both in their conceptualization of the relationship between structures and actors, or agency, and in the extent to which their underlying assumptions are primarily political, economic or sociological.

Neorealism and the structure of international politics

The assumptions of structural realism (or neorealism), as developed by Kenneth Waltz (1979), are primarily political. Waltz's focus is the international political system, the organizing principle of which (anarchy) determines the behaviour of the units (states). In consequence, the sources of behaviour are to be found not in the differing characteristics, or volition, of states but in their fundamental need, in an anarchical system, 'to compete with and adjust to one another if they are to survive and flourish' (Waltz 1979:72). In these circumstances relative power capability is the only significant factor differentiating between states. Hence the interests of states, and ultimately their behaviour, are externally given and, in principle, predictable; they derive from the distribution of power in the international system. Thus, as Dessler (1989) has pointed out, neorealism is essentially a positional model, in which the policy options available to individual state actors are, to a significant extent, determined by their position in the power structure.

From this perspective, the emergence of the European Community was permitted because the Cold War bipolar structure served both to diminish the importance of the West European 'powers' and mitigate the conditions of anarchy in which they operated. While other obstacles remained, an important impediment to cooperation was removed – that is 'the fear that the greater advantage of one would be translated into military force to be used against the others' (Waltz 1979:70). This analysis provides useful insights into the creation of the EC, but can offer, at best, only a partial explanation for a period when creative political responses to the opportunities offered by bipolarity were of great significance.

Our concern, of course, is with the contemporary EU; and in the post-Cold War context structural realism gives only limited guidance.[4] From this perspective the most likely outcome of the ending of bipolarity would be dissolution of the EU and renationalization of security by its Member States, in some 'back to the future' scenario (Mearsheimer 1990). Alternatively the Member States might seek to maximize their collective status through providing the EU with a credible military capability. An 'emerging united Europe' would thereby attain the status of a powerful state, perhaps then forming one pole of a tripolar system (Jervis 1991/2:42). It is difficult to see how this outcome could be predicted, however, on the basis of neorealist assumptions of an adversarial, self-help international system.

Undoubtedly the ending of the Cold War bipolar system has had a significant impact upon the EU. In particular the emergence of conflict and instability in Eastern Europe has posed major challenges. However these have not been met by individual Member State initiatives, nor by plans to increase national defence expenditure, but by a range of financial assistance and diplomatic initiatives coordinated by the EU; and, indeed, by proposals for the development of an EU military capability. Nevertheless, while commitment remains to some form of collective response, there are significant divisions between EU Member States on questions ranging from enlargement to the East to the vexed issue of defence. However these divisions are not easily explained from the perspective of structural realism. While it might be predicted that an EU military capability would be supported only by the smaller, 'less powerful' Member States, in practice the situation is very much more complex. Divisions on this issue, for example between the UK and France (or indeed between Ireland and Belgium), do not reflect power differentials.

Ultimately the divergent responses of EU Member States to the end of bipolarity can only be understood when account is taken of the different historical experiences, and contemporary policy preferences, of the individual Member States: that is, when consideration is given to the interaction between agency and structure. Moreover neorealism, with its primary focus upon political/military power, fails adequately to account for the economic, and indeed, ideological bases of power. Since the EU's role in external economic relations is of considerably greater significance than any military role it might acquire in the foreseeable future, analyses which focus upon economic structures will clearly have relevance to our discussion.

Neo-Marxist conceptions of structure

To a significant extent structural analyses which focus upon economic factors derive from Marxist and neo-Marxist assumptions. Their primary focus is upon the structure of a capitalist economy which has become increasingly integrated in its operation, and extensive in its scope. From this perspective the state retains a significant, although not fully autonomous, role; thus the state is, to varying degrees, conceived as subordinate to the needs and interests of capital. As in the case of neorealism, international relations is portrayed as a struggle for power; but here power is conceived in terms of economic advantage or dominance. There are considerable divergences between theorists adopting a broadly neo-Marxist perspective, and here we briefly examine the implications, for EU actorness, of two such approaches – the 'world-systems theory' of Immanuel Wallerstein and the neo-Gramscian approach of Robert Cox.

Wallerstein (1984) discerned the roots of a 'capitalist world-economy' in the sixteenth and seventeenth centuries and considers the capitalist economy to have become global in scope by the end of the nineteenth century. His concern is to describe and explain the broad historical evolution or 'cyclical rhythm' of the world-system (Wallerstein 1991:8). This perspective encourages us to see significant events, such as the end of the Cold War, in the context of phases of expansion and stagnation in the world economy. A key factor, here, is the decline of US economic preeminence, which reflects 'the normal entropy of monopolistic advantage within capitalism' (*ibid*:53). Here a role for the EC emerges in maximizing the potential of Western European states – both in challenging US hegemony in the early years and in gaining benefits from hegemonic decline in the 1970s.

By the mid 1980s it had become clear that the economic advantage of 'Europe' had diminished and that European firms were 'losing ground to Japan and the USA in crucial sectors for future development in the late twentieth century' – in particular information technology, telecommunications and biotechnology (Commission 1991c:10). It is in these areas that it is necessary, in Wallerstein's terms (1991:55), 'to gain monopolistic edges that will guarantee the direction of flows of surplus ... clearly it must be of concern to Europe that she will come a poor second in the race'. These concerns underlay the creation of the Single European Market (SEM) and the associated development of an EC technology policy, which included substantial Community funding for research in these key sectors.[5] Such concerns are also reflected in the words of the Cecchini Report, which provided the rationale for the single market programme –

> if they [Europeans] respond robustly, the continent's citizens, companies and governments will do more than realise their collective economic potential as Europeans. They will propel Europe into the blustery world stage of the 1990s in a position of competitive strength and on an upward trajectory of economic growth lasting into the next century.
>
> (Cecchini, Catinat and Jacquemin 1988:xvii)

While it is, of course, to the (West European) Member States of the EC that Cecchini *et al.* refer when discussing 'Europe', it is interesting to note that Wallerstein speculated in 1988 (when his 1991 essay was originally published) about the possibilities for and implications of 'European unity' through EC enlargement to the East. This, he concluded, would 'breathe considerable new life into the existing capitalist world-economy' (1991:63). It would also perpetuate a system in which 'a large portion of the world's population would still be outrageously exploited, perhaps more than ever (*ibid*). The prescience of Wallerstein's speculations is evident, as we shall see in Chapter 5, from the diversion of EC financial assistance, in the 1990s, from 'Third World' to Central and East European countries.

While also focusing upon economic structures at the highest level, Robert Cox (1993) sees the emergence of a global capitalist economy as a contemporary and still incomplete phenomenon. In consequence his attention focuses more directly upon the specifics of contemporary change in Europe, rather than upon its location in the panorama of world historical events. In this sense the perspectives of Cox and Wallerstein are complementary. In Wallerstein's analysis, however, the determining role attributed to economic structures is almost complete; little space is left for creative political action and, as in the case of neorealism, differences between states are unimportant. For Cox, however, differences in domestic political arrangements, or forms of state, are highly significant (Cox 1986). A central concern is that state autonomy, and the related ability to maintain alternatives to the neoliberal state form, has been eroded through a process of 'internationalisation'. Thus, increasingly, 'states must become the instruments for adjusting national economic activities to the exigencies of the global economy' (Cox 1993:260). In consequence, in the context of Europe, he is concerned with the ability of the social democratic state to withstand the pressures of economic globalization.

Cox's analysis has considerable relevance for our discussion. The emergence of 'macro-regional economic spheres' has been a necessary response to economic globalization and has been associated, in turn, with the emergence of complex, multi-layered systems of governance which challenge Westphalian assumptions of sovereignty and territoriality and which might be considered as a new form of state, or 'international state' (Cox 1986; 1993). Of particular significance, here, is the increasing disjuncture between political/military power, which remains territorially based (the latter most particularly in the USA) and economic power, which is both more widely dispersed and less amenable to regulation at the level of the state. For the EU the consequences of this disjuncture are particularly acute: their impact is twofold.

First, economic globalization has generated considerable pressure for the transfer of economic management functions to the EC level. Here tensions between neoliberal and social democratic forms of governance can be resolved in circumstances which are largely divorced from public scrutiny.[6] This separation of economic oversight from domestic political systems is a crucial factor in disrupting a strong European tradition of political control over economic processes; in consequence it is likely to be maintained (Cox 1993:284). The implication for our discussion of actorness is that there is no impetus towards the provision of overall political direction for EC/EU external activities. On the contrary, the interests of global economic liberalism are best served by a continued separation of 'political' foreign policy and external economic relations. There is some evidence to support this argument, for example disputes during 1997 over Burma's accession to the Association of South-East Asian Nations (ASEAN), in which proposals emanating from the Common Foreign and Security Policy (CFSP) of the EU that relations with ASEAN be interrupted in protest at Burma's human rights record were vigorously opposed by the Commission (Interview). However there is much evidence, too, of major disputes *within* the Commission on issues of this nature. This indicates, again, the need for analysis of the interaction between external demands and internal tensions.

Second, the increasing separation between the economic and political/military dimensions has resulted in an implicit division of global management tasks between the US and the EU. Thus major policy decisions at the global level on non-military matters such as trade or environment require, at minimum, US acquiescence; where military enforcement is at issue the US plays a leading role. The EU, for its part, is increasingly expected to pay a large proportion of the cost, while gaining little political advantage. This is evident in the Middle East, former Yugoslavia and in the broader area of humanitarian assistance. It is not well known, for example, that the European Community Humanitarian Office (ECHO) is now the world's largest single donor of humanitarian aid (ECHO 1996). In this analysis, the EU's role as a 'civilian power' paymaster is assigned rather than deliberately chosen.

Through their focus on the EU's position within global political and economic structures, these analyses contribute in important, and distinctive, ways to our understanding of EU actorness. They also share an emphasis upon external determinants of actor capability and, in particular, the constraints which structural factors impose upon the roles and policy options available to the EU. Clearly this provides a necessary antidote to behavioural approaches which conceive of actorness as primarily a function of political will and the availability of resources. Nevertheless structural explanations provide only one side of a complex story. Bipolarity doubtless permitted, and economic globalization encouraged, the development of cooperation in Europe. However the European Union as a political form is entirely unique; its creation reflects a combination of external demands and opportunities, and political will and imagination on the part of its founders. The subsequent development of the EU also reflects, we believe, a complex yet dynamic relationship between structure and agency. In short, there is a need for an approach which emphasizes neither structure, nor agency, but the relationship between them. As Alexander Wendt has famously observed (1994:388) 'Anarchy is what states make of it'.

International structures as socially constructed

Constructivist accounts which seek to reconcile structural and behavioural approaches to explanation are largely derived from sociological theory.[7] They arise from, and attempt to resolve, what Alvin Gouldner (1971:54) has termed 'the unique contradiction distinctive of sociology'; that human beings inhabit a social world, which they have themselves created but to which they are also subject. In addressing this contradiction, constructivists seek explicitly to redress the determinism of analyses emanating both from the Marxian and Durkheimian traditions. Thus structures are seen as providing opportunities as well as constraints, they are potentially enabling; at the same time actors have agency – that is they are rule makers as well as rule takers.

Structures, in constructivist analyses, are not defined in material terms, rather they are intersubjective. Thus, in relation to the international system –

> Intersubjective systemic structures consist of shared understandings, expectations and social knowledge embedded in international institutions . . . Intersubjective structures give meaning to material ones, and it is in terms of meanings that actors act.
>
> (Wendt 1994:389)

In this analysis, structures do not determine outcomes but provide 'action settings' or distinct patterns of opportunity and constraint within which agency is displayed. Moreover actors are, to varying extents, knowledgeable about the settings within which they are located and are potentially able to change them (Hay 1995:200). The potential for agency to be displayed reflects the extent to which actors are 'strategically well placed', in that structures are more open to some types of strategy than others, and innovative – for example 'the architects of the "Europe of 1992"' (Carlsnaes 1992:262).

Constructivists thus posit a dialectical relationship between agency and structure; actions have consequences, both intended and unintended, and structures evolve through the renegotiation and reinterpretation of international rules and practices. However constructivists see structure and agency as mutually constitutive, and hence only *'theoretically* separable' (Hay 1995:200, original emphasis). In an analysis of the external role of the EU, however, it is precisely the interaction between structure and agency which is of interest, hence we find useful Carlsnaes' notion (1992:260) of:

> a continuous cycle of action-structure interactions, a dialectical process which not only serves to provide both continuity and change to social systems, but also can be penetrated analytically as a consequence of its essentially sequential thrust in societal transformation.

Thus, in any given context, structures must logically both precede and follow action – however this reflects temporal sequencing rather than ontological prioritorization. It is, thus, to a cyclical process of social construction and reconstruction that we refer in employing the concept of structuration. Within this process, we believe, only actors, that is entities having the capacity to formulate goals, have causal powers. However, the capacity to act, or actorness, is a function both of external opportunities, including those associated with the international legal and institutional framework; and internal capabilities, which include the availability of policy instruments and the capacity and legitimacy of decision making processes.

For a number of reasons we have found a constructivist approach useful to our attempts to conceptualize EU actorness. Thus, in addition to considering the evolving practices and procedures which constitute EU external policy, our research has placed particular emphasis upon the perceptions and actions of third parties. These, we believe, contribute significantly to the shared understandings framing the policy environment, and hence shaping the practices, of Member State governments, EU officials and third parties alike.

As we have observed, the EU is unique, both in conception and evolution. Its creation reflected the dynamic interaction between innovative political actors and the opportunities and constraints afforded by changing international and domestic structures. The subsequent evolution of its external role, with which we are specifically concerned, reflects a similar dynamic – but with the added dimension that the EC's emergence as an international actor itself contributed to the evolution of the meanings and practices which constitute intersubjective international structures. The EC's contribution, in this respect, has been a function not only of intentional decisions or purposive actions but also of its existence, or presence, as a new form of international actor which defies categorization. Here it is instructive to examine the process by which, for purposes of environmental negotiations, the EC was accorded the status of Regional Economic Integration Organization (REIO), a UN category having a membership of one (see Chapter 3).

In some respects the uniqueness of the EU has been an impediment to the development of actorness. There is, for example, a significant difference between the formal and informal treatment of the EU by third parties. Thus, while there has frequently been reluctance to accord formal status in international fora to what is seen as a hybrid entity (more than an intergovernmental organization, less than a state) the perceptions and everyday practices of the third party representatives we interviewed demonstrated, repeatedly, that the EU is already considered to be an important global actor.[8]

It is to be expected that these changing practices and evolving, shared understandings will precede formal recognition or codification of EU actorness. This applies equally to the internal dynamics of policy formulation – as we shall see (in Chapters 2, 4 and 5) from the Commission's unacknowledged but very evident involvement in foreign policy under the guise of external economic relations, and (in Chapter 6) from the almost imperceptible process of 'Brusselsization' of foreign policy. Here an example of the evolution of international practices is provided in a speech by Alain Juppé to a Conference of Ambassadors in September 1994 –

> It is your role as ambassadors of France, both to assert the identity of the European Union and to explain the specific positions defended by France within the institutions thereof. It is without reservations, therefore, that you will endeavour, wherever you are, to affirm the political identity of the Union.
>
> (Quoted in de La Serre 1996:36–7)

Despite such informal practices, reflected in extensive cooperation between Member State missions in third countries, there is considerable resistance to formalizing these arrangements through the establishment of joint representations – as evidenced by the delays and controversies surrounding establishment of common consular facilities in Abuja, Nigeria, which continue to affect the project after five years of discussion.

In several respects the formalization of informal practices has tended to be especially problematic in the case of the EU, not least because the EU's existence challenges the assumptions upon which the interstate system is based – that is, the principles of sovereignty and territoriality. The pervasiveness and influence of these ideas is such that they both inform international practices

in relation to the EU and frame academic debate concerning its development and role. Thus, whether it is concluded that the EU undermines the
state (Marquand 1989) or strengthens it (Milward 1992), the state is
overwhelmingly the template against which the EU is measured.

Nevertheless the development of the EU has itself engendered considerable debate about the changing meaning of international practices and
principles. It has, for example, become commonplace both for politicians
and academics to conceive of sovereignty as divisible.[9] For Keohane and
Hoffman (1991:13) the EU is 'essentially organized as a network that
involves the pooling or sharing of sovereignty'. This network analogy,
which is commonly applied to the EU, also has the effect of challenging
territoriality. Here, however, commentators have been relatively slow in
coming to terms with the notion that political forms may be, in some senses,
post-territorial.[10] As Ruggie has observed (1993:140), it is rare in scholarly
treatments of the EU to find –

> so much as a hint that the institutional, juridical, and spatial complexes
> associated with the community may constitute nothing less than the
> emergence of the first truly postmodern international political form.

Ruggie's notion of the EU as a 'multiperspectival polity' (1993:172) is
a useful one, which captures something of the complexity of the EU's
external personality. As we shall see in the chapters which follow, the EU is
a multi-faceted actor; indeed it can appear to be several different actors,
sometimes simultaneously. It has, moreover, a confusing propensity to
change its character, or the persona it presents to third parties – as we shall
see from the discussion of environmental negotiations in Chapter 3. Thus, in
some circumstances the EU resembles an international organization (indeed,
as already indicated, it is regarded by International Lawyers as an international organization *sui generis*). In other circumstances it has state-like
qualities which cannot be divorced from territoriality, in the sense that
stringent rules operate in relation to the flow of goods, and of people, into its
space. Moreover, as representatives of states applying for EU membership
would confirm, the EU as a 'network' is remarkably impenetrable. The eligibility criteria constructed by the EU are an aspect of its emerging collective
identity – a matter which is discussed in Chapter 8.

To conceptualize the development of the EU's external role in terms of
cyclical relationships between agency and structures, defined as intersubjective systems of meaning, allows us to accommodate the complexity of the
EU's external personality and to question the assumptions which underlie
approaches to actorness in International Relations. For academic commentators, however, the persistent influence of state-centric perspectives has
made it extraordinarily difficult to avoid seeking 'Miniature state-like structures, situated in Brussels' (Caporaso 1996:33). Practitioners dealing with
the EU on a daily basis, however, already encounter (or employ) a range of

practices which include or accommodate understandings about the EC/EU as an actor. Thus, for example, Commission negotiators, in dealing with third parties, exploit the complexity and opaqueness of EC decision processes as a bargaining asset. While our interview material suggests that this ploy contributes to the reputation of Commission officials as formidable negotiators, there is also evidence of reciprocity, in this respect, on the part of the Commission's interlocutors. Thus, in the course of negotiations –

> some third parties, while having a very clear idea of the state of affairs at any given time, nevertheless professed *'faux naif'* bewilderment in an endeavour to draw diplomatic advantage from the Community's uncertainties and ambiguities.
>
> (Nuttall 1996a:130)

In a very real sense, understandings about the EU, its roles, responsibilities and limitations, form a part of the intersubjective international structures which provide the 'action settings' of global politics. At the same time the EU contributes to the processes of constructing intersubjective international structures, both as a purposive actor and through its unique presence. It is to these issues that we now turn.

PRESENCE AND ACTORNESS: CONSTRUCTING THE EXTERNAL ROLES OF THE EU

We have already noted a number of pitfalls which are likely to beset attempts to assign roles to the EU. These include the pervasive influence of assumptions concerning the state-like characteristics required by actors, and the exclusively behavioural basis of many explanations of actorness. Consequently, in his discussion of its external activities, Christopher Hill cautions against attempting to identify a distinctive role for the EC. This is because the idea of a role –

> assumes that an actor can and should find for itself something approximating to a part played on a stage, namely a distinctive, high-profile and coherent identity. But if all were to seek this in international relations, then nationalism inexorably would follow . . .
>
> (Hill 1993:307)

While sharing Hill's caution we do not share his fears, which appear to be based upon the traditional state-centric assumptions he seeks to avoid. Moreover we do not conceive of roles as self-evidently available or freely chosen. Roles, we believe, are socially constructed through the interaction of agency and structural factors and are, to varying extents, *available* to actors. The actor's capacity (or failure) to exploit available opportunities will itself contribute to the development of mutual understandings, and hence expectations, concerning future performance. Thus the notion of role implies some degree of action; roles do not simply denote position, or status, in the international system. Our central concern is with actorness, and hence with purposive action and its consequences. Nevertheless we are also concerned with the implications and impacts of the EU's status, or presence, in world politics.

In their discussion of 'Western Europe's status and impact within the contemporary international arena' Allen and Smith (1990:19) explicitly attempt to avoid treating the EC as 'an international actor of the conventional state-like kind'. Thus, in order to resist the temptation of reverting to a 'states as actors' approach, they abandon the concept of actor altogether, employing instead the concept of 'presence'. Thus presence 'is not the prerogative solely of 'actors' centred on people and institutions, but can be a property of ideas, notions, expectations and imaginations' (*ibid*:22). We are comfortable with this formulation, which accords with our own preference for a social constructivist approach to analysis in which ideas and expectations are accorded significance. In Allen and Smith's analysis, however, it is evident that presence serves as a substitute for, and extension of, the concept of actor. Thus –

A particular presence, then, is defined by a combination of factors: credentials and legitimacy, the capacity to act and mobilize resources, the place it occupies in the perceptions and expectations of policy makers.
(Allen and Smith 1990:21)

We consider that it is unhelpful to conflate presence and actorness in this way. Actorness relates to the capacity to act; presence is a function of *being* rather than action. Presence manifests itself through subtle forms of influence; but it also produces tangible impacts. Clearly there is a relationship between presence and actorness, in that actorness logically presupposes presence, which is thus a precondition for actorness. In consequence, presence denotes latent actorness. Moreover, presence can also *promote* actorness: thus presence may generate an active response from third parties which, in turn, produces demands for action by the EU. While this is particularly evident from the 'magnet' effect of the Single Market, the EU's presence has significant impacts in other policy areas. For example its 'environmental presence', as the world's second largest emitter of carbon dioxide, has generated expectations of coherent action by the EU in the sphere of global environmental politics. In addition to the (largely) unintended external impacts of internal policies or processes, we also consider an important aspect of the EU's presence to lie in its influence as a model – of regional economic integration or as an 'island of peace'.

The complex interaction between presence and actorness contributes to processes of structuration. These, in turn, are reflected in roles which are available to the EU: however, the desire or capacity to exploit this potential is necessarily, also, a function of agency. Below we briefly survey a range of roles offered to, or played by, the EU.

External 'roles' of the EU

The role of the EU can be conceptualized, in the broadest sense, as contributing to overall 'Western' policy, in terms of maintenance within and extension beyond the West of values and beliefs which are the product of an essentially European culture and, more specifically, of the European Enlightenment. These include optimism concerning the possibility of progress through human endeavour, belief in the worth and dignity of the human individual, liberal-democratic political arrangements and the capitalist economic system. The EU, as presence, has contributed significantly to consolidation of these values and principles in Western Europe.

Since the end of the Cold War the EU has been increasingly active in promoting these values as an aspect of its external policy. They are formally enshrined in the Common Provisions of the 1993 Treaty on European Union and, as we shall see, cooperation and association agreements concluded since the end of the Cold War have incorporated a range of conditionalities, including compliance with human rights and 'democratic governance' criteria, economic liberalization and privatization. These measures accord with conditionalities imposed elsewhere, both bilaterally and through Western dominated multilateral organizations such as the International Monetary Fund and the World Bank. In these circumstances the EU could be regarded as merely an instrument for promulgation of a broader, Western approach – or, indeed, an adjunct of the external policy of key Member States. An example, here, would be the early period of 'development cooperation', when policy outcomes largely reflected the interests of the French government. However, it is our contention that the EC/EU has developed, over the years, a distinctive presence, and distinctive roles, which have enabled it to contribute to the development of the international system.

To a significant extent the creation of the EC, and the external roles it began to fulfil, reflected the constraints and opportunities offered by its external environment – that is, the context created by the evolving structures of East/West and North/South relations. However the distinctive nature of the Community contributed to its ability to act within that context. Thus the EC, as a new body, was relatively untainted by the stigma of colonialism attaching to the Member States; moreover it had no pretensions to superpower status – not only did it lack military capability, it did not even resemble a state. In consequence the EC was relatively acceptable to neutral and non-aligned countries and was able to develop distinctive relationships with, for example, the Nordic countries, the Arab League and (then) Yugoslavia. Moreover the inauguration of the Conference on Security and

Cooperation in Europe (CSCE) process in 1973 provided the EC with the opportunity to play a role in East/West dialogue, particularly in relation to economic and human rights issues.

In the sphere of North/South relations, the EC provided a framework for decolonization in Africa, a potentially difficult process in the light of Cold War tensions, and subsequently maintained close relationships with former colonies in a manner judged (in the South) to be relatively positive. Moreover, in contrast with the US and several Member State governments, during the Cold War the EC maintained links with socialist regimes in Ethiopia, Angola and Mozambique and, in the 1980s, developed links with Nicaragua despite the strong disapproval of the US government. Thus, during the Cold War period, the EC came to occupy a distinctive position in the international system; providing, through a combination of presence and actorness, a focus for Western policy which was different from, and provided an alternative to, the US position.[11]

Alongside these broad and relatively intangible developments, however, the EC had increasingly come to occupy a prominent position in relation to the global economy. Indeed the Community's economic presence, and its role in world trade, is fundamental to its external activities overall (as Chapter 2 demonstrates). Here a number of roles might be considered for the EC – for example as partner/competitor with the United States in the management of world trade. Susan Strange has put the matter succinctly – the EC's 'task is to compete with Japan and the United States' (quoted in Hill 1993:307). Particularly in relation to climate change issues, a more recent, but potentially important, role for the EC/EU lies in the aspiration to environmental leadership (see Chapter 3).

In areas where the EC potentially serves as a model, the relationship between presence and actorness is, again, important. Regional economic cooperation has undoubtedly proved an attractive response to economic globalization – as is evident from the creation of ASEAN and the North American Free Trade Agreement (NAFTA). At the same time the EC has actively promoted the development of such arrangements – thus, for example, the Interregional Framework Agreement between the EU and Mercosur (Mercado de Sur) strongly supports the development of regional economic integration in Latin America.

In the aftermath of the Cold War the EU again provides a model – as an 'island of peace' for less stable regions to the East and South. Moreover it is actively involved, through the development of an array of multi-faceted association and cooperation agreements, in attempting to export stability beyond its borders. Nevertheless, here, the challenges and expectations from the 'near abroad', not least the proposals for enlargement of the EU to the East and the South, may prove beyond its capacity as an actor. Moreover the limitations to a conventional security role for the EU have already been demonstrated – by the dismal failure of its policy towards former Yugoslavia in the early 1990s. As will be evident from Chapters 6 and 7, the EU's role in traditional foreign and security policy matters remains uncertain and contested. Nevertheless the EC/EU is developing new roles which accord with its 'civilian' status in the international system. Thus, as already noted, the EC has become the world's most important deliverer of humanitarian assistance, developing novel ways of working with a network of some 60 non-governmental organizations (ECHO 1996).

In each of the policy areas outlined above the EC/EU is actively involved, to a greater or lesser extent. However actorness, and more particularly the capacity to act coherently and effectively, depends not only upon the constraints and opportunities afforded by structural factors, but upon the ability of actors to respond. We have yet to examine the resource base of EU actorness.

THE BASES OF EU ACTORNESS

Judgements concerning EU actorness abound, although systematic analyses of the bases of actorness are relatively uncommon. In many cases, viewed externally, the EU is simply assumed to be an important actor. 'No longer is the United States a hegemon with the EC orbiting in its sphere . . . the US and EC have entered the 1990s on a much more equal basis' (Featherstone and Ginsberg 1996:3) conveys rather nicely the simplification, and reification, frequently employed in such discussion. It also implies, of course, that the EC/EU possesses the characteristics and capability of an important international actor; a large state or, indeed, 'a superpower in the making' as Johan Galtung once argued (1973). While, in 1973, Galtung's arguments were controversial, discussion of the EU as a global power with global responsibilities is no longer remarkable (Buchan 1993; Piening 1997). Nowhere is this more evident than from the ubiquitous 'Europe must act now' approach of contemporary journalism.[12]

These depictions of the EU as a significant global actor are based, sometimes explicitly, upon the assumption that the basis of EU actorness is primarily economic. Thus, for Piening (1997:196), the EU 'may not be a superpower (a term that implies the possession of great military power as well as economic strength) but it is certainly a global power'. This conclusion reflects earlier thinking, notably by François Duchêne, about the EC's nature and role. Duchêne argued that, in circumstances of increasing economic interdependence, when 'lacking military power was not the handicap it once was', the EC as a 'civilian power . . . could play a very important and potentially constructive role . . . a new role for a new world' (1972:43–4). Ultimately, as we argue in Chapter 7, any conclusion that the EU is a significant actor in global politics must accept the assumption that 'civilian power' matters.

Not all commentators do accept this assumption, however. We have referred, above, to Hedley Bull's (1983) robust response to Duchêne's arguments – 'civilian power Europe: a contradiction in terms'. More recently Christopher Hill has echoed Bull's sentiments. In his study of the EC as an international actor, Hill finds a number of deficiencies in actor capability, but concludes that the EC 'could conceivably reach the position of being able to act purposefully and as one while eschewing a military capability'. Nevertheless he remains convinced that, ultimately, 'defence is the key to the development of the Community's place in the world' (Hill 1993:318). Despite an explicit attempt to avoid the 'spectre of statehood' (*ibid*:309) this conclusion demonstrates that the conceptual template against which the EU is measured remains the state. Indeed, as Caporaso has pointed out (1996:34), it derives from an 'idealized model of the Westphalian state' which has rarely, if ever, existed in practice.

By locating the EU within debates concerning the historical and contemporary evolution of the state, Caporaso provides a number of valuable insights. For example his discussion of the EU as a 'post-modern polity' provides a metaphor which discourages its perception as an aberrant, hybrid form (part intergovernmental, part supranational); or as an embryonic state which lacks, as yet, the attributes of a 'fully fledged' international actor. Moreover the postmodern metaphor captures, almost celebrates, the complexity, or polymorphic structure, of the EU. In this view it is necessary neither to choose between intergovernmentalism and supra-nationalism, nor to supersede the distinction – 'both logics operate' (Caporaso 1996:47). In consequence, the notion of the EU as a postmodern polity is by no means inconsistent with an approach which includes detailed empirical analysis of the EU's operation. If it is to be considered a global actor, a postmodern polity, like any other, must meet the essential prerequisites for actorness; that is the ability to formulate and pursue goals. Moreover, if it is to act effectively, it will need to satisfy more than these basic prerequisites.

Requisites for actorness

The most fully elaborated approach, here, undoubtedly remains the complex scheme developed by Gunnar Sjöstedt (1977) explicitly in relation to the EC.[13] Despite its overwhelmingly behavioural assumptions, Sjöstedt's analysis retains some useful features. He begins by assuming that the EC meets two basic prerequisites for actorness – that it is 'discernible from its environment' and that it enjoys a 'minimal degree of internal cohesion' (Sjöstedt 1977:15). This allows him to conclude (as did Cosgrove and Twitchett in 1970) that the EC enjoyed a degree of autonomy necessary for it to be considered an international actor. However autonomy is a necessary, but not a sufficient, requirement for actorness. For Sjöstedt the challenge was then to identify, and attempt to measure, the components of actor capability. Sjöstedt's complex scheme is not elaborated here, rather we propose five basic requirements for actorness –

1   Shared commitment to a set of overarching values and principles.
2   The ability to identify policy priorities and to formulate coherent policies.
3   The ability effectively to negotiate with other actors in the international system.
4   The availability of, and capacity to utilize, policy instruments.
5   Domestic legitimation of decision processes, and priorities, relating to external policy.

The first of these requisites is not problematic. The Common Provisions of the Treaty on European Union set out very clearly the values and principles to which the EU and its Member States are committed. These range from economic and social progress and sustainable development to democratic governance and the rule of law. Moreover the 1997 Treaty of Amsterdam introduces procedures for suspension or partial suspension of Member States which fail to respect the democracy and human rights aspects of the Common Provisions.

As will be evident from the chapters which follow, the ability, *in principle*, to identify policy priorities and formulate coherent policies is not in question. In question, rather, is the extent to which this ability is realized; and this varies considerably according to issue area and policy sector. Inevitably, as in any complex decision making system, divergent interests generate tensions over the identification and prioritization of goals, hence impeding policy formulation. Nevertheless policy coordination within the EC/EU system is affected by difficulties which flow from its unique character. We refer to these, following usage common within the EU, as the problems of consistency and coherence.

Consistency denotes the extent to which the bilateral external policies of Member States are consistent with each other, and complementary to those of the EC/EU. Hence consistency is a measure both of Member State political commitment to common policies and of the overall impact of the EU and its Member States. In those areas of external economic relations where there is full Community competence, and common policies are entrenched, consistency is not a major problem. Nevertheless Member State governments continue to pursue bilateral trade/investment promotion efforts in third countries. In areas of environmental policy, however, consistency becomes very much an issue; while in relation to development policy and foreign policy, consistency is of central importance. Put another way, claims that the 'EU' is the world's largest trading bloc have a rather different meaning from claims that it is the world's second largest emitter of carbon dioxide, or the world's largest donor of development assistance. In this last case (which should not be confused with EC humanitarian aid efforts referred to above) the development assistance total on which this claim is based amalgamates EC aid with Member States' bilateral aid. As we shall see in Chapter 4, while Member State governments have made a specific commitment to ensure consistency in this area, this has been pursued to only a limited extent in practice. Clearly, in this and other areas, lack of consistency impinges upon EU actorness – not least as perceived by third parties.

A related issue, here, is increasing tolerance of 'flexibility'. Thus the TEU, in permitting the UK and Denmark to opt out of important policy areas, notably Economic and Monetary Union (EMU), established notions of differentiated integration, which were also reflected in provisions permitting 'closer cooperation' between two or more Member States in the area of Justice and Home affairs (TEU K.7); a provision which is somewhat strengthened by the TOA (K12 [TEU 40]). The TOA also introduces the concept of constructive abstention in the area of Common Foreign and Security Policy (J.13 [23]). These provisions are likely to have mixed impacts, in that they remove impediments to policy integration or coordination internally, and potentially to actorness externally, but also impact negatively upon overall presence. Future enlargements are certain to compound this paradoxical effect.

Coherence refers to the internal policy processes of the EC/EU. In many respects the problems, here, are analogous to those affecting any pluralistic political system. Tensions between trade policy and environment policy, for example, are endemic; as are controversies over the extent to which sectors of the economy, in particular agriculture, can or should be protected from external competition. Nevertheless there are aspects of the EC/EU policy system which generate particular coherence problems. The first of these is the Pillar structure itself which, as we argue in Chapter 6, impinges significantly upon the coherence of external policy as a whole.

Within the EC Pillar, aspects of the contemporary operation of the Commission are an impediment to coherence. First among these is the fragmentation of external policy, which is currently divided between five external relations Directorates-General (Relex DGs) – see Figure 1.1.[14] There are tensions and jealousies between officials of Relex DGs at all levels; and these are reflected in the College of Commissioners.[15] This problem is exacerbated, at present, by the absence of a satisfactory mechanism for resolving disputes between Commissioners. There is widespread acknowledgement of this problem, and proposals to reform the organization and functioning of the Commission in this respect (Commission 1997e) have been accepted. In consequence, when the new Commission takes office in 2000, the President will have enhanced powers in respect of the allocation and reallocation of portfolios. Moreover it is proposed that the number of portfolios will be substantially reduced, with some Commissioners fulfilling 'support functions'. This will effectively provide the President with powers of promotion and demotion. With specific reference to external policy, there will be, from 2000, a Vice-President with overall responsibility for external affairs and a corresponding reorganization of external relations departments. These reforms, aspects of which are summarized in Declaration 32, annexed to the

Directorate-General I
(Commissioner Sir Leon Brittan)

> Common Commercial Policy
>
> Relations with North America, Japan, China, South Korea, Hong Kong, Macao and Taiwan

Directorate-General IA
(Commissioner Hans van den Broek)

> Common Foreign and Security Policy
>
> Responsibility for EC Delegations to third countries
>
> Relations with the Central and East European Countries (CEEC) and New Independent States (NIS)
>
> Relations with Turkey, Cyprus and Malta

Directorate-General IB
(Commissioner Manuel Marin)

> Relations with the Southern Mediterranean countries, Middle and Near East and most of developing Asia

Directorate-General VIII
(Commissioner João de Deus Pinheiro)

> Oversight of the Lomé Convention, relations with the African, Caribbean and Pacific (ACP) countries
>
> Relations with non-governmental organizations (NGOs)

European Community Humanitarian Office (ECHO)
(Commissioner Emma Bonino)

> Humanitarian assistance and emergency aid

Figure 1.1 Directorates-General of the European Commission having responsibility for external relations (Relex DGs): 1995–9.

Treaty of Amsterdam, should go some way towards addressing the coherence problem, at least within Pillar I. However much will depend upon imponderables such as the political skills of the next Commission President.

In the context of external relations, the ability to negotiate with other actors in the international system is fundamental; indeed it is a condition of entry to the system itself. 'Policy making' in international fora contrasts significantly with the legislative processes of domestic political systems: it is, for the most part, a function of formal negotiation between legally recognized entities. In consequence 'the ability to negotiate' is determined by the interaction between external and internal factors. Thus accordance to the EC of international legal status, or personality, provides a formal right of entry to the system in circumstances where the EC enjoys exclusive competence internally. In practice, however, the unwillingness of Member State governments to transfer competence to the Community in policy areas considered 'sensitive' means that competence is frequently mixed (shared between the EC and the Member States), disputed or unclear. This lack of internal cohesion provides the opportunity for third parties to raise objections to participation by the EC/EU, or even withhold recognition of the right of the Commission or the Presidency to negotiate on behalf of the Member States. This is a particularly troublesome issue in environmental negotiations, as Chapter 3 will demonstrate.

For almost all explicitly EC external activity, negotiation is central – whether in the multilateral setting of the World Trade Organization or in constructing bilateral association or cooperation agreements with third parties globally. Here the issue is not the ability to negotiate, rather it is the effectiveness of the negotiators; and again internal and external factors interact in constructing actorness. Internally, the structural impediments to agreeing a coherent mandate for negotiation are almost invariably apparent, as will be evident in several of the chapters which follow. A particular problem, here, is the lack of flexibility accorded to Commission negotiators in circumstances where changes to the mandate have to be renegotiated internally between 15 Member States. While this can delay or even jeopardize conclusion of negotiations, as in the case of the Europe Agreements with CEE countries (see Chapter 5), it can also have the effect of strengthening the Commission's negotiating position. Thus, in circumstances where the Community's economic presence looms large, and third parties are unwilling to take risks, the Community as a negotiator appears truly formidable. Indeed it was evident from interviews both with Commission officials and third parties that the EC uses its structural inflexibility as a negotiating ploy. Typical perceptions of the Commission's approach among third party representatives were – 'there are no free lunches'; 'we've cooked up a deal, take it or leave it'. Even among representatives of large third countries there was a sense of the Commission as a formidable negotiating partner. Without doubt, in circumstances where the economic weight of the EC can be utilized, the Commission is an effective negotiator.

That the policy instruments available to the EC/EU are overwhelmingly economic is the most obvious point to make in relation to the fourth requirement for actorness – availability of and capacity to utilize policy instruments. Routine use of the economic presence of the EC in the furtherance of broad policy aims is evident from most of the chapters which follow. Thus, as we shall see from Chapter 2, the accordance of various forms of privileged access to the Single Market reflects political priorities to a considerable extent; more recently insertion of explicit political conditionalities into aid and trade agreements has become routine, and increasingly intrusive. Non-compliance has, in a number of cases, led to full or partial suspension of privileges (see Chapters 4 and 5). As Piening has observed (1997:10) the weight of the EC can be formidable when displeasure is incurred.

As a consequence of increased economic integration, the imposition of formal economic sanctions has inevitably become a matter for the EC/EU.

Prior to entry into force of the TEU, this was achieved under existing trade provisions of the Treaty establishing the European Community (TEC). However the TEU introduced specific provision for the imposition of economic sanctions (Article 228a TEC [301]) and financial sanctions (Article 73g TEC [60]), in the context of joint actions under the CFSP and in order that the EU can speedily comply with UN decisions to impose sanctions.[16] These provisions are wide ranging but not without problems, since this is an area which straddles the Pillars of the Union; thus the decision to impose sanctions falls within Pillar II and the instruments of policy within Pillar I. In the case of UN sanctions this has not been a serious problem; however cross-pillar tensions have arisen over sanctions proposals arising in the context of CFSP particularly in the area of development cooperation.

As noted above, the EU's lack of assured access to military instruments is considered by some commentators to be a significant impediment to actor capability. In Chapter 7 we discuss this issue with particular reference to the security environment of post-Cold War Europe. We conclude that, while the new measures for constructive abstention introduced by the TOA might increase the potential for CFSP joint actions to include limited use of military personnel in pursuit of peacekeeping or conflict management tasks, this is unlikely to be a significant aspect of EU activities in the foreseeable future. In consequence economic instruments will remain central to EU actor capability.

The inclusion of domestic legitimacy as our final requirement for actorness reflects a number of factors, not least the growing significance of policy making at the EU level – in terms both of internal and external matters. This policy 'deepening' raises issues of legitimacy for two principal reasons. First there is a perception that, despite insistence upon adherence to democratic principles on the part of Member States and third parties, the EU itself suffers a democratic deficit. Second it is evident that, as EU policies impinge more directly upon the daily lives of individuals, policy implementation will increasingly be dependent upon public consent, forbearance and even active support. Economic and Monetary Union is only the most obvious example here.

In recent years a number of commentators have expressed concern that the EU is suffering a 'legitimacy crisis' (García 1993; Laffan 1996; Obradovic 1996). To the extent that such a crisis exists, it is likely to undermine the credibility of the EU and hence impede its capacity to act externally. In Chapter 8 we discuss this issue in some detail, both in relation to the overall legitimacy of the EU as a policy system and specifically in relation to external policy. Our conclusions are mixed. While there is little evidence of the popular identification with the EU that unquestioned overall legitimacy would imply, there appears to be widespread acceptance of the need for the EU to act in areas where Member State action is perceived to be inadequate. Overwhelmingly these are external policy areas (Taylor 1996; Leonard 1997).

External perceptions and expectations

The basic requirements for actorness outlined above relate to internal procedures and capabilities. However, as we have pointed out, the extent to which capabilities can be used effectively, or indeed at all, is also a function of opportunity to act, which we have linked to structural factors. Even from Sjöstedt's behavioural perspective, actor performance in any given situation requires consideration of 'influencing factors' emanating from the decision making environment (1977:75–6). While this is not central to Sjöstedt's analysis, we place great emphasis upon external influencing factors in the construction of intersubjective structures. Hence we have paid considerable attention to the perceptions and expectations of third parties.

In discussion of EU 'actorness', a number of persistent themes emerged. Interviewees referred, without exception, to the considerable challenges involved in interacting with the EC/EU, which is 'quite unlike dealing with an individual state government'. The complexity of the EC/EU, and the related difficulty of ascertaining the cause of policy blockages, was one theme; a second the extremely hard bargaining positions adopted by Commission negotiators (see the discussion of negotiation above). Moreover distinctions were frequently drawn between the effectiveness of the Commission and the uncertainty and inconsistency attending dealings with the Presidency. Here there is no doubt that the Commission's relative permanence and more ready access to economic policy instruments provide considerable advantages over the rotating Presidency.

It is of interest to note that, while a number of interviewees commented upon the lack of overall political direction and impetus to external policy, the absence of military capability was not identified as an issue by any of the third party representatives interviewed – all of whom nevertheless considered the EU to be a significant actor. Frequent reference was made, however, to the EU's failure to derive political benefits, in terms of recognition and influence, commensurate with its economic investment. While the EU's role in the Middle East was most commonly identified in this respect, there are a number of other areas, including humanitarian aid, where the EU's contribution has been largely unacknowledged. The overall thrust of these comments indicates that the EU is perceived, by those knowledgeable third party representatives whom we interviewed, to be more significant as an actor than is generally apparent; despite the failure fully to realize the political potential of its economic presence. It is our view that these perceptions contribute in important ways to understandings, expectations and practices relating to the EU as a global actor.

CONCLUSION

This chapter has surveyed a range of approaches to actors and actorness from International Law and from International Relations. The attempt to apply these approaches to the EU has revealed two sets of problems, which are interrelated. The first of these relates to ontological and epistemological questions concerning the nature of, and criteria for, actorness; and the second flows from the unique and complex character of the EU itself.

We have defined an actor as an entity capable of volition; that is, of formulating and acting upon decisions; and have argued that only actors have causal powers, or agency. Nevertheless we do not see agency as unlimited, rather we consider that the capacity to act reflects the interaction between internal capabilities and external opportunities. In examining the patterns of constraint and opportunity which contextualize agency, consideration was given to a range of structural analyses which essentially conceive of actors as subordinate to structures. Ultimately, however, our preference is for a social constructivist perspective which conceives of structure and agency as interacting dialectically. In this analysis structures are intersubjective; they comprise shared understandings which give meaning to, and provide the context for, agency. Since structures continually evolve, and provide opportunities as well as constraints, this analysis can accommodate change and even permits novelty. Clearly this is a major advantage when considering the EU.

The unique character of the EU has proved a major challenge to IR scholars. Despite the development, from the 1970s, of a 'mixed actor' focus to analysis, it has proved difficult to accommodate a multi-faceted entity which is neither an intergovernmental organization nor a state, but which operates globally across a range of policy areas. Consequently the temptation to use the state as comparator when discussing the EU has proved difficult to resist.

In our view comparisons between the EU and other actors in the global system are likely to produce only limited insights. The EU is an actor *sui generis*. We conceive of it as a multi-perspectival polity whose construction reflects both the experimentation of policy entrepreneurs and the opportunities afforded by the changing structures of the international system. Essentially, therefore, the EU remains in course of construction. This approach accommodates its evolution over time and its shifting character at any one time; it also leaves open the question of its future destination. Despite this, the conclusion that the EU should be considered as a single, albeit multi-faceted, actor remains problematic. In some policy areas, as we shall see, this is a tenable proposition, in others the EC/EU bifurcation and the complex and shifting relationships between the Community and its Member States might suggest several actors. Here issues of internal coherence and consistency assume importance.

In the following chapters we examine, across a range of policy areas, the complex interaction between internal and external factors in the construction of EU actorness. Two issues are of central importance – the relationship between internal coherence/consistency (which to a significant extent reflects political will to act), and perceptions of the EC's presence; and the mechanisms by which presence, in turn, contributes to the construction of actorness. This enables us to think in overall terms about the status of the EU in the global system, the sources of its influence and the impact of the evolving perceptions and expectations of third parties. Thus are the roles of the EU as a global actor socially constructed and reconstructed.

2 The EU as an economic power and trade actor

> The European Union is the world's largest trading bloc. The sheer size of its
> market gives it incomparable influence on international trade issues.
>
> (FCO/DTI 1996:18)

Within the tariff walls of the Single Market live 368.7 million consumers
with an aggregate GDP, in 1993, of 5.8 trillion ECUs. In terms of sheer
economic presence, the Union is only, at the moment, rivalled by the United
States. Comparable figures for the USA show a significantly smaller population of 258.3 million people but a slightly larger economy with a GDP of
6.052 trillion ECUs (Commission 1995h:18). Although the US and EU
currently constitute the largest economic entities on earth in GDP terms
(Japan has a GDP of 2.43 trillion ECUs), they have only 4.6 per cent and 6.6
per cent of global population respectively.[1]

Economic presence, as it has developed from a customs union of six
nations to a Single Market of 15, has not been entirely matched by the
development of a capacity to behave as a single purposive actor in the world
system. The foundations of such a capacity were legally provided by the
Treaty of Rome, which granted exclusive Community competence in the
management of external trade in goods as a necessary corollary to the creation of a customs union with a Common Customs Tariff (CCT). Since 1961
the Community has fully developed its potential as a trade policy actor in
ways which were extensively determined by the structural influence of the
world trade regime. The comments, by a largely 'eurosceptic' British government, that it has 'an incomparable influence on international trade issues'
are testimony to this. However, trade in goods is only one aspect of the
contemporary global economy, and one which has declined in relative significance since the establishment of the Community. In these other areas –
services, investment and monetary affairs – the burgeoning presence of the
EU has not yet been reflected in the creation of an equivalent capacity to act
as a single player. The relationship between economic presence and different
forms and degrees of external 'actorness' are the subject of the first part of
this chapter.

Based, at least initially, on its position as a trade policy actor, the Union (or more properly the EC) has developed a repertoire of roles in the world political economy. Most evident, to the very large number of states that rely upon trading access to the Single Market, is its role as gatekeeper and negotiator of access to the markets of others. The utilization of various degrees of preferential access to the Single Market, which we discuss in the second part of this chapter, positions the EC at the centre of a web of bilateral links. For those outsiders at the periphery of this system the EC, and indeed particular parts of the Commission, appears as a very potent, sometimes inscrutable, and on occasion domineering, single actor.

The EU is also a key contestant in the often conflictual relations between the major blocs in the world economy. 'With the end of the Cold War,' wrote the Director of Economic Studies at the US Council for Foreign Relations, 'US trade policy is becoming high foreign policy even if policy-makers in Washington do not always recognize it' (Aho 1993:19). If this is so for the only remaining military superpower, it is likely to be an even more relevant observation for Europeans. Thus in the third section of this chapter we consider the role of the EC/EU as 'big power' in relation to Japan and, most significantly, the United States. A notable element of this transatlantic interaction is the way in which US administrations, despite continuing quarrels over the specifics of trade policy, have increasingly 'constructed' the European actor as an equal with which to conduct a whole range of economic and political business. The final part of this chapter is very much an extension of the EU's 'big power' role, in that we consider the Union as a multilateral negotiator in the context of the GATT/WTO. The focus is upon the Uruguay Round negotiations, which provided the most severe test of the EC's coherence and consistency as an actor.

TRADE: FOUNDATION OF PRESENCE AND ACTORNESS

This most fundamental aspect of Community presence derives from the initial creation of a customs union. The method employed, under GATT rules, was to establish a Common Customs Tariff calculated by taking the average of all the existing tariffs of the original six members.[2] As soon as this was put in place it had real impacts for outsiders in terms of what economists describe as trade diversionary effects. The stimulation of trade and economic growth within the union was, of course, the main reason for its establishment. Trade statistics indicate that the customs union was effective in bringing about a reversal of the ratio between internal and external trade. In 1958 the trade between EC members was 35 per cent of their overall total, by 1975 it was 49 per cent and by 1992, 59 per cent (Heidensohn 1995:10). These figures are somewhat misleading because over this period the Community enlarged from six to 12 members – automatically transferring trade from the category of external to internal. This, at the same time, greatly added to the presence of the EC in the world economy. The accession of Britain in 1973, with its high dependence on overseas trade and its extensive system of ex-imperial preference (which necessitated a new EC relationship with the African, Caribbean and Pacific (ACP) countries) was particularly significant.

The Community, and now the Union, has remained the world's largest trading entity. Despite all the shifts in the volume and composition of world merchandise trade, its share of global imports and exports has remained relatively stable at around 20 per cent (see Figures 2.1 and 2.2). At present 9 per cent of EU GDP and 10 per cent of all employment within the Single Market is directly attributable to external trade (WTO 1997a:11). The composition and direction of EU merchandise trade are described in Figure 2.3 and in the accompanying list of the EU's top 20 trading partners (Table 2.1).

A key set of indicators of presence are those measuring the dependence of trading partners on the EU market. This can be very extensive indeed for some European and African economies. The 1995 average for the Central and East European Countries (CEEC) was 63 per cent, with Slovenia conducting 78.8 per cent of its trade with the EU (Commission 1997g:5–7) while in Africa some comparable figures are Uganda 75 per cent, Mauretania 79 per cent and Equatorial Guinea 99 per cent (Commission 1997d:56–7). While, despite the effects of the customs union, trade with the other industrialized countries has generally increased since 1961, the major losers appear to have been the non-oil exporting non-newly industrializing countries (NICs) whose share of imports into the EC has dropped from a 1958 figure of 46 per cent to a 1992 level of 30 per cent (Heidensohn 1995:8). This, however, is more reflective of a general trend in the world economy

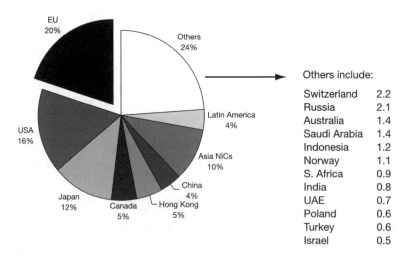

Figure 2.1 Shares of world merchandise exports (excluding EU intra-trade), 1995. (*Source:* Commission 1996a, 12:33)

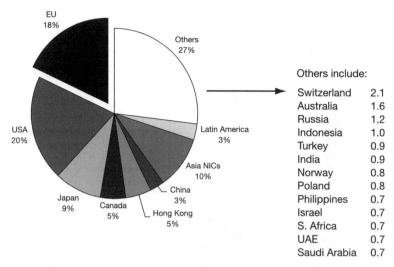

EU
18%

Others
27%

Others include:

Switzerland	2.1
Australia	1.6
Russia	1.2
Indonesia	1.0
Turkey	0.9
India	0.9
Norway	0.8
Poland	0.8
Philippines	0.7
Israel	0.7
S. Africa	0.7
UAE	0.7
Saudi Arabia	0.7

USA
20%

Latin America
3%

Asia NICs
10%

China
3%

Japan
9%

Canada
5%

Hong Kong
5%

Figure 2.2 Shares of world merchandise imports (excluding EU intra-trade), 1995. (*Source:* Commission 1996a, 12:34)

than any particular impediments imposed by the creation of the EC, which has indeed made strenuous, if not altogether successful, efforts to enhance the access of the ACP associates and other less developed countries to the European market (see Chapter 4).

The creation of a customs union and the setting of a CCT necessarily involved the granting of competence to the Commission to negotiate tariff levels with third parties. This continues to provide the basis for the oldest and most potent manifestation of the EC as an actor, the Common Commercial Policy (CCP), which has been effective since 1961. At that time the EC, in the shape of the Commission, was almost immediately involved in developing its role as a trade actor, as its trading partners sought to negotiate on the effects of the customs union. The GATT 'Dillon Round' of 1960–1 was largely devoted to this.

As the Common Commercial Policy developed, the Commission exhibited a significant degree of autonomy from the Member States, and a real capacity to behave in a deliberate way in relation to other actors. This is evident both from the legal ascription of competence and in actual practice, which has on occasion moved well beyond the 'letter of the law'. The legal foundation is provided by the exclusive competence in trade granted to the Community in the Common Commercial Policy established by Article 113 [133] of the Treaty of Rome. This 'most frequently used Treaty provision in the exercise of the European Community's powers in the field of external relations' (Macleod, Hendry and Hyett 1996:266) transfers the making and implementation of trade policy to the Community level, where there will be a common policy on tariff rates, international negotiations, liberalization,

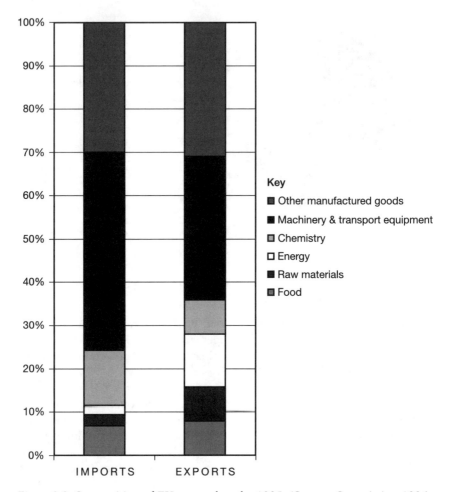

Figure 2.3 Composition of EU external trade, 1995. (*Source:* Commission 1996a, 12:37)

exports and trade protection measures; all based on uniform principles. On this basis the Community now has in excess of 9000 separate tariff lines and a very extensive corpus of Community trade rules and policy instruments, mostly in the form of Council Regulations.[3]

In the Common Commercial Policy (and also in agriculture) the Commission has the right to initiate policy and to propose negotiations, while the Council has the right to approve or disapprove acting by Qualified Majority Vote (QMV). Nevertheless, in the final analysis, where the national interests of Member States are severely at risk, a *de facto* consensus may be required. In a negotiation the Commission will propose, and the Council approve, a mandate which provides the brief from which the Commission will actually conduct the talks. Even when representatives of the Member States are

Table 2.1 Top twenty trading partners of the EU, 1995.

	Exports			Imports		
Rank		%	Σ%		%	Σ%
1	USA	17.8	17.8	USA	19.0	19.0
2	Switzerland	9.0	26.7	Japan	10.0	29.0
3	Japan	5.8	32.5	Switzerland	8.0	37.0
4	Norway	3.0	35.5	China	4.8	41.9
5	Russia	2.8	38.4	Norway	4.7	46.5
6	Hong Kong	2.8	41.1	Russia	4.0	50.6
7	Poland	2.7	43.8	Poland	2.2	52.8
8	China	2.6	46.4	Taiwan	2.2	55.0
9	Turkey	2.4	48.7	Canada	2.1	57.1
10	South Korea	2.2	50.9	South Korea	2.0	59.1
11	Czech Republic	2.0	52.9	Brazil	2.0	61.1
12	Brazil	2.0	54.9	Turkey	1.7	62.8
13	Singapore	1.9	56.8	Malaysia	1.7	64.5
14	Australia	1.8	58.7	Czech Republic	1.7	66.1
15	Canada	1.8	60.5	Singapore	1.6	67.7
16	Taiwan	1.8	62.2	Saudi Arabia	1.6	69.3
17	Israel	1.7	63.9	India	1.4	70.8
18	India	1.7	65.6	South Africa	1.4	72.2
19	Hungary	1.5	67.1	Hungary	1.4	73.6
20	Saudi Arabia	1.5	68.7	Hong Kong	1.3	74.9

Source: Commission 1996a, 12:38–9.

physically present (as, for example, at GATT/WTO meetings) they will remain silent while the Commission articulates the Community position. At the end of the negotiation the Commission will propose the conclusion of any agreement reached to the Council.

The Commission, for the purposes of the Common Commercial Policy, is DGI which, at least in relation to other DGs, has usually been associated with free trading and an essentially liberal approach, especially under the leadership of Vice-President Sir Leon Brittan. Significantly, there is no formal Trade Council composed of national trade ministers within the regular schedule of Community business as there is, for example, an Agricultural or Environment Council. Instead the Council that deals with trade, alongside a great many other issues, is the General Affairs Council (GAC) composed of Member State foreign ministers. They will benefit from a wider view of external policy (as opposed to what the Community defines as external relations) but they do not have the tightly focused sectoral interest in merchandise trade issues that the Agricultural Council has with regard to the farming industry.[4] Trade ministers do, however, meet as the Council within the context of GATT/WTO meetings, where Member States are contracting parties/members and where they are able to adjust the Commission's negotiating mandate 'on the spot'.

The European Parliament has not been allowed to play a formal role in the negotiation or conclusion of trade agreements under Article 113 [133]. Despite extending the scope of parliamentary powers elsewhere, the Maastricht Treaty maintained the rule that, although the Council was required to consult the Parliament where other international agreements were being made, this should not be the case for the Common Commercial Policy (TEC Art.228(3) [300(3)]). An extensive set of informal practices have, however, grown up involving consultation with the relevant parliamentary committees during external negotiations, including trade negotiations.[5]

In the Common Commercial Policy, as in other areas, there has always been a degree of tension, not to say distrust, between the Member States and the Commission. Sir Roy Denman, then a British trade official, observed one of the early forays of the European actor into trade diplomacy: 'a Commission representative would sometimes turn up for negotiations, flanked by French and German officials who appeared to have him under a kind of house arrest' (quoted in Buchan 1993:13). This was in the very early 1960s, during the transition period. By the end of the decade a more institutionalized means whereby Member States could monitor the external negotiating activities of the Commission was established. This had a treaty basis in Article 113(3) [133], where the Commission was charged with the conduct of negotiations 'in consultation with a special committee appointed by the Council to assist the Commission in this task . . .'.

The Article 113 Committee, as it became known, has been a significant body in the conduct of the Community's trade diplomacy ever since, in many ways obviating the need for a formal Trade Council. It meets in two formations: monthly at the level of 'full members' who are senior national trade officials assisted by their advisors, partly home and partly Brussels based, and more regularly at the level of deputies, who cope with the technical detail. The Commission is similarly represented at the meetings and at the more specialized *ad hoc* working groups that the 113 Committee spawns. Working relationships become close and informal and a 'club like atmosphere' pertains (Hayes-Renshaw and Wallace 1997:90). Although the original function of the Article 113 Committee was to monitor the Commission, it has become a close policy collaborator, relating the views of Member State governments to the Commission on a day-to-day basis.

The Common Commercial Policy has evolved through a complex interaction between the shifting composition of international trade, the external demands of various GATT rounds and adjudicative decisions of the European Court of Justice (ECJ) that have fleshed out the meaning of the sparse Treaty clauses.[6] These were bound to be disputed because the wording of Article 113 [133] is not 'exhaustive' in delimiting the categories of trade that are included within the Common Commercial Policy. The operative clause simply reads:

The common commercial policy shall be based on uniform principles, particularly in regard to changes in tariff rates, the conclusion of tariff and trade agreements, the achievement of uniformity in measures of liberalization, export policy and measures to protect trade such as those to be taken in the event of dumping or subsidies.

While, in 1957, the substance of what constituted trade was relatively well understood, by the time of the Uruguay Round, with the potentialities of liberalized trade in goods largely played out and with vast alterations in an increasingly globalized economy under way, this was no longer the case.

The Common Agricultural Policy

The historic counterpart of the creation of the common market was the Common Agricultural Policy (CAP). The basic mechanism of this policy, which sought to increase food production and raise farming incomes, ensured that there would also be external consequences. Artificially high prices within the EC were maintained by the imposition of a 'variable levy' on imports, which served to adjust their price up to the high level set for European produce. The receipts went into the Agricultural Guidance and Guarantee Fund (EAGGF) and were used to intervene in the market to maintain high prices, thereby guaranteeing farm incomes.

Although the CAP soon became a budgetary nightmare (swallowing at one point around 75 per cent of the EC's financial resources) it achieved runaway success in encouraging ever higher levels of food production – way beyond that which could be absorbed by the domestic market. Obligated under the CAP to intervene and purchase the surpluses, the Community sought alternatives to expensive stockpiling in the infamous 'wine lakes' and 'butter mountains'. The economic answer was to subsidize the export of the surpluses through export restitution payments, which made it possible to sell high priced EC food on world markets.

The EC soon moved from being largely a food importer to the status of a major exporter. For example, its share of the world wheat flour market increased from 24 per cent in 1963–4 to 62 per cent in 1980–1, while the corresponding US share fell from 40 per cent to 18 per cent (Paemen and Bensch 1995:24). Not the least dimension of the Community's presence in the global system, and certainly the most objectionable for third parties, has thus been its position in world agricultural markets. This was a function, not of externally orientated policy, but a series of internal developments and actions to cope with the burgeoning CAP, which essentially served to offload some of its problems on to outsiders. The United States, faced with the economic damage done to its agricultural exports, proceeded to retaliate with its own system of farm subsidies, further driving down world prices and worsening the terms of trade of those countries most dependent upon agricultural exports. The worst affected countries were those, like Argentina and Brazil, reliant upon the export of temperate products – cereals, beef, citrus fruits – falling within the remit of the CAP (*ibid*). The EC has, of course, no interest in interfering with free trade in tropical products, which have duty free access to the European market. It is the misfortune of cane sugar producers that there is also a temperate, Community grown and subsidized version of their product – beet sugar.

Bringing agricultural trade within the disciplines of the General Agreement on Tariffs and Trade was a principal and highly controversial aim of the US and others during the Uruguay Round. Partly as a consequence of the negotiations, reform of the CAP, involving direct income support for farmers rather than production subsidies, is under way. However progress has been slow. The level of EC agricultural protection remains high, with an average tariff rate of over 20 per cent (compared with an industrial goods rate of 4.9 per cent) and significant tariff 'peaks' for certain commodities. Use of quota restrictions also continues (WTO 1997a:7).

Agriculture was the other important area in which the Community was initially granted exclusive competence in the Treaty of Rome. The main concern here was the massive internal task of creating the CAP but, as indicated above, the EC's agricultural presence was soon to have extensive external impact. An external dimension to the CAP was envisaged at the outset in terms of 'machinery for stabilising exports and imports' (TEC Art.40 [34]). Agricultural products do not, however, fall within the scope of the Common Commercial Policy and are the responsibility of DGVI of the Commission (as opposed to DGI for trade) and the Agricultural Council (as opposed to the General Affairs Council).[7] For a long period this distinction was relatively unimportant, although there were agricultural trade elements to the Community's many preferential agreements. It became very significant, as we shall see, during the Uruguay Round.

The international trade regime

The evolution of the Common Commercial Policy and the EC as a trade actor can only be understood with reference to the trade regime, initiated in 1947. For half a century the General Agreement on Tariffs and Trade (GATT) has provided the basis of multilateral rule-based regime. Its fundamental norms have been 'most favoured nation treatment' (Art.I) in terms of the tariffs set by members against each other and 'national treatment' of imported goods once customs duties at the border have been paid (Art.III). Other important GATT provisions, sometimes honoured in their breach rather than observance, are the outlawing of quotas, non-tariff barriers (Arts.XI–XIV) and trade distorting subsidies (Art.XVI). The regime has been developed by successive rounds of reciprocal tariff cutting negotiations in which, as we have seen, the EC has been involved since its inception. The whole edifice is underpinned by a unique rule enforcement system of dispute panels in which the EC has also been a frequent litigant.

As we have seen, the original Common Commercial Policy of the EC was something of a *tabula rasa*: its development and the understandings and practices adopted by the Community as it emerged as a trade actor were very much the outcome of a mutual process of structuration. That is to say EC agency was constructed in terms of the disciplines and institutional setting of the GATT regime, but equally the regime itself was moulded to the requirements of one of its most powerful participants. Of primary significance here is GATT Article XXIV concerning the creation of customs unions and free trade areas (FTAs). As well as permitting the creation of the customs union in the first place it provides the framework within which the EC's many association agreements with outsiders have been constructed.

EC practice across the whole range of its trade activities and policy instruments has been framed not only by the legal 'disciplines' but also by the common intersubjective understandings of the regime. DGI describes the trade regime as 'the central' anchor of the Community's external role and applauds its 'implementation of the right policies' (WTO 1997a:12). More-over, in the words of the Chairperson of a WTO trade policy review meeting, 'the trade policies and actions of the EU do not leave any WTO member indifferent' (WTO 1997b:8).

The original 1947 GATT was an agreement between 'contracting parties' not an international organization – indeed an International Trade Organization (ITO) had been explicitly rejected by the US Congress.[8] After the creation of the EEC this gave rise to the anomaly that only the Member State contracting parties had full legal status and responsibility for carrying out obligations, while at the same time in terms of internal Community law the EC had succeeded them as participants in the GATT (Macleod, Hendry and Hyett 1996:179). Notwithstanding, the Commission exercised its exclusive competence in trade matters in the decision making procedures of the regime – where the EC from the beginning has operated and been accepted as a single actor. A strong Commission presence was established in Geneva, the base of the GATT (and now WTO) Secretariat and Council meetings, where the *Maison de l'Europe* housed both the Commission's delegation and the ambassadors of the Member States to the GATT.[9] An important outcome of the Uruguay Round was the creation of a new body, the World Trade Organization. This provided a proper organizational framework for GATT activities and, in the process, regularized the position of the EC by making it a member on the same basis as the original contracting parties (WTO, Art.XI, Original Membership).[10]

BEYOND TRADE IN GOODS

During the life of the Community, merchandise trade *per se*, as covered by the original Common Commercial Policy, diminished in significance as a clearly delineated international economy gave way to an increasingly globalized one. According to the World Bank, by 1990 40 per cent of visible world trade was actually intra-trade within transnational firms (*Financial Times*, 2 June 1992). Moreover the startling growth of financial markets moving funds around in cyberspace is largely unrelated to 'real trade'. The Single Market, in common with other developed economies, has been increasingly dominated by tertiary sector invisible trade across frontiers. The service sector has proved difficult to define adequately, provoking major questions as to the extent of Community competence under Article 113 [133].[11]

The Uruguay Round forced these matters on to the agenda. Previous rounds had covered tariffs and codes for merchandise trade with which the original EC arrangements were well equipped to deal. Now, however, not only was agriculture included in the Uruguay Round, but new agreements on trade in services (GATS), intellectual property (TRIPS) and investment (TRIMS) were proposed. If any or all the latter were to be defined as part of the Common Commercial Policy then they would be subject to exclusive community competence, something that a number of Member States were unwilling to countenance. On the other hand, the negotiations had to be pursued. Accordingly, for the duration of the Round, Member States agreed an *ad hoc* arrangement that they could be handled using the normal procedures of the Common Commercial Policy. Given the complex interlinkage between issues at the talks and the 'globality' rule that nothing would be settled until everything was settled, it would pragmatically have been difficult to proceed in any other way. However, the end of the negotiations was soured by accusations, from some Member States, that the Commission had exceeded its authority and had not been entirely open about its negotiating strategy. This was compounded by DGI's decision, endorsed by the College of Commissioners, to proceed with an undifferentiated implementation of the results of Uruguay (claiming that they all fell within the scope of Article 113 [133]) and to meet Member State objections by recourse to a European Court ruling. This was, from the Commission's point of view, a serious mistake.[12] The result was Opinion 1/94 a somewhat bizarre 'judgement of Solomon' in which the ECJ refused to accept the Commission's arguments and held that only certain aspects of trade in services and intellectual property were part of the Common Commercial Policy. In terms of trade in services, which had been categorized in the GATS by four modes of supply, only one mode, involving the actual crossing of frontiers, was included (Macleod, Hendry and Hyett 1996:269–71).

The problem of Community competence, the Commission's prerogatives and the new forms of international trade persisted into the Intergovernmental Conference that negotiated the 1997 Treaty of Amsterdam. A draft text before the IGC proposed a new article (113a) giving the Community competence for services, intellectual property and investment within the context of multilateral negotiations, but with the express proviso that Member States would retain internal competence in these areas. This was to have been supported by a declaration that the Commission would in future conduct negotiations with the 'maximum transparency' *vis à vis* Member States.[13] In the event the apparent trade-off between increased competence and transparency did not succeed as the French government insisted upon numerous exclusions. This drove the Commission to the conclusion that it had nothing to gain by the new clause (Interview, Commission, DGI, July 1997). The Conference result, which does not settle the issue, merely adds wording that the Council, acting unanimously, may decide to extend the application of Article 113 [133] 'to international agreements and negotiations and agreements on services and intellectual property' (TEC Art.133(5)).[14] The problem will not diminish, as subsequent WTO meetings have enlarged still further the definition of what can be legitimately discussed under the heading of trade. The so-called 'new trade issues' include investment, competition policy, trade and the environment and, most contentious of all, trade and labour standards (Woolcock 1996).

The Single Market

The original Common Market, despite the removal of all internal tariff barriers by mid 1967, never yielded the full benefits in terms of internal cross-frontier economic activity of which it was assumed to be capable. Many impediments remained, including disparities in national standards, border controls and national purchasing and tendering arrangements. In order to sweep these away and revitalize the European economy, the '1992' project for the completion of the internal market was put in train. Implicit in this project was an understanding that far reaching measures were required if Europe was to compete effectively with the United States and Japan. It had enormous implications for the outside world. For the EFTA countries it gave rise to the calculation that most of them could no longer prosper outside the Community and, in a process permitted by the ending of the Cold War, led to the accession of Austria, Sweden and Finland.

Presence is as much a matter of external perception as economic statistics, and in the United States the reaction to the completion of the Single Market, which was frequently dubbed 'fortress Europe', was both excessive and politically significant. It helped to stimulate a new US approach to the EC which increasingly focused upon the provisions of the 1992 project which, although not strictly related to trade, had significant and largely unintended impacts within the US and elsewhere. National service industries such as banking and telecommunications have traditionally been heavily protected, and a major part of the 1992 programme was to liberalize such markets within the EC. This had implications for EC presence in the global economy – indeed the intention was to improve European competitiveness. At the forefront were a number of 'market access' issues that confronted outsiders who would have to deal with the new Single Market. In the banking sector, for example, the EC Second Banking directive of 1988 implied that those countries wishing to participate in the EC market must offer comparable access to their own. This placed pressure on US state-based banking regulations, where the Federal authorities were not in a position to offer such reciprocal access. As Hocking and Smith (1997:55) note:

> while the EC was moving regulation from national to Community level, in the USA there was no parallel state or state-like regulatory structure. The challenge to the executive on these 'behind the border' issues arose not only from the nature of the SMP [Single Market Programme] but also from the diffusion of regulatory power in the USA itself.

In this and other ways the 1992 programme established a new and formidable competitive presence. As we shall see, the response of the United States was both to engage the EC in the traditional way, through well-worn trade channels, and also to open a multi-level dialogue with the Community in an attempt to set regulatory agendas and almost become part of the internal policy making process. This had implications for the external actorness of the EC which were far removed from the relatively simple concerns of the original Common Commercial Policy. At the level of the international trading regime the experience of perfecting the Single Market has, it is generally acknowleged by trading partners, been highly influential in shaping subsequent liberalization on a world scale, where the Single Market process and multilateral liberalization have been mutually supportive.[15]

A major reason for the EC's competitors to be concerned over the completion of the Single Market was that their corporations were already amongst the largest players within its boundaries. In the past 30 years there has been an enormous growth in flows of foreign direct investment (FDI).[16] The original creation of the Community led many corporations based in the US, Japan and elsewhere to establish subsidiaries within the tariff wall, in order to avoid the competitive disadvantages of exporting to the Community as opposed to producing within it. Between 1985 and 1990, for example, over 500 Japanese firms established themselves within the EC market (Commission 1991c:6). The presence of the Single Market thus continues to serve as a magnet to investment flows. European firms of 'American parentage', as they are tactfully described, would include within their number most major US corporations. This situation poses a novel problem for the US government (and indeed other governments) in dealing with the Community, in so far as the interests of American firms within the EC may directly contradict those of American exporters. Nor should it be forgotten that the EU is a major source of finance for the rest of the world. During the Asian economic crisis of 1997–8, for example, it was pointed out by the British Chancellor of the Exchequer that the exposure of European banks was greater than that of the US and Japan combined.[17] The EU is not, however, a single actor in this area, despite its close relationship to trade. The primary reason is simply that there is no common policy on investment. Nonetheless, the EU cannot avoid involvement in attempts to create an international investment regime parallel to the GATT/WTO.[18]

Economic and Monetary Union

From the beginning the Member States of the Community have been charged with the coordination of their macroeconomic policies and the ECOFIN formation of the Council of Ministers provides the necessary forum. However, while the EC has massive presence as a trade bloc, and many significant policy functions have been transferred to the Community level, the essential fiscal and monetary levers of macroeconomic management are still in national hands. Above all, although there have been long-run aspirations towards Economic and Monetary Union (EMU), and serious attempts to create the necessary policies from 1970, they did not prosper until the 1990s. Consequently the Union has exhibited a peculiarly unbalanced economic presence, where a coherent trade bloc and investment market contrasted starkly with a fragmented fiscal and monetary order.

Recognition of the significance of the EC as an economic entity for the purposes of global macroeconomic coordination has been evident since 1980, when the President of the Commission was first invited to attend G7 summit meetings. Since the ratification of the Maastricht Treaty extensive preparations have been in hand for the institution of a single currency and the creation of a single European monetary entity. The Euro began trading on international markets on 1 January 1999 and will challenge the dollar as the major international reserve currency. The EC has begun to pursue this end. In 1998 it struck a deal on improved trade access with the Chinese government under which 40 per cent of the latter's reserve assets will be held in Euros (*The Guardian*, April 1998).

With the attainment of Economic and Monetary Union the EU will enjoy a comprehensive and coherent global economic presence with important consequent changes in its capacity to act. This was already emergent in the late 1990s, as Member States adjusted their policies to meet the Maastricht convergence criteria for membership of the new monetary union. Finance ministers of the Member States, meeting in the ECOFIN Council, increasingly concert their monetary and macroeconomic policy. Although the EC is not a member of the IMF the larger Member States are amongst the major shareholders and ECOFIN meets 'in the margin' of IMF and related meetings in order to coordinate a European position. To this must be added the various international meetings dealing with the financial stabilization of the post-Communist economies (Hayes-Renshaw and Wallace 1997:31–2) and more recently the attempts to cope with monetary consequences of the collapse of Asian financial markets in 1997–8. In all this activity the finance minister who is 'president in office' has a key role in representing the Union at G7 and other meetings. While the G7 continues to meet at the level of the finance ministers and central bank governors of the major industrialized countries (USA, Canada, Japan, Italy, France, Germany and UK), it has been expanded for other purposes to become the G8, through the addition of Russia. Most notably what used to be the G7 annual summit meeting is now a G8 meeting. Here the arrangement is that when a G8 member holds the EU presidency they should also chair and host the summit during their term of office.

The EU has begun to acquire actor-like characteristics in global monetary politics even if the approach continues to be intergovernmental and the EC has no formal standing at the IMF. Yet the situation is changing rapidly with the onset of Economic and Monetary Union and a single currency. The Community and its new central bank will succeed the Member States at the IMF. The new Article 109 [111] of the TEC negotiated at Maastricht provides for Council decisions on these matters.[19] The introduction of EMU and a single currency will in all likelihood constitute the most significant strengthening of the Union's position as an economic actor since the development of the Common Commercial Policy. However, the mechanisms that will be used for international monetary negotiation will not be akin to the familiar trade procedures of Article 113 [133]. Although the Commission has a right of initiative it is not provided with an autonomous right to negotiate. In a phrase reminiscent of the Common Foreign and Security Policy (the CFSP is covered in Chapter 6) it is merely to be 'fully associated' with negotiations (TEC Art.109(3) [111(3)]).

GATEKEEPER OF THE SINGLE MARKET

The everyday economic role of the Community in the world system, and the role in which most countries have direct experience of the EC as an actor, is as gatekeeper of the Single Market and regulator of trade relations. It also now aspires to a more offensive role, as opener of overseas markets, under the Commission's 1996 Market Access Strategy.[20] The first line of defence at the border is through the use of tariffs, which have been progressively reduced – at least on industrial goods. There are also quantitative restrictions or quotas which, although contrary to GATT principles, are frequently imposed upon textiles and agriculture products. Both the latter have not, until the Uruguay Round, been subject to the disciplines of the trade regime. There have also been 'grey area' restrictions on imports of products such as cars and electronic goods negotiated in the form of Voluntary Export Restraints (VERs) by Member State governments. The Commission has been relatively successful in the gradual elimination of this area of inconsistency in EU trade policy (WTO 1997a:17).

The GATT/WTO regime can be regarded as a disarmament agreement in which competing nations agree to a reciprocal reduction of their trade defences. In doing this they are also permitted a range of 'safeguard' measures for the 'contingent protection' of national economies. These include the use of countervailing duties (Art.VI), emergency protection of industries through quantitative restrictions on imports (Art.XIX) and anti-dumping measures. The latter has been the preferred instrument for the Commission's defence of the European market against 'unfair' competition and the 'EU remains the second most important user of anti-dumping procedures' (WTO 1997a:17).[21] The relevant GATT Article VI recognizes that 'dumping, by which products from one country are introduced into the commerce of another at less than the normal value is to be condemned if it causes or threatens material injury to an established industry'. Under these circumstances contracting parties are permitted to levy an anti-dumping duty. The controversial element in anti-dumping policy, as executed by a large staff in DGI Directorates C and D, is that it is very difficult to obtain objective measures establishing that dumping has occurred and that, in the view of critics, numerous fanciful calculations are performed to serve protectionist ends (Hindley 1992). It is significant that the GATS agreement does not include an anti-dumping clause; however, while the new GATT 1994 agreement attempts to bring more discipline to anti-dumping activity, it does not eliminate it as a potent and frequently used weapon in bilateral trade policy.

Association and preference

In acting out its role as gatekeeper, the Community benefits from its position at the centre of a complicated web of institutionalized bilateral links. They are provided for by Article 238 [310] of the TEC, whereby the Community may establish 'an association involving reciprocal rights and obligations, common action and special procedures'. The common element in all these agreements is trade and, usually, some form of discrimination or preference. They are also increasingly 'trade plus' agreements which can include a great deal more than an agreed removal or realignment of tariffs. Association Agreements, for example, include Association Councils, annual meetings at ministerial level plus Association Committees of senior civil servants, and there may even be a parliamentary element. From the earliest arrangements with Greece and Turkey the number and scope of agreements have increased markedly, especially since the 1980s, and renegotiated 'second and third generation' agreements have further broadened the range of items covered. These now include elements of human rights and political conditionality, cultural and technical/scientific cooperation. Few of the more recent agreements negotiated by the Commission fall exclusively within the purview of the Common Commercial Policy. Rather, they are 'mixed' in the sense that both the Community and Member States will be parties. Furthermore, items within the agreement will not only be beyond exclusive Community competence, but may, as in the case of political dialogue clauses, be beyond Community competence altogether (Macleod, Hendry and Hyett 1996:372).[22]

The coverage of such agreements is so extensive that the majority of states comprising the contemporary international system are now in some form of institutionalized preferential trade relationship with the EC. At the last count the EC had preferential (non-MFN) agreements with no fewer than 117 states (Stevens 1997:1).

> The EU's system of non-multilateral trade policy is so complex as almost to defy systematic, across the board analysis. Not only does Europe have more than two dozen agreements that provide non-multilateral access (tariff and non-tariff) – each with its own rules of origin – but the accords must be studied in detail to identify the level of preference. Moreover, the tariff levels keep changing.
>
> *(ibid:2)*

The EC's association and cooperation agreements have gone through a number of generations detailed in Figure 2.4, perform a range of functions and are at the heart of the Community's relationships with the developing world and its near neighbours which we discuss in Chapters 4 and 5 below. Those excluded from this extensive network of formalized links are the Commmunity's principal interlocutors within the WTO: the United States, Japan and Australia and New Zealand.

The Association Agreements are based on preferential trade arrangments which appear to violate the liberal and non-discriminatory principles of the international trade regime. They are, however, legitimized as either free trade areas or customs unions which are permitted under GATT Article XXIV.[23] The unwillingness of GATT contracting parties, over the years, to exercise rigorous scrutiny and disallow such arrangements (Hoekman and Kostecki 1995:219) has allowed the EC to construct what many observers have described as a 'pyramid of preferences' attaching large areas of the globe, and especially Europe's 'near abroad' in the Mediterranean and the old Soviet bloc countries, to the Community.

At the top of the pyramid are the remaining members of EFTA – Norway, Iceland and Liechtenstein – which under the European Economic Area Agreements are essentially within the Single Market. Below them are the CEEC, which have been granted a phased preferential access but one which is sharply curtailed in 'sensitive' areas where they might, under conditions of free trade, be expected to enjoy a comparative advantage; agricultural products, steel and textiles. They are still, of course, in a better position *vis à vis* the Single Market than other industrialized countries – whose exports are subjected to the CCT on the basis of the, in the circumstances, ironical GATT notion of 'most favoured nation status'. However, it should be

Evolution of EC agreements[1]
First generation trade agreements (1970s). Sectorally based, preferential or non-preferential.

Second generation trade and cooperation agreements (1980s). Added financial and technical cooperation to basic trade relationship.

Agreements with European non-member countries and other developed countries:
    Association Agreements – Cyprus, Malta, European Economic Area (Iceland, Leichtenstein, Norway); Trade/ Cooperation Agreements – Australia, Canada, New Zealand, Switzerland

Contemporary agreements reflecting TEU provisions
on development cooperation (Art. 130u [177])
Third generation cooperation agreements – provide for extensive cooperation on economic policy, employment generation, social and environmental issues, etc.

    Agreements with Asian and Latin American countries (ALA); Albania; interregional agreements with ASEAN, Gulf Cooperation Council, Andean Pact and Mercosur

Mixed Association Agreements – include all features of other third generation agreements plus dialogue on CFSP and JHA matters. Require Member State ratification.

    Europe Agreements with Central and East European countries (CEEC)

    Partnership and Cooperation Agreements with New Independent States (NIS) of former Soviet Union.[2]

    Euro-Med Association Agreements with Maghreb and Mashreq countries, Israel and Palestinian Authority.[3]

[1] Two important exceptions are the Lomé relationship with ACP countries (see Chapter 4) and the Association Agreement, now Customs Union, with Turkey (see Chapter 5), both of which involved in-depth cooperation from the outset.
[2] In practice these relationships vary in intensity. Their current status is shown in Table 5.1.
[3] For the current status of these agreements see Table 5.2.

Figure 2.4 Patterns of association and preference.

remembered that these, in reality 'least favoured' trading partners of the Union account for the bulk of the Community's imports (Commission 1997j:3).

Preferential access to the Single Market is only the beginning of the story. Not the least of the loopholes in GATT Article XXIV, which refers optimistically to the removal of 'substantially all' trade barriers, are the 'safeguard' and 'rules of origin' clauses that are a standard part of the EC's preferential arrangements. The safeguard clauses allow the EC to resort to unspecified measures against imports of 'sensitive' products if there is 'serious injury' to European producers or 'serious disturbance or difficulties which could bring about serious deterioration in the economic situation of a region within the EU' (Heidensohn 1995:60; citing Art.30 of the Europe Agreements). Bilateral FTA agreements between a central customs union and various individual economies have a 'hub and spoke' character in which specific exclusions of 'sensitive' sectors and the use of safeguard clauses can be utilized by import competing industrial lobbies to fend off effective trade liberalization (Hoekman and Kostecki 1995:226–7). Trade agreements will also typically include a local content or 'rules of origin' requirement. Normally this will require that the exporting country must have added at least 60 per cent of the value of a product in order to qualify for preferential access to the Single Market (Heidensohn 1995:60). This is to prevent a situation where parties outside the FTA would gain preferential access through re-exportation of a product. However, the effect may well be to force exporters within an FTA to seek higher priced sources of supply in order to comply with the 'rules of origin'. On top of all this, FTA members will also be subject to 'anti-dumping' action.

Bilateralism, actorness and power

It would be much more difficult to advance such protectionist interests under a multilateral FTA. The 'hub and spoke' character of the EC's preferential arrangements thus bestows a great deal of structural power on the centre in relation to the periphery, in which the EC is potentially able to dominate a divided set of supplicants and trade partners.[24] For most of the participants in these bilateral arrangements the Community is an often dominant actor whose external face is the Commission.

When interviewed, members of the missions in Brussels, professionally concerned with the management of 'trade plus' issues, were in little doubt as to the EC's 'actorness'. The EC is, of course, inordinately more complex than a state and, as one Ambassador put it, the move from negotiating with a government in a national capital to negotiating with the EC in Brussels 'is like changing from playing draughts to playing chess' (Interview, June 1996). An often repeated view, expressed by another trade diplomat, was that frequently the Commission would not be open to negotiation at all, but would simply 'agree a position and push it down our throats . . . sometimes we say no but only occasionally'. 'The typical Commission position is "we've cooked up a deal [with the Member States] take it or leave it"' and Commission officials will sometimes say 'if you want one word different we will have to go back to the Council' (Interview, January 1996).

Behind this lies not only the difficult internal arrangements of the Union, but, more brutally, the immense structural economic power of the hub, represented by the Commission, as opposed to even quite substantial trading nations located at the ends of the 'spokes'. For a Trade Counsellor of one such nation it was simply the case that his country was not an equal partner and lacked the muscle to engage in 'aggressive reciprocity' on trade issues; for another diplomat his countrymen's view was 'that ministers had to go to Brussels wearing trousers with reinforced knees' (Interview, January 1996).

The Commission does not solely rely upon an obduracy founded on the difficulty of persuading 15 Member States to agree. In trade matters DGI has long experience and competence in every sense of the word, and is quite capable of successfully pursuing its own view even if individual Member States may be uncomfortable.[25] It was a common view amongst the personnel of the Brussels missions that the Commission could, indeed, behave in an unaccountable way 'it had power but it was not under control', especially in the implementation of external policy.[26]

The EU is unusually difficult to deal with because ultimate decision making authority within the Common Commercial Policy rests with the Member States in Council and with their permanent representatives in COREPER. The latter was seen by outsiders as particularly opaque – 'a dark animal' (Interview, January 1996). As one trade counsellor put it:

> If you could get to represent your case at COREPER it would be ideal, but you have to rely upon your representatives lobbying Member States. It's like being unable to lobby a ministry when dealing with a national state. You don't cross COREPER and you have more chance of finding out what goes on in Council than in COREPER.
>
> (Interview, January 1996)

Decisions at COREPER, and ultimately in the Council, are bedeviled by what trade theorists have called the 'restaurant bill problem' (Winters 1994). This uses the analogy of a group of self-interested (even greedy) diners who know that they will have to share a single restaurant bill and therefore have an incentive to maximize their own gastronomic pleasure by ordering the most expensive dishes on the menu. In a customs union all members bear the welfare costs of protection but there are individual incentives to obtain protection for the particular products in which a country specializes. Under QMV rules in the Council there is space for a degree of bargaining and reciprocity which, while they may satisfy the immediate political requirements of Member States, will lead to outcomes which are protectionist and, in the view of bilateral trade partners, mean-spirited. Portugal, for example, will not benefit from the restrictions on imported vehicles backed by the French and Italian governments with auto industries to sustain; but can set against this measures to protect its own textile sector. For their part, French, Italians and consumers right across the Single Market will be paying higher prices for clothing as well as cars. In bilateral relations it will often be difficult for a partner, who does not have access to the intergovernmental horse-trading which lies at the heart of the EU system, to understand the reasons for discrimination:

> In negotiating with the EU one has to find out which country is obstructing progress and there is a problem of pinpointing which Member [for example Portugal and textiles] is opposing and work on them. Also Member States blame each other. Sometimes it is difficult to pinpoint

what is blocking agreement – countries may, for example, veto an issue as a bargaining chip related to some other concern. A deal that you reach is blocked somewhere else for extraneous reasons.

(Interview, external Mission, January 1996)

For another external observer: 'The incentive structure is all wrong. Agricultural ministers play to their constituencies and don't take the consequences of their actions' (Interview, external Mission, January 1996). In bilateral relations with a large set of smaller economies the kind of constraints to the expression of the rather narrow national interests of Member States – that might exist in a more equal relationship or a fully multilateral framework – are not present. This goes some way to account for the evident gap between free trade rhetoric and mercantilist behaviour on the part of the EU (something it shares in full measure with the US) and the embarrassing pettiness of some of its external dealings. The latter is particularly evident in the treatment of agricultural produce from developing or transitional countries, which the EU is committed to assist, but whose grapes or raspberries are excluded from the Single Market at the behest of specific commercial interests in one or more Member States.[27]

Liberal economists will decry the deleterious effects of such arrangements in terms of obstacles to trade liberalization, protectionist 'rent-seeking' at the centre and a general reduction of what they define as welfare. The political analyst will have an overlapping concern with the lobbying process, whereby particular interests can influence the Commission and ministers in the Council in shaping and operating the various agreements. Yet there is also a wider political view in which the Union as an actor has consciously arranged its trade preferences according to a set of political and strategic rather than simply economic purposes.

THE EU AS A 'BIG POWER'

There is a qualitative difference between the rather lop-sided and dependent relations that have been described in the previous section and those that exist between the EU, US and Japan and also, to a lesser extent, Canada, Australia and New Zealand. These countries (except for Canada which has a cooperation agreement dating from 1976) are not formally linked with the Union. They do, however, have very significant dealings with it on a number of dimensions, of which trade has traditionally been the most important. The multiple channels connecting these 'advanced' societies, involving high levels of direct foreign investment; increasingly seamless transnational financial markets; extensive interchanges of people and ideas and long established and intimate defence relationships, are well described by Keohane and Nye's (1977) concept of 'complex interdependence'.

It is certainly possible to observe the extremely high level of mutual interdependence between Japan, the United States and Western Europe, but a more mercantilist perspective on recent trends in the global political economy would identify the growth of a three-bloc configuration in the emerging structure of the global economic system. The creation of NAFTA involving the US, Canada and Mexico with a possible further extension into Latin America; and Japanese dominance in the Asia Pacific can be portrayed as two points of this triangular structure. The third most coherent and equally expansionist point is represented by the EU. The Union has itself favoured the institutionalization of interbloc and certainly interregional relationships with ASEAN, Mercosur and other regional organizations. Economic diplomacy within this tripolar world is often portrayed as being poised between the extension of multilateralism and global free trade through the WTO and a retreat into a world of neomercantilist trade blocs. Both trends are observable and there was certainly a relationship between the conclusion of the Uruguay Round and threats by the United States to concentrate upon liberalization within its spheres of economic influence.[28]

A significant characteristic of most of the commentary on these issues is that 'Europe' is normally assumed, without much question, to be an integrated, economic great power. For example:

> as Japan and Europe have caught up with the United States, the dominance of the US economy in the international system has been eroded, and with this the hegemony of the United States has been weakened. It has not been replaced by either Japanese or European hegemony, which would provide a framework into which institutions for promoting global cooperation could be fitted.
>
> (Currie and Vines, 1992:589)

Arguably the EU is regarded as a 'great power' (if not the biggest power) in the global political economy in just the same way that Austria–Hungary, whatever its internal peculiarities, was seen as one of the 'powers' in analyses of the nineteenth century politico-military balance. Whatever the interpretation of recent developments, few would dispute the significance of Japan–EU and US–EU relations for the future development of the global economy.

Japan

Japan is frequently regarded as an economic superpower, but it is worth remembering that its emergence as a leading exporter of manufactures has been relatively recent and that it accounts for just under 9 per cent of world trade (8.7 per cent in 1995, Commission 1996a:35). Also, whatever the potential of some future Japanese-led grouping in Asia, there is as yet no Asian equivalent to NAFTA and certainly none comparable to the European Union (the Asia-Pacific Economic Conference [APEC] is dedicated to 'open regionalism' and includes the United States). The problem for both the EU and USA is not only a highly adverse visible trade balance but also the concentration of Japanese export success in key sectors such as automobiles and consumer electronics. The EU continues to run a serious trade deficit with Japan of 21.4 billion ECU in 1995 reducing to 16.8 billion ECU in 1996 (Eurostat 1997). The closed nature of the Japanese home market, protected by a range of non-tariff barriers, some of which are both subtle and culturally specific, alongside very unsubtle agricultural protectionism, has contributed to the unbalanced pattern of EU–Japanese trade. For the Commission this has been a structural consequence of:

> Japan's incomplete integration into the multilateral trading system. Japan has reaped considerable economic benefit from access to world markets which the system makes available. But its domestic market has not generally offered comparable opportunities to Japan's trading partners.
>
> (Commission 1995h:26)

At the strategic level the EC called for action to 'rebalance' trade relations with Japan and in particular to open up the Japanese internal market. In the move towards creation of the Single Market, and particularly in various Community research programmes in high technology, *le défi japonais* was a significant spur to action and even emulation. At a more tactical level, Member States and the Commission, themselves often at loggerheads, have been involved since the 1970s in frequently acrimonious attempts to limit Japanese manufactured imports into the European market. Specific Japanese products became a regular target for anti-dumping surveillance and action, and GATT panels were invoked on such issues as Japanese discrimination against Scotch whisky. Member states also attempted to throw up non-tariff barriers (the celebrated funnelling of video recorder imports through a single customs post in Alençon) or to negotiate Voluntary Export Restraint agreements. By the late 1980s, in the automobile sector, this had resulted in a national patchwork of Japanese market penetration ranging from 2 per cent in the Italian market to 42 per cent of the unprotected Irish market (Lehmann 1992:45). Britain, which had initially joined France and Italy in utilizing strict VER-based quotas, now adopted a more collaborative approach by inviting Nissan, Honda and Toyota along with numerous other Japanese corporations, to set up manufacturing plants within the European market. The evident tensions cruelly exposed the limitations of the Community's external economic (as opposed to trade) policy as Member State representatives in Tokyo competitively touted for Japanese inward investment (Nuttall 1996b:110). Japanese corporations were keen to respond, and a degree of collaboration emerged alongside the ongoing conflicts. Appreciation of the Yen through the mid 1980s, the completion of the Single Market and the prospects of avoiding anti-dumping actions and VERs, led many

Japanese corporations, as we have seen, into direct investment in manufacturing plant located within the Single Market. However, just as for trade, FDI flows are not mutual and balanced. In 1993 EU-sourced investment in Japan was only 7.6 per cent of the equivalent Japanese investment in the EU (Commission 1995h:22).

The Commission had long been attempting, unsuccessfully, to negotiate on trade issues with Japan. A new Community-based trade relationship was negotiated in 1991, although insufficient use was made of Japanese anxieties concerning the impact of the 1992 programme to extract concessions on market access. A key element of the new relationship was not a formal agreement at all, but an EC–Japan 'consensus' on vehicles which created a European-wide VER quota of 8 per cent of the market (pending full liberalization at the end of 1999 and complemented by supposedly agreed targets for Japanese, European-based production). This would leave Japanese corporations with around 16 per cent of the European vehicle market (Lehmann 1992:47–9). There are comparable VERs for ball bearings, cotton fabrics, forklift trucks, machine tools and steel products (Heidensohn 1995:123). More formally, a Trade Assessment Mechanism was set up to allow mutual monitoring of the performance of Japanese and European firms in each other's markets, and to institutionalize regular discussions between officials. This was supplemented in 1994 by a new dialogue on deregulation, something of particular importance given the Community's long-standing complaints about access to the Japanese market (Nuttall 1996b:112–14).

The EU–Japan relationship has remained almost exclusively trade focused. Up until the early 1990s there were few formal links (although there were mutual parliamentary and other visits) and it was significant that the head of the EC Delegation in Tokyo was not granted the usual full ambassadorial status and accreditation to the Emperor. A continuing coolness may not have been entirely unconnected to the well publicized remarks about 'a country of workaholics who live in . . . rabbit hutches' made by one Delegation head (cited in Piening 1997:152).

In the 1990s serious attempts have been made to develop a relationship that goes beyond arguments about VERs, market access and dumping; based on the 1991 EC–Japan Declaration and involving the creation of an institutionalized political dialogue. According to Buchan (1993:139), 1991 marks an important turning point for the Japanese who, unlike the US, had no geopolitical interest in the European Union and had previously preferred to deal indirectly through Member State governments. Commission President Delors 'was received by the Emperor, conferring on him virtual head of state status'. Diplomatic relations were also upgraded and the Commission perceived, in responding to the Japanese desire for a political declaration, that there was a certain complementarity of interest between the 'two fledgling superpowers' both 'at a similar stage in taking up their responsibilities on the world stage' (*ibid*). The non-economic aspects of the nascent dialogue have so far proved disappointing for the Commission and 'there have been few examples of concrete cooperation' (Commission 1995h:7). Yet as Piening (1997:154) observes, the really significant aspects of the EU–Japan relationship remain economic and involve market access:

> For European business, Japan remains a potential prize of enormous value. 'Fortress Europe' was an illusion that never materialized; the walls of fortress Japan, while cracking, have still to be fully breached.

The United States

The multi-dimensional transatlantic relationship has been studied and agonized over since the days of Henry Kissinger's (1966) *Troubled Partnership*. At the onset of the Cold War the United States was instrumental in the foundation of the European enterprise and its representatives, from Kennedy to Clinton, have expressed a desire to do business with a European partner on a basis of equality. The only sense in which this was possible, in an otherwise subordinate and fragmented set of relationships, was economic. In contrast to relationships with Japan, the US–EU side of the triangle of economic superpowers remains remarkably balanced and interdependent. Both constitute economies of similar size (EU GNP = $7300 bn and US GNP = $6400 bn) and are each other's most significant trading partner. The US sends 17.8 per cent of its exports to and receives 19.0 per cent of its imports from the EU. Equivalent figures for the Union are 21.2 per cent and 17.8 per cent (Commission 1996a:36). Despite earlier US deficits, trade in manufactures has been essentially in balance during the mid 1990s and is, furthermore, balanced in its composition.[29] That is to say that, despite some sector-specific imbalances, there is a broad two-way exchange of both agricultural products, raw materials and industrial manufactures – in contrast with the skewed US–Japan relationship where high technology goods are traded for raw materials (Piening 1997:104; Heidensohn 1995:124–7).

Investment interdependence remains very extensive and has not been subject to the frictions that have bedevilled the trade relationship. Over 50 per cent of all FDI in the US is sourced from EU countries, while the comparable US share of inward investment to Europe is of the order of 40 per cent, the respective totals for 1994 are $237 billion and $225 billion (US Mission to the European Union 1996:63). Most of the major US corporations have a direct presence within the Single Market, describing themselves as 'European firms of American parentage'. This had interesting consequences for US Government agencies attempting to respond to the policies of the European Union. While US exporters were alarmed at the 'fortress Europe' potential of the Single Market, US-owned corporations within that market had a significant interest in the completion of the 1992 programme.[30]

Since 1961 the United States has been obliged to deal with a single European trading entity of which the embodiment was DGI of the Commission.

A symmetrical and in many ways symbiotic relationship has developed over the years, in which the primary interface has been between the EC External Relations Commissioner and the United States Trade Representative (USTR). In strict trade policy terms, commentators have argued that the EC has enjoyed a much more defined policy and coherent decision making system, less open to manipulation by special interests, than its US partner (Heidensohn 1995:127; Peterson 1996:111). There are, as we shall see in consideration of the Uruguay Round, real problems in obtaining a Council of Ministers consensus on trade policy and in reconciling the views of different parts of the Commission particularly if, as with DGVI, there is strong support for a sectoral interest. However, the US side is often even less coherent and subject to the competition between State Department, USTR, Department of Commerce and, above all, to the requirements of special interests within Congress.

The history of US–EU bilateral trade relations has been one of continuing specific conflict. The pattern was initiated by the celebrated 'chicken war' of 1963–4, in which the US side invoked GATT compensation rules for the loss of markets for poultry exports attendant upon the erection of the Customs Union. Since then the record of GATT disputes panels exhibits many high profile EU–US cases, often bitterly contested, over subsidized steel exports, wheat, canned fruit, oilseed, bananas and bovine growth hormones. There has also been less institutionalized trade conflict whereby the United States administration, usually under Congressional pressure, has utilized 'Section 301' legislation, which provides for specific, targeted retaliation and 'aggressive reciprocity' against the 'unfair' trading practices of other nations. Inevitably, the EC was one of the targets, and responded with its own surveillance and retaliatory mechanism – the 'New Commercial Policy Instrument' (Heidensohn 1995:54).

The game of trade threat, counter-threat and retaliation may have interesting consequences for EU policy making, where US action is aimed at the particular Member State believed to be obstructing a solution and the 'US retaliation list comes off the fax machine while the 113 Committee is in session' (Interview, Commission DGI, July 1997). Thus an agreement on oilseed was blocked in 1990–1 by French and Irish objections and US retaliation threats were accordingly targeted 'very precisely' at Cognac and Irish whiskey exports. Alas, modern commercial conditions often invalidate such precision, for as British representatives explained to their American counterparts, production of these beverages was dominated by UK-based firms (Interview, Commission DGI, July 1997).

The military analogies sometimes used to describe US–EU bilateral trade conflicts are essentially misplaced, because they occur within a complex multi-dimensional relationship which, in the last analysis, has always ensured that even the most acrimonious disputes have been settled. While, from an American perspective, the 1992 programme for the completion of the Single Market was initially, and mistakenly, viewed in terms of new tariff walls and 'fortress Europe', its real implications were more far reaching. They involved the transatlantic effects of EU policies, in 'beyond the border' areas such as financial regulation and technical standard setting, which had real implications for US competitiveness but could not be accommodated within the well established trade policy relationship. This posed what Hocking and Smith (1997:56) have described as a 'challenge of conceptualisation':

> was the EC to be treated as proto-state, as a complex set of functional networks or as a type of federal system in which the member states were analogous to the American states?

The answer to this question was an attempt at wide-ranging engagement with the EU on a range of policy dimensions that went well beyond the Community's exclusive competence under the Common Commercial Policy. American objectives were not simply to negotiate with the relevant parts of the European entity but actively to set agendas and to be closely involved with the formulation of policy. In strictly economic terms this was a result of the challenging presence of the Single Market as well as a requirement for collaboration in the face of Japanese industrial/technological competition (Peterson 1996:121–3).

The broader political context was the new politico-strategic situation that confronted the Atlantic Alliance at the end of the Cold War. The 1990 Transatlantic Declaration sought to institutionalize an impressive range of bilateral meetings and consultative procedures from presidential down to 'technical' levels. What distinguished this emergent relationship from the normal run of the Union's cooperation agreements with third parties was not only its scale and scope but the heavy emphasis that was placed, especially after Maastricht, on non-trade issues and on the Union as an explicitly political actor (these matters are dealt with in Chapter 6).

The EU–US relationship was further developed in the New Transatlantic Agenda (NTA) and Joint US–EU Action Plan, agreed at the Madrid Summit of December 1995. The intention was to move beyond consultation to a programme of joint action. In the words of the, then, US Ambassador to the European Union, Stewart Eizenstat:

> Most importantly for the United States, the agenda marks the first time we have dealt comprehensively with the European Union as a political force able to join with the United States as a full equal partner.
>
> (*European Voice*, 25–31 January 1996:14)

The NTA and the Action Plan had four major elements involving global political collaboration, responses to environmental, crime and health 'challenges', economic expansion and construction of transatlantic cultural, educational and scientific exchanges. One such 'bridge building' activity predated the Madrid Summit. This was the 'Transatlantic Business Dialogue' a series of private sector meetings sponsored by the Commission and the US Secretary of Commerce, which served to generate a number of the business oriented recommendations to be found in the NTA. Alongside a joint commitment to cooperation in the development of the WTO, the NTA aimed to create 'The New Transatlantic Marketplace'. This somewhat grandiose concept falls far short of a formal design for a transatlantic free trade area. Instead it contains a range of joint studies and projected specific agreements designed to remove some of the obstacles to trade and investment, particularly in the area of technical standards, certification, customs procedures and information technology (IT) and telecommunications policies.

The NTA demonstrates, in contrast with the Japanese relationship, the multi-dimensionality of US–EU links. Yet bilateral conflicts continue, not only over the usual range of market access issues, but perhaps most acrimoniously at the interface of politics and economic policy. A particular source of European irritation is the tendency of the US Administration and Congress to take extra-territorial action against overseas business interests in support of political foreign policy objectives. In the early 1980s the EC was involved with the Reagan Administration's embargo on firms contracting to build a Soviet gas pipeline. There have been a number of subsequent difficulties relating to trade with Iran and Libya and notably the Helms-Burton Act of 1996, which attempted to use the US courts to penalize European and other firms trading with Cuba.

Over the years the United States has come to recognize and treat with the European Union as an actor in its own right. Initially the only area in which this could occur was trade, as narrowly defined in the Common Commercial Policy. The Single Market programme served as a stimulus to a much broader engagement in a whole range of areas covered by the European treaties. Perhaps most important of all, in the wake of the Cold War, was a very conscious American decision, initially by Secretary Baker, but confirmed by the Clinton Administration, to deal politically with the Union and to make political cooperation the first element in the NTA – before trade, scientific and other links. Transatlantic interdependence and economic dialogue have thus done much to shape the characteristics of the European actor. Initially much of the traffic was one way, as the Community responded to US expectations, but as the conflictual/cooperative relationship has developed there has been more reciprocity – evidenced particularly by the way in which the creation of the Single Market challenged the structure and practices of the US as an international economic actor.

If, as we have argued, identity and actorness are shaped through interaction with and the perceptions of others, then shifting US practice in relation to the European entity has been significant indeed. From the period of the Marshall Plan onwards, the dominant view amongst the US policy making establishment has been that, whatever the trade difficulties, the US has a long-term national interest in the establishment of a more unified and coherent European partner. This has been reflected in an expanding conceptualization of the capabilities of the European entity and, indeed, in the organization of their diplomatic effort, which in the mid 1990s, shifted posts from embassies in Member State capitals to the Brussels Mission (Interview, external mission, January 1996).

THE COMMUNITY AS MULTILATERAL TRADE NEGOTIATOR: THE URUGUAY ROUND

Multilateral trade negotiator is the oldest of all the Community's external roles – dating back to the Dillon Round of the early 1960s. Since then the EC has been periodically involved in bargaining about the trade framework, a very different activity from its day-to-day bilateral dealings, but one which sometimes became synonymous with the transatlantic relationship. The GATT Uruguay Round, which commenced in 1986 at Punte del Este and only concluded at Marrakesh in 1994, provided the most searching test of actor capability.

The negotiation was conducted at various levels. The detailed work on what was ultimately to become 26,000 pages of text was done at expert level by 15 working groups located at GATT headquarters in Geneva. Commission officials negotiated for the Community in these groups, although Member State representatives were always on hand and sometimes chaired working groups. The Round was punctuated by higher level ministerial meetings where Member State trade ministers would attend and form the Council for the purposes of directing the Commission, which would then formally represent the Community (in their absence national officials would form the 113 Committee). At an informal level at Geneva, at ministerials and elsewhere, 'Quadrilateral' meetings between trade ministers or their officials provided a forum for influential exchanges of view which, although not negotiations in themselves, had a clear bearing upon progress. 'Quad' meetings involved the USTR, EC External Relations Commissioner and trade ministers of Japan and Canada or their chief negotiators or officials.[31] It was to become evident that the crucial relationship was the bilateral one between the US and EC members of the 'Quad'.

Community negotiators had to cope with what became the most extensive multilateral negotiation in history where, because of the extreme difficulty of reforming the Common Agricultural Policy in ways that would satisfy both Member States and trading partners, they were frequently isolated and accused of bringing the world trading system to an impasse. There was deadlock on agriculture at the mid-term review of the Round in 1988 and at the Brussels Ministerial Meeting that was supposed to conclude negotiations in 1990. Only in 1992 did internal proposals for the reform of the policy, and the election of a new US President, open the way for the conclusion of an EU–US (pre) agreement on agriculture at Blair House.[32] The Commission struck this deal without the full formal backing of the Council and in the face of French opposition. It was to be a source of severe internal tension within the EC for the subsequent year, leaving the outcome of the whole Round hanging in the balance. Although, through complex politicking in Brussels, the agreement was finally accepted by the Council, Blair House has continued to cause bad blood between the Commission and some of the Member States. When DGI officials wish to advise against initiatives that 'get ahead' of Member States, the form of words apparently used is 'Not another Blair House Commissioner?' (Interview, DGI, July 1997).

Although agriculture seized the headlines, the proposals for the Uruguay Round also contained many areas of potential advantage for EC Member States in which the Community was able to take a consistent and even leading position. The most significant innovation was to be found in the attempt to bring services within the ambit of the trading regime for the first time. This was an area in which, alongside the US, Community countries possessed substantial comparative advantage. By the same token Southern 'developing' members of the GATT were loath to open their heavily protected national markets. For this reason, services were not simply added to the existing GATT but negotiated within a separate General Agreement on Trade in Services.

A key element in the complex deal that facilitated Southern participation was a Northern agreement to phase out the disgracefully protectionist Multifibre Agreement (MFA), which had limited the access of Southern textile producers to the rich markets of the developed world. This was to create more difficulties within the European Community because a group of members – Portugal, Spain, Greece and Italy – had substantial textile industries which would experience severe competition following the abolition of the MFA. Alongside the phased removal of the MFA there was also an EC led agreement to remove any restrictions on the importation of tropical products. Also included in the negotiations were the standard GATT topics of reciprocal tariff cutting and subsidies plus two important new items involving the trade related aspects of intellectual property rights (TRIPS) and investment measures (TRIMS).[33] A source of suspicion in the South, they tended to represent a joint interest of the US and the EC, particularly in terms of the protection of patents and copyright. The outcome of the negotiations was ultimately governed by the principle – agreed at the outset – of 'globality'. This was a new concept for the well-worn negotiating rule that 'nothing is finally settled until everything is settled'.[34]

Actor capability in the Uruguay Round

There can be no doubting the significance of the EC as a participant in the Round. Stripped to its essentials the Uruguay Round was hardly a multilateral negotiation at all – for long periods it was a bilateral confrontation between what Jacques Delors referred to, in 1992, as the 'two elephants on the world market' (Buchan 1993:9). This was obviously the case in the high profile agricultural dispute, but the central contest between the US and EC infected many other areas of the negotiation – in intellectual property rights, services and elsewhere – in which they might have been expected to have common interests. This tendency was accentuated by the very low negotiating profile adopted by the other behemoth of world trade – Japan. The whole complex negotiating machinery of the GATT was often becalmed while US and EC officials tried to resolve their differences – some of which, like the disputes over soya beans or civil aircraft subsidies, had a strictly bilateral character. Once agreements were struck, as with the 'Tokyo Scheme' on tariffs, there was a requirement to 're-multilateralize' the process and involve all the other GATT parties.[35] The EC–US struggle went on to the end. Aspects of the Blair House (pre) agreement and other issues were still being haggled over by Mickey Kantor and Sir Leon Brittan at the eleventh hour while the other participants waited in Geneva to initial the agreement (Paemen and Bensch 1995:247).

In some respects the importance of the EC served only to highlight the negotiating inadequacies arising from its ambivalent position as an actor – even in the area of trade policy – where it might be expected to be at its most consistent and coherent. This view was commonly and effectively deployed by the US side to blame the internal disagreements of the Community on agriculture for various impasses in the long Uruguay process. Those on the Community side were more than aware of the vulnerability of 12 states operating by EC rules, with mandates and conclusions dependent on qualified majorities subject, always, to the threat of national veto under the Luxembourg compromise.[36]

Differences between Member States were mainly evident in two areas of the Uruguay Round, textiles and agriculture. On textiles and the dismantling of the MFA, Greece, Italy and Portugal initially gave the Commission no negotiating flexibility and were later to treat it with the greatest suspicion (Paemen and Bensch 1995:136). There were parallel disputes between the Northern and Southern Member States over the reform of anti-dumping rules.[37]

It was, of course, the concerns not just of France but of a number of Member States including Germany and Ireland over the fate of the CAP that gave rise to the greatest diplomatic embarrassment and lack of negotiating flexibility. This was at no time more evident than in the dramatic failure of the 1990 Brussels Ministerial Meeting, after which even Member State representatives joined in the general public denunciation of the Community's position, or rather lack of position. Virtually throughout the Round agriculture was the EC's Achilles heel, where it generally proved impossible to develop and sustain an effective tactical line, and where the obverse of Member State demands for more transparency was a lack of confidentiality inimical to successful negotiation. The problem was not just one of well entrenched national interest groups ranged in defence of the CAP, but the very structure of the EC policy making system, which leaves the supervision of the Common Commercial Policy to the General Affairs Council, rightly preoccupied with matters far removed from the Uruguay Round, but allows the Agricultural Council to pursue its own agenda when there is an agricultural dimension to negotiations.

Yet such problems are not unique to the EU. The famous Blair House meeting was marked by a falling out between the USTR, Carla Hills, and the Secretary for Agriculture, who felt that too much was being conceded to the EC. For this reason the two EC Commissioners left Blair House without an agreement, only to be informed later by telephone that the President had resolved the matter in favour of the US Trade Representative (Paemen and Bensch 1995:215–18). Divisions within the EC were not capable of such speedy resolution despite resort to 'Jumbo Councils' involving both Foreign and Agriculture ministers.[38]

The politics of the final year of the Uruguay Round were inordinately complex and involved political shifts within both France and Germany. A definitive vote on the Blair House (pre) agreement was studiously avoided and, despite the probable existence of a qualified majority, the Council acted by consensus. By withholding endorsement until the very end, the French government and its allies were actually able to reopen aspects of Blair House and to obtain some final US concessions (Keeler 1996:144–5; Paemen and Bensch 1995:240–7; Woolcock and Hodges 1996:318–21). In a sense there was a parallel between the pressures each side could exert on the other. US negotiators frequently use the demands of Congress on a well intentioned executive and warn of the way in which, without progress, Presidential 'fast track authority' to negotiate will expire or be withheld. In the same way, Commission negotiators can refer to problems with their mandate from the Council and the well known obduracy of certain Member States.

Agriculture represents a mere 11 per cent of world trade and a smaller percentage of EC–US trade. This should place the long drawn out wrangling over farm subsidies and soya beans in perspective. While there were early Community divisions on textiles and dumping, and continuing ones over agriculture, which clearly did serve to render the EC inconsistent and relatively ineffective as a negotiating actor, a concentration upon these areas obscures the EC's performance across the much more significant and greater part of the Round. Woolcock and Hodges (1996) make a useful distinction between the 'technocratic' and 'political' control of policy. In most of the 15 working groups of the Round the EC operated in 'technocratic' mode. The Commission was given the latitude to negotiate in collaboration with the 113 Committee, and the General Affairs Council merely rubber-stamped the results. The alternative mode applied to only a few high profile areas, like agriculture, where there was active 'political' involvement and open controversy.

There is substantial evidence that, operating in 'technocratic' mode across most of the Round, the EC was an effective, coherent and frequently innovative negotiator. According to one commentator; 'it was possible to reach an agreement largely because the European Union negotiated as a unit and showed itself willing and able to take on a global leadership role' (Leonard 1997:18). Such was the record in tropical products, the phase-out of the MFA, trade in services and the IPR, along with the creation of the new World Trade Organization (Woolcock and Hodges 1996:309–10; Paemen and Bensch 1995:146–75). In the words of Peter Sutherland, GATT Director General at the end of the Round, and admittedly also a former EC Commissioner, 'We wouldn't have a WTO if the European Union did not have a common commercial policy and did not negotiate with one voice' (*New Statesman and Society*, 18 October 1996).[39]

CONCLUSION

The growing economic presence of the European Union has ensured that in many respects it can be regarded as a great power, rivalling the United States. Initial Community competence for the Common Commercial Policy has ensured that in the field of trade relations, narrowly defined, the Union has developed an equivalent capacity to act. Elsewhere, changes in the global economy and the growth of the Union's economic presence in areas such as services and investment, have exerted pressure for the EU to find some way of representing itself externally.

The expanding scope of actorness is clear from the record, but the form that it takes is less consistent. There has been sustained resistance by Member States to the simple extension of basic trade competence into new areas which ensures that, although the EC increasingly appears to outsiders as a single economic entity, its external representation and capacity to act will still vary widely.

Trade policy provides the best example of the Union as a consistent actor across its various roles. Member States long ago granted exclusive competence to the Community, and where there have been difficulties arising from different national policies (as with VERs against Japanese vehicle imports) they have been resolved. In negotiations where substantial national economic interests are at stake, the Uruguay Round experience suggests that in the end there is inexorable pressure to reach a common negotiating position, although the process may be difficult. Beyond trade in goods there is much more inconsistency. Exclusive competence has not been granted for trade in services and intellectual property, and there have been clear differences of Member State approach within the WTO on post-Uruguay issues such as trade and labour standards. Resolving such problems is seen as highly significant by Commission officials because, as one put it, 'If the EU is not achieving coherence in WTO then the rest is nothing' (Interview, DGI, July 1997).

Member States continue to compete with one another in attempts to secure inward investment, but in monetary policy there are evident indications of increasing consistency as EMU approaches. This will not result in exclusive monetary competence for the Community, but it will be a dramatic step towards the creation of a fully consistent international economic, as opposed to trade, actor.

Coherence – which in EU parlance denotes the internal consistency of the Union's policy processes – will always cause problems for any large economic actor with many constituencies to please. During the Uruguay Round it was the disjuncture between trade and agricultural policy and related internal decision making procedures, as much as the rooted national interests of some Member States, that created such difficulties. In trade policy the fragmentation of the Commission can be 'disastrous, but if the Commission can articulate a coherent position then the Member States will generally follow' if not 'then they will pursue their own interests' (Interview, DGI, July 1997).

The Community itself maintains 127 overseas Delegations and in return 164 states have established permanent diplomatic Missions to the Community/Union. They may deal with a range of bilateral issues, but the essential reason for their existence remains the management of trade and aid relations. Community competence in these areas provides the essential basis of the environmental, developmental and regional roles which we discuss in the next three chapters. It is likewise the threat of interruption of these and other economic transactions which, in the absence of dedicated armed forces, constitutes the main deterrent or punitive instrument available to an emergent Common Foreign and Security Policy.[40]

3 International environmental diplomacy

The Union's growing role

By any standards the countries of the European Union cast a long ecological shadow. The scale of industry, transport, energy consumption and agriculture within the EU ensures that, while not perhaps matching the United States in critical areas such as carbon emissions, it is amongst the largest polluters and resource exploiters on earth.

At the time of the signature of the Vienna Convention on the protection of the stratospheric ozone layer the (then) 12 members of the European Community were responsible for in excess of 45 per cent of world chlorofluorocarbon (CFC) production. Over one-third of this was exported, making the EC 'unchallenged in world markets' (Benedick 1991:26–7). In 1990–1 the EC accounted for around 13 per cent of global fossil carbon emissions (Nitze 1990:16) and 15.7 per cent of world commercial energy consumption (UNDP 1994:203) The 1995 estimate of carbon dioxide emissions for all 15 members of the EU was 3.328 million metric tonnes (Commission 1997k, Table 5:57). Additionally, some 2 billion tonnes of industrial and other waste have to be dealt with annually within the Union.

In many other areas the countries of the EU exploit a substantial slice of the earth's resources. The scale of the European fishing 'effort' provides an obvious example, as EU-based trawlers range far beyond those depleted waters subject to the Common Fisheries Policy.[1] Enlargement to more than 20 members, some with particularly difficult pollution problems, can only increase the impact of EU environmental presence. Such presence is most directly experienced by the Union's immediate neighbours in Central and Eastern Europe and the Mediterranean, but there has been an increasing realization that an economy the size of the EU's has major responsibilities on a global scale: for stratospheric ozone depletion, climate change, desertification and species loss.

In the first decade of the European Community's existence, such matters were almost entirely absent from considerations of Europe's role in the world system.[2] One reason for this is that there were, at that time, no common environmental policies; another, that the salience of environmental questions for international politics was not yet widely apparent. The process whereby environmental questions became the subject of international and even 'high' politics merits study in its own right (Vogler 1997). It is in large part a reaction to scientific understanding and public awareness of the gravity of transboundary environmental impacts (for example 'acid rain' deposition) and, during the 1980s, of a burgeoning concern with change and degradation on a global scale which coincided with the ending of the Cold War. The emergence of environmental issues on the international agenda was marked by the United Nations Conference on the Human Environment, held at Stockholm in 1972. Twenty years later its successor, the Rio Earth Summit, agreed *Agenda 21* – a blueprint for sustainable development – and provided the stage for the signature of the Framework Convention on Climate Change (FCCC) and the Convention on Biodiversity. The growth of EC environment policy and its related forays into the new environmental diplomacy closely paralleled these developments. The year 1972 marked the beginning of the EC's environment policy, while the 1992 Maastricht Treaty added 'sustainable' growth to the purposes of the Community and Union (TEC Art.2, TEU Art.B [2]).

In the beginning the Treaty of Rome was silent upon environmental matters. Significantly it required the 1972 Stockholm conference to persuade the leaders of the European Communities, meeting in Paris, to take the first steps towards an environmental policy. But it is also probable that concerns about the trade implications of recently introduced German environmental legislation were equally significant (Somsen 1996:183). The immediate result was the first Environmental Action Programme of 1973 (there have since been four more). It provided the impetus for the progressive adoption of over 100 relevant policy instruments in the period up until 1987 (Commission 1990a:19). Areas in which extensive legislation, usually in the form of directives, has been adopted, and Community competence established, include: air and water quality, waste treatment, noise abatement, protection from hazardous chemicals and the conservation of wildlife and habitats. Originally action was based on specific directives and emissions controls. The current trend is to consolidate these into 'framework directives' (for air and water) and to adopt a more integrated and horizontal approach to the maintenance of environmental quality, with increasing reliance upon 'market-based' instruments such as eco-labelling and green taxes.[3]

The initial thrust of environmental policy was to remove trade distortions arising from different national standards and policies although measures were also introduced with the sole purpose of promoting the conservation of the environment.[4] The Single European Act of 1987 (Title VII – Environment) strengthened the latter, by according explicit treaty status to the Community's environmental objectives: to preserve, protect and improve the quality of the environment, to contribute towards human health and to ensure a prudent and rational utilization of resources (TEC Art.130r [174]). It also established under this article the principles of prevention and that the polluter should pay, along with the stipulation that environmental concerns 'shall be a component of the Community's other policies'. Subsequent to the

Single Act there has been a cascade of legislation, making the environment the area in which there was the greatest increase in Community activity; and in which national policies were increasingly determined at the European level (Sbragia 1996:243).

Environmental policy has a markedly intersectoral quality which goes well beyond the strict responsibilities of the Commission's DGXI for Environment, Nuclear Safety and Civil Protection. It evidently involves trade, agriculture, industry, taxation, energy, transport, aid and scientific research.[5] In this, as in many other ways, climate change policy provides the most extensive and difficult example of intersectoral policy coordination, involving a substantial number of Commission DGs across a wide range of policy concerns.[6]

The link between trade and environment has become increasingly salient, with high profile international disputes such as the Tuna–Dolphin case involving the EC as a protagonist. In this instance the EC followed Mexico in mounting a successful challenge to the United States using the GATT disputes procedure. The Community and Mexico objected that a US ban on importing tuna which had been caught using nets which incidentally snared dolphins was a form of protectionism; and the EC particularly objected to the 'secondary embargo' imposed by US law, whereby European companies dealing in Mexican tuna were also barred.[7]

Trade-related issues can cause serious problems for policy coordination and coherence within the Commission itself and between the Council and Commission. A leading example is provided by the long-running saga of 'leghold traps' which pitted DGXI and the animal welfare lobby against DGI. The source of the problem was a 1991 Regulation to ban the import of furs from countries which had not outlawed the use of leghold traps (Canada, Russia and the USA). These barbaric instruments subject animals to a cruel and often prolonged death. The internal arguments involved the animal welfare competence of DGXI and the trade competence of DGI. Arguing the adverse trade implications, and possibility of reference to the GATT/WTO disputes procedure, DGI was able to win an intra-Commission struggle to prevent the implementation of the ban – which had already been agreed by the Environment Council. This aroused the ire of Members of the European Parliament, who threatened legal action against the Commission. Meanwhile, in order to resolve the issue, a draft agreement on trapping standards was negotiated with Russia and Canada (but not the US) which was widely regarded as inadequate by the animal welfare lobby, and which the June 1997 Environment Council failed to approve (Interview, UK Department of the Environment, May 1997 and *European Voice*, 23–27 June 1997). Finally, in early 1998 agreements were concluded with the fur exporting countries.

In terms of the international environmental role of the Community, one common policy deserves special mention. A common fisheries policy had a basis in the Treaty of Rome, in that fish were defined as an agricultural product (TEC Art.32 [38]). However it took until the early 1980s, under the stimulus of a worldwide extension of Exclusive Economic Zones to 200 miles from national coasts, to create a common policy for the management and marketing of the fish stocks in EC waters. Almost immediately, the number of fishermen and the tonnage of trawlers subject to the policy more than doubled with the accession of Spain and Portugal to the Community. Continuous over-fishing and the desperate need to conserve stocks both within and beyond EU waters has meant that fisheries policy, administered by DGXIV, is environmental policy. It is also probably the most politically sensitive area of environmental policy, with a clear international dimension arising from EC participation in no fewer than 26 bilateral fisheries agreements and many of the major multilateral fisheries Commissions. The potential of fisheries questions to escalate to wider diplomatic confrontation was evidenced by the serious dispute with Canada in 1995 over the waters off Newfoundland.

Environmental policy has also been beset with problems of consistency between Member States. This is hardly surprising given their differing locations, degree of modernization and varying administrative traditions. However it is also possible for large industrialized Member States at similar levels of development to have fundamental policy differences. British–German disagreement over the requirements for and approaches to pollution control provide a case in point (Weale 1992:66–92). In general the Germans and Scandinavians have been 'pioneers' in the setting of high standards of environmental protection (Andersen and Liefferink 1997).

The situation is further complicated by the variety of Community decision making procedures and shared competences to which environmental policy is subject. This may be seen, in part, as a consequence of the slow and somewhat *ad hoc* development of environmental policy – in comparison, for instance, to the initial establishment of Community competence for trade. Complexity also results from various bargained compromises between a range of interests eager, on the one hand, to restrain the expansion of the Community's competence and, on the other, to advance green legislation while ensuring that common policies do not provide a brake on progressive national developments.

The Single European Act, while formally establishing the environmental policies of the Community, also made it subject to differing allocation of competences and decision making procedures depending upon which article of the Treaty was being used as the basis for action.[8] The Treaty on European Union served to further complicate what was already a difficult area. Under the revised Article 130s [175] at least four different procedures can now apply, depending on the issue area under discussion – with further variants if energy or taxation is involved. Thus, not only does environmental policy touch virtually the entire scope of the Community's policy competences, it can also be subject to almost the whole range of the EC's variegated decision making procedures. This, as we shall see, is of some importance for the EC/EU performance as an actor in international environmental politics; not least as a source of bewilderment for third parties.

EXTERNALIZATION OF THE EC'S ENVIRONMENTAL POLICIES

The same dynamics that have driven the production of environmental policies at Community level also served to internationalize them. There are two main forces at work here. First, the pressure to respond to trans-boundary pollution and, increasingly, to global scale environmental changes; and, second, what may be broadly regarded as the trade implications of environmental policy.

The need to respond to transboundary threats provided the impetus for the earliest major international negotiations in which the EC was engaged, that is, the negotiation of the Long Range Transboundary Air Pollution (LRTAP) Convention of 1979 and its subsequent protocols relating to transboundary fluxes of nitrous and sulphuric oxides. These negotiations, involving over 30 North American and European states, were linked to those relating to acid rain deposition within the Community, which resulted in the Large Combustion Plant Directive. An essentially similar point can be made about increasing Community involvement in marine pollution control, which physically must involve both Member States and third parties in the North Sea and the Mediterranean. The EC has also participated in negotiations relating to the sustainability of shared 'common pool' resources. Here, as we have seen, the EC has exclusive competence for the negotiation of fisheries agreements, both bilaterally and in such multilateral UN negotiations as those relating to 'Straddling Stocks'. The EC is also a signatory to the 1982 (in force from 1995) Third Law of the Sea Convention and to the 1980 Convention on the Conservation of Antarctic Marine Living Resources.

Direct interest in the global change phenomena which achieved such prominence in the 1980s is, perhaps, less immediately evident. In the case of stratospheric ozone depletion, the EC was slow to respond initially and beset by internal competence problems and the special interests of its chemical industries. However, European publics soon became aware that the dangers of UV/B induced skin cancers and genetic mutations were not confined to the high latitudes of the Southern Hemisphere and the EC had, by the end of the 1980s, assumed a much more proactive stance.

Climate change issues associated with the enhanced greenhouse effect dominated the international environmental agenda during the early 1990s. The EU was not amongst those most obviously at risk, although low-lying coastal areas (the Netherlands and East Anglia) would be subject to inundation under current Intergovernmental Panel on Climate Change (IPCC) estimates. Moreover it is not always remembered that some of the overseas island territories of Member States would be likely to disappear, along with the members of the Alliance of Small Island States (AOSIS). Given the responsibilities of developed countries for the problem of global warming, it would have been unthinkable that the Member States should not have been involved from the beginning with the negotiation and development of the 1992 Framework Convention on Climate Change, and in providing financial and other support for the IPCC. The EC/EU has also been an important participant in the other 'global change' Conventions on biodiversity and desertification.

The second source of internationalization derives from the fact that implementation of measures to counter environmental threats, or promote good practice at national (or at EU) level, will inevitably impact upon trade, investment and other flows across national boundaries. This provided much of the motivation for the initial inclusion of environmental concerns in the EC's policy making, and the need to ensure a 'level playing field' remains a major incentive for the Community to negotiate with third parties on environmental issues. Similarly, although there are genuine long-term concerns about climate change, the fact that energy questions – vital to international competitiveness – are under discussion provides a very real short-run incentive to participate in the Climate Change Convention. The 1992 Biodiversity Convention also has significant commercial implications. At the same time, as briefly discussed in the previous chapter, the trade environment nexus is now under active discussion as one of the 'new trade issues' within the WTO.

In consequence of all this activity, and much that has not been mentioned (for example the preservation of wildlife and endangered species) the Community is now a signatory to, and participates in, no less than 31 major multilateral environmental agreements (excluding their sometimes numerous protocols) detailed in Figure 3.1. The precise way in which this occurs is subject to considerable variation – sometimes during the course of a single day in a particular negotiation. Thus the question of EU actorness is altogether more complex in the area of international environmental politics than it is in the field of trade. The familiar Article 113 [133] type procedures do occur where exclusive community competence has been established; as, for example, in negotiations about the conservation of fish stocks or where matters under discussion clearly fall within the Common Commercial Policy or the Common Agricultural Policy. At the other extreme, there may be exclusive Member State competence equivalent to the Common Foreign and Security Policy within Pillar II. This will involve unanimity voting in the Council, giving each of the Member States an effective veto. The Commission will have a subordinate and implementing role, while the duties of spokesperson and leader of the EU will be assumed by the representative of the Member State which currently holds the Presidency, assisted by the previous and next holders of the office (the 'troika').

Because of the way in which EU environmental policy has evolved, and

Atmosphere

C. on long-range transboundary air pollution GENEVA 1979 & Protocols 1984, 1988, 1991 & 1994.

C. for the protection of the Ozone Layer VIENNA 1985 & Protocol 1987 MONTREAL & Amendments 1990 & 1992.

Transboundary impacts

C. on Environmental Impact Assessment in a transboundary context ESPOO 1991.

C. on transboundary effects of industrial accidents HELSINKI 1992.

Animals and habitats

C. on the conservation of migratory species of wild animals BONN 1979.

C. on the conservation of European wildlife and natural habitats BERN 1979.

C. on the conservation of Antarctic marine living resources CANBERRA 1980.

European C. for the protection of vertebrate animals used for experimental and other scientific purposes STRASBOURG 1985.

C. on the protection of the Alps SALZBURG 1991 & 3 Protocols 1994.

UN A. on the conservation of small cetaceans of the Baltic and North Seas NEW YORK 1992.

Marine pollution

C. for the prevention of marine pollution from land-based sources PARIS 1974 & Protocol 1986.

C. for the protection of the Mediterranean Sea against pollution BARCELONA 1976 & Protocols 1976, 1976, 1980, 1982.

C. on the Law of the Sea MONTEGO BAY 1982.

C. for the protection and development of the marine environment of the wider Caribbean region CARTEGENA DE INDIAS 1983 & Protocol 1983.

A. for cooperation in dealing with pollution of the North Sea by oil and other harmful substances BONN 1983.

C. for the protection, management, and development of the marine and coastal environment of the East African region. NAIROBI 1985 & Protocols 1985, 1986.

Cooperation A. for the protection of the coasts and waters of the North East Atlantic against accidental pollution LISBON 1990.

C. for the protection of the marine environment of the Baltic Sea area. HELSINKI 1992.

C. for the protection of the marine environment of the Baltic Sea area HELSINKI 1972. (EC accession pending)

C. for the protection of the marine environment of the North East Atlantic PARIS 1992.

Watercourses

C. for the protection of the Rhine against chemical pollution BONN 1976.

A. between the Federal Republic of Germany and the EEC, on the one hand and the Republic of Austria on the other, on cooperation and the management of water resources in the Danube basin REGENSBURG 1987. (To be cancelled)

C. on the International Commission for the protection of the Elbe MAGDEBURG 1980 & Protocol 1991.

C. on the protection and use of transboundary watercourses and international lakes 1992

C. on the cooperation for the protection and sustainable use of the Danube SOFIA 1994.

Hazardous wastes

C. on the control of transboundary movements of hazardous wastes and their disposal BASEL 1989.

Climate change

UN Framework C. on Climate Change NEW YORK 1992.

Biodiversity
UN C. on Biological Diversity RIO 1992.

Deserts
UN C. on Desertification PARIS 1994.

Fisheries
(not listed by DGXI)
C. on future multilateral cooperation in fisheries in the North West Atlantic 1978.

C. on future multilateral cooperation in North East Atlantic fisheries 1980.

C. for the conservation of salmon in the North Atlantic area 1982.

C. on fishing and conservation of the living resources in the Baltic Sea and Belts 1973. (EC Accession 1992)

Others
(not listed by DGXI)
Under this heading are the significant agreements with environmental clauses.

Economic Cooperation Agreements.

The Europe Agreements.

EEA Agreement 1994 Arts.73–5, 78.

Fourth ACP–EC Conversion (Lomé IV) Arts.33–41.

Energy Charger Agreement 1994, Art.19.

Source: except where stated: Commission DGXI.A.4., CONVL12.DOC, Brussels: 11.12.95

The EC is a signatory to all the agreements listed but Council Conclusion may not yet have been achieved in recent Conventions.

Figure 3.1 EC participation in multilateral environmental agreements.

because of the 'cross cutting' nature of the subject matter of this relatively new area of diplomacy, most negotiations will not align neatly with either the exclusive Community or Member State competence models. Instead, they are 'mixed'; Member States and the Community having 'concurrent' powers. The exact mixture, and hence the degree of EU actorness, will depend upon, and be disputed in relation to, the location of internal competence and the granting of external recognition.

Internal and external competence

Initially, as we have seen, exclusive competence for the Community was limited to one or two areas in which it was expressly provided in the Treaty of Rome. However, as the Community's policies developed, conflicts began to emerge between internal legislation and the external agreements made by Member States. In an important 'leading case', the European Road Transport Agreement (ERTA) judgement of 1970, the ECJ went well beyond the provisions of the Treaty of Rome by establishing the doctrine of 'parallelism', that is to say when the Community acquires internal competence over a subject it also acquires external competence – *'in interno in foro externo'*.[9] This had major and continuing implications for the conduct of external environmental policy, which had not even been mentioned in the original Treaties.[10] The ERTA case and subsequent judgements and practice have provided the legal basis upon which the Commission has asserted its right to be involved in the conduct of international environmental negotiations (for example the LRTAP mentioned above where there was internal community competence in relation to atmospheric pollution). The most important of these subsequent rulings involved 'potential competence'. This extended ERTA principles to areas where, although there were no common rules in existence, participation of the Community in an international agreement 'is necessary for the attainment of one of the objectives of the Community'.[11]

It is not the case that competences can be precisely listed, because the issues involved in each new negotiation will be different and the internal situation within the Union may alter. The adoption of the subsidiarity principle at Maastricht may mean that, whereas there has in the past been a trend towards increasing Community competence, there may in future be movements in the other direction, with powers reverting to Member States and equivalent changes in external competence. Each new negotiation raises the question of determining competence, which can prove a controversial matter with Member State governments. The determination of competence will rely, *inter alia*, upon interpretation of the Treaties, judicial rulings and, most significantly, on judgements concerning the fulfilment of the purposes of the Treaties (teleology). Although taking judicial form it will also, of course, be an intensely political process given the differing views of Member State governments as to the proper extent of Community powers.

If questions under consideration relate entirely to trade or to fisheries, then there is exclusive Community competence and Article 113 [133] procedures apply. Thus, at the recent UN Conference on Straddling Stocks and Highly Migratory Fish Stocks, concluded in August 1995, the EC had exclusive competence and the Commission negotiated for the Community on a Council mandate.[12] Even here there can be some politico-legal pettiness. When the EC acceded to the 1980 Convention on the Conservation of Antarctic Marine Living Resources (CCAMLR), Member States objected to exclusive competence on grounds of teleology. The CCAMLR is a very advanced fisheries agreement because its Article II involves a total ecosystem view of marine conservation. Thus its purpose is manifestly not just to preserve fish stocks (a Community competence) but also to protect other forms of life dependent upon them – notably penguins. Penguins are, of course, birds. However Community competence for the preservation of birds under its Bird Directive only extends to Europe, not the Southern Ocean. It was, thus, that objections were made to exclusive Community competence in relation to the CCAMLR (Macrory and Hession 1996:132).

As described in TEU Article 130r [174], most environmental issues involve mixed agreements and concurrent competence, where representation is legally shared between the Presidency and the Commission. For example, trade and air pollution issues in the stratospheric ozone negotiations fell within Community competence, while other matters were reserved to Member States. As Benedick's (1991) rather hostile account makes clear, the extent of competence was under active dispute within the Community delegation during the negotiation of the Montreal Protocol. These negotiations were in part conducted during the formulation of the Single European Act, which evidently reduced the number of areas in which Member States alone could make agreements. Since then competence has been rather less contested and external parties, especially the United States, but also a post-Cold War Russia, have been happier to see the Commission as a player in its own right (Interview, DGXI, June 1996).

A good current example is provided by the Basel Convention on hazardous waste. It has trade aspects (where there is full Community competence), science and development assistance aspects (where there is Member State competence), and environmental aspects – where mixed competence prevails. The Biodiversity Convention negotiations were also marked by divided competences, with a strong Community position on trade and intellectual property, but Member State competence in other areas. At the beginning of the process of negotiating the Climate Change Convention there was little Community competence and the Commission was not a formal participant in the Intergovernmental Negotiating Committee (INC). This has changed, but competence remains a problem because the taxation instruments that the Community might employ, in order to give substance to Article 4 commitments to reduce emissions of greenhouse gases, fall within the jealously guarded area of national fiscal competence.

Finally, there are instances where, although clear Community competence is established, external actors will not afford recognition and participation rights to the EC as opposed to its Member States. Under these circumstances it is understood that Article 5 [10] of the Treaty of Rome imposes a 'duty of solidarity' on Member States to pursue a common Community position. This serves to highlight the importance of external conceptions of the European entity and the willingness that exists to recognize and treat with it.

External recognition

Sovereign states alone were the traditional parties to public international law, but since the Second World War international organizations have acquired 'objective' legal personality – that is to say a status that exists even if denied by the governments of some sovereign states. The European Economic Community was provided with such a personality in the Treaty of Rome, along with the right, subsequently extended to cover environmental questions, to conclude international agreements in specific areas. Application is confined to areas over which the Community has competence, and thus it will be noted that the European Economic Community (since 1993 simply 'the European

Community') appears as a signatory of various multilateral environmental agreements; the Montreal Protocol, the Framework Convention on Climate Change and the Convention on Biodiversity, alongside the Member States. The European Union, as established by the Maastricht Treaty of 1993, does not have personality in international law, although there were unsuccessful attempts at Amsterdam to endow it with such status.[13]

The actual development of the EC as a negotiating actor in the environmental field has also depended upon the extent to which this has been accepted by third parties. Moreover the EC's own Member States have not always been willing to allow separate representation of the Community. There have been continuing conflicts and disagreements as the Commission has sought to extend its external competence and provide the Community with a distinct voice in environmental diplomacy.

An important foundation was laid during the negotiations for the 1979 LRTAP Convention. As we have seen, this marked the first foray of the EC into a major multilateral environmental negotiation. Here the Commission was necessarily involved alongside Member States because it had acquired competence in matters of atmospheric pollution. Initially the Soviet Union was opposed to any EC participation (see fuller discussion of the USSR's attitude towards the Community in Chapter 5) but was subsequently prepared to agree to a new formulation, that of Regional Economic Integration Organization (REIO), which allowed recognition of the Community. The LRTAP itself was very much part of the Helsinki Conference on Security and Cooperation in Europe (CSCE) process, which attempted to construct bridges across a divided Europe, and the Soviet concession was apparently in the expectation that similar status would be accorded to Comecon – a long-standing ambition (Interview, DGXI, June 1996). In such a way the concept that has covered EC recognition in all subsequent major multilateral environmental conventions was born. Soviet aims were never realized and, to date, the EC is the only extant example of the REIO provided for in negotiations and in the text of conventions.

Having REIO status has come to mean that the EC can be party to a convention without any of its Member States being a party. However, when one or more of the latter are also parties 'the organization and its Member States shall decide on their respective responsibilities for the performance of their obligations under the convention or protocol' (Vienna Convention 1985: Art.13(2)). Furthermore, the REIO must declare its competence in the instruments of ratification and provide information on any subsequent changes to its status (Vienna Convention Art.13(3)). Voting rights are accorded equivalent to the number of states that are parties, subject to the proviso that the organization shall not exercise its right at the same time as any Member State and *vice versa* (Vienna Convention Art.15). As one US diplomat rather wearily put it, 'We don't mind what they do as long as they all don't want to vote at the same time' (Interview, January 1996).

Development of the REIO concept was not easy, particularly during the stratospheric ozone negotiations of 1985–7. Since that time, however, the REIO provisions have been repeated, practically verbatim, in the FCCC and Biodiversity Conventions.[14] While third parties may be concerned about the voting rights accorded by REIO status, and the establishment of clear responsibility for the implementation of any agreements, Member State governments are sometimes exercised by the internal implications of the signature and ratification of an agreement by the EC as an REIO. Before the 1993 Council 'conclusion' (the ratification procedure under Art.228 [300]) on the Climate Convention, the UK government indicated that it might simply proceed with a national ratification if EC ratification was to be linked to the introduction of a carbon tax (Haigh 1996:167).

Aside from the REIO pattern that has been established for multilateral negotiations, the EC has no automatic right of participation. Such rights have been negotiated on a case-by-case basis; and have been contested by Member States. In practice the EC currently has full member status in only three international organizations (as opposed to treaty-based organizations such as the United Nations Conference on Trade and Development (UNCTAD) or various 'Conferences of the Parties' in which the EC operates as an REIO). They are the Food and Agriculture Organization (FAO), the European Bank for Reconstruction and Development (EBRD) and the World Trade Organization (McGoldrick 1997:32–3). The FAO has a role in international environmental politics, particularly in relation to the conserva-tion of fish stocks, while the impact of the WTO is potentially enormous, although the activities of its environment committee to date have largely been confined to discussion of the conflicts principles of environmental conventions and the trading regime.

Much high profile environmental diplomacy is conducted under the aus-pices of the UN General Assembly. Here the EC has had a very incomplete and ambivalent status as an actor, which extends only to its participation in conferences and the deliberations of the Economic and Social Committee and Specialized Agencies. The relevant 1974 General Assembly Resolution merely grants the EC observer rights.[15] Just before the UN Conference on Environment and Development (UNCED) in April 1992 the EC was finally granted 'full participant status', in an amendment to the draft rules of pro-cedure, on the express understanding that this applied only to the forth-coming 'Earth Summit' and not beyond (Brinkhorst 1994:612; Mensah 1996:32). This meant that the EC briefly acquired rights equivalent to those of participating states, except for voting and the submission of procedural motions. This was the result of what a DGXI official has described as a 'huge battle' with Member States arising from the possible implication for the EC's status at the UN (Interview, June 1996). A permanent memorial is to be found on the first page of *Agenda 21* which contains the footnote:

When the term Governments is used, it will be deemed to include the European Economic Community within its areas of competence.

In relation to *Agenda 21* these areas of competence are, indeed, extensive – ranging across a great deal of the ground covered by that huge document. Thus the Community, in the guise of the Commission, has submitted an extensive review document of its own, alongside those of Member States (Commission 1997k). Although the same formula was used for EC partici- pation in subsequent UN conferences on Habitat, Health and Environment and the Food Summit of 1996, it took three weeks of preparatory discussion to insert it into the documentation for the June 1997 General Assembly Special Session (UNGASS), which reviewed progress towards sustainability since UNCED. Not only were some Member State governments unhappy, but there were also objections from regional groups, such as the Latin Americam Mercosur, which regarded the treatment afforded to the EC as discriminatory. Commission officials also had to ensure that President Jacques Santer was given equivalent status to other heads of state and government attending (Interview, DGXI, June 1996).

Similar rights were sought in relation to participation in the Commission for Sustainable Development (CSD) (established as a follow-up to UNCED) and a two-year long argument ensued within the Economic and Social Council of the UN (ECOSOC), the parent body of the new CSD. To the usual disputes about competence and voting strength was added a new con- sideration arising from the fact that membership of the CSD was to be limited to 53. This meant that the European Commission was demanding full membership of a body to which only some of the EU's constituent Member States would be elected. The issue was only resolved in 1995 after the CSD had already held two sessions. 'Full participation' by the EC was defined as speaking rights, the right to put propositions but not to vote; and all this on the understanding that there would be no increase in the represen- tation to which members of the Community would otherwise be entitled (Mensah 1996:32).

The situation in terms of participation rights is, thus, not static, and Com- mission officials have to argue continuously for the extension and main- tenance of the EC's status. For example, at a recent UNEP/FAO sponsored conference on 'prior informed consent' for the movement of hazardous chemicals, the EC initially attended as an observer but eventually obtained the right to vote on the grounds that it was a full FAO member with com- petence for agriculture – despite the fact that 'with 130 countries present there are always bound to be some that will oppose EC participation' (Interview, DGXI, June 1996).[16]

Environmental diplomacy and the conduct of negotiations

The mechanics of entering into and conducting a 'mixed' negotiation can be complex. According to Article 228 [300] of the Treaty of Rome, as extended and amended by Maastricht, the process of negotiating an international agreement starts with a right of initiative for the Commission in seeking a mandate from the Council of Ministers 'which shall authorize the Commission to open the necessary negotiations'. In environmental policy areas the preliminary phase of formulating the Commission's approach will usually involve 'interservice' consultations between the various interested DGs, analogous in many ways to the interdepartmental policy coordination (or bureaucratic politics) that is the stuff of national foreign policy making.

DGXI, responsible for much, but by no means all, environmental policy, is surprisingly small in size compared with national ministries and other Commission DGs. This, coupled with the intersectoral character of much environmental policy, can make the 'internal' deliberations quite extensive and often difficult (Sbragia 1996:244–6). Such deliberations will, of course, differ from national models and, indeed, from what one might strictly expect on a reading of Article 228 [300] with regard to the involvement of the Presidency and Member States. 'Much of the recent political science literature on lobbying within the EU arena . . . ignores the fact that member state governments, especially those of the forthcoming Presidency, also lobby the Commission' (Wurzel 1996:277). This is necessitated by the Commission's right of initiative and by the problems involved in changing a Commission proposal once it has been formalized.

In some areas, notably climate change, the Commission will not have extensive competence and may be relatively inactive (in most negotiations there is some existing legislative base to sustain a Commission mandate but this has not proved to be the case in ongoing climate change negotiations). Here there is reliance upon a 'lead country approach', involving inputs from key Member States which have particular interests and expertise (Interview, Council Secretariat DGI, July 1997).[17] In practice fewer than half the Member States are usually active and three or four positions are likely to emerge, rather than 15. Where there can be no Commission proposal for a mandate, the formal responsibility falls upon the Member State holding the Council Presidency (assisted by an informal version of the CFSP troika involving past and future presidencies). Hence, for example, the March 1997 Council decision on the EU position for the Kyoto climate change conference (FCCC CoP 3) was engineered by the Dutch Presidency. If a small Member State, such as Luxembourg, holds the Presidency it may only be able to employ two or three of its officials to specialize in environmental matters and there will necessarily be a greater reliance upon other Member States and upon DGI of the General Secretariat of the Council.[18] Depending upon the issues under discussion, the Commission will also be consulted. Here cooperation is seen as markedly better than under the analogous CFSP Pillar II procedures (see Chapter 6). It is also worth noting that negotiations are not isolated events. They occur within the context of existing international organizations and secretariats with which the Commission has a continuous and active relationship, usually involving technical and financial matters.[19]

Third party governments, especially those like the US which are in continual environmental policy dialogue with the EC, and have missions which are equipped to cope with its internal complexities, will also attempt to obtain intelligence upon and influence this phase of EC decision making. For them the Commission may appear as a body that prides itself on its distinct approach to environmental questions and which is difficult to penetrate:

> There is no other organization like the EU – it operates differently – the dynamics of policy are different. The Commission itself is a very politically sensitive body. Which nationality gets which post in a DG is crucial. The US, in dealing with the Commission, is typically drawn to the UK and Irish with a similar cultural outlook and to Germans and Scandinavians. The French and the Southern Europeans are more reticent. Unofficial 'finding out on the Brussels circuit' is very important. Sometimes people at the Commission will tell you which Member State to square. You have to be very vigilant in Brussels – so much is going on that it is difficult to keep your finger on the pulse of every issue.
>
> (Interview, external Mission, January 1996)

When a proposal emerges it goes to the Council Working Group on the Environment, which is one level down from COREPER and does the detailed work on the mandate for the Council. The negotiating mandate which is finally agreed by the Council is a confidential document. Under the revised terms of Article 228 [300] it will be adopted by different decision making procedures depending upon the issues under consideration. The mandate will establish competences in what is usually a 'mixed' negotiation, provide a set of binding directives and give greater or lesser freedom of manocuvrc to thc Commission, and of course to itself, in the conduct of negotiations (Macrory and Hession 1996:135–6). Preparation for a conference involves the same basic procedures. However there will be no mandate but, instead, a 'common platform'.

In a 'mixed' negotiation there are likely to be difficulties at the margins of competence, for the actual course that the talks will take and the issues that arise cannot always be predicted. On occasion it may be possible for a direct link to be established between the EU delegation and the Council or COREPER, especially when negotiations extend over a long period.[20] But generally this will not be possible and issues will have to be resolved in coordination meetings between officials attending the negotiations.

The manifestation of the Union that other parties to an international environmental negotiation see across the table will also be determined by the Council acting with reference to Article 228 [300]. If Community competence is exclusive, the Commission will negotiate but the delegation will include at least one Member State representative, and there may even be a full Article 113 type committee dealing with the Commission in much the same way as in a standard trade negotiation. Otherwise, in a 'mixed' negotiation, there will be separate Commission and Member State delegations who will divide up responsibilities according to their competence.

Normally, when there is a common position which is not covered by exclusive Community competence, the Presidency will speak for all. This is especially important in cases (such as the INC negotiations to create the Climate Change Convention) where the EC does not have full rights of participation and the Presidency will speak using the formula, 'On behalf of the Community and its Member States' (Macrory and Hession 1996:136).

After some early problems, members of EC delegations and third parties have come to live with the 'bicephalous' arrangements in mixed negotiations. Once a coordination meeting has taken up a position all are bound by it. Both Member State and Commission sources have attested to the improvement in Community/Member State consistency at negotiations. One Member State negotiator observed to us that over the past three years, in which he had been an active participant, there had been a notable 'tightening up' allowing Member States 'less space to go their own way' (Interview, UK Department of the Environment, September 1997).

Most difficulties seem to occur within UN General Assembly fora where, as we have seen, the EC's status remains problematic and where there is a certain 'lack of Community discipline'. The growth of green politics in a UN context alongside the extension of the EC's policy has meant that inter-governmental diplomats have been faced with novel interventions from 'little environmental women who say "Sorry, I will talk on this matter because it falls within Community competence"' (Interview, DGXI, June 1996). The precise division of competence in any negotiation is a confidential and often difficult matter, but it can sometimes be turned to advantage. As one member of an EC delegation at recent negotiations put it:

> Negotiation is a three card game. We don't tell third parties which articles are covered by Community competence and which Member States. They would never let you say this and it allows us to wash our dirty linen in private.
>
> (Interview, DGXI, July 1997)

The 'washing of dirty linen' and the day-to-day planning of negotiating strategy is conducted in EC coordination meetings. These are held every morning during a negotiation but sometimes at midday and in the evening too. This can be onerous for Member State representatives who may find themselves rising at 6 a.m. and being forced to hold national delegation meetings late at night (Interview, UK Department of Environment, September 1997). Much depends upon the leadership role of whichever Member State holds the Presidency. If the Presidency is not strong the Commission sees its role as 'doing the work for them' and also acting as a 'sheepdog' to round up straying Member State representatives (Interview, DGXI, June 1996). On the other hand even a 'strong' Presidency will, on occasion, see the need to delegate responsibility for making first drafts of EC positions to Member State representatives who either volunteer or are requested to 'take the lead'. This may also suit the Commission, which may itself lack the resources to undertake the task. In such circumstances Member State representatives assist the Presidency but do not supplant it as formal negotiator.

The final stage involves signature and ratification. Article 228 [300] does not mention the signature of agreements, but the practice is to seek Council approval for this. There is then the ratification procedure, which in EC terminology is described as a 'Council Conclusion'. An important aspect of this conclusion is that the Council will make a formal statement of the legal bases upon which the agreement is concluded, involving citation of the relevant Treaty articles. Normally the decision making procedure involves qualified majority voting and consultation of the European Parliament within a strict timetable (McGoldrick 1997:91–2; Macrory and Hession 1996:138–9). Implementing legislation, if this is required, must be on the table at the same time and the process can extend over two years or more.

EXTERNAL ENVIRONMENTAL ROLES

Presence might be expected to provide the essential basis for the development of actorness. With respect to regional environmental questions this has evidently been the case. As we have seen, it was in attempting to solve transboundary atmospheric problems that the Community 'cut its teeth' as an international environmental actor. In attempts to manage regional seas, rivers and other shared ecosystems there has been a similar pattern. The Community has been obligated by its presence, by its close ecological interdependence with neighbouring states, and indeed, by the expectations and requirements of their governments, to develop an active regional role.

What is more intriguing and problematic, is the clear aspiration of the Commission and certain Member State governments to move well beyond such essentially regional concerns and to adopt a global leadership and 'agenda setting' role. This has been evident across the whole raft of 'global' environmental issues – stratospheric ozone, climate change, desertification and biodiversity – that have emerged over the past decade or more. Even though, in a general sense, the scale of the Single Market ensures that the EU will be a necessary participant in global negotiations, there is not the kind of direct link between presence and actorness that exists in the regional context. Given its internal disparities, and the problems of mixed competence, the aspiration to leadership might well be regarded as perverse.

The EU as regional environmental actor

Just as the presence of the Single Market exerts enormous sway over its immediate neighbours, so the related environmental policies and standards of the Community will be very influential. This may be because access to the market requires the attainment of certain environmental standards (phytosanitary regulations or product or emission standards). Or it may also be the case that a comparative advantage is sought by undercutting EC internal levels of environmental protection in third country export production. As well as the exercise of its gatekeeping role, the EC can also deploy a range of other instruments in support of its environmental policy objectives in relation to its neighbours. Access to scientific advice and information is significant but, above all, the critical instrument has been the provision of financial aid.

Union environmental policy operates at several regional levels. The EC is a signatory to large-scale international agreements directly affecting the territories of its Member States – the 1979 LRTAP and its associated protocols creating a regional air quality regime have already been mentioned. At a sub-regional level are agreements relating to the management of seas; notably the 1976 Barcelona Convention for the Protection of the Mediterranean Sea against Pollution and the 1983 Bonn Agreement, which provides a framework for international cooperation in tackling oil and other pollution of the North Sea.

The most potent manifestation of the Union as environmental policy actor in a regional context is, however, in its largely bilateral dealings with what we have described as its 'near abroad'. This has emerged most dramatically, following the end of the Cold War, in the Union's dealings with the countries of the old Soviet bloc. At the same time, and in some ways counterbalancing the new Eastern policy, there exists a continuing environmental relationship with the countries of North Africa and the Eastern Mediterranean. Both Eastern Europe and the Mediterranean are of great significance for the Union, on a number of policy dimensions, and form the subject of Chapter 5 below. What follows, extracts just one of these dimensions.

During the Soviet era, Eastern Europe and the USSR itself were renowned for their profligacy with natural resources and their neglect of good environmental housekeeping. This had the most dramatic and direct impact upon the countries of the Community in 1986, when the explosion of a nuclear reactor at Chernobyl in the Ukraine caused radioactive debris to be blown on the wind as far as the most westerly parts of the EC. Unsurprisingly, the major part (56 per cent in financial terms) of the Union's immediate post-Cold War environmental policy towards its Eastern neighbours has involved financial and technical assistance with improving the safety of nuclear installations and, indeed, with the closure of the Chernobyl complex itself.[21]

Other aspects of Union policy towards the East developed from 1991 in the context of the 'Dobris assessment' of the state of the European environment, which launched a process of consultations and biannual Ministerial meetings in which the Community has played a leading role. The Environment Programme for Europe (agreed at the Sofia Ministerial Meeting of 1995) was not, as some in Eastern Europe had hoped, an 'environmental Marshall Plan' (Liberatore 1997:201). Instead, the Community contribution was initially, between 1991 and 1995, to fund a specific series of projects and activities within the Phare (Poland–Hungary: Aid for Reconstruction of the Economy) programme for Central and Eastern Europe and the Tacis (Technical Assistance to the Commonwealth of Independent States) programme for the countries of the former Soviet Union. In practice, however, only 9 per cent of the 5417 million ECU committed falls under the heading of environment and nuclear safety. In the case of Tacis (2268 million ECU committed by 1995), the equivalent figure is 19 per cent (Commission 1997k:147–51).

The relationship of the Union towards the Central and East European Countries (CEEC) has been transformed since the end of 1994 by preparations for accession. Not only are Phare funds increasingly directed towards this end, but there has been greater emphasis on investment in new power generation and other environmentally related facilities, which can be portrayed as offering mutual advantages. The marginal costs of reducing pollution levels in Eastern Europe are much less than within the existing countries of the Union, whose industries will also benefit from supplying 'state of the art' environmental technologies to the East. Undoubtedly the greatest impact made by Union policies on its aspirant neighbours will simply be that they will, over time, have to adopt them. Accession requires that the environmental *acquis* of the Community, the whole body of law built up since the early 1970s (some 300 legal acts) be 'approximated' in the national legislation of new members.[22] The required changes in environmental policy and performance are extensive and costly. For all ten CEEC candidates for membership the investment costs of implementing the *acquis* are currently estimated by the Commission at 120 billion ECU. The bulk of the spending would be in air pollution abatement (40 per cent), water and sewage management (40 per cent) and solid and hazardous waste management (20 per cent) (*Enlarging the Environment*, 6 September 1997:6).

With the CEEC, the Union has now entered into an intensive process to force the pace of change. This new role is markedly different from that of 'catalyst' of environmental modernization and good practice that the Commission has more usually ascribed to itself in its dealings with neighbouring states (Liberatore 1997:200). A current example is provided by the Short and Medium Term Action Plan for the Mediterranean or SMAP. As part of the Euro–Mediterranean Partnership, agreed at Barcelona in 1995 (see Chapter 5), this plan represents the latest stage in a long sequence of EC activity designed to promote international collaboration in saving the threatened ecology of the Mediterranean Sea. Its southern Member States have, of course, a very direct interest in this, and a less immediate, but still significant, concern with combatting the spreading desertification of North Africa. The SMAP covers five priority fields of action: integrated water and waste management, dealing with 'hot spot' areas of heavy pollution and with threats to biodiversity, integrated coastal zone management and countering desertification. The Programme involves the Union and its 12

Mediterranean partners in a continuing consultative network which will not only 'promote the transfer of Community experience in the field of financing techniques, legislation and environmental monitoring and integration of environmental concerns in all policies' but also provide financial incentives via the Mediterranean Assistance (MEDA) instrument and European Investment Bank (Commission 1998a).

The EU as global leader?

In the politics of global environmental change, the Union's representatives have quite self-consciously claimed the mantle of leadership – whether in developing the climate change regime, strengthening the Montreal Protocol, creating the Intergovernmental Panel on Forests, promoting the Basel Convention on hazardous waste or 'greening' the WTO (Commission 1997k: 40,48,60,102,14). Inevitably, as in the field of trade, comparison is made with an inactive Japan and an inconsistent but dominant United States. One Commission official put it like this:

> In areas where the political impetus comes from the US the substantive result is predefined by the Union because the latter is so slow to come to a position because of the need to integrate different views, legal traditions etc. It takes a long time to arrive at a position and it is unlikely to change radically. By contrast the US can change from one day to the next. The US is a strong political actor, whereas the EU is a slow moving but weighty ship. The Community position has more weight in the long term. The US often cannot define a credible negotiating platform – they cannot think of all the North–South ramifications as the Community can. In climate, forests and biodiversity the EU is the only leader. Here the US is absent, blocking or destructive. This places the burden of leadership on the EU's slow moving ship.
>
> (Interview, DGXI, June 1996)

Such substantial claims are easy to comprehend in areas where Community competence has been long established and which are a natural extension of the Community's role as the largest actor in world trade. In 1992 the Community was the first to adopt legislation on the export and import of certain dangerous chemicals and has been in the forefront of negotiations to establish a binding prior informed consent procedure (PIC) for the movement of hazardous chemicals such as asbestos and pesticides across frontiers. It has also pressed other signatories of the Basel Convention on the matter of a total ban on the export of hazardous wastes from OECD to non-OECD countries.

Important though such trade-related questions may be, they are not the stuff of global environmental change. The most significant global negotiations have been in the areas of stratospheric ozone depletion and climate change. As we have already seen, it is in these areas that Community competence and the status of the EU as an actor has been problematic.

Stratospheric ozone

The record of the stratospheric ozone negotiations and the development of the Montreal Protocol provides some useful indications of the progress made by the Union since the mid 1980s. At the outset the attempt to respond to scientific findings on the depletion of the stratospheric ozone layer was clearly led by the United States which, in conjunction with an 'epistemic community' of concerned scientists and policy makers, pressed for the creation of an international regime to control the production and export of ozone-destroying chemicals, notably CFCs. The US chemical industry already had an interest in extending the domestic constraints on its own production (subsequent to 1977 Congressional action to ban the use of CFCs in aerosols) to its international competitors. The Member States of the EC were divided. Denmark and Germany pressed for immediate and extensive action while British and French governments, in line with the interests of national chemical industries currently responsible for a substantial share of world CFC exports, took a more negative initial attitude.

Richard E. Benedick, the chief American negotiator, is scathing in his personal account *Ozone Diplomacy: New Directions in Safeguarding the Planet*. For him, uncertainty about Community competence and the laborious, not to say contentious, procedures of the EC delegation and their masters in Brussels proved a tiresome obstruction in the path of the enlightened agreement sought by the American side –

> In its approach to CFC regulation throughout the negotiations leading up to Montreal, the EC Commission seemed to many observers generally more concerned about European political and economic union than about the urgency of protecting the ozone layer ... In accord with its expanding federal role, the EC Commission insisted on being sole speaker for all 12 countries at the negotiating table. It could not enforce this discipline, however, when the frustrations of individual delegations became too intense ... Bitter behind-the-scenes struggles occurred at internal EC caucuses that preceded, and often accompanied, the negotiating sessions.
>
> (Benedick 1991:35)

The author goes on to provide extensive detail on the problems of the EC Presidency during the negotiations, the difficulty of obtaining a mandate for the Commission from the Council and the general inflexibility that resulted. It is also charged that the delay in entry into force of the Protocol stemmed from EC demands that its members ratify simultaneously.[23]

The view from the other side of the table has been put by UK delegation leader Fiona McConnell. Criticizing the inevitable one-sidedness of Benedick's account, she paints an altogether different picture, where 'The Commission's relations with Member States in general and the UK in particular were smooth and harmonious throughout the Montreal meeting' (McConnell 1991:319). This seems very much a matter of perspective, but McConnell makes two further points which are worthy of note. First, that the problems of reaching consensus are hardly unique to the EC. Second, that the real problem for the Community may be that its procedures are simply misunderstood by others. Referring to a number of 'misapprehensions as to Community procedure' on Benedick's part, she writes that 'if someone of his distinction, working cheek by jowl with us for so long, can make such fundamental errors of interpretation, then the Community should ask itself why it is still misunderstood' (*ibid*). Without doubt there continues to be a problem here. In the diplomatic community there are, we were told, a small minority of 'cognoscenti' in EU matters (mostly trade specialists). Beyond the Missions in Brussels there is a great deal of ignorance of the niceties of EU procedure and much time is spent by those posted to Brussels explaining to home departments the complications of the system and the way it might be influenced (Interview, external Mission, January 1996).

The most critical point relates to the divergence between Member State positions, summarized in a well-worn phrase about 'convoys moving at the speed of the slowest vessel'. This had some force when the Council voted by unanimity but, as we have seen, the effect of the 1987 SEA and 1993 TEU was to greatly expand the areas covered by qualified majority voting. The 'convoy' analogy was, thus, appropriate to the beginning of the Montreal negotiations – with the EC passive and 'condemned to immobility without being able to react to compromise proposals' (Jachtenfuchs 1991:265). Certainly Benedick and others can point with some pride to the impetus provided by the initial US demands for CFC production cuts. However, it should be recalled that this was only after substantial internal conflicts and changes of direction in US policy – that Benedick himself documents.

Proponents of the EC's side can reply with some justification that the final comprehensive package involving production and consumption cuts, and subsequently a phase-out, owed much to the Europeans; and produced a more extensive and effective agreement than had initially been on offer. As Haigh (1996:246) notes, it was the Community that was able, in the end, to come to a rapid decision, made by the Council in December 1990, to exceed the requirements of the Protocol and opt for a complete phase-out of CFCs by 1997.

In the 1990s the EC has taken a proactive role in developing the ozone regime. On the tenth anniversary of the Montreal Protocol, for example, it went further than the USA and most other industrialized states in pressing for action in respect of the accelerated phase-out of the consumption of

HCFCs (the less ozone-depleting successors to CFCs) and the introduction of production controls.[24]

Climate change

The problem of climate change, produced by human activities, has an all-encompassing character. It has dominated international environmental diplomacy for over a decade. The main focus has been on the need to control emissions of the three principal 'greenhouse gases' – carbon dioxide, methane and nitrous oxide (there are three other industrial gases, hydrofluorocarbons, perfluorocarbons and sulphur hexafluoride). Carbon dioxide is seen as the principal culprit – responsible for some 80 per cent of global warming potential – but there is no simple answer equivalent to that available for the ozone regime, where the offending chemicals could simply be banned. Neither are there 'end of pipe' solutions of the type found in the long-range transboundary air pollution regime, where the chemicals responsible for acidification can be removed at source. Instead there is a need to reduce the use of those fossil fuels which provide the energy and transport bases of industrial society.

Effective action would range across many areas of national and Community policy – involving taxation, planning, transport infrastructure and alternative energy sources. The costs are extensive, but not prohibitive. Current Commission estimates of the price of achieving the EU greenhouse gas reductions proposed in its pre-Kyoto negotiating position vary between 15,000 and 35,000 million ECU or 0.2–0.4 of Union GDP in 2010 (Commission 1997l). However, it has long been the EU position that a commitment to reductions cannot be unilateral, but must be negotiated as part of a global regime involving, in the first instance, all the EU's main developed country competitors; to ensure that no competitive disadvantage ensues –

> Implementing reductions in greenhouse gas emissions that will imply significant changes in production and consumption patterns, is not possible for individual countries or groups of countries such as the European Community. Many industries operate in an environment with increasing global competition where relatively small cost margins are important. More and more economic sectors compete for capital in a global market where short term profit is important. And several important industrial sectors in Europe have faced or are facing overcapacity that make changes difficult to achieve.
>
> (*ibid*)

This problem is compounded by the fact that the scientific basis of the enhanced greenhouse effect continues to be disputed, despite the increasing certainty of successive IPCC assessments of the trend of global mean temperatures. Action will still, therefore, have to be based upon the precautionary principle. Further very difficult dimensions of the problem arise once the developing countries and their likely contribution to global warming over the next century are brought into consideration. A related and equally controversial matter is the need to conserve forests – owing, in part, to their role as 'sinks' for carbon dioxide. The ramifications potentially go far beyond the current concern with reducing gas emissions, and call into question the sustainability of the world trade and monetary regimes – thus, by implication, involving many of the external roles of the EC/EU.

The EC/EU has been a major participant in the attempt to create an international climate change regime since its inception in the late 1980s. This was despite the fact that climate change policy remains an area in which the main competences rest with the Member States. In the initial Intergovernmental Negotiating Committee, which created the 1992 UN Framework Convention on Climate Change, the Community was not formally represented, although it did become a signatory to the FCCC alongside the Member States. At subsequent Conferences of the Parties at Berlin in 1995, Geneva in 1996 and Kyoto in 1997, and at the important interim negotiations (especially the Ad Hoc Group on the Berlin Mandate) the EU 'negotiated as 16 – 15 Member States and the Commission' (Interview, DoE, December 1997).

The development of the climate change regime is now the subject of a substantial literature (Vellinga and Grubb 1993; Mintzer and Leonard 1994; Nilsson and Pitt 1994; O'Riordan and Jager 1996; Paterson 1996). This is not the place to examine the long-drawn-out and complex negotiations or, indeed, the difficult internal disputes that attended them. What is clear from all the accounts, however, is that the EU is routinely regarded as an entity with the capability to act. This is particularly striking in the light of inconsistencies between Member State taxation and energy policies, and internal difficulties over competence.

It is even more striking that the Union can lay serious claim to have been a leader in climate change policy – at least in comparison with the passivity of the United States and its JUSCANZ partners (Japan, Canada, Australia and New Zealand). From before the 1992 Rio Summit which witnessed the signature of the FCCC, EC Member States, notably Germany and Denmark, have been in the vanguard as far as carbon dioxide emissions reduction targets are concerned, with 1990 projected cuts of 25 and 20 per cent respectively in the period to 2005.[25]

Prior to the signature of the FCCC the common EC position was for binding commitments to emission targets. However American opposition, in an election year, led to the negotiation of a much weaker Article 4 of the FCCC, which merely expressed the 'aim (for Western industrialized countries) of returning individually or jointly to their 1990 levels of . . . anthropogenic emissions of carbon dioxide and other greenhouse gases'. The 1995

Berlin Conference of the Parties formally judged this to be unsatisfactory and set itself the target of producing new commitments by December 1997. At this meeting, in the view of one observer:

> The EU countries remained the most proactive with the EU as a group – now with the full backing of the UK – seeking specific commitments in emission reductions below 1990 levels on specific 'targets and time-tables'. They were also the most sympathetic to the insistence by developing countries that it would be inequitable to expect additional commitments from developing countries at this stage, and that the industrialized world had yet to demonstrate that it was taking an adequate lead as required in the Convention.
>
> (Grubb 1995:3)

The Achilles heel of such leadership, and one well known to the EU's negotiating partners, is that there has been no agreed internal strategy and clear line of responsibility for actually delivering the ambitious declaratory targets for greenhouse gas emissions. This is not to underestimate the achievement of obtaining a common negotiating position in the first place. Here, operating through Community institutions has served to aggregate the interests of 15 states and to reconcile differences between economies at different levels of development. The mechanism employed is the 'bubble' concept, whereby regional partners negotiate differential contributions to a common target for emission reductions. First devised within the EC as a means of successfully concluding the Large Combustion Plant Directive (Nitze 1990:24–5), it has provided a framework within which very different national requirements for greenhouse gas emission reductions (or in the case of the Southern members of the Union – increases) can be accommodated.

In advance of the Kyoto Conference of the FCCC Parties, the Council agreed to a negotiating position that sought emission reductions (for a three-gas 'basket' of carbon dioxide, methane and nitrous oxide) of 15 per cent (on 1990 levels) by 2010. This was based on highly differentiated national 'contributions' from the 15 Member States. Heavily industrialized countries with the most polluting industries – Luxembourg, Germany, Austria and Denmark – agreed 25 per cent reductions, while Belgium, the Netherlands and UK undertook cuts of 10 per cent. France and Finland, deemed to be low polluters, would stabilize at 1990 levels while the 'developing' states of the Union: Greece, Portugal, Spain and Ireland were allowed small increases (*The Times*, 4 March 1997).

This was impressive and remained, until September 1997, not only the most progressive but the 'only figure on the table' for consideration by the Parties. It was subject to criticism by the US and others on the grounds that the 'bubble' had no basis in EC legal competence and that, under such circumstances, they could not be expected to negotiate and exchange binding commitments as they would with a legally accountable state (Interview, DoE September 1997).

More damaging was the absence of common internal policies to achieve the 'bubble' targets. The whole area of common carbon/energy taxation and energy saving measures has been fraught with problems, and the subject of extensive industrial lobbying, since before the Rio Conference (Skjaerseth 1994). Member States are extremely wary of transfers of competence in taxation and energy. The failure of the first attempt to legislate a carbon tax was the occasion of the well publicized refusal to attend of the, then, Environment Commissioner Carlo Ripa de Meana.[26] At Berlin in 1995 the EU's internal controversies over carbon taxation 'undermined the EU's credibility as an international environmental leader' (Liberatore 1997:205). There is now very little likelihood of such a tax coming into being and a recent survey finds that, given the lack of collective political will, emission reductions will depend primarily upon national action by Member States (Collier 1996).[27]

The question of emissions targets has had the highest visibility, but many other aspects of the FCCC have been subject to often difficult negotiation. These include the responsibilities of developing countries, the relationship between sinks and sources of emissions, the review of national inventories and commitments and the introduction of carbon trading and joint implementation which might allow industrialized countries to offset some of their national obligations to reduce omissions. The latter were very much part of US policy in advance of Kyoto, along with a commitment merely to return emission levels to 1990 levels by the period 2008–12, and a controversial demand from the Senate that any agreement be dependent upon commitments to emission reductions by developing countries. The Japanese position – a 5 per cent reduction on 1990 levels by 2008–12 – occupied the middle ground between the US and EU.

The EU was able to maintain its discipline as a unit at Kyoto despite attempts to disaggregate its common position (*The Guardian*, 5 December 1997). The Kyoto Protocol to the FCCC was inevitably a compromise, but one which reflects the influence of the EU as a major protagonist. The industrialized countries agreed to an average 5.2 per cent cut in emissions for a basket of six greenhouse gases by 2008–12. The parties committed themselves to different targets – the US, 7 per cent, Japan 6 per cent and the EU 8 per cent overall. While these figures are not too far away from the EU interim target of 7.5 per cent by 2005, there are elements of 'flexibility' within the Protocol which reflect US objectives involving emissions trading and the 'factoring in' of savings made by re-afforestation.[28] Inevitably, the full implications of the Protocol will only become clear when the various mechanisms for its implementation are put in place and when, crucially, Member State and EC policies to deliver the promised emission reductions are operative.

CONCLUSION

The European Community has developed a wide-ranging set of environmental policies to deal with questions of air and water pollution, waste management and the conservation of nature. The external aspects of these competences meant that, by the end of the 1970s, the Community had begun to establish itself as an international environmental actor – and the first, and indeed only, recognized REIO.

The creation of a significant regional role reflected both the environmental presence of the Community and its close and increasing interdependence with its neighbours. As the conservation aspects of trade and fishing came increasingly to the fore the EC became a truly international player. Much of this was uncontentious because, given competence under the Common Commercial or Fisheries policies, only the EC (as opposed to the Member States) was in a position to comply with the requirements of international regulatory regimes. In what was described to us by a DGXI official as a 'good second phase', from the late 1980s, there has been an acceptance by insiders, and increasingly an expectation on the part of third parties, that Community competence must come into play across a wide range of environmental negotiations. Moreover, it is seen as providing 'added value' as well as complications (Interview, DGXI, June 1996). The most recent regional role played by the Union is altogether more directive than its other external environmental activities – involving the wholesale transfer of its internal standards and policies to the CEEC.

The development of the EC/EU as an international environmental actor has been extensively shaped by the attitudes and behaviour of third parties. This is evident, most obviously, in the differential willingness of various international organizations to recognize the EC as a party distinct from the national representation of the Member States. Less obviously, the development of international conceptions of environmental policy and sustainability has provided opportunities for the assertion of actorness by the EC. In particular the very recent development of global environmental diplomacy, centred upon the UNCED process, has provided the Union with a new stage. While the form in which it would be represented has proved contentious, there has been an evident ambition to develop a leadership role for the EU.

The period between the Stockholm and Rio conferences was marked by a paradigm shift, which extended environmental attention from localized and transboundary to global ecological interdependence, and today the EU's aspirations to a leadership role cover the whole range of global environmental topics. These ambitions cannot adequately be explained by reference to the EU's environmental presence. While aspects of EC competence are necessarily involved, and the EC/EU can claim an unrivalled range of policies and interests in relation to 'sustainable development' in all regions of the world (as we shall see in Chapter 4), there is not a close and immediate connection between presence and environmental 'actorness'.

Part of the explanation for the attempt to assume a global leadership role is internal pressure, in particular from a number of environmentally progressive 'lead states', which are always to the fore in the international game of declaring targets for emission reductions and exceeding the environmental standards set by the Community itself. Indeed, for all the Member States there are definite advantages in approaching global environmental issues via a common position, even if this is not strictly required by the letter of EC law. The EU when acting in a concerted way has equivalent weight in international fora to the United States, and has recently been in a position to set the pace in global negotiations. It is also worth remembering that the rotating Presidency provides individual Member States with previously undreamt of diplomatic opportunities. Thus, at the 1997 Kyoto Conference of the Parties of the FCCC it fell to Luxembourg to articulate the EU position alongside the US, Japan and China.

The global leadership role is still not entirely convincing. A primary problem remains that, in contrast to the Common Commercial Policy, competence is normally shared between Community and Member States and agreements and negotiations are 'mixed'. This raises particular, and on occasion niggling, coordination difficulties in the conduct of environmental diplomacy and provides scope for divergence between Member States, laying Union policy open to charges of immobility and reduction to the lowest common denominator. That this has not always been the case, especially in areas where competence remains largely with Member States and QMV does not apply, is a tribute to Community solidarity and to the influence of 'lead states' with a progressive environmental agenda. While the Community approach to negotiations may be criticized in terms of its slowness, it does serve to aggregate the interests of 15 states, thereby simplifying what may be described as the geometry of negotiations.

At the implementation stage of international agreements, it is obviously more desirable that common provisions be enacted for a whole region simultaneously than for 15 states to go their own way at their own pace. Thus, for the Montreal Protocol, the Commission initiated and the Council agreed a regulation binding on all members which precisely followed the requirements of the Protocol. However, as most commentators agree, there is also a significant 'implementation deficit' once agreements have been made.[29] The EU is engaged in a two-level, or often three-level, process, where Directives and Regulations agreed at Union level have to be made effective in concrete ways through the enforcement and monitoring of rules at national and local levels. As the 'completion' of the Single Market demonstrated, this is never easy. Although the EU procedures for monitoring and enforcing the compliance of its Member States are considerably in advance of those to be found in any other international organization, this is not the standard against which they will be judged. Inevitably, the comparison will be with large industrialized sovereign states and here, as the US side pointed out in the climate negotiations, there are continuing grounds for concern.

International environmental politics provides an expanding and, on occasion, very high profile arena of external action that could not have been envisaged at the time of the Treaty of Rome. The absence of a common environmental policy has meant that the external persona of the European actor, as they have developed in this area, are often differentiated and complex. 'Mixed' negotiations cause difficulties for insiders and outsiders alike, and there are inevitable problems of coherence between the range of EU policies touched by environmental considerations and consistency between Member States in those very significant areas where there is no Community competence. Even under such circumstances, however, the extent to which press reporting and academic commentary now routinely ascribes the status of single purposive actor to the Union bears striking testament to the development of 'actorness' in this new field of diplomacy.

4 Development cooperation
The EC in North/South relations

In the late 1990s the European Community and its Member States accounted for 60 per cent of world aid. Moreover the EC itself, 'as a distinct entity apart from the bilateral aid programmes of the individual Member States, has become *the world's fifth largest aid donor*' (Cox and Koning 1997:xiii, emphasis in original). Not only has the EC acquired a role as an aid donor, however. The 40 years since the EC was created have seen the evolution of increasingly complex relationships with developing countries in all parts of the world; they denote an important role for the EC as a development agency. Indeed the EC's significance as an actor in North/ South relations is underlined by the agreements it has recently made, with the World Bank and the United Nations Development Programme, to produce common development strategies. The first of these, between the EU and UNDP, will focus upon the Great Lakes region of Central Africa. 'The EU and UN said other big aid donors, such as the US, were welcome to join' (*The Guardian*, 7 April 1998).

The proactive role today played by the EC/EU in development matters reflects, in part, the opportunities provided by the end of Cold War bipolarity. The intention to develop such a role is clearly indicated in the Treaty on European Union – both in the general sense of the Union's aspiration to 'assert its identity on the international scene' (Art.B[2]); and because the TEU, for the first time, explicitly provided for a Community policy on development cooperation. This aims to foster –

the sustainable economic and social development of the developing countries, and more particularly the most disadvantaged among them;

the smooth and gradual integration of the developing countries into the world economy;

the campaign against poverty in the developing countries.

the general objective of developing and consolidating democracy and the rule of law, and of respecting human rights and fundamental freedoms.

(Art.130u [TEC 177])

These provisions clearly reflect the post-Cold War ideological climate in which the TEU was formulated. The accordance of Treaty status to this policy area undoubtedly reinforced the EC's role as patron/mentor in relation to 'cooperation partners'. It also provided the basis for increased politicization of development policy, as we shall see. Nevertheless, despite the absence of explicit Treaty provisions until 1993, the Community had been involved in development policy from the beginning. By 1982 its role had evolved to the extent that the Commission was to claim –

> Development policy is a cornerstone of European integration . . . The policy is an important one because of the institutional, financial, technical and trade resources it deploys; because of the number of countries it reaches; because of the novel forms of international cooperation it has pioneered. Today it is a manifestation of Europe's identity in the world at large and a major plank in he Community's external policies generally.
>
> (Commission 1982:8)

This evolution of an explicitly *Community* development policy, alongside the policies of the Member States, is attributable to several factors – all of which reflect aspects of EC presence. Thus, for example, introduction of the Community's Common Agricultural Policy established, from 1967, a very significant EC involvement in food aid, particularly as implementation of the CAP led increasingly to surplus production.[1] Food aid was originally managed in the context of the CAP, but became the responsibility of the Food Aid Service in DGVIII from 1986.[2]

More generally, the economic presence of the EC, in terms of the attraction of its market, has been central to policies seeking to promote 'development' through economic diversification and, in particular, industrialization.[3] This has involved use of trade incentives to encourage the industrial export sectors of developing countries. Trade policy instruments, of course, lie within Community competence, thus necessitating active EC involvement in trade-related aspects of development cooperation. Today, bilateral and multilateral agreements between the EC and third parties, in all regions of the South, typically include a range of differentiated and highly complex trade provisions. Moreover, from 1971, the Community's GATT-related Generalized System of Preferences (GSP) accorded to all developing countries preferential access to EC markets for industrial products and a range of processed foods. From 1980, and in particular since their most recent revision in 1995, the terms of the GSP reflect considerable differentiation between less developed countries (LDCs) and least developed countries (LLDCs). In a reflection of TEU provisions, the latter are accorded very much more generous treatment, provided labour standards and other conditionalites are observed, while a 'graduation' mechanism permits withdrawal of GSP benefits in cases where LDC exports are deemed to have reached appropriate standards of competitiveness (Piening 1997:175).

Finally, and most importantly, the Community's role in development cooperation originated from the colonial ties of its Member States. Both the EC's presence in North/South relations, as the political and cultural 'metropolis' at the centre of a network of dependency relationships, and its associated role as patron/mentor, were largely prefigured in the colonial era. Indeed, the EC's initial involvement in development matters grew directly from colonialism. In consequence, although reference is made to the full range of EC activities in this policy area, our focus is primarily upon the highly structured 'association' relationship, governed by the Lomé Conventions, between the EC and the African, Caribbean and Pacific former colonies of its Member States (the ACP Group).

This focus is merited, we believe, because it is here that the EC's presence is most apparent. ACP trade is overwhelmingly oriented towards the EC; the Community provides more than 30 per cent of all aid to sub-Saharan Africa, which remains at the centre of EC development cooperation; and the countries of the Pacific and Caribbean are highly dependent upon ACP membership for representation in Europe. More particularly, it is in the strategy of association that a distinctive, Community approach to development cooperation is most apparent – and most controversial. Here, assessments of the nature and significance of the EC's role have varied considerably. When the first Lomé Convention was negotiated in the 1970s, commentators seemed in no doubt that the Community was a significant actor in North/South relations. At that time there were concerns that the EC would become a major imperialist power; an instrument for collective exploitation of the South (Galtung 1973; Shaw 1979).[4] In the 1990s, however, liberal commentators have dismissed the EC's association strategy as both insignificant and anachronistic (Davenport 1992; Ravenhill 1993).

While evidently a reflection of competing ideological perspectives, these diverging opinions also reflect the passage of time. In this policy area, the interaction between ideas, beliefs and historical events has been of particular significance in constructing the shared meanings which have shaped EC relations with the South. Thus, despite core elements of continuity in EC development cooperation, a number of factors have precipitated change. In particular ideological shifts in the conceptualization of North/South relations, most recently the growing significance of neoliberal ideas, have interacted both with the changing character of the EC/EU itself and with developments in the external environment.

A survey of the EC's evolving relationship with its 'association partners' in the South suggests three periods when historical events and ideological preferences were of great significance in shaping the practice of development cooperation, and hence EC actorness, in this policy area. First the late colonial period, when the ideology and policy of associationism was constructed. Second, the period of Third World anti-imperialist political activism in the early 1970s, when the first Lomé Convention was signed. And third the dominance of neoliberalism in the early post-Cold War period when the Treaty on European Union was formulated and the fourth Lomé Convention negotiated.

ASSOCIATIONISM: SOURCE OF EC DEVELOPMENT POLICY

Community involvement in North/South relations originated from the need to accommodate the remaining colonial interests of Member States, in particular French colonies in Africa.[5] It was thus inevitable that the ideological preferences and policy priorities of French officials, representing both the dominant partner during the early stages of integration and the major colonial power, would shape the Community's initial approach to North/South relations.

From the early nineteenth century, French policy towards Africa had coalesced around the essentially ideological notion of 'Eurafrica'. This concept encapsulated the belief that the destinies of Europe and Africa were inextricably entwined; linked through the complementarity of their cultural, social, economic and political spheres in a relationship of mutual dependence, even symbiosis. During the twentieth century the Eurafrica concept was formalized through a system of 'association', which established a separate political identity for the colonial territory and afforded a degree of guided autonomy to indigenous elites, while ensuring French access to African raw materials and markets.

The almost mystical ideas associated with Eurafricanism were reflected in early EC involvement in North/South relations. Thus, despite opposition from the Dutch and German governments, which would have preferred a more global approach to North/South relations, the principles of associationism formed the basis of Community development cooperation.[6] Subsequent events, not least successive enlargements of EC membership, have inevitably weakened the influence of Eurafricanism. Nevertheless its vestiges can be discerned in the thinking of French policy makers and Francophone African officials (Interviews: external Mission, February 1996; DGVIII June 1996).[7]

Formal expression of the ideas underlying Community development cooperation can be found in the Treaty of Rome. At the insistence of the French government, Articles 131–6 [182–7] provided for 'association of non-European countries and territories with which Member States have special relations'. From these provisions the principles and practices of association evolved, that is, 'cooperation partnership' and a range of trade and aid instruments. Despite numerous complicated refinements, these three elements have remained the basis of EC development policy.

Financial assistance is provided through a fund established for this purpose – the European Development Fund (EDF). In recognition of different levels of Member State commitment to this policy area, the EDF derives from national funding rather than the Community budget. Each EDF is of five years' duration, and Member State contributions have been the subject of regular, often difficult, renegotiation. Following agreement of the global amount by the Council, the EDF is managed by the Commission. We discuss below the contemporary procedures for EDF disbursement.

In relation to trade, the associated countries were given privileged access to EC markets which placed them above other developing countries in the Community's system of preferences. This system effectively discriminated against the exports of non-associated developing countries and was, consequently, of dubious legality under GATT rules. Despite introduction and refinement of the GSP from 1971 the issue of differentiated Community preference continues to generate dissatisfaction among non-preferred countries, especially in Latin America, as recent controversy over bananas has demonstrated.[8] After more than 40 years, the issue of GATT/WTO legality also remains a problem.

In addition to its trade and financial assistance elements, association involved the establishment of formal relationships between the Member States collectively and their remaining colonies and overseas territories. In 1957, as we have noted, these were largely French dependencies, predominantly in sub-Saharan Africa.[9] In a very real sense the EC was to be associated with French policy towards Africa; to share with France some of the potential trade benefits, but also the financial burden, of French colonialism – and subsequently of the decolonization process and its aftermath. Consequently it is appropriate, in the early years, to regard the EC role in North/South relations as an adjunct to French policy rather than a distinctive Community approach to development.

EVOLUTION OF EC POLICY: THE YAOUNDÉ AND LOMÉ CONVENTIONS

Shortly after the EC's creation the meaning of association was challenged by anti-imperialist and pan-African movements sharply critical of EC policy,[10] and by the early 1960s a reassessment of association had become a necessity. This resulted in the formulation of a formal treaty or Convention of Association, referred to as Yaoundé I after the Cameroonian capital in which it was signed, which entered into force in 1964. It linked the six Member States of the EC and 18 Associated African States and Madagascar (AASM), and was of five years' duration.

In political terms the Convention acknowledged the new, legally independent status of the associates, while maintaining the core economic aspects of the existing arrangements. The reality of economic dependence is reflected by the fact that, in 1960, approximately 80 per cent of the associated countries' trade was with EC Member States and 98 per cent of aid to associated countries was EC related (Grilli 1993:15). The second Yaoundé Convention entered into force in 1971. Table 4.1 charts the evolution of the Yaoundé relationship and its successor (Lomé) Conventions.

The political innovations of the Convention were initially modest in impact. However they created important precedents. Unlike the previous agreements, which had simply been imposed upon the associates, the terms of the Conventions were the subject of negotiation – albeit highly asymmetrical – between the parties. The Convention enjoyed contractual status and was subject to formal ratification by all participating states. To facilitate the processes of negotiation, and the administration of the Conventions, joint institutions were established, including an Association Council and a parliamentary assembly composed of AASM representatives and Members of the European Parliament.

These innovations created conditions under which a complex, bilateral relationship could develop between the EC and the AASM. This provided a forum for AASM countries to coordinate and articulate their demands in the context of the evident failure of the Yaoundé Conventions to meet their needs.[11] It also facilitated their contribution to broader demands – by the increasingly assertive Third World lobby operating as the Group of 77 (G77) within the United Nations system – for a New International Economic Order (NIEO). This was to be based *inter alia* on radically altered terms

Table 4.1 Evolution of the EC–AASM/ACP relationship.

Year	Event	No. of countries	
		AASM/ACP	*EC*
1957	Creation of European Economic Community. TEC provision for association of countries having special relations with EC Member States	–	6
1964	Yaoundé I Convention between EC and Associated African States and Madagascar (AASM)	18	6
1969	Yaoundé II Convention, EC–AASM	18	6
1975	Lomé I Convention between EC and African, Caribbean and Pacific countries. Establishment of ACP Group	46	9
1980	Lomé II Convention, EC–ACP	58	9
1985	Lomé III Convention, EC–ACP	65	10
1990	Lomé IV Convention, EC–ACP	68	12
1995	Lomé IV *bis*, EC–ACP	70[1]	15

Note
1 ACP membership 71 following accession of South Africa in 1997.

of trade, which would ensure both more generous and more stable receipts for primary product exports, a range of measures to support economic diversification in the South and substantially increased financial assistance.

Strengthened by the significant increase in oil prices imposed by the Organization of Petroleum Exporting Countries (OPEC) in 1973, Southern demands for a more equitable North/South balance considerably influenced the renegotiation of Yaoundé necessitated by UK accession to the EC,[12] thus ensuring that the Yaoundé formula was comprehensively upgraded. Eventually signed in 1975, the first Lomé Convention linked the EC with 46 associates from Africa, the Caribbean and the Pacific. Again it was to be subject to renegotiation at five-year intervals.

The current membership (of Lomé IV) is set out in Table 4.2, which also shows the 1997 UNDP *Human Development Index* ranking of the ACP countries. Figure 4.1 shows the present geographical scope of the ACP, an artificial 'bloc' effectively created by the Community. The ACP Group nevertheless has separate legal status as an international organization, governed by the Georgetown Agreement of 1975. Thus the EC is unable to impose new members upon the ACP nor, indeed, can it disband the Group.

The original Lomé Convention contained important innovations, some of which reflected aspects of the NIEO programme.[13] Indeed its Preamble proclaimed the establishment of –

> a new model for relations between developed and developing States, compatible with the aspirations of the international community towards a more just and more balanced economic order;
>
> (Preamble, Lomé I Convention)

In economic terms, the existing formula of EDF assistance and trade concessions was enhanced. In relation to trade, two important changes partially reflected NIEO demands. First, the requirement for reciprocity in trade concessions was abandoned; in future Community concessions to ACP states would be unilateral. Second, measures were introduced to ameliorate the impact of price fluctuations on export earnings. The System for the Stabilization of Export Earnings (Stabex) provided for compensation payments, funded from the EDF, in respect of a range of specified agricultural products which fall outside the Common Agricultural Policy. A drop in price of more than 7.5 per cent was to trigger Stabex payments. In subsequent Conventions this threshold was both reduced and differentiated, so that by Lomé IV the Stabex trigger had reduced to 1 per cent for least developed ACP countries.[14]

For a number of products considered 'sensitive' because they are potentially in competition with Community products, but which have particular significance for specific groups of ACP countries, additional Protocols have been negotiated. These introduce special arrangements for sugar, bananas, rum and, most recently, beef and veal. Of these the Sugar Protocol has been

Table 4.2 Current ACP membership and human development index (HDI) ranking[1] – by region.

Country[2]	HDI ranking 1995	HDI ranking 1997	Country[2]	HDI ranking 1995	HDI ranking 1997
Africa (46 countries)					
Angola	164	157	Lesotho	131	137
Benin	155	146	Liberia	159	
Botswana	74	97	Madagascar	135	152
Burkina Faso	169	172	Malawi	157	161
Burundi	165	169	Mali	172	171
Cameroun	127	133	Mauritania	150	150
Cape Verde		123	Mauritius	60	61
Central African Republic	149	151	Mozambique	167	166
Chad	162	164	Namibia	108	118
Comoros	139	140	Niger	174	173
Congo	122	130	Nigeria	141	141
Côte d'Ivoire	145	145	Rwanda	156	174
Democratic Republic of			São Tomé and Principe	133	125
Congo (former Zaire)	143	142	Senegal	152	160
Djibouti	154	162	Somalia	166	
Equatorial Guinea	142	135	South Africa	95	90
Eritrea		168	Sudan	144	158
Ethiopia	171	170	Swaziland	124	
Gabon	114	120	Tanzania	147	149
Gambia	161	165	Togo	140	147
Ghana	129	132	Uganda	158	159
Guinea	168	167	Zambia	136	143
Guinea Bissau	163	163	Zimbabwe	136	129
Kenya	130	134			
Caribbean (15 countries)					
Antigua and Barbuda	55	29	Haiti	148	156
Bahamas	26	28	Jamaica	88	83
Barbados	25	25	St Kitts and Nevis	37	49
Belize	29	63	St Lucia	84	56
Dominica	69	41	St Vincent	79	57
Dominican Republic	96	87	Surinam	77	66
Grenada	67	54	Trinidad and Tobago	39	40
Guyana	105	104			
Pacific (8 countries)					
Fiji	46	46	Tonga		
Kiribati			Tuvalu		
Papua New Guinea	126	128	Vanatu	119	124
Solomon Islands	125	122	Western Samoa	102	96

Notes
1 The HDI ranking is taken from the United Nations Development Programme (UNDP) (1995 and 1997) *Human Development Report*, Oxford: Oxford University Press. The HDI is based on three criteria: gross domestic product *per capita*, adjusted to take account of purchasing power: life expectancy at birth; and level of education.
2 Number of countries listed was 174 in 1995; 175 in 1997. Gaps indicate data not available.

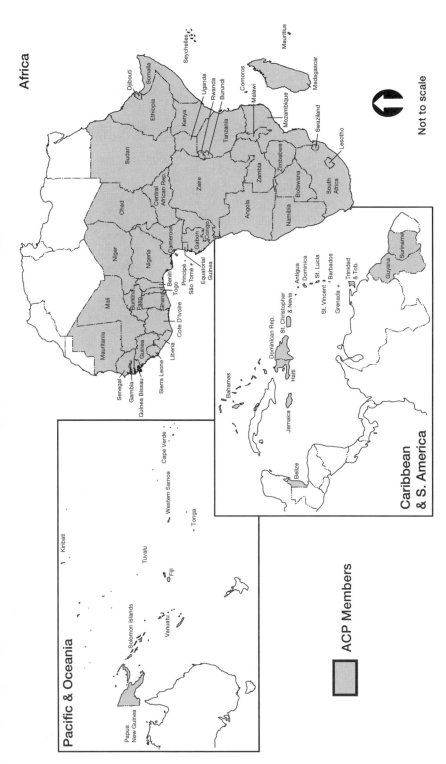

Figure 4.1 The ACP Group. (Figure © LJMU Cartographic Unit 1998)

the most significant, and historically the most controversial.[15] Politically, the Protocols have proved useful to ACP negotiators, since they facilitate discussion between Commission officials and sub-groups of the ACP having a common interest (Interview, ACP Secretariat, June 1996).[16]

In acknowledgement of the robust stance of ACP negotiators, the new model accorded greater importance to the notion of partnership. ACP members were to have full responsibility for their own internal political arrangements and development strategies, and there would be no tied or conditional assistance. In consequence the rhetoric surrounding the launch of Lomé I proclaimed the establishment of 'a relationship very much based on equal terms between the two partners' (*The Courier* 1975:3). To accommodate the 'partnership' concept the institutions of association were strengthened; an important innovation being establishment of the ACP Committee of Ambassadors, which is responsible for detailed negotiation of the overall Lomé package with Commission representatives.

The launch of the first Lomé Convention was heralded as a revolutionary approach to North/South relations and 'one of the greatest achievements of the Commission' (*Die Zeit* quoted in Erridge 1981:9). Although subsequent evaluations have been mixed, as we shall see, there is no doubt that creation of the Lomé system, with its complex provisions and strengthened institutions, consolidated a distinctive, Community approach to development cooperation.

Lomé IV: the changing context of North/South relations

The environment surrounding the negotiations for Lomé I was singularly propitious for the ACP Group; they were never again to achieve similar levels of bargaining power. The model of OPEC commodity power had not proved transferable to other commodities; indeed the cohesion of OPEC itself had not endured. Moreover the effects of oil price rises on the economies of Third World oil importers, which included the majority of ACP, were disastrous – causing chronic balance of payments difficulties and deepening debt. The Lomé provisions were not sufficiently flexible to meet these growing problems. While Stabex payments have, in practice, been used to ameliorate balance of payments deficits, the sums involved are modest in relation to need. EDF funding itself is largely project related. In consequence the Lomé relationship became less central to the needs of ACP governments, which were increasingly obliged to seek assistance from other sources, in particular the World Bank. Moreover, the ideological climate of the 1980s was very different from that of the 1970s. Given the increasing influence of neoliberal views, which saw market liberalization and foreign direct investment as the most appropriate route to economic development, the ACP 'equal partners' of Lomé I were anxious to maintain the concessions gained in 1975. There were, in consequence, few innovations in Lomé II (1980) and III (1985).[17]

While its essential elements remained intact, the Lomé relationship lost much of its impetus. This reflected not only the weakened position of ACP members, but also preoccupation, on the part of the EC, with internal matters. Thus the accession of Greece, Spain and Portugal increased pressure for a broader focus to development policy to include Latin American and Mediterranean non-member countries. Even more significant for the ACP was the Community's Single Market programme, which generated fears of an introspective 'fortress Europe'. While the Single Market might, in principle, have provided stimulus to ACP countries seeking to increase and/or diversify their exports, in practice their ability to take advantage of such opportunities was severely constrained by economic weakness as a result of falling commodity prices and escalating debt.[18] Moreover the Single Market programme introduced additional impediments to ACP exports, such as compliance with new unified product standards and consumer protection measures, which required levels of investment largely unavailable to ACP countries.

During this period the domestic liberalization of the Single Market process was mirrored by proposals under discussion in the GATT Uruguay Round. In particular, the extension of trade liberalization measures to agricultural products threatened seriously to erode ACP preferences. Thus the principles underlying the entire edifice of Community development cooperation were increasingly challenged by the influence of neoliberal economic orthodoxy, with its reliance upon non-interventionist, market strategies. '*La pensée unique*' as one Commission official observed (Interview, DGVIII, June 1996).

The negotiations for Lomé IV, in 1988–9, took place in an environment which was hostile to the ACP. However the very weakness of the ACP may, paradoxically, have been a source of strength. There is evidence that ACP representatives successfully used the prospect of further economic decline, and its social and political implications, as a bargaining device; and that similar arguments were used, in turn, by the Commission in urging Member State governments to increase the size of the EDF (Ravenhill 1993:45). Thus the Lomé IV negotiations provided an important indication that, as the ACP's significance for the Community declined, the EC's continuing presence as the metropolitan centre of a dependency network would necessitate continuance of the relationship in some form. In this policy area, presence may have the effect of circumscribing rather than enabling action.

In the event, Lomé IV saw a number of innovations. First, the Convention itself was of ten years' duration with a mid-term review, rather than full renegotiation, at the end of five years. This was ostensibly to provide extra stability in order to facilitate long-term planning, although the EDF was agreed by the Member States only for five years.[19]

With minor revisions to accommodate changing needs – for example introduction of the ill-fated Banana Protocol and use of a proportion of the

EDF to support World Bank imposed adjustment programmes – the basic trade and aid formula persisted into Lomé IV. There was, however, a perceptible shift in approach to cooperation partnership – in that, for the first time, explicit political conditionality was introduced. This took the form of a Human Rights clause (Article 5).[20] Inclusion of this measure, which had been strongly resisted by ACP governments in the past, demonstrates their weakness in the new negotiating climate.

Further innovations of potential significance were measures intended to acknowledge and enhance the role of women in development, and a new Title dealing with the environment.[21] Subsequently there has been disappointment at the lack of progress, in particular with regard to the gender provisions. This apparently reflects resource constraints, which have prevented the appointment to the Development Directorate-General (DGVIII) of staff with special expertise in this area (van Reisen 1997a:168).[22]

Lomé IV was signed on 15 December 1989. During the final months of the negotiations momentous changes had occurred in Europe, culminating in the symbolic breaching of the Berlin Wall on 9 November. These events inevitably cast a shadow over the signing ceremony, as Togolese President, Gnasingbe Eyadema, indicated in his speech to delegates. He called upon the Community –

> not to abandon their friends of the South for the benefit of their brothers of the East, whose opening to the Community market will basically change the fundamental element of North–South cooperation.
>
> (Quoted in *The Courier* 1990:4)

These concerns had not diminished by the time of the 1995 mid-term review of Lomé IV. Indeed, during the intervening period, Central and Eastern Europe had become an increasingly central focus of EC/EU activity, and the position of the ACP correspondingly weaker.

The mid-term review and Lomé IV *bis*

Reflecting entry into force of the TEU, the revised Fourth Lomé Convention, signed in Mauritius in November 1995, explicitly refers, for the first time, to 'the objectives and priorities of the Community's cooperation policy' (Article 4). Previously only the priorities of ACP States were referred to. Again reflecting TEU provisions, the Article 5 reference to human rights was expanded to include 'application of democratic principles, the consolidation of the rule of law and good governance ... good governance shall be a particular aim of cooperation operations'. These provisions encroach substantially upon the principle of equal partnership. As with the more focused human rights provisions, non-observance of these broad conditions could lead to suspension of assistance.[23]

A further innovation in relation to financial assistance also provides increased scope for supervision of the Convention's operation. Thus grant-related EDF payments are subject to a two-tranche system, under which 70 per cent of funding is released initially; the remaining 30 per cent is conditional upon progress with the first phase of agreed projects and the level of preparedness for the second phase. This provision was strongly resisted by ACP representatives. In the event they succeeded in reversing the proportions of funding to be released in each tranche (Interview, DGVIII, June 1996).[24]

In accordance with tradition, negotiation of the EDF – the central aspect of the review process – was the most controversial. In 1995 there were serious, public disagreements between the French, German and UK governments. The French government, which occupied the EU Presidency for the first six months of 1995, was eager to increase the value of the new EDF (the eighth) above the level of inflation.[25] However the German and UK governments were seeking to reduce their EDF contributions.[26] Eventually agreement was reached at the Cannes Summit in June, at the end of the French (EU) Presidency, for an EDF only marginally smaller than that originally proposed. This was reported as a 'goodwill gesture' to President Chirac (*The Guardian*, 22 June 1995). In the case of the UK government, however, the gesture was not unduly generous. The UK was the only country to reduce its contribution to the EDF – by 23 per cent. (Member State contributions to the eighth EDF are shown in Table 4.3.) There were subsequently considerable delays in ratifying Lomé IV *bis*, to the extent that the Commission now estimates that it will not be able to call on the eighth EDF until 2002 (van Reisen 1997a:177). These problems are indicative of a general lack of commitment to the Lomé system on the part of EU Member States.

The difficult negotiations for Lomé IV *bis* were affected not only by the evident shift of EU/EC commitment to the 'near abroad' but also by a more general sense that the Lomé relationship was an increasingly irrelevant remnant of Europe's colonial past. In a post-Cold War world where 'global free trade by the year 2020' was seen by some as a central policy aim, and a solution to all development problems (FCO, DTI 1996:*passim*), a structured relationship with 70 of the world's poorest countries seemed unappealing. Thus even before Lomé *bis* was signed there was considerable speculation about its continuation beyond 2000. In 1997 the Commission published a Green Paper inviting discussion of a number of options for the future. Before considering the future options, however, we briefly assess the operation of the Lomé system to date.

THE RECORD OF LOMÉ

In some respects EC associationism has been characterized by remarkable continuity. The core elements of associationism – financial assistance, trade preferences, and partnership – endured for many years. Trade and aid polices, albeit subject to increasingly daunting bureaucracy and ever more

Table 4.3 Profile of aid from EU Member States and the EC.

Member State	Bilateral (% of DAC aid) 1995	of which % tied[1]	EC Budget % 1994	Eighth EDF % 1995/2000	Policy consistency with EC[2]
Austria[3]	1.27	41	2.7	2.6	No policy known
Belgium	1.76	50.8	3.8	3.9	Partial
Denmark	2.77	50	1.9	2.1	Yes
Finland[3]	0.66	17.5	1.4	1.5	No
France	14.37	30.5	18.3	24.3	No
Germany	12.74	37.4	29.5	23.4	Declaratory
Greece	–	–	1.4	1.2	N/A
Ireland	0.24	nil	0.8	0.6	Partial
Italy	2.59	18.2	13.3	12.5	No
Luxembourg	–	–	0.2	0.3	N/A
Netherlands	5.66	2.2	6.1	5.2	Yes
Portugal	0.46	3.3	1.6	1.0	No
Spain	2.23	33.0	7.7	5.8	No
Sweden[3]	3.21	14.8	2.5	2.7	Declaratory
UK	5.42	26.6[4]	15.5	12.7	No
EC	9.37	nil			

Sources: Cox & Koning (1997); Commission (1997f); van Reisen (1997a).

Notes
1 That is, proportion of aid which must be used to buy goods or services emanating from the donor country.
2 Extent to which Member States have adopted policies intended to ensure consistency between bilateral and EC programmes. 'Yes' and 'Partial' indicate existence of some mechanisms to ensure consistency.
3 Contributions of Austria, Finland and Sweden to EC budget are for 1995, the year of their accession to the EU.
4 In November 1997 the UK government announced a change in policy on this issue.

complex provisions, have remained central to the association. Despite the maintenance of a multi-faceted institutional relationship, however, 'partnership' has ceased to mean that the political arrangements and development strategies of ACP countries remain the responsibility of their own governments.[27] Increasingly the EC has concerned itself with the promotion of democratic governance and market reforms among its associates.

While the EC–ACP instruments have endured, a cursory glance at Table 4.2 demonstrates that in the majority of cases the fundamental aim of assisting their political, social and economic development has not been realized. Having enjoyed up to 40 years of development cooperation with the Community, ACP countries remain among the poorest in the world; indeed 41 ACP members are classified as 'least developed' countries. In seeking explanations for this failure, we briefly examine the impact of each of the three elements of cooperation.

With regard to trade, ACP preferential access to Community markets has undoubtedly privileged these countries' products over all others.[28] Despite this, ACP exports to the EC have not fared well in relation to exports from non-preferred competitors, particularly from Latin America and Asia. Between 1976 and 1992, while ACP exports grew at an average annual rate of 2.28 per cent, those of Latin America and Asia grew at rates of 5.97 per cent and 11.7 per cent respectively (Cosgrove 1994:224–7). Table 4.4 shows the declining position of the ACP in trade between the EU and developing countries.

There are numerous reasons for the poor performance of ACP exports.[29] Indeed neoliberals argue that trade preferences confer only minimal advantages; and that discontinuation of preferences would advantage the ACP in the long run by obliging them to be more competitive (Davenport 1992). While there is undoubtedly a need to increase the competitiveness of ACP exports it is not immediately evident how this is to be achieved. Expertise, technology and investment are woefully inadequate in most ACP countries:

Table 4.4 (a) Trade between the EU and developing countries, by region, 1976–94; (b) ACP trade dependence.

(a) *Imports into EU* (ECU billion)	1976	1980	1985	1990	1992	1994
ACP	10,5	19,4	26,8	21,9	18	18,6
Asia	6,7	16	26	50,9	66,4	83,9
Latin America	8,3	13,7	25,8	25,7	24,8	26,7
Exports from EU (ECU billion)						
ACP	9,6	15,7	17,4	16,6	17	14,9
Asia	7,5	13,1	29,4	41	47,1	70,7
Latin America	7,7	12	13,5	15,6	20,4	28,4
Share of total imports to EU (per cent)						
ACP	6.7	7.2	6.7	4.7	3.7	3.4
Asia	4.2	5.9	6.5	11.0	13.6	15.5
Latin America	5.3	5.1	6.5	5.6	5.1	4.9

(b) *Exports to EU as percentage of world (selected examples)*

Africa	Cameroun	74.38
	Central African Republic	82.17
	Equatorial Guinea	99.05
	Uganda	75.00
Caribbean	St Lucia	70.42
Pacific	Vanuatu	53.15
ACP average		41.00

Source: Commission (1997d).

these inadequacies tend both to impede efforts to enhance the competitiveness of traditional exports and to preclude economic diversification. Thus in the case of bananas, for example, it is difficult to see how ACP bananas – which are organically grown on small farms, often in difficult terrain – can compete with the aggressively marketed Chiquita Banana.[30]

For the poorest ACP Member States, the trade provisions of Lomé are almost entirely irrelevant; these countries are only marginally involved in export activities. Consequently in many cases financial assistance has been, and remains, the core of the association system. Figure 4.2, which shows the composition of the EDF for 1995–2000, gives an indication of its size and complexity. Both these aspects of the EC's assistance programme have attracted criticism.

The overall amount of the EDF has increased substantially at each five-year renewal. However, while it has kept up with inflation, it has not expanded in relation to the enlargement of the EC/EU, or the extension of ACP membership; nor has it kept pace with demographic growth in ACP countries. The Lomé *bis* financial protocol was for 12 billion ECU over a five-year period. Given a current ACP population of approximately six million, this provides little more than five ECU per person per year (*The Courier* 1996:23). Moreover, as Table 4.5 indicates, assistance to the ACP group has declined as a proportion of the overall EC aid effort. This largely reflects the EC's new priorities in Central and East Europe and the Mediterranean.

The complexity of the EDF system can be demonstrated by a brief outline of its operation. EC Member States make payments to the EDF annually on the basis of a Commission forecast of expenditure and are 'always in arrears' (Interview, Council Secretariat DGE, July 1997).[31] Division of programmable (project-related) aid between ACP Member States is determined

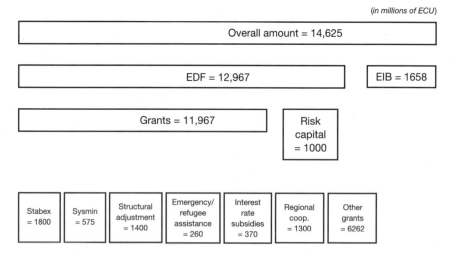

Figure 4.2 Composition of the eighth European Development Fund.

Table 4.5 Regional distribution of EC aid, 1986–95.

	1986	1987	1988	1989	1990	1991	1992	1993	1994	1995
Committed										
(million ECU)										
ACP	1141	2632	2869	1994	1362	2123	2765	2774	3514	2599
S. Africa	7	19	30	25	31	58	81	91	103	125
Asia	140	257	236	426	317	383	470	504	451	696
Latin America	160	156	159	210	222	286	338	401	390	486
Med./Mid. East	401	149	309	511	386	1133	655	711	757	869
CEEC	–	2	1	52	683	845	1238	1588	1294	1446
NIS	–	–	20	–	5	615	679	592	593	821
Unspent in year	704	643	582	96	249	124	370	185	213	301
Share (%)										
ACP	44.7	68.2	68.4	60.2	41.9	38.1	41.9	40.5	48.0	35.4
S. Africa	0.3	0.5	0.7	0.8	0.9	1.0	1.2	1.3	1.4	1.7
Asia	5.5	6.7	5.4	12.9	9.8	6.9	7.1	7.4	6.2	9.5
Latin America	6.3	4.0	3.8	6.3	6.8	5.1	5.1	5.9	5.3	6.6
Med./Mid. East	15.7	3.9	7.4	15.4	11.9	20.3	9.9	10.4	10.4	11.8
CEEC	–	0.1	–	1.6	21.0	15.2	18.8	23.2	17.7	19.7
NIS	–	–	0.5	–	0.2	11.0	10.3	8.7	8.1	11.2
Unspent in year	27.6	16.7	13.9	2.9	7.7	2.2	5.6	2.7	2.9	4.1

Source: adapted from Cox and Koning 1997:7.

Abbreviations
ACP: African, Caribbean and Pacific Group
CEEC: Central and East European countries
NIS: New Independent States (of former Soviet Union)

by the Commission, which subsequently negotiates – bilaterally with ACP representatives – the terms of National Indicative Programmes (NIPs) for its utilization. These cover the five-year period of the EDF and are subject to approval by the Development Council, by QMV. Individual project proposals are discussed bilaterally between ACP representatives and Commission officials, both locally in EC Delegations and in Brussels.[32] At the end of this arduous process, award of contracts for works and services is the responsibility of ACP governments.[33] This provision contrasts markedly with Member State bilateral aid, a substantial proportion of which is tied to the purchase of goods or services (as indicated by Table 4.3, which provides a profile of Member State aid).

For ACP governments and their Permanent Representatives in Brussels, the 'very, very complicated' EDF procedures have produced 'an administrative nightmare' which taxes the capacity, not only of ACP countries but also of the Commission. There is also a strong sense of lack of transparency – of working in a situation where 'non-decisions are taken over non-lunches over non-papers by non-people' (Interview, Euro–CIDSE, June 1996). In relation to the funding process, ACP criticisms have focused, in particular, upon delays and uncertainties experienced in dealing with DGVIII officials. While this reflects staffing constraints in the Commission, there is no doubt that it affects the morale of ACP representatives.[34] 'Delay is the deadliest form of denial' as one ACP Ambassador commented (Interview, June 1996).

Criticisms from EU Member States have focused upon inadequate supervision of agreed projects; hence the introduction of the two-tranche funding process in the mid-term review. Nevertheless DGVIII has paid considerable attention to evaluation of projects, including use of independent evaluators, and recent Court of Auditors' reports on the use of the EDF have been favourable (*Official Journal of the European Communities*, C343, C395, 1996).

Despite its shortcomings, there is no doubt that the EDF has provided a substantial amount of financial assistance over many years. Its failure to halt the economic decline of ACP countries is only in part a function of its inadequacies. Many of the problems besetting ACP States stem from major changes in the international environment since the mid 1970s; and from the failure of policy makers, both within the EC and the ACP, to respond effectively to these changes. The failure to anticipate or address the problem of ACP debt is central here.

Partnership, the third element of the Lomé system, has arguably been the most significant. Certainly it is this aspect of Lomé which distinguishes it from EC relations with other developing areas. The Community effectively created the ACP to facilitate its interaction with a large and diverse group of former colonies, the majority of which were small in size and/or economically weak. In consequence the Lomé system encapsulated, from the outset, an inherently asymmetrical relationship. In recent years this asymmetry has increased markedly. The success of the ACP Group in pursuing collective interests has, in consequence, been mixed.

A further factor affecting ACP success is that the interests of so large and heterogeneous a group are inevitably diverse. In addition to differences associated with level of economic development, there are a number of political tensions between ACP members. The most notable of these is the historical divide between Francophone and Anglophone states, which has persisted. Such divisions impede policy coordination within the ACP and are reflected in the internal politics of its Secretariat.[35] Nevertheless, the ACP Group has provided a means, which its members would not otherwise have had, of collective representation and bargaining. The Lomé relationship cannot be characterized simply as collective exploitation; it also represents a rational response, on behalf of ACP governments, to their situation of political and economic weakness. As one Permanent Representative commented, 'the Community is a world power and it helps to have a mechanism to deal with it' (Interview, Caribbean Mission, June 1996). Another highlighted the relatively sympathetic treatment of ACP governments by the EC, when compared with the World Bank. In the case of the World Bank conditionality is 'really excessive'; here recipient governments are allowed sufficient space for 'about one minute's decision making' (Interview, African Mission, February 1996).

The ACP has endured. No members have left the Group; indeed membership has grown considerably (from 46 in 1975 to 71 in 1997). The newest member of the ACP Group is South Africa, which acceded to the Lomé Convention in April 1997. However South Africa is only partially involved in the Lomé system, since both its trade and aid relationships with the EC are the subject of special, bilateral arrangements.[36] Nevertheless the application for membership by South Africa shortly after the ending of apartheid provides further evidence of the attractiveness of the ACP which is, itself, an indicator of success.[37] There is no doubt that, despite criticisms of its shortcomings, the Lomé system is valued by its ACP members. This was evident in our discussions with Permanent Representatives, not least from their concerns over Lomé's future.

The 1997 Green Paper and the future of Lomé

The Commission's Green Paper examines all aspects of the Lomé relationship, including its geographical scope. This is a particularly sensitive issue since it impinges upon the composition of the ACP Group. Two of the Commission's proposed options would maintain the existing arrangements – the status quo and the status quo supplemented by increased bilateral differentiation. The two further proposals would effectively end the EC–ACP relationship.

First among these is a focus on least developed countries; an approach favoured by several Member State governments, including those of the UK and the Scandinavian countries. According to non-governmental development organization (NGDO) representatives this would have the effect of 'ghettoizing' Africa, although inclusion of countries such as Bangladesh, Laos and Cambodia is under consideration. In practice, however, most LLDCs outside Lomé receive broadly similar aid and trade advantages from the EC under separate 'cooperation' arrangements.[38] Consequently the issue is not that non-Lomé LLDCs are disadvantaged; but that Lomé advantages are enjoyed by non-LLDCs. It is difficult for the NGDOs to argue against poverty eradication but this approach, which would effectively reduce Lomé from a development programme to an aid conduit, would allow the EC 'to take the moral high ground and save money at the same time' (Interview, Euro–CIDSE, June 1996). It would also deprive any successor to the ACP Group of expertise from the relatively developed countries, particularly in the Caribbean, which has proved an important asset in ACP negotiations.

Also under consideration are proposals that Lomé should be broken into a set of regional arrangements. Emphasis on regional initiatives is already included in the Convention but has had little impact.[39] However the new approach would move beyond exhortation and encouragement – to *create* regional groups with which the EC would in future interact. Since one proposal is that the Caribbean ACP members should join with Central American countries in forming a regional group, this would have the effect both of breaking up the ACP and introducing new members to the post-Lomé arrangements.

ACP reactions to these proposals varied. Francophone African representatives were confident that 'the French government will not let Lomé die'.[40] They also commented positively on the proposed regional focus of future cooperation (Interviews, February 1996). Concern about the future of Lomé was greatest among Caribbean representatives. Focus on the least developed would exclude most Caribbean states and there was little optimism about the potential for regional initiatives involving Central American countries (Interview, Caribbean Mission, June 1996). Despite their relatively better economic performance, their small size makes Caribbean countries extremely vulnerable, in particular to changes in the external economic environment.

Despite differences of emphasis among ACP representatives, there was agreement that membership of the ACP has brought benefits, not least the increased weight of negotiating as a bloc rather than singly. Lobbying in the complex policy environment of the Community has proved daunting even to third party Missions having large staffs and substantial financial resources. ACP Missions do not have these advantages. While the Lomé institutions and DGVIII's management of the Lomé system help to reduce the complexity of the policy environment for the ACP, it was still experienced as 'confusing and complicated' (Interview, Caribbean Mission, June 1996). A typical ACP Mission has only three diplomats and is accredited to the Benelux countries and several other Member States in addition to the EC. Without the support of the ACP Secretariat, and the potential to maximize the expertise of individual Missions through the Committee of Ambassadors, few ACP countries would be in a position to maintain an effective relationship with the EC. Their voices would simply not be heard in Brussels.

The ACP Group itself has expressed strong commitment to a continuation of the Lomé relationship. The 1997 Libreville Declaration, adopted by the First Summit of ACP Heads of State and Government, envisages a 'new and even more vigorous relationship with the European Union and its Member States'. Moreover there was a desire to 'strengthen the unity and solidarity of the [ACP] Group and retain it as a geographical entity'. Here there was an intention that, in addition to participating in a 'reinforced' Lomé relationship, the Group would in future act outside the ACP–EU context 'as a politically cohesive force in international relations and in such fora as the United Nations and the WTO' (http://www.oneworld.org/acpsec/gabon: 7 November 1997). This broader role has long been an aspiration among sections of the ACP Group (Interview, Caribbean Mission, June 1996). If achieved it would provide the Group with a more distinct personality, 'enabling it perhaps to negotiate with Japan or China'. There was a sense that 'having relations elsewhere would strengthen the ACP's negotiating hand' in dealing with the EU. 'The EU has taken the ACP for granted, but we deserve it.' In order to succeed, however, the ACP Group needs stronger leadership and a willingness to abandon 'outdated theories – of Kaunda, Nyerere, socialism and the LSE' (Interview, external Mission, June 1996).

The Green Paper addresses all three components of the Lomé system – partnership, trade and aid.[41] A major theme, which is evident in all areas of potential cooperation, is the strong emphasis on the overall aims of EU/EC external policy. Thus, in relation to 'partnership', greatly increased emphasis is placed upon the need for political reform within ACP countries; and upon the conditional nature of future cooperation. Indeed, it is stated that –

> the EU can commit itself to supporting only economic and social organ-
> ization models which contribute to the objectives of its cooperation
> policy and which comply with the political and social values which it
> means to promote.
>
> (Commission 1997a:25)

These proposals reflect the EU's new assertiveness in the political environment of the 1990s and following entry into force of the TEU. They suggest a very significant role as 'patron/mentor' in shaping the future development and political direction of the EU's Southern 'partners'.

This new assertiveness is also evident from the recent evolution of EC development policy beyond the associates – that is, in relations with Asian and Latin American countries (ALA).[42] Also of significance in the post-Cold War period has been the rapid growth in the operations of the European Community Humanitarian Office (ECHO). We briefly outline these developments, in order to demonstrate the EC's increasingly important role in North/South relations, before assessing the consistency and coherence of development cooperation policy as a whole.

DEVELOPMENT COOPERATION BEYOND THE ASSOCIATES

As we have seen, inclusion of the concept of association in the Treaty of Rome, and the subsequent evolution of the Yaoundé and Lomé relationships, established a regional approach to development policy which privileged Africa in particular. Thus in ALA countries (and especially in Latin America) there has been strong resentment of the EC's discriminatory practices.[43]

UK accession in 1973 did not immediately disturb the regional focus of development cooperation; however it reinforced pressure for a broader focus to Community policy. Consequently, in 1976, the EC negotiated a series of bilateral agreements with ALA countries. These did not include the 'partnership' dimension of Lomé and were less advantageous than Lomé arrangements in other ways – for example financial assistance was provided on an annual basis rather than as part of a multi-annual programme. Subsequently, in recognition of their particular problems, the EC introduced an 'extended GSP' for the benefit of non-associated LLDCs, together with a compensatory scheme for loss of export earnings (Compex, which mirrors Stabex). Bangladesh has been the principal beneficiary of this arrangement, which was introduced in 1987.[44] In contrast with the Lomé arrangements, these programmes are funded from the Community budget; moreover they do not fall within the responsibility of DGVIII (see Figure 1.1).

Since the mid 1980s EC relations with Latin America have strengthened considerably, partly as a result of the accession of Portugal and Spain in 1986. However the relaxation of Cold War tensions was also significant, since it enabled the EC to pursue a more proactive political role in a region traditionally seen as the preserve of US policy. Thus the EC contributed to conflict resolution in Central America through the San José process, which was launched in 1984 and involved political dialogue supported by development assistance. Of particular significance, here, is the Commission's insistence, in the face of strenuous opposition from the UK government, on including Nicaragua in this programme.[45] Subsequently Nicaragua has remained among the major recipients of EC aid in Latin America. The EC's willingness to encroach upon areas sensitive to US foreign policy is further evidenced by the development of tentative links with Cuba during the 1990s. Indeed in 1995 approximately 80 per cent of humanitarian aid to Latin America went to Cuba (Euro–CIDSE 1996 March–April:20).[46]

In 1995 the Commission formulated a comprehensive policy toward Latin America. This involves a two-pronged approach combining provision of development assistance to the poorest countries and strengthening links, in a broad range of policy areas, with economically vibrant countries. Thus agreements have recently been negotiated with Chile, Mexico and the Mercosur (Mercado de Sur) countries (Argentina, Brazil, Paraguay and Uruguay) with whom the EU–Mercosur Interregional Framework Agreement was concluded in December 1995. Chile has subsequently joined Mercosur (in January 1997) and Bolivia has signed a preferential tariff agreement. A major focus of EC assistance to the group is to promote market integration. The reasons for this focus are clearly acknowledged; the Community 'is striving to consolidate and improve its trading and technological position in a region with strong growth potential' (Commission 1995c:6).

The Commission has also shown increased interest in Asia since 1994, when an 'Asia Strategy' was adopted. Here, however, the differences in approach to LDCs and newly industrializing countries (NICs) are particularly marked. This reflects the very considerable economic divergence in the region.[47] For almost 20 years, until the early 1990s, the EC operated an overtly hostile trade policy towards the Asian NICs. Somewhat belatedly the Commission, in particular Sir Leon Brittan, has become 'seized with the importance of Asia' and has made strenuous efforts to improve relations with ASEAN in particular (Interview, external Mission, January 1996).[48] In relation to LDCs, the Community concluded broadly focused cooperation agreements with Vietnam and Nepal in 1996. These agreements emphasize employment generation, primary health care and the role of women. This last area has received special emphasis in Asian programmes, where projects have included provision of credit for women, often combined with training in technical or business skills (Cox and Koning 1997:85–8). There has also been emphasis upon environmental provisions which reflects, in part, an EC commitment to the conservation of tropical forests, agreed in 1992. This provides for 10 per cent of funding to be allocated to environmental projects (*ibid*:90).

In accordance with TEU provisions, the now customary human rights and good governance conditionalities have been included in the increasingly broadly based 'third generation' cooperation agreements concluded with ALA countries in the 1990s.

In addition to these regional programmes, the European Community Humanitarian Office deals with aspects of development policy on a global scale. Established in 1992 to enable the EC to respond to the humanitarian crises of the post-Cold War period, particularly in ex-Yugoslavia and the Great Lakes Region of Africa, ECHO has grown very rapidly in terms of scope of activities and expenditure. It is responsible for preservation of life during emergencies and longer-term assistance thereafter, including rehabilitation and reconstruction, and the welfare of refugees and returnees (ECHO 1996). The operation of ECHO has been subject to criticism, however. There is evidence of overlap between the activities of ECHO and the longer-term assistance provided by development cooperation programmes. There are fears, too, that the new focus and considerable expenditure (almost 657 million ECU in 1996) on crisis measures are diverting resources from the painstaking development work which would help to prevent crises from occurring (ACTIONAID 1995:101; van Reisen 1997a:169).

The establishment of ECHO clearly reflects political priorities, in particular the need to respond to high profile crises where there is a media-led demand that something be done. However the overlapping, and potentially conflicting, aims of crisis management and development cooperation are indicative of the inadequate coordination and lack of coherence which affects external policy generally. These problems, which impinge significantly upon EU actorness, were explicitly addressed by the Treaty on European Union.

EU ACTORNESS: CONSISTENCY/COHERENCE OF DEVELOPMENT POLICY?

The TEU aims to give overall political direction to all aspects of external policy. Thus, in a key Article (C[3]) the Union is given responsibility for ensuring 'the consistency of its external activities as a whole in the context of its external relations, security, economic and development policies'. The European Council and the Commission are jointly charged with ensuring such consistency.[49] In relation to development cooperation, the provisions which link Community practice with the fundamental political objectives of the Union are those concerning democracy and the rule of law, and respect for human rights and fundamental freedoms. These guiding principles are common both to Community development cooperation and the Union's Common Foreign and Security Policy.

Our outline of the evolution of EC development policy demonstrates that these principles have indeed guided practice, in that political conditionality clauses have been inserted in all recent EC agreements with third parties – appearing in Lomé IV *bis*, and the new 'third generation' agreements concluded with ALA countries from 1994. Problems have tended to arise, however, when these conditions are deemed not to have been met, and when decisions to impose penalties for non-compliance have been taken in the context of CFSP, on an intergovernmental basis. Inevitably CFSP decisions of this nature require implementation by the Commission. Since development cooperation falls within EC competence, and the Commission would normally have sole right of policy initiation in this area, there have been several occasions when a CFSP decision has been the subject of tension between the Council and the Commission.[50]

In development policy as elsewhere, tensions between Pillars, and within Pillar I, tend to impede overall policy coherence. Within the Community Pillar there are coordination problems not only between the Relex DGs, but also between Relex DGs and DGs having horizontal responsibilities. This applies, in particular, to agriculture (DGVI) and fisheries (DGXIV).[51] In June 1997 the Development Council adopted a resolution on coherence, which covers the areas of conflict prevention and peace building, food security, fisheries and migration, and calls upon the Commission to devise procedures to ensure coherence in these areas (Council 1997b). Potentially this would address a number of problem areas, for example the unclear division of responsibility between ECHO and the regionally focused DGs. However policy coherence is a sensitive issue for the present, deeply divided Commission. While co-location in the centrally located Charlemagne Building of policy level staff from the previously dispersed Relex DGs (from 1998) may be a step in the right direction, progress toward greater policy coherence is likely to remain limited pending reform of the Commission's organization in 2000. (The Commission's reform proposals are discussed more fully in Chapter 6.)

Despite the problems which undoubtedly arise, lack of coherence is not the most significant impediment to EC actorness in this policy area. Rather it is lack of consistency, arising from the operation of parallel development policies by the Member States, which diminishes the importance of the EC's role. The TEU both acknowledges and perpetuates this situation. Community policy, according to Article 130u [177] 'shall be complementary to the policies pursued by the Member states'. This makes clear that EC policies are intended to co-exist with rather than to replace those of the Member States. Thus, in legal terms, there is concurrent or parallel competence (Macleod, Hendry and Hyett 1996:343). Effectively, the EC operates a 'sixteenth' development policy alongside the policies of the Member States.[52]

This parallelism avoids competence problems of the magnitude encountered in environmental negotiations (see Chapter 3). Moreover, in a further contrast with environmental issue areas, the very broad competence enjoyed by the EC to introduce measures contributing to 'economic and social development' in third countries is not dependent upon the prior adoption of such measures internally (Macleod, Hendry and Hyett 1996:341–2). Nevertheless the co-existence of EC and Member State policies inevitably impinges upon the effectiveness of development cooperation. In this key issue of policy consistency the legal view, as confirmed by the European Court of Justice, is that Member States are not prevented from acting 'in relation to the same matters' outside the EC framework – however their policies must not conflict with or undermine the objectives of EC policies (*ibid*:343).

The issue of consistency is dealt with in the TEU through the provision that –

> The Community and the Member States shall coordinate their policies on development cooperation and shall consult each other on their aid programmes, including in international organizations and during international conferences ... The Commission may take any useful initiative to promote the coordination referred to ...
>
> (Art.130x [180 TEC])

This provision is potentially very important. In 1995 the EC and its Member States provided 53.50 per cent of the total aid from Development Assistance Countries (DAC), but of this total only 9.37 per cent was EC aid. These figures exclude the substantial EC aid to Central and East Europe, which is not classified as development assistance. For comparative purposes, Table 4.6 shows all DAC contributions for 1995. It is notable that two EU Member States, France and Germany, operate bilateral programmes greater in size than the total EC programme. Effectively coordinated, development assistance emanating from combined EU sources would have considerable impact. However, uncoordinated efforts result in situations such as has occurred in Burkina Faso, where ten Member States and the EC are

Table 4.6 Official development assistance[1] of DAC countries, 1995.

Country	ODA 1995 as % of total DAC	ODA 1995 as % of GNP
Australia	1.95	0.34
Austria	1.27	0.32
Belgium	1.76	0.38
Canada	3.60	0.39
Denmark	2.77	0.97
Finland	0.31	0.32
France	14.37	0.55
Germany	12.74	0.31
Ireland	0.24	0.27
Italy	2.59	0.14
Japan	24.45	0.28
Luxembourg	0.00	0.00
Netherlands	5.66	0.80
New Zealand	0.21	0.23
Norway	2.12	0.87
Portugal	0.46	0.27
Spain	2.23	0.23
Sweden	3.21	0.85
Switzerland	1.85	0.34
United Kingdom	5.42	0.29
United States	12.44	0.10
EU Member States	53.50	0.38
of which EC	9.37	

Source: Adapted from Commission (1997f).

Note
1 Does not include Official Aid to CEEC and NIS.

operating aid programmes simultaneously. In such situations, EC Delegation staff attempt to assist with coordination on the ground. However this cannot remove the pressure on the administration of a very poor country obliged to interact with 11 different donors (Interview, Council Secretariat DGE, July 1997).

Success in achieving the necessary strategic coordination of development programmes has been modest. There have been attempts, for example, to ensure that both the EC and Member States are not 'covering health' in a particular country (Interview). This reflects Council resolutions in 1994 and 1995 exhorting the Commission and the Member States to ensure consistency in this and other areas, including food security, education and training, human and social development and the integration of gender (van Reisen 1997a:174). Few Member States have taken practical steps to implement these resolutions, however. Indeed a recent survey of Member State development policies found that seven had made no statement whatsoever concerning consistency with EC objectives, while only Denmark and the Netherlands had comprehensive policies which included mechanisms for implementation (Table 4.3, in giving a profile of EC aid, indicates the findings of this survey). In general it was evident that the position of Member State governments was –

> predicated on a view of the EC development cooperation as an extension of the country's position. Elements that contradict national views are generally dismissed as irrelevant.
>
> (van Reisen 1997a:175)

In a few cases the aims of Member State development policy are already consistent with those of the EC. Where there is divergence, however, national priorities dominate. Moreover commercial interests continue to have significance in many bilateral programmes, as Table 4.3 shows. Thus, while increased consistency has been achieved in specified areas such as policy on HIV/AIDS (Interview, Council Secretariat DGE, July 1997), overall consistency of development policy is a distant goal.

Ultimately, while problems of policy coherence within the EC may be mitigated through reforms in the future, consistency between Member State and EC policies is likely to remain a problem area. Moreover there seems to be little prospect of a major shift of emphasis from bilateral aid to EC development cooperation. Thus, although Member States appear to have increased the EC focus of their overseas assistance, this has not been at the expense of bilateral aid; it represents a diversion of funding from other multilateral programmes, in particular those operated by the United Nations (van Reisen 1997a:171–2).

CONCLUSION

The past 40 years have seen the evolution of relationships between the EC and developing countries in all parts of the world, many of them former colonies of the Member States. At the centre of these relationships has been a multi-faceted and highly institutionalized system of development cooperation involving a significant number (currently 71) of the world's poorest countries, collectively known as the ACP.

This chapter has focused disproportionately upon the ACP–EC relationship. This emphasis is justified, we believe, because it is here that a distinctive, Community approach to development policy is most apparent. Particularly evident here, too, is the interaction between agency and structure in the processes and practices which have shaped the evolution of the EC–ACP relationship. Creation of the ACP to facilitate ACP–EC interaction, and the subsequent growth in size of that grouping, is itself an indication both of EC actorness and of its significant presence.

A further manifestation of actorness lies in the increasingly prescriptive nature of Lomé provisions in the 1990s. In future political conditionality, and penalties for failure to meet EC prescriptions, are likely to be central to development cooperation, as the Commission's 1997 Green Paper demonstrates. Indeed the Green Paper proposals for the future of the ACP–EC relationship after 2000 have very significant implications for ACP members, and for North/South relations more broadly. For example, should the Lomé review process result in establishment of a set of EC–regional relationships, this would have a major impact on the future of Caribbean and Pacific countries, and upon embryonic regional cooperation in Southern Africa. In the context of the very sensitive relations which characterize this region, the significance of the EC/EU, as presence and actor, is indicated by the conclusion that –

> In any calculation of the future . . . a major player in both the national aspirations of South Africa and the regional hopes of southern Africa will be the European Union.
>
> (Kibble, Goodison and Balefi 1995:42)

Since creating the Lomé system, the Community has developed relationships with many other Southern countries. However Lomé itself is unique. The highly institutionalized Lomé arrangements have not been replicated in the EC's relations with ALA countries, which are the subject of more traditional, bilateral arrangements. Nevertheless, during the 1990s, EC–ALA agreements have become increasingly broad in focus, incorporating a range of political and other conditionalities which mirror recent Lomé provisions. In the case of non-associated countries, however, the relationship with the EC does not have the centrality of the EC–ACP relationship – for ALA countries the EC is a relatively minor player.

Following entry into force of the TEU, we have noted increasing consistency in the broad objectives of EC development cooperation. Moreover it is evident that the EU's political priorities underlie the changed orientation of development policy generally, whether through the increased political conditionality of Lomé IV *bis* or the highly focused cooperation agreements recently concluded with ALA countries. While there has always been a political dimension to EC development policy,[53] its contemporary, generalized politicization represents a discernible shift from an approach which aimed to assist favoured groups or regions, selected according to political criteria, to policies intended to shape the political complexion and policy preferences of recipient governments. This shift is a product of the ideological hegemony of liberalism since the end of the Cold War; and a clear reflection of principles and priorities enshrined in the Treaty on European Union.

Despite its global scope, and increasing importance, EC development cooperation has evolved alongside, and in addition to, the development policies of the Member States. Indeed their bilateral arrangements have remained the major focus of Member State policies; they have neither been subsumed within Community policy nor effectively coordinated at the Community level. This continuing significance of Member States' policies serves to divert resources, and distract attention, from the Community's efforts. Thus the full potential for EC actorness in this policy area could be realized only if greater consistency was achieved between EC and Member State policies.

The development of a distinctive Community approach to development policy is important, nevertheless, in establishing the EC's role as a relatively benign 'patron/mentor' in relation to the South.[54] It has attempted, however imperfectly, to develop models of partnership and cooperation; and has avoided the practice of tying aid to commercial interests. It would be unfortunate if EC development cooperation was abandoned in favour of exclusively market oriented approaches; or reduced to an aid conduit for regions that Member State governments would prefer to forget. Nevertheless, while the ending of Lomé IV in 2000 provides the opportunity for reprioritization of policy, the EC's significant presence in North/South relations, and the responsibilities thereby entailed, precludes the option of abandoning its Southern 'partners'.

5   Ever closer association?

Relations with the 'near abroad'

In contrast with the declining importance, for the EU, of cooperation with its ACP 'partners' (the subject of the preceding chapter), the significance of the EU's relations with its two peripheries – to the East and the South – has increased enormously since the end of the Cold War. This is particularly evident in the case of the EU's Eastern neighbours, both because of the constrained nature of relations with Eastern Europe during the Cold War, and of the perceived need to respond urgently to the dramatic events which characterized its end. Thus, the Commission observed in 1990 –

> The peaceful revolution which swept Eastern Europe in 1989 is probably the most significant event in global terms of the past 45 years. It is happening on the very doorstep of the European Community. It represents a challenge and an opportunity to which the EC has given an immediate response.
>
> (Commission 1990c:5)

While less momentous than the events in the East, a number of factors ensured that EC relations with the Mediterranean region also attained increasing salience in the late 1980s. Firstly, the accession of Greece in 1981 and of Spain and Portugal in 1986 increased the Mediterranean focus of the EC itself. Subsequently concerns about the poor economic performance of the region, and the associated potential for social unrest (evidenced by serious riots in Algeria in 1988) prompted a Commission proposal in 1989 for a 'renovated Mediterranean policy' (Marks 1996:11). During the 1990–1 Gulf crisis the increasing radicalization and anti-Western focus of Arab/Islamic public opinion, even in the most pro-Western countries in the region, further alarmed policy makers within the EC.

In consequence, as we shall see, there has been an evident parallelism in EC/EU policies towards the two peripheries since 1989. This reflects the priorities for 'urgent foreign policy cooperation' identified by the Lisbon European Council in June 1992 –

geographical proximity, overwhelming interest in the political and economic stability of a region or state, and existence of a potential threat to the Union's security interests.

(Piening 1997:91)

These criteria evidently accord priority status to the regions comprising the 'near abroad'.[1] Responses by the EC/EU, since 1989, have been both incremental and differentiated, as we shall see. Nevertheless policy towards both regions has been broadly similar, in that it has focused upon forging links intended to draw the countries of each region, to a greater or lesser extent, within the ambit of the Union. Thus in both cases, complex and multi-faceted relationships have been constructed, in which financial assistance and 'cooperation' have included political matters (democratic reform and human rights issues) and a cultural dimension, in addition to broadly focused approaches to economic transition and development. This has involved a series of wide-ranging bilateral agreements with individual countries, contextualized within a broader regional framework.

While differing policy emphases and outcomes between and within the two regions have inevitably reflected prioritization by EU policy makers, and hence EU actorness, they have also been significantly affected by third party perceptions of the desirability/necessity of establishing or enhancing links with the EU. Indeed relations with the near abroad provide a particularly clear demonstration of the relationship between presence and actorness; and of the importance of intersubjective structures in shaping action. Moreover, while it could be argued that relations with the near abroad are regional rather than global in focus, their significance extends more widely. Thus the need to manage the proposed enlargement to the East in a manner that will avoid creating destabilizing tensions, not least in relations with Russia and Turkey, is undoubtedly among the most difficult challenges facing EU policy makers today.

Below we consider separately the evolution of relations with each region, as a prelude to assessing the overall implications for EU actorness.

RELATIONS WITH THE EASTERN NEIGHBOURS

In the context of the Cold War, relations between the EC *per se* and Eastern Europe were minimal.[2] This reflects the fact that the EC's creation and development was, in part, a response to Cold War bipolarity; its function in this respect to provide a model of successful capitalism for Europe *as a whole*. Thus the Treaty of Rome (Art.237)[3] explicitly stated that 'any European state may apply to become a member'.[4] Given the EC's function as a capitalist 'role model' (Commission 1990c:10) it is unsurprising that, although the Council for Mutual Economic Assistance (CMEA) had been established since 1949,[5] the creation of the EC in 1957 was condemned by the Soviet government – and West European 'Imperialist integration' was routinely denounced thereafter.

By 1972, however, the economic presence of the Community had begun to cast its shadow. It was then evident that bilateral trade agreements between EC Member States and CMEA countries would shortly be replaced by the EC's Common Commercial Policy (this was finally achieved in late 1975). Consequently, in an attempt to minimize the negative impacts of this development, the Soviet government indicated its willingness to recognize the EC, provided that the EC in turn recognized the CMEA. This overture was rejected by the EC on the grounds that the two regional organizations were founded upon incompatible principles, in that the CMEA was merely an instrument of Soviet economic policy which lacked the institutional machinery to act on behalf of its members. There was, in consequence, no comparable body having competence for external economic relations with which the Commission could interact; in the judgement of the Commission (1990c:7), the CMEA 'did not have the structure or authority to be an equal partner'.[6] This opinion, as we shall see, presages recent EU policies intended to shape the transformation of the Eastern neighbours in the image of the Union.

An EC initiative, in 1974, to replace expiring Member State bilateral trade agreements with bilateral arrangements between the EC and individual CMEA countries also failed as a result of Soviet insistence that all EC relations with the East must be conducted through the CMEA.[7] Thus it was only with the Yugoslav Republic, an associate member of the CMEA, that the EC concluded preferential trade and cooperation arrangements. Elsewhere EC relations with Eastern Europe were mediated by 'an impressive and restrictive unilateral Community trade policy machinery' (Maresceau 1992:95). This ensured that, by the early 1980s, 50 per cent of the EC's notorious anti-dumping actions (see Chapter 2 for fuller discussion of these matters) were directed against a region which represented only 7 per cent of its total external trade (*ibid*:115).

The parallel development of, and lack of formal dialogue between, the EC and the CMEA are central to understanding how perceptions of the EC's presence developed in the East during the Cold War period. Thus among East European elites knowledge of the EC was partial and distorted – they were distanced from the more frustrating aspects of the EC's complex procedures and decision processes but were acutely conscious of its relative economic success. Indeed, by the mid 1980s the EC had clearly demonstrated its attractiveness, having doubled its membership and more than doubled the size of its economy. This political and economic dynamism contrasted sharply with the stifling political climate and economic stagnation which prevailed in the East during the Brezhnev years (1964–82) and beyond. Moreover the EC's Single Market programme represented a major deepening of the integration process which both highlighted the dynamism of the Community and threatened further to marginalize the CMEA bloc.

In the new climate of East/West relations which characterized the Gorbachev era (from 1985), the estrangement between the EC and the CMEA was resolved, in June 1988, by a Joint Declaration establishing mutual recognition. The immediate practical effect of recognition was the accreditation of formal missions to the EC by CMEA countries, and the conclusion of bilateral trade and commercial cooperation agreements between the EC and individual CMEA members. These were traditional 'first generation' agreements, which reduced quota restrictions but did not give preferential access to the EC market. Nor did they include provision for financial assistance. Nevertheless they were important – in that they established the EC's preferred 'hub and spokes' approach to external relations, which had long been resisted by the Soviet government, and that they were for the most part negotiated, and in some cases concluded, prior to the 'velvet revolutions' of 1989.[8] Negotiation of such far-reaching agreements with 'socialist' or 'state-trading' countries was, at that time, still regarded as surprising, attesting to the rapidity of change in Eastern Europe (Maresceau 1992:95–6). It also demonstrated the willingness of the EC to respond quickly and positively to the new situation – albeit in traditional ways which, as we shall see, would almost immediately prove inadequate to meet the needs of the East European countries.

Of particular importance for EC actorness was the decision of the Luxembourg European Council in April 1989 that policy towards Eastern Europe would be coordinated within the EC framework. Shortly afterwards the EC's role was confirmed and enhanced by the Group of 7 (G7) decision, in July 1989, that the European Commission should be responsible for coordinating financial assistance, provided by the Group of 24 (G24) Western donors, to support the processes of reform in Eastern Europe. This was the first occasion on which the Commission had been accorded such a role by an external body. Thus, for Nuttall (1996a:142) 'This was a new kind of legitimacy . . . for the first time, the Commission was a foreign policy actor in its own right.'[9] In the context of the G24 decision, the EC established its own assistance programme in January 1990. Entitled Phare (original meaning 'Poland–Hungary: Aid for Reconstruction of the Economy') it now extends to 13 Central and Eastern European countries; thus its title should be considered a 'brand name' rather than an acronym.[10]

These decisions, taken by mid 1989 prior to the fall of the Berlin Wall in November that year, provided a basis for EC action towards Eastern Europe. The subsequent development of EC/EU policy reflects a number of factors, including the varying circumstances of the East European countries and the evolution of, and interaction between, attitudes and perceptions in West and East Europe. Thus there commenced, from the outset, a highly political process, involving politicians and commentators both in the East and West, of constructing distinctions – and implicitly hierarchies of EC/EU preference – between the countries of Eastern Europe.[11]

By mid 1989 the expression 'Central and East Europe' had become common in EC usage, although the meaning of this term has never been made explicit. Initially it was thought to imply a distinction between the Soviet Union and other CMEA members (Maresceau 1992); however, evolving usage since the dissolution of the USSR does not support this contention. In contemporary EU publications the term Central and East European Countries (CEEC) refers to 'a geographical region, encompassing altogether 15 countries' (Commission 1997g:3). Significantly, however, elucidation of the sensitive distinction between 'Central' and 'East' has been carefully avoided in materials published by the Commission.[12] Academic commentators have been very much less circumspect.[13] As Figure 5.1 indicates, the Commission's notion of a 'geographical region' is fairly subjective; for example there appears to be no strong *geographical* rationale for the exclusion of Ukraine or, indeed, Belarus. Nevertheless the inclusion of so wide a range of countries within the CEEC category reflects a concern to avoid an exclusionary dynamic which could impact negatively upon security and stability (see Chapter 7 for further discussion of this issue). In practice, however, the Commission makes a distinction between the ten CEEC which have applied for EU membership and the five which have not yet done so – that is Albania and the countries of the former Yugoslavia (except Slovenia).[14] It is

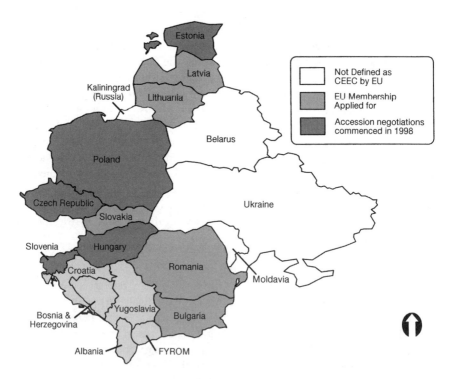

Figure 5.1 The Central and East European Countries. (Figure © LJMU Cartographic Unit 1998)

upon the 'CEEC10' that our discussion of EU–CEEC relations will focus (former Yugoslavia and Albania are discussed in Chapter 7).

Following the dissolution of the Soviet Union in 1991 the EC referred, collectively, to the former Soviet Republics in terms of their membership of the Commonwealth of Independent States (CIS). Thus the EC's assistance programme for the former Soviet Republics, established in 1991 immediately following the dissolution of the Soviet Union, was entitled Tacis (Technical Assistance to the CIS). It is noteworthy that the Baltic Republics received Tacis funding in 1991 but were subsequently transferred to the Phare programme, whereupon they became CEEC.[15] Contemporarily the CIS countries are referred to as New Independent States (NIS), a title preferred by their governments. Given this change of terminology, Tacis, like Phare, should also now be considered a 'brand name' (Interview, DGIA, February 1998).[16]

The CEEC/NIS distinction is an important one; it differentiates between countries likely to be subject to 'ever closer association' and those (the NIS) where the development of 'second generation' Partnership and Cooperation Agreements is in progress (see Table 5.1) but relations are unlikely to develop beyond this stage in the foreseeable future. Here it is significant that a major emphasis of Tacis has been nuclear safety and the environment, which in 1996 received almost triple the allocation given to economic restructuring (Commission 1997i:8). There are, in addition, very significant differences in the intensity of relations between the EU and the various NIS, with the Russian Federation, followed by Ukraine, evidently the most important partners.[17] These differences are reflected in Tacis funding, as Table 5.1 indicates.

Table 5.1 New Independent States: Partnership and Cooperation Agreements (PCA) and Tacis funding status.

Country	PCA	Indicative programme 1996–9 (ECU million)
Armenia	Signed 22 April 1996	28
Azerbaijan	Signed 22 April 1996	32
Belarus	Signed 6 March 1995	
Georgia	Signed 22 April 1996	32
Kazakhstan	Signed 23 January 1995	57
Kyrgyzstan	EP assent 30 November 1995	26
Moldova	EP assent 30 November 1995	36
Russian Fed.	EP assent 30 November 1995	600
Tajikstan		14
Turkmenistan		20
Ukraine	EP assent 30 November 1995	165
Uzbekistan	Signed 21 June 1996	57

Source: Commission (1997i)

The EU–NIS relationship is an aspect of the EU's increasingly important role in external policy. A clear manifestation of actorness, here, is the application of conditionalities intended to shape the development of NIS countries. Thus, for example, the absence of funding proposals for Belarus reflects EU disapproval of the record of democratic reform in that country; while the modest funding approved for Tajikistan reflects its 'comparative instability and lack of economic reform' (Commission 1997i:6). However it is in the intense relations between the EU and the CEEC10 that the ability of the EU to shape policy outcomes in third countries is most apparent, and a very particular relationship between EU presence and actorness is demonstrated in these cases. Consequently it is upon these relations that we focus below.

EU–CEEC relations after the Cold War

Despite the breadth of the EU's contemporary definition of Central and East Europe, in the closing phase of the Cold War attention focused primarily upon five countries – Hungary, where economic reforms had preceded the end of the Soviet era, Czechoslovakia, Poland and, to a lesser extent, Bulgaria and Romania. In these countries perceptions of the EC formed during the Cold War were, for the most part, strongly positive; albeit founded upon 'a combination of myths, stereotypes, anxieties and hopes' (Szajkowski 1997:164). There was considerable optimism concerning the prospects for an imminent 'return to Europe', and early EC membership became a central policy priority of the new CEEC governments. At this time the significance of the idea of 'rejoining Europe' was very great. It denoted not only a desire for increased economic well-being, but provided a set of ideas and aspirations to fill the political and ideological vacuum created by the demise of the Soviet system. Thus the European idea –

> acted successfully as a political-cultural as well as an economic template ... an ideological shorthand standing for participatory democracy, the market economy, the rule of law, constitutional order and social citizenship ... The east Europeans believe that as long as they adhere to this formula then entry to the EU is assured.
>
> (Kolankiewicz 1994:481)

The enthusiasm to test the TEC commitment that 'any European state' would be considered for membership led the Commission to conclude (1990c:31) that, for the peoples of Central and Eastern Europe, 'The European Community has what might be termed a mystical attraction'. Clearly in CEE countries perceptions of the Community's presence were strong indeed; moreover they generated demands to which the EC, and the Member States, were obliged to respond.

The challenges facing the Community at the end of 1989 were both daunting and unique. The EC itself was undergoing a major process of internal deepening, with the Single Market partially completed and parallel Inter-governmental Conferences (IGCs) on economic and political union – which ultimately produced the TEU – about to begin. Inevitably there were concerns, in the Commission and some Member State governments, that the EC's response to events in Eastern Europe should not disrupt these ongoing internal processes. Despite these reservations, the December 1989 Strasbourg European Council reiterated commitment to a central role for the Community as 'the corner-stone of a new European architecture'. A number of significant decisions were taken at this Council – on support for the unification of Germany (which would constitute a *de facto* enlargement to the East); on the establishment of the European Bank for Reconstruction and Development (EBRD);[18] and on the need for a new form of association with CEEC undergoing reform. Consequently the Commission was requested, in 1990, to produce proposals for a new type of association agreement which would be appropriate to the developing EC/CEEC relationship.

The decision to adopt the EC's traditional association strategy in relation to the CEEC seemed eminently sensible from the Community's perspective. Utilizing a familiar model, it provided a breathing space during which ongoing negotiations with the EFTA countries concerning the European Economic Area (EEA) could be completed, EC internal reforms finalized, and the political and economic situation within CEEC be stabilized.[19] From the perspective of CEE governments, however, association was an inadequate and potentially destabilizing formula – not least because contrasting outcomes of earlier association agreements, in relation to Greece and Turkey, served as a constant reminder of the importance of belonging to 'Central' rather than 'Eastern' Europe.

The bilateral Association, or Europe Agreements[20] eventually negotiated with the CEEC moved beyond the traditional 'trade plus' formula. The preamble to each agreement acknowledges that EU membership is the ultimate goal of the associated country, although it contains no formal commitment by the EU. The economic provisions are wide ranging and there is provision for technical assistance in 'approximating' legislation – that is bringing CEE legislation into conformity with that of the EC. An important innovation is the inclusion of political dialogue (a reference to foreign policy) and cultural cooperation. Since these matters fall outside Community competence the Europe Agreements heralded a new generation of 'mixed' agreements, negotiated by the Commission on behalf of the EC and the Member States, which required ratification by each Member State.[21] The usual institutions of association (Association Council, Association Committee, Parliamentary Committee) were established and reference was made to consultation at Ministerial level on foreign policy matters. The first Europe Agreements were concluded with Poland, Hungary and Czechoslovakia in 1991.[22] The current status of Europe Agreements and membership applications for the CEEC10 is indicated in Figure 5.1.

The difficult negotiations for the Europe Agreements are considered below in our discussion of actorness. For CEEC representatives, exposure to EC negotiating procedures proved a sobering experience, in which the EC evidently lost much of its 'mystical attraction' (Interview, external Mission, June 1996). Following conclusion of the negotiations there remained a number of areas of dissatisfaction with the EC position, including lack of formal commitment to enlargement, failure to address issues concerning the movement of people, and resentment of the EC's traditional reservations on market access in relation to 'sensitive' products (steel, textiles and agricultural products). As one CEE trade Counsellor commented, 'Negotiations on agricultural products were very, very difficult. There is no flexibility in DGVI' (Interview, external Mission, June 1996). CEEC anxieties concerning market access have to be understood in the context of the very substantial reorientation of their trade from the CMEA region to the EC from 1989.[23]

A number of factors combined to ensure that unmet CEEC demands and aspirations continued to be heard after negotiations for the first Europe Agreements were concluded in December 1991. Fears of conflict and instability in Europe had been greatly fuelled, during 1991, by the attempted coup against President Gorbachev and the subsequent disintegration of the Soviet Union; by the contemporaneous eruption of violent conflict in Yugoslavia, and the division of that country; and by the growing tensions which led to the division of Czechoslovakia the following year. These events gave weight to the demands of CEE governments, and their supporters in the West, that the EC should do more to support the extremely difficult, and painful, processes of transformation in the CEE countries.[24] However they also reinforced fears that early accession of CEE countries would risk importing into the Community the instability which was increasingly evident in Eastern Europe.[25] While, essentially, CEE governments required a formal commitment to enlargement, and a firm timetable for accession, policy makers within the EC proved more ready to commit themselves to the former than the latter.

During 1992 it became increasingly clear that there was acceptance, within the EC, both that the provisions of the Europe Agreements required enhancement, and that some or all of the CEEC would eventually proceed to full membership. Here the June 1993 European Council in Copenhagen marked a turning point, in that it formally and explicitly endorsed the principle of CEEC membership. The Copenhagen Council also adopted membership criteria for application to CEE countries, that is –

- Possession of stable institutions guaranteeing democracy, the rule of law, human rights and protection of minorities.
- The existence of a functioning market economy and the capacity to cope with competitive pressures within the EC.
- The ability to adopt the *acquis communautaire*, including adherence to the aims of political, economic and monetary union.

In addition, it was confirmed, enlargement was conditional upon the ability of the EC to absorb new members. Thus it was made clear that the ongoing process of integration internally, including the TEU provisions on Economic and Monetary Union, Common Foreign and Security Policy and Justice and Home Affairs, should not be jeopardized by the projected enlargement. Effectively the CEEC were facing a moving target; a problem that will be compounded upon entry into force of the Amsterdam Treaty, particularly in relation to Justice and Home Affairs matters.

The Copenhagen Council also decided that the market access provisions of the Europe Agreements should be enhanced (a central CEEC demand) and made recommendations for increased dialogue between the parties. These included a new emphasis upon multilateral discussions to complement the existing, essentially bilateral framework provided by the Europe Agreements. This initiative was prompted by EC concerns about the 'atmosphere of competition' prevailing between CEEC, which could be prejudicial to their ability, following accession, to achieve the levels of cooperation required of Member State governments (Interview, DGII, September 1996).[26] This proposal was given concrete form as part of the pre-accession strategy devised by the Commission and endorsed by the Essen European Council in 1994, becoming known as the 'structured dialogue'.[27] The second dimension of the pre-accession strategy, preparation for integration of CEEC into the internal market, was subsequently the subject of a White Paper advising on the alignment of CEEC and EC legislation on Single Market matters, which was seen as a prerequisite for membership (Commission 1995e).

These decisions having been taken, the Commission was charged, by the 1995 Madrid European Council, with two major tasks – assessing the readiness of CEE countries for accession;[28] and assessing the potential impact of enlargement upon the EU itself. The results of this major effort were presented, in June 1997, in the form of *Agenda 2000*, the Commission's multi-volume study of the prospects for and impact of enlargement (Commission 1997a–c).[29] The Commission's recommendation that accession negotiations should open early in 1998 with five CEEC – the Czech Republic, Estonia, Hungary, Poland and Slovenia; and that reinforced pre-accession strategies should be adopted simultaneously in respect of all ten CEEC, was endorsed by the Luxembourg European Council in December 1997.[30] The 'reinforced strategies' involve creation of a new EU instrument, the Accession Partnership, which will have the effect of focusing all existing programmes and processes on the EU's priorities for accession. Thus, for example, there will be a reorientation of the Phare programme to an accession driven, rather than demand driven, mode.[31]

Accession Partnerships are to be extended to all the CEEC10 – that is the five which opened accession negotiations in March 1998 and the 'pre-ins' awaiting judgement on their 'progress' before commencement of accession negotiations. The Partnerships will be 'serious for all countries', and additional funding is to be made available, from previously undisbursed Phare sources, to support 'catch-up strategies for the pre-ins' (Interview, DGIA, February 1998). Accession Partnerships will necessitate a continuous bilateral dialogue between individual CEEC and the Commission in order to identify the priority areas for attention, both prior to accession and beyond. The agreed priorities will, of course, be subject to Council approval.

This is a completely new procedure for the EU – 'never before have all the accession priorities been identified and then applied in this manner' (Interview, DGIA, February 1998). Provision has been made for regular reviews of progress, of which was the first delivered before the end of 1998, in the form of 'mini opinions'. Since areas where progress has been satisfactory will be omitted, for reasons of efficiency, these interim opinions are likely to give the impression of negativity (Interview, DGIA, February 1998). As in the past, no firm timetable for accession has been given, although there is an expectation among CEE governments that the first accessions will take place not later than 2003. The order of accession of the candidate countries will, in principle, depend upon the Commission's opinion concerning their readiness. However Member State governments may well also consider broader political and security issues when making final decisions on this highly sensitive matter.[32]

EU–CEEC relations: implications for actorness

Our outline of EU–CEEC relations since the end of the Cold War has demonstrated a clear relationship between presence and actorness. In the early period the attraction of the Community was based upon perceptions of its success, and its apparent desirability as a model. For the new CEE political elites, orientation towards the EC appeared to offer the most promising solution, perhaps the only available solution, to the problems they faced. Thus the Community's formidable presence was originally constructed from a mixture of hopes and myths, and was relatively uninformed by detailed knowledge or close experience. Expectations of EC actorness were, in consequence, unrealistic, and it was almost inevitable that the Community's initial policy responses would prove disappointing. Thus, from 1991, disillusionment with the EC grew among CEE elites and publics – as a result both of the perceived inadequacy of the EC's policy towards the East and of exposure to information concerning the EC's internal procedures and problems, for example the difficult TEU ratification process. Moreover changing public attitudes towards the EC (charted by Central and Eastern Eurobarometer from 1990) impacted, in turn, upon the legitimacy of political elites who had so strongly advanced the notion of 'rejoining Europe' (Kolankiewicz 1994:478–9).

Despite this evaporation of the EC's 'mystical attraction', the Community's presence in relation to the CEEC has not diminished; rather it has assumed the more traditional form of economic presence and associated dependency relationships. This reflects not only the major reorientation of CEEC trade referred to above, but also the fact that, despite the broader commitment of G24 countries, financial assistance and foreign direct investment have emanated overwhelmingly from EU sources.[33] Dependency relationships entail responsibilities, as we saw in the previous chapter; moreover the demands of the CEEC cannot be ignored, since the failure of their transformation processes would impact directly and negatively on EU countries. These circumstances have necessitated an active response; indeed they have provided the context for unprecedented actorness on the part of the EU.

The EU–CEEC relationship has been, from the outset, highly asymmetrical. Indeed the dependency relationship, here, is particularly strong, since CEE governments have few other sources of assistance or support. Despite tentative moves to strengthen the CEFTA relationship (see note 26) CEE governments share a sense of there being no alternative to EU membership if future stability and prosperity are to be assured. In the case of Slovenia, for example, a recent economic analysis which evaluated a range of policy options concluded that –

> there seems to be not much choice for a small European country in transition like Slovenia . . . In theory there are other options but in practice they do not appear viable.
>
> Stanovnik and Svetličič (1996:16)

The incremental manner in which the EC/EU has responded to CEEC demands has also contributed to the construction of their role as supplicants and, more particularly, as apprentices. This latter aspect of the relationship has been greatly strengthened by the EU's commitment, in principle, to enlargement – but without providing guarantees or timetables. In the resulting prolonged period of uncertainty, the policy of CEE governments, and indeed the behaviour of private actors, has increasingly been shaped by the EU's 'pre-accession' requirements. This evolving mentor–apprentice relationship has included many areas of EC and EU policy competence. It has also extended Commission involvement into areas outside formal EC competence – democratic procedures, observance of human rights and treatment of minorities and, in particular, administrative and legal capacity. Involvement in these latter areas, which are of great concern to the Commission since they are central to the CEE countries' ability to apply the ever expanding *acquis communautaire*, demonstrates rather nicely the presence-actorness relationship involved in the transition from 'template' or reference point to active policy promoter.[34]

In short, the evolution of the EU–CEEC relationship has been characterized, not only by increasing intensity, but by the EU's increasingly active attempts to shape policy decisions within CEE countries. As one Czech diplomat commented, 'What can we do? If we want to become members of the Union, we have to accept what is decided' (Vaclav Kuklik, quoted in *The European*, 12–18 September 1996). The publication of *Agenda 2000*, while not resolving uncertainties concerning accession, marked a further shift in EU–CEEC relations. In future these are to be explicitly oriented towards the EU's pre-accession requirements; thus heralding a considerable intensification of the 'learning' experience of CEEC in the final stages of their membership apprenticeship.

The ability to shape policy preferences and, indeed, the broad processes of transition in CEE countries, is a function both of presence and of actorness, as we have seen. This has been, from the outset, an area in which the Member States have chosen, to a considerable extent, to coordinate their policies through the EC/EU.[35] An important consequence of this has been the role accorded to the Commission in 'political' areas which are elsewhere jealously guarded by the Presidency and the Member States. This is evidenced, in particular, by the Commission's role in negotiating the Europe Agreements, which contrasts significantly with 'mixed competence' aspects of global environmental negotiations (see Chapter 3). The apparently strong manifestations of actorness in this policy area are not necessarily based upon consistency between Member State and EU approaches, however; nor upon the development of coherent strategies by the EC/EU.

EC–CEEC negotiations: issues of consistency and coherence

The decision to entrust the Community with policy towards the Eastern neighbours is not indicative of consensus between the Member States; rather it reflected the urgent need to 'do something' in the absence of a common strategy. Thus the recourse, in 1989, to traditional Community trade and aid instruments initiated a process in which the EC's role was constructed through the interaction of complex demands and opportunities. The subsequent expansion of EC involvement, and in particular of the Commission's role, flowed from the gradual evolution of an understanding that enlargement was inevitable; that CEE countries were, indeed, 'central' to Europe.[36] This understanding has shaped EC/EU action despite a lack of strong commitment to enlargement among Member State governments and, indeed, within the Commission.

Examination of the 1991 negotiations for the first Europe Agreements is instructive, in that they revealed the underlying, and enduring, problems of coherence and consistency impeding the formulation of policy towards the CEE countries. This was reflected in the decision to negotiate association agreements with CEE governments whose primary demand was for high level political commitment to enlargement. The negotiations were opened by the Commission, on behalf of the Community and the Member States, on a Council mandate which afforded little room for flexibility on any of the three areas of central concern to CEE governments. At this time only the UK government was prepared to make a firm commitment to enlargement, a position which reflected both opposition to further deepening of the integration process and the fact that the UK had little to lose in making concessions on the other areas of CEEC interest – trade in 'sensitive' products and movement of people. This last affected Germany in particular, while most Member State governments entertained reservations concerning trade issues (although objections from France, Spain and Portugal were the strongest and most sustained).[37]

There has been a tendency to portray Member State positions during the Europe Agreement negotiations as indicative of a particular lack of generosity towards CEEC (Sedelmeier 1994). In practice, however, the trade negotiations followed a familiar pattern of narrowly focused discussions between technical experts, effectively divorced from the broader political context.[38] In the event, following breakdown of the negotiations, the Commission was twice obliged to seek a broader negotiating mandate from the Council. The concessions contained in the final Agreements represented a political compromise approved at the level of the European Council; nevertheless they were, for the most part, symbolic rather than substantive. It was only at a late stage that the broader political importance of EC–CEEC relations impinged significantly upon the progress of the negotiations.[39] During 1991 political attention within the EC had been very much internally focused – upon the ongoing Intergovernmental Conferences on Political Union and Economic and Monetary Union. However mounting evidence of instability in East Europe demonstrated, to all participants, the importance of a successful conclusion to the negotiations.

Clearly the competing priorities of deepening and widening were a source of division within the EC during 1991. Moreover internal policy development was prioritized both by the Commission and several Member States. Thus Commission President, Jacques Delors, expressed concern that enlargement might lead to the Community being 'diluted', while the Belgian Prime Minister voiced fears that the Community might be 'melting away under the warm glow of pan-Europeanism' (Wilfred Martens, quoted in Buchan 1993:33). These concerns persist, and are reflected in the formal insistence, repeated in *Agenda 2000*, that acceding countries adopt the *acquis* in its entirety. The extent to which this position will be maintained in practice remains to be seen; there is evidently an unresolved tension between those who fear a dilution of EC policy and proponents of early CEEC accession. Increasingly this centres upon a distinction, which is implied in the Commission 1995 White Paper, between regulatory frameworks governing product standards and those focusing upon the processes of production. For some academic commentators process regulation is very definitely not a priority for the CEE countries; nor, apparently, for the EC, since –

> It is possible to argue that there is simply no economic case for harmonisation of environmental and social policy at any stage of European integration, and that opt-outs should be permanently permitted . . .

Some groups of European citizens could choose to create competitive advantages for themselves by accepting lower environmental quality or poorer social protection.

(Smith *et al.* 1996:5)

Such issues are central to the future character of the EU; exemplifying the fundamental nature of the challenges raised by the prospect of an Eastern enlargement. Consequently inconsistencies are likely to remain between Member States and within the Commission; and to impede the formulation of coherent, long-term policies in this area.[40] Paradoxically, the uncertainties thereby created have tended to strengthen the EU's influence, or presence, in relation to CEE countries.

A further division between Member States has concerned the relative significance of relations with the Eastern and Southern neighbours. For the French and Spanish governments, in particular, the Mediterranean non-member countries are an important priority. Consequently, at the insistence of these governments, the development of the EU–CEEC relationship has been paralleled by an intensification of EU–Mediterranean relations. It is to this area that we now turn.

RELATIONS WITH MEDITERRANEAN NON-MEMBER COUNTRIES (MNC)

The Mediterranean region is the EU's second highest external policy priority after Central and Eastern Europe.[41] While there have been a number of parallels between relations with the two peripheries since 1989, EU–Mediterranean relations differ in significant ways from those with the Eastern neighbours. This reflects not only the different characteristics of the regions themselves, but also significant historical differences in their relationships with the EC/EU.

At the time of the EC's creation close economic, political and cultural links existed between the Member States, in particular France and Italy, and non-member Mediterranean countries. Indeed Tunisia and Morocco had attained independence from France only in 1956, and Algeria remained a French Department until 1962. In this latter case the complex and highly sensitive nature of Franco–Algerian relations has impinged upon the EC's relationship with Algeria, which has 'always been difficult' (Interview, DGIB, February 1998).[42]

The EC's presence in the region, from 1957, reflected pre-existing patterns of interaction and, in particular, the MNCs' export dependence upon West European markets. This economic presence was consolidated by formulation of the Common Commercial Policy and, subsequently, the Common Agricultural Policy. Indeed the CAP impacted heavily upon MNC exports of Mediterranean products (citrus fruits, vegetables, olive oil and wine) which were in direct competition with French and Italian produce. This extensive overlap in agricultural production both complicated and delayed the establishment of preferential agreements with the Maghreb countries in particular (see note 47). In consequence, although a Declaration of Intent annexed to the Rome Treaty promised special treatment for Morocco, Tunisia and Libya, it was not until 1969 that limited association agreements were concluded with Tunisia and Morocco.[43] This contrasts with the treatment of sub-Saharan African countries (see Chapter 4), whose exports of tropical products were complementary to rather than in competition with EC production. Thus, from the outset, there has been a sense of unequal treatment of the Maghreb countries. Moreover, by 1969, the EC had already concluded highly favourable association agreements with Greece (1961) and Turkey (1963). These were of unlimited duration and envisaged a process of 'ever closer association', with the ultimate goal of EC membership. More limited association agreements were subsequently concluded with Malta (1970) and Cyprus (1972). Alongside these association agreements, the EC also concluded a series of bilateral, and somewhat differentiated, trade agreements with Israel (1964), Lebanon (1965), Yugoslavia (1970), Spain (1970), Egypt (1972) and Portugal (1972).[44]

Thus, by 1972, the EC had negotiated some form of economic agreement with the majority of MNC. However the uncoordinated and *ad hoc* development of these agreements had become a source of concern within the EC. In 1971 the European Parliament criticized the 'disorderly' character of EC–MNC relations and called for the formulation of a systematic policy towards the Mediterranean region (Siotis 1974:77). A year later, at the October 1972 Paris summit, a Global Mediterranean Policy (GMP) was announced. Strongly supported by the Commission and the French government, the GMP proposal reflected the importance, *for the EC*, of the Mediterranean region.

EC–MNC relations cannot be conceptualized solely in terms of a dependency relationship based on the colonial legacy and the EC's economic presence. Not only has the Mediterranean region traditionally provided an important market for EC products – in 1993 still almost twice the value of EC exports to CEEC (Commission 1995e:25) – but the EC has been and remains dependent upon the Mediterranean region for more than a quarter of its energy imports.[45] In consequence, throughout the Cold War, the Mediterranean region was considered by Western governments to be of great strategic importance. Thus it is in the context of their membership of NATO that the EC's early, favourable treatment of Greece and Turkey can best be understood. As Grilli has argued (1993:184) –

> In dealing generously with both Greece and Turkey from the economic point of view, the Community countries were shouldering part of their collective responsibilities as members of the Western alliance.

In 1973, the EC's strategic and economic interests in the region were sharply emphasized by the Arab–Israeli October War and the subsequent oil crisis. While these events may have given impetus to the newly announced GMP, their principal effect was to underline the differentiated patterns of dependency in the region. Thus they generated a specific response – the Euro–Arab Dialogue – which continued intermittently for a decade without significant results (Piening 1997:74–6). This, however, had the effect of separating the Middle East conflict (and currently the Peace Process) from attempts to create an overarching EC–Mediterranean relationship. While this separation has proved positive in the longer term, as we shall see, in the 1970s the initiation of the Euro–Arab dialogue served to divert attention from the broader, GMP initiative.

Ultimately the GMP proved disappointing to all parties. The Commission had hoped to apply to the MNC the Lomé Convention model negotiated with the ACP countries (see Chapter 4). However it did not prove possible, in the case of the MNC, to negotiate an arrangement having 'the solidity and political value of a collective contract' (Commission 1982:13). The collective clientelism of the Lomé model was explicitly rejected by MNC governments and EC–MNC negotiations were, in consequence, strictly bilateral. Moreover MNC governments, 'emboldened by the vision of "commodity power" in the roaring years of OPEC', were seeking major trade concessions which the Community, in the changing economic and political climate of the mid 1970s, was not prepared to concede (Grilli 1993:189).[46] In the event Cooperation Agreements, having broadly similar features – albeit subject to individual variations – in terms of trade, financial assistance and (bilateral) common institutions, were concluded with Algeria, Morocco and Tunisia in 1976 and with Egypt, Lebanon, Jordan and Syria in 1977.

The 'GMP' thus produced a rather more coherent situation than had previously pertained; nevertheless it fell far short of a global strategy. In particular, it differentiated between countries considered likely, in future, to accede to the Community – Greece, Turkey, Cyprus, Malta, Spain and Portugal – where association and/or accession strategies were pursued, and the Maghreb and Mashreq regions, where, as we have seen, Cooperation Agreements were concluded.[47] There has evidently been, also, a distinction between the Maghreb and Mashreq countries, reflecting the fact that the former are more closely linked to several EC Member States (but in particular France) and are more dependent upon EC markets.

The trade privileges accorded to MNC in the Cooperation Agreements of the mid 1970s fell short of Lomé preferences from the outset. In 1979 they were subject to considerable erosion as a consequence of the EC's overall tariff reductions, agreed during the GATT Tokyo Round. Accession to the EC of Greece, Spain and Portugal was even more damaging to MNC preferences, owing to the greatly increased production of Mediterranean products within the EC. In consequence, from the mid 1980s, MNC governments 'were left with the prospect that the GMP would soon be giving them a preferential share of nothing' (Pomfret 1992:79).

This was the situation at the commencement of the Single Market programme, which threatened further to decrease MNC market shares. In consequence the governments of MNC countries whose trade dependence on the EC was greatest felt obliged, as did EFTA governments, to reconsider their relationship with the EC. Thus, while there was little reaction from Mashreq countries, in 1987 Morocco applied for EC membership. Following the rejection of this application, on the grounds that Morocco was not a European country, the Maghreb countries sought to enhance cooperation within their own region through establishment of the Arab Maghreb Union.[48] In 1989 Turkey applied for EC membership, followed by Cyprus and Malta in 1990. By this time, however, events in Eastern Europe threatened remaining MNC privileges, as CEE countries sought to 'replace their previous least-favoured status' with preferential trade agreements with the EC (Pomfret 1992:80).

Clearly the end of the Cold War also necessitated a major reconsideration, by the EC, of relations with the near abroad. Consequently since 1989 the French and Spanish governments, with support from the Commission, have pressed for a degree of parallelism in policy towards the EC's two peripheries. This reflects perceptions of the Community's growing presence in the post-Cold War period, in that –

> The European Community is now seen as the main focus for peace, democracy and growth by all Europe and the neighbouring countries to the South and East ... What is required is a new regional policy ... [which] embraces the Community's immediate neighbours, from the Baltic to Morocco.
>
> (Commission 1989, quoted in Marks 1996:5–6)

In the case of the Mediterranean region, the incremental development of a new policy approach, intended to parallel and complement the developing EC–CEEC relationship, began with the Commission's proposal for a redirected Mediterranean policy, which stressed the importance of the region for European security 'in the broadest sense' (Commission 1990d:2). The 'redirected policy', which was agreed in 1991, found expression in enhanced market access, particularly for Moroccan and Tunisian products, and increased financial assistance, which primarily benefited Algeria, Egypt, Morocco and Tunisia (Cox and Koning 1997:73). The MED Programme also introduced a new focus on 'horizontal' or decentralized cooperation, intended to promote multilateral and cross-border initiatives and to involve non-governmental actors.[49]

Despite these measures, the Maghreb governments (and in particular the Moroccan government) were dissatisfied by the EC's 'redirected' policy. The performance of the Arab Maghreb Union had been poor and in the early

1990s the Maghreb governments, with the support of Mediterranean Member State governments, began demanding parity of treatment with CEE countries. From this time external demands combined with internal pressures in constructing expectations, and ultimately a shared acceptance, of a measure of parallelism in policy towards MNC and CEEC. It is in the context of this process that the EU's Mediterranean Partnership initiative developed.

Below we discuss policy towards the region as a whole, contemporarily expressed through the overarching Euro–Mediterranean Partnership, before considering the particular issues associated with those countries seeking accession – that is, in the light of the temporary withdrawal of the Maltese application in 1996, Turkey and Cyprus.[50]

The Euro–Mediterranean partnership

The 1992 Lisbon European Council's prioritization of foreign policy objectives – in terms of geographical areas where political or economic stability could pose a security threat to the EC – added weight to arguments for an enhanced Mediterranean policy. Initially this was to be realized, in response to the immediacy of demands from Maghreb countries, through a Euro–Maghreb partnership and free trade area.[51] Subsequently this initiative was greatly expanded, both in content and in scope, finding expression in ambitious proposals for 'Establishing a Euro–Mediterranean Partnership' (Commission 1995f).

Here it is important to note that EU policy towards the Mediterranean region reflects expectations of actorness which are less firmly based upon the EU's presence than is the case for CEE countries. In the Mediterranean region, even where economic presence is substantial, as in relations with Israel[52] and the Maghreb countries, this does not necessarily provide a basis for political influence. Nevertheless, in 1994, several factors combined to suggest that a comprehensive approach to the Mediterranean region might be possible. First, of course, entry into force of the TEU in November 1993 provided impetus for an explicitly political dimension to the EU's 'partnerships' generally. Second, the Commission's experience with EC–CEEC relations, since 1989, suggested that 'a similar all-encompassing strategy' would be appropriate for the Mediterranean region (Piening 1997:80). Finally, and perhaps most importantly in the Mediterranean context, progress in the Middle East Peace Process at that time permitted adoption of an overarching approach.[53]

In terms of scope, the Partnership was to include Algeria, Morocco and Tunisia, the Mashreq countries, the Palestinian Authority and Israel, together with Turkey, Cyprus and Malta. Figure 5.2 shows the MNC membership of the Euro–Mediterranean Partnership, now known as the 'Med 12'. In terms of content, a process of increasingly close political and economic cooperation was envisaged, leading to an end state described by the

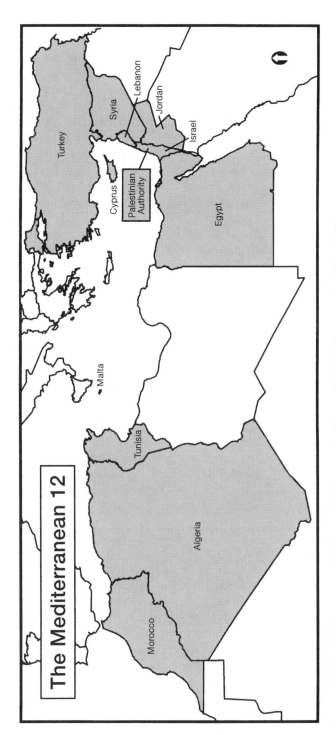

Figure 5.2 The Mediterranean 12 (Euro–Med Partners). (Figure © LJMU Cartographic Unit 1998)

Commission, somewhat coyly, as 'a close association, the content of which will be jointly defined' (Commission 1995f:8). At the centre of the association process would be progress towards free trade, supported by greatly increased financial aid. The now standard reference to political dialogue (covering respect for democracy, good governance and human rights) was to be 'extended to security issues', with the overall aim of establishing 'a Euro–Mediterranean zone of peace and stability' (*ibid*).

Proposals for a Euro–Mediterranean Partnership were approved, in principle, by the Essen European Council in December 1994, and the French and Spanish Presidencies the following year saw a period of intense diplomatic activity in preparation for its formal launch in November 1995. The three elements of the Partnership – financial cooperation, bilateral association and multilateral dialogue – essentially mirror the EU–CEEC relationship; albeit with important differences, as we shall see.

In relation to financial cooperation, the 1995 Cannes Summit approved funding to MNC for the 1995–9 period of 4685 million ECU, a substantial increase on previous funding.[54] Also agreed was the replacement of existing bilateral and regional programmes by a single MEDA budget line, originally from January 1997.[55] In organizational terms, MEDA provides a unified framework for the Mediterranean programmes, with the intention of promoting increased efficiency of management and coherence of approach. More politically, the EU's priorities for the MEDA programme are very evident, and funding will 'first and foremost benefit the MNC embarking on modernizing and reforming their economies to culminate in free trade' (Commission 1995g:33). Moreover the new system of three-year rolling indicative programmes introduced by MEDA provides for annual updating, and may be amended on the basis of 'progress in structural reform, macro-economic stabilization and social progress achieved by the Mediterranean partners' (Council MEDA Regulation reproduced in Commission 1995g:33). In principle, the new basis of funding allocation for MEDA provides enhanced opportunities for the EU's objectives to be pursued, and hence for EU actorness.

The second element of the Euro–Med Partnership will be a series of upgraded bilateral agreements. Except in the special cases of Turkey, Cyprus and Malta, these will take the form of Euro–Mediterranean Association Agreements. In practice, negotiations for association agreements with the countries most dependent on EC trade – Israel, Morocco and Tunisia – were already well advanced when the Euro–Med initiative was agreed. However it provided impetus for a conclusion to the negotiations which, in the case of Morocco, were stalled because of failure to reach agreement on the traditionally sensitive area of trade in agricultural products (Marquina 1995). These negotiations are considered below in our discussion of actorness in this policy area.

Following conclusion of the first Euro–Mediterranean Agreements, an EU priority has been to negotiate similar agreements with the other

Mediterranean 'partners'. Table 5.2 indicates the current status of Euro–Mediterranean Agreements. The core of the Agreements is economic cooperation, with a major emphasis upon movement towards free trade in industrial goods and services. The Agreements also contain political and social/cultural elements, and provide for establishment of the usual association institutions. However, there is evidently an intention that bilateral dialogue on these matters should be downgraded – to 'technical level' – and that 'political level' ministerial meetings should be held within the context of the multilateral Partnership process. Nevertheless, in part to accommodate the Moroccan government's desire to strengthen bilateral relations, there is also an assurance that multilateral dialogue will 'supplement but not replace' bilateral dialogue (Presidency Conclusions, Cannes European Council, reproduced in Commission 1995g:68).

Two of the three elements of the Euro–Mediterranean Partnership were already substantially agreed when the Partnership Initiative was formally launched, in November 1995, at the Barcelona Euro–Mediterranean Ministerial Conference.[56] The ensuing Barcelona Declaration and Work Programme for multilateral dialogue was agreed (but, tellingly, not signed) by all 27 participants. Using a formula considered to be reminiscent of the CSCE process (Barbé 1996:26), the Declaration divided the partnership into three chapters – political and security;[57] economic and financial (including establishment of a free trade area by 2010); social, cultural and human affairs.[58] These chapters include matters covered by all three Pillars of the Union, although at all stages the dominance of the partnership's economic core is evident.

The Work Programme provided for periodic meetings of Ministers for Foreign Affairs and *ad hoc* thematic meetings of Ministers, senior officials

Table 5.2 Euro–Mediterranean Association Agreements: progress of negotiations.

Partner	Conclusion of negotiations	Signature of Agreement	Entry into force
Tunisia	June 1995	July 1995	March 1998
Israel	September 1995	November 1995	
Morocco	November 1995	February 1996	
Palestinian Authority	December 1996	February 1997	July 1997
Jordan	April 1997	November 1997	
Egypt	Negotiations in progress		
Lebanon	Negotiations in progress		
Algeria	Negotiations in progress		
Syria	Mandate in course of preparation		

Source: Commission (1998b)

and experts. These meetings include representatives from all 27 partners. A 'Euro–Mediterranean Committee for the Barcelona process' (at senior official level), comprising the EU troika and one representative from each of the 'Med 12', was established to provide general oversight of the partnership process and carry out preparatory work for Euro–Med Ministerial Conferences. To provide an indication of the ongoing 'Barcelona process', Figure 5.3 summarizes Euro–Med events up to the Second Ministerial Conference in April 1997, and Table 5.3 sets out the 'Calendar of Priority Actions' for the first semester of 1998. This complex multilateral process is intended to provide an overarching framework and strategic direction for the Euro–Mediterranean Partnership generally.

Political and security aspects

Senior Officials meetings, March, May, July, October, November 1996; January, March 1997.

Seminars for diplomats (Malta 1996, Egypt 1997).

Economic and financial aspects

Statistics cooperation: Directors General Seminars (two).

Customs cooperation: Officials meetings on rules of origin (three).

Information Society: Workshops (three); Ministerial Conference, May 1996; Conference on Maritime Information, June 1996.

Tourism: Ministerial Conference, May 1996.

Private Investment and Industry: Industrial Federations conferences (two); Working Group meetings (five); Industry Ministers meeting, June 1996; Meeting of Economic Institutes, March 1997; Conference on Private Investment, May 1997.

Energy: Conference of Energy Ministers, June 1996.

Environment: Experts meeting on wetlands, June 1996.

Transport: Experts meeting, maritime transport, October 1996.

Water: Conference on local management, November 1996.

Fishing: Experts meeting on fish stocks, July 1996; Diplomatic Conference on fish stocks, November 1996.

Science and Technology: Monitoring Committee (two meetings).

Social, cultural and human affairs

Dialogue among Cultures and Civilizations: Workshops on cultural heritage (three); Ministerial Conference, April 1996; Conference on European/Islamic relations, June 1996.

Social Development: Conference on work, enterprise, training, May 1996; Conference on Governance, March 1997.

Dialogue on Human Rights: Workshop, January 1997.

Drugs/organized crime: Officials Meeting, June 1996.

Summits of Economic and Social Committees: 1995, 1996.

Figure 5.3 Euro–Mediterranean events between First and Second Ministerial Conferences.

Table 5.3 Calendar of agreed priority actions of the Barcelona Process for first semester, 1998. (Dates/venues to be finalized in some cases.)

Date	Event	Location
25 Feb.	Senior Officials meeting on Political and Security questions	Brussels
26 Feb.	Euro–Mediterranean Committee for the Barcelona Process	Brussels
4–7 March	Seminar on use of the Internet	Cyprus
26 March	Euro–Mediterranean Conference on capital markets	London
6–7 April	Meeting of Euro–Mediterranean Energy Forum at Director level	Malta
23 April	Workshop on dialogue between cultures and civilizations	Stockholm
April	Information session for diplomats	Malta
11 May	Euro–Mediterranean Conference of Energy Ministers	Brussels
27 May	Senior Officials meeting on Political and Security questions	Brussels
28 May	Euro–Mediterranean Committee on the Barcelona Process	Brussels
?	Seminar of persons with politico-military responsibilities relating to humanitarian tasks	Rome
?	Steering Committee, project on prevention of natural and human catastrophes	?
?	Institutes of Defence Studies meeting	Paris
?	Workshop for diplomats on cultural dialogue	Cairo
?	Experts meeting on migration	?
?	Workshop on technology innovation	Brindisi
?	Industry Ministers Working Groups: 1 development of industrial fabric 2 legal and administrative frameworks	?
June	Informal Foreign Ministers meeting	Italy

Source: Commission (1998b).

The Euro–Med partnership: implications for actorness

The Euro–Med Partnership initiative is an ambitious, long-term strategy. The EU is attempting, through its presence, to provide a common anchor which will ensure the stability of its Southern neighbours. At the same time it is actively seeking to promote cooperation between them; indeed the Partnership is an attempt to apply the EC model of functional cooperation to the construction of peaceful relations in the Mediterranean region. Thus the Barcelona process provides a framework, however fragile, for meetings involving representatives of countries, not least Israel and Syria, who rarely interact in other fora. There is said to be a desire on the part of all participants 'to separate the long term Euro–Med process from the Middle East Peace Process, which essentially involves a sub-region' (Interview, DGIB, February 1998).

Inevitably this has not always proved possible – in November 1997, for example, the Moroccan government cancelled a ministerial conference in protest at lack of progress in the Peace Process. Nevertheless, most meetings focus upon 'highly technical' matters and do make progress (Interview, Commission DGIB, February 1998). In consequence the Barcelona process differs from the EU/CEEC structured dialogue in that it provides a forum which, despite its low profile, is valued for the unique opportunity it provides to establish contacts across a highly volatile region. Perhaps its importance is demonstrated by the fact that the US government wished to participate fully and Russia requested observer status. Ultimately it was decided to limit the process to the Med 12 plus the EC and its Member States (Barbé 1996:34).

While EU actorness in the Mediterranean has evidently increased in recent years, it is impeded both by relative lack of presence in relation to MNC (when compared with CEEC and ACP) and by problems of consistency and coherence pertaining to the EC/EU itself. This latter reflects a broadly North/South divide between Member States concerning both policy prioritization between the Eastern and Southern peripheries and the direction of policy towards the Mediterranean region itself.[59] Nevertheless, in terms of consistency between Member State and EU efforts, a divided approach to the Mediterranean region is not clearly evident from the composition of Member States' bilateral aid programmes. Although France, Spain and Italy evidently prioritize MNC over CEE countries, a reverse process in favour of CEEC is apparent only in the case of Austria (Randel and German 1997). Here, as in other policy areas, the Commission acknowledges the need for 'improved strategic and operational coordination' and has pledged 'energetically to promote that objective' (Commission 1995g:41). However in circumstances where individual Member States have long established bilateral relations with various MNC this is not easily accomplished.

With regard to policy coherence, the EU's internal North/South divide is reflected in contrasting approaches to EU–MNC economic cooperation, at least in principle. Thus Northern Member States support increased market access for MNC agricultural exports, while Southern Member States have traditionally argued for a policy of encouraging food self-sufficiency (rather than increased exports) alongside substantial financial assistance for MNC. These divisions were clearly reflected in debates over the Euro–Med package, with the outcome an inevitable compromise between the two positions. In practice, however, negotiation of the Euro–Med Agreements[60] revealed a familiar pattern of protectionism which cuts across this internal North/South divide. In the case of the negotiations with Morocco, for example, the Commission's negotiating position was constrained as much by Belgian, Dutch and German sensitivity over tomatoes and cut flowers as by Spanish preoccupation with fish (Marquina 1995; Barbé 1996). As in the case of the Europe Agreements, minor additional concessions were granted at the eleventh hour in the context of broader strategic debates – in the Mediterranean context, the decision to launch the Euro–Med Initiative.

As we have seen, the financial cooperation and Association elements of the Partnership have yet to come fully into effect. These policy instruments are interlinked, in that 'associated' countries are likely to be prioritized in allocating funding assistance and possibly, also, in attracting foreign investment. Thus, in principle, the Euro–Med package would appear to increase the leverage of the EU in its bilateral relations with MNC. Here progress in ratifying and implementing the Euro–Med Agreement will be of interest, since, as Marks (1996:14) has noted, 'The prospect of creating a free trade zone was met with modified rapture across the region'.[61] In the past, however, there has been reticence in attempting to exploit the EC's economic presence. This is partly because relations with MNC have traditionally been complicated and difficult, creating 'a very slippery stage' for EC actorness (Grilli 1993:210). Contemporary evidence of a relatively cautious approach to MNC (when compared with ACP or CEE countries) can be found in the approach to political conditionality. Thus, in the context of EU–MNC relations, to take action on democracy/rule of law issues would be considered an 'extremely grave step' (Interview, DGIB, February 1998). This contrasts with the treatment of other 'partners', as we have seen.

The sensitivity of EU–MNC relations reflects a number of factors – among which, of course, is the range of external perceptions and expectations of the EU. Thus, in contrast with EU–CEEC relations, for most of the Med 12 there is neither a prospect nor a desire for EU membership, and hence a correspondingly reduced opportunity for political influence on the part of the EU. Moreover, the EU is not the only interested external actor in this strategically important region. In the Middle East, in particular, the EC's considerable economic presence in relation to Israel and the Palestinian Authority is not translated into political influence; here the United States remains the most important external actor. Indeed it is only in respect of Turkey and Cyprus, where there is an aspiration to accede to membership, that significant actorness might be anticipated – and even here EU influence is problematic.

Relations with Turkey and Cyprus

The early development of relations with Turkey reflected, as we have seen, Cold War strategic priorities. In the post-Cold War environment Turkey has remained strategically important to Western governments; indeed there have been expectations that Turkey would make an important contribution to stability in Central Asia, the Caucasus and the Balkans (Craig Nation 1996). As one Turkish diplomat commented, Turkey is seen as 'a buffer against everything' (Interview, June 1996). This raises the central problem affecting EU–Turkish relations. Turkey, as a Western oriented, secular,

Islamic country, is expected to play a role in protecting European interests; but does not receive in return acceptance – required to maintain the position of modernizing, secular elites – that Turkey is part of Europe.[62] In this context membership of NATO, the CSCE, the OECD and the Council of Europe, and most particularly Turkey's application for EU membership, represent 'an attempt to gain recognition of Turkey's European status by joining all the right clubs' (Müftüler-Bac 1997:53).

The 1964 Ankara (Association) Agreement provided for phased introduction of a customs union and the possibility of future accession to the EC – when Turkey was deemed ready to take on the obligations of membership. For a variety of reasons, implementation of the Ankara Agreement was not energetically pursued by either party. The Turkish government was unenthusiastic about economic liberalization, preferring to pursue import-substitution strategies behind tariff barriers. On the EC side, 'sensitive' products remained sensitive; and the provision for free movement of workers between Turkey and the EC, due to take effect from December 1986, was notable for its non-observance.

While lack of progress on economic cooperation contributed to the Turkish government's distrust of EC intentions, the most significant impediments to progress in EC–Turkish relations have been political. Tensions over Cyprus have been a complicating factor since Turkey's military intervention in 1974, but were greatly exacerbated by the accession of Greece to the EC in 1981. The internal political situation in Turkey has proved an even greater impediment to closer EU–Turkish relations, however. On numerous occasions the Council of Europe and the EC have drawn attention to human rights abuses and the treatment of the Kurdish minority. Perhaps of even greater significance has been the fragility of democratic processes, evidenced by the close involvement of the military in Turkish politics. Since signature of the Ankara Agreement the military has on three occasions intervened in the political system – in 1971 forcing the resignation of the government; in 1980 taking over the government and maintaining military rule until 1983; and in 1997 intervening to reverse the policies and ultimately force from office the pro-Islamist minority government of the Welfare Party. The Turkish constitutional court subsequently disbanded the Welfare Party on the grounds of 'actions against the principles of the secular republic' (Chief Justice Ahmet Necdet Suzer, quoted in *The Guardian*, 17 January 1998).

The growing political instability in Turkey which prompted this most recent military intervention is partly attributable to the EC's negative response to Turkey's 1987 membership application. The decision to seek membership was originally taken by the 1980–3 military government – as a response to Greek accession in 1981 and in the light of Turkey's strong economic growth of over 5 per cent a year (Töre 1990:9). The restitution of civilian rule thus reflected this decision. It brought into office a strongly Western oriented government which embarked upon a programme of economic liberalization in preparation for Turkey's formal application for EC membership. The rejection of this application, based upon the Commission's (1989) Opinion, emphasized, alongside economic obstacles to Turkish accession, human rights and minorities issues and the dispute with Greece over Cyprus. Turkish opinion was inevitably offended by –

> the political analysis and comment levelled at Turkey – which did not feature in earlier Opinions in connection with the applications of the last three members, Greece, Spain and Portugal, themselves hardly paragons of democracy before they joined the Community.
>
> (Töre 1990:10)

In the light of subsequent developments, it is ironic that the Community's rejection of the Turkish application was widely interpreted, in 1990, as 'a disguised attempt to put Turkey in the same bracket as the East Europeans' (*ibid*).

As an alternative to Turkish accession, the Commission recommended that the long delayed customs union with Turkey be speedily completed. This was achieved and the customs union entered into force in December 1995, with the consequence that Turkey became the non-member country most fully integrated into Community structures (Kramer 1996a). Nevertheless, attendance at the Customs Code and Standards Committees is not a substitute for EC membership; ultimately the Turkish government is obliged to implement decisions adopted by the Council of Ministers, where it has no representation. This political asymmetry is mirrored by the economic impacts of the customs union, which applies only to industrial products. As anticipated this has resulted in unequal distribution of costs and benefits, which is likely to continue in the medium term.[63] It was intended that Turkey would receive EC financial assistance to offset the cost of implementing the customs union (Commission 1989:8). However disbursement of funding has subsequently been blocked by the Greek government. Consequently Kramer's (1996a:73) fears that the customs union would destabilize Turkish–EU relations proved to be well founded.

EU–Turkish relations are further complicated by tensions over Cyprus. In 1990 the government of the Republic of Cyprus formally applied, on behalf of both parts of the divided island, for membership of the EC. However the legality of this application is disputed by officials of the Turkish Republic of Northern Cyprus (TRNC), and by the Turkish government, which is alone in officially recognizing the TRNC. In its Opinion on the Cypriot application, the Commission confirmed the eligibility of Cyprus for membership, subject to progress towards settlement of the intercommunal dispute (Commission 1993:17). The Commission also recommended that, in the event of continuing failure of UN mediation efforts, the Cypriot application should be reconsidered in January 1995 (*ibid*:18). This reconsideration resulted in a complicated trade-off, in which an undertaking was given that accession negotiations with Cyprus would begin six months following the conclusion of the 1996–7 IGC – in return for Greek approval of the customs union with Turkey.

As a consequence of this trade-off the EU is now faced with an extraordinarily challenging situation. Accession negotiations with the Republic of Cyprus opened at the end of March 1998, alongside those with the Czech Republic, Estonia, Hungary, Poland and Slovenia, as recommended in *Agenda 2000*. Despite reiteration of Turkey's eligibility, in principle, for EU membership, *Agenda 2000* did not recommend commencement of accession negotiations, nor initiation of pre-accession strategies, hence effectively prioritizing all of the CEEC10 and Cyprus over Turkey. Thus the outrage of the Turkish government at exclusion from the current phase of enlargement was compounded by the opening of accession negotiations with the Greek Cypriot government despite the objections of the TRNC authorities.

Relations with Turkey and Cyprus: implications for actorness

EU policy in this area is indicative of a complex and highly problematic relationship between actorness and presence. It also illuminates, very clearly, the extent to which consistency problems can impede effective policy formulation.

In the early years of its development, the EC was significant primarily in the context of Turkey's broader orientation towards Western institutions. It was not until the 1980s that the EC became a sustained and important focus of Turkish policy. While this reflected the EC's increased economic presence as a consequence of the Single Market process, it was strongly influenced by the accession of Greece to the EC and the (well founded) belief that this would be damaging to Turkish interests. Thus the EC's 'presence', for Turkey, reflects a highly charged political dynamic.

Since the end of the Cold War the EC/EU's importance for Turkey has increased, and the EU has supplanted NATO as the principal focus of policy in Europe. Today, the relationship with the EU is more than ever necessary to Turkey's secular elites – in the face of deep internal divisions between Islamist and secular forces and external pressures and demands placed upon Turkey as a consequence of post-Cold War regional instabilities. Conversely, maintenance of a stable, secular regime in Turkey reflects Western strategic interests; hence the EU has experienced external pressure, not least from the US government, to maintain and enhance its links with Turkey. Despite these strong incentives for a proactive EU policy towards Turkey, outcomes have, in practice, been mixed.

In some respects the EC/EU has been influential in shaping domestic political developments in Turkey. This was particularly evident during and after the 1980 military takeover, when the EC exerted considerable economic and diplomatic pressure for a return to civilian rule. The extent to which EC displeasure influenced Turkish policy during this period is demonstrated by the early release of political prisoners, at EC insistence, and by the visit of the Turkish foreign minister to the Commission in 1982 to present and discuss the draft of Turkey's new democratic constitution (Müftüler-Bac 1997:80). After return to civilian rule, and prior to Turkey's membership application, a number of further reforms were carried out, again at EC insistence. These included removal of restrictions on political activity by persons considered by the military to have been extremists – including the Islamist politician Necmettin Erbakan who was removed from office as Prime Minister following military pressure in 1997. The EU is thus faced with the conundrum that secular rule in Turkey, which it approves, is sustained by military involvement in the political system, which it does not. The ability of the EU to respond adequately to the needs of Turkey's secular elites is thus constrained, in part, by the nature of the Turkish political system. However EU actorness in this area is also greatly impeded by internal problems of consistency and coherence.

The concerns and interests of individual Member State governments have intruded in relations with Turkey since the outset – the 1964 Ankara Agreement provision for free movement of labour was an early casualty of Member State sensitivity. From 1972, when the German government banned recruitment of non-EC workers, immigration into the EC has been possible for Turks only in cases of family reunion. From this time the German government, 'with the silent accord of all its partners in the EC' has actively impeded full implementation of the Ankara Agreement (Kramer 1996b:206). While originally the German government's position reflected primarily economic considerations, more recently there has been a tendency to emphasize cultural and religious factors as impediments to Turkey's 'European vocation'. Thus, at a conference of the (Christian Democrat) European People's Party in March 1997, Chancellor Kohl and other prominent Christian Democrats plainly stated that Turkey could never be admitted to the predominantly Christian EU. These statements caused a crisis in German–Turkish relations, which remain cool.

While difficult bilateral relations between Germany and Turkey have impeded EU actorness in this area, the attitude of the Greek government since 1981 has ensured that EC/EU policy towards Turkey has been largely confined to exhortation, criticism and economic penalties. The ability to offer financial assistance as incentive or reward has been severely curtailed, and the ultimate incentive of future EU membership for Turkey appears less viable today than it did in 1964. In these circumstances the presence and actorness of the EU in relation to Turkey, and by extension to Cyprus, is insignificant when compared with the EU–CEEC relationship.[64]

CONCLUSION

Examination of the EU's increasingly close and complex relations with its two peripheries highlights a number of factors concerning EU actorness. While economic presence is a significant factor in both regions, the relationship between presence and actorness is mediated, to a considerable extent, by differing demands and expectations – in respect of third parties and of actors within the EU policy system itself.

In both regions the end of the Cold War has impacted decisively. And the evolving dynamic of post-Cold War interactions has resulted in the construction of highly significant shared understandings – that enlargement of the EU to the East is inevitable; and that this enlargement must be balanced by enhanced relations with the Mediterranean non-member countries. While different emphases are apparent in both cases, it is only in regard to EU–Turkish relations that shared understandings are absent.

Relations with CEE countries reflect a formidable EC/EU presence which has to a considerable extent shaped perceptions and expectations; not least the perception, on the part of CEE elites, that there is no alternative to EU membership. The corresponding perception that enlargement is inevitable, but not necessarily desirable, has provided a strong basis for EU actorness in shaping CEE transition processes during the prolonged pre-accession period. Hence, in this region, actorness has been displayed through the role of increasingly stern mentor. Indicative of the uncompromising stance of Community officials charged with managing the new Accession Partnerships with CEEC is the statement 'Opt-outs are for us, not for them' (François Lamoureux of DGIA, quoted in *The Guardian*, 28 March 1998).

Relations with the Mediterranean countries have historically been difficult. Here the complex and uncertain links between presence and actorness reflect the fact that EC/EU relationships with MNCs are characterized by elements both of interdependence and dependency; and that, in this region, other external actors have played an important role as a focus for demands and expectations. Most importantly, perhaps, divisions within the EU have impeded or even prevented the formulation of coherent policies towards MNC. Nevertheless, changes since the end of the Cold War, in particular the development of the EU's *Östpolitik*, have contributed to a perception, increasingly shared, that relations with the EU's Southern periphery must similarly be prioritized. The ensuing Euro–Mediterranean Initiative represents a significant policy development for the EU.

Policy towards the 'near abroad' since 1989 is undoubtedly indicative of enhanced EU actorness. However this has been founded upon perceptions of necessity and inevitability; it does not indicate the achievement by the EU of high levels of consistency and coherence. Here the dismal failure of policy towards Turkey represents the nadir of EU actorness. Inability to address this issue may ultimately undermine the EU's broader strategy of closer association with the near abroad.

6   Towards a common foreign and security policy?

Our discussion of relations with the near abroad demonstrated both the complexity and the uncertainty of the relationship between presence and actorness. While this is, in part, a function of differing external perceptions and expectations of the EU, it also reflects an inability to agree, internally, on measures which would provide overall strategic direction for EC/EU external activities. Here, the attempt to create a common foreign and security policy for the EU is central to our concerns. If the Union is fully to realize the potential of its significant presence, it is vital that the economic power of the European Community is articulated to a stronger sense of collective political purpose. A well coordinated and fully functioning common foreign policy would have this effect.

The Community, as we have seen, lies at the centre of a vast network of trade relationships and association arrangements which span the globe. In the spheres of trade and (to a lesser extent) environmental policy, the EC undoubtedly plays an important, global role. Even in these areas, however, we have identified problems of inconsistency between the EC and the Member States, and incoherence within the Community itself, which impede policy formulation and implementation. In the policy areas which are the subject of this chapter, the impediments to the overall coherence and effectiveness of external policy are more starkly evident.

Title V of the TEU begins with the declaration 'A common foreign and security policy is hereby established'. This bold claim is misleading, however. The Common Foreign and Security Policy (CFSP) cannot be regarded as a common policy in a sense analogous to the Common Commercial Policy; rather it is a highly institutionalized and complex process of consultation and cooperation between Member State governments. This reflects a traditional view of foreign policy – as pursuit of national interests and state security through formal, intergovernmental relations. Regarded as a specialized and essentially political policy area – frequently referred to as 'high politics' – foreign and security policy has traditionally been considered as entirely distinct from the mundane 'low politics' of external economic relations. In practice, of course, this distinction has always been blurred. It is increasingly so today, given the significance of the economic instruments of statecraft and of 'soft', non-military security, where the EC/EU has an important role. As is pointed out in *Agenda 2000* –

> The interdependence of modern economies and the increased importance of transnational factors mean that an active and effective foreign policy cannot be limited to the more traditional aspects of international relations. This applies in particular to the Union, characterised by its strong economic dimension.
>
> (Commission 1997b:28)

While there is evidently considerable overlap between these policy areas, in practice a division between external economic policy and 'political' foreign policy became deeply entrenched in the course of the Community's evolution. It is formally enshrined in the Treaties and reflected in the parallel development of two separate, externally oriented bureaucracies. This has resulted in duplication of effort and extraordinary difficulty in achieving overall coordination and coherence of external policy.

Despite the reluctance of Member State governments to countenance policy integration in 'sensitive' areas of foreign policy, there has been a gradual evolution in the commitment to and capacity for cooperation. Indeed, today, there are very few areas of foreign policy where the EU refrains from making a statement of some sort.[1] However, the practice of issuing joint statements on issues of the day is indicative of a largely reactive approach to foreign policy, which has all too frequently remained at the declaratory stage. If the EU is to develop a foreign policy capable of providing overall political direction to its external activities, it will need both the political will to define and pursue common objectives, and the capacity to formulate and implement proactive policy initiatives.

To a significant extent, political will on the part of Member State governments is the key to successful formulation of foreign policy at the EU level. Nevertheless here, as in other policy areas, the growing presence of the EC interacts with external perceptions and demands, thus creating expectations of, and a perceived need for, a common approach to third parties.[2] As we have seen from previous chapters, the significance of the EC as an economic actor has generated increased expectations of coherent policy initiatives from the EC/EU, whether as a participant in intergovernmental trade or environmental negotiations, or in providing support for the processes of economic development or transition. Moreover, in the area of foreign policy, the impact of these interlinked internal and external factors must be assessed in the context of a significantly changed international environment in which Member State governments are, themselves, reformulating foreign policy approaches and priorities.

In this context it is interesting to note the 1996 White Paper issued by the, then, UK Conservative government. Entitled *Free Trade and Foreign Policy: A Global Vision*, this joint publication by the Foreign and Commonwealth

Office (FCO) and Department of Trade and Industry (DTI) proclaimed as its purpose –

> to state the Government's commitment to global free trade and open markets as a major policy objective and as a fundamental national interest.
>
> (FCO, DTI 1996:3)

In the White Paper the case for a coherent approach to all aspects of external policy is strongly argued. Moreover there is acknowledgement that the UK national interest (as defined in the White Paper) is well served by coherent and effective policies at the EU level. Indeed, in an implicit reference to the Community's economic presence, it is argued that the EU provides access to 'incomparable influence' (FCO, DTI 1996:18).

Pronouncements of this type are important, since they contribute to the construction of understandings about foreign policy and its conduct. And acknowledgement that 'fundamental national interests' can most effectively be pursued at the EU level is a first step towards creating the political will necessary to give concrete expression to these understandings. It is by no means sufficient, however, for the formulation of a proactive, common foreign policy which moves beyond the lowest common denominator of disparate 'national' interests. This would require identification of common interests, the ability to define and prioritize specific policy aims and access to the instruments of joint policy implementation.

Identification of common interests, in the sense of overarching principles, is not a problem. The Union's Common Foreign and Security Policy has the following declared objectives –

> to safeguard the common values, fundamental interests, independence and integrity of the Union . . .
>
> to strengthen the security of the Union in all ways;
>
> to preserve peace and strengthen international security . . .
>
> to promote international cooperation . . .
>
> to develop and consolidate democracy and the rule of law, and respect for human rights and fundamental freedoms.
>
> (TEU J.1 [11])

These broad objectives are not, in themselves, controversial – and there is no doubt that they are pursued, in a general sense, in the course of the EU's external activities. Moreover there is explicit reliance upon the EC's economic presence in furtherance of these political aims. Thus, for example, all Cooperation and Association Agreements concluded since entry into force of the TEU contain 'political conditionality' clauses, which provide for suspension of all or part of the agreement in the event of non-fulfilment of 'good governance', human rights and other obligations. In addition to this general use of conditionality, issues of rights and freedoms are also raised in specific cases – where reliance on the EC's economic weight is evident in attempts to threaten or cajole. Here an example is provided by the warning addressed to the Croatian President by UK Foreign Office Minister Tony Lloyd, on behalf of the Presidency, that progress on minority rights issues 'will be a key factor in the development of closer relations between Croatia and the European Union' (*UK Presidency on the Internet*, 27 February 1998). Such matters have also achieved prominence in the context of the EU–ASEAN relationship, which has been interrupted, by the EU, as a result of ASEAN insistence on the inclusion of Burmese observers at meetings of the Joint Cooperation Council. EU members object to the human rights record of Burma (*Agence Europe*, 13 November 1997).

Agreement on whether or how to pursue such matters beyond declaratory statements is by no means assured, however. The decision to resist Burma's membership of ASEAN was taken only after great controversy (Interview, UK Permanent Representation to the EU, October 1997); in other cases it has proved impossible to agree on concrete measures in furtherance of CFSP objectives. Our central concern, in consequence, is the extent to which there is a will, and ability, to formulate and implement specific, common policies capable of giving overall direction to the EU's external activities.

Below we focus on two interrelated problems which impede the development of a coherent and effective EU foreign policy. The first of these, inadequate coordination between and within policy issue areas, is the most fundamental. It reflects both low levels of Member State commitment and tensions between Member States and the Commission – problems which are endemic in this policy area – and is evidenced by difficulties both in formulating and implementing policy. This fundamental problem is, to a large extent, the source of a further impediment to policy effectiveness – lack of clarity in external representation – which, in impeding development of a strong and positive EU collective identity, impinges upon third party perceptions of EU actorness.[3]

The source of these persistent problems is revealed by the history of attempts to provide the EC/EU with a meaningful foreign policy dimension. We outline the evolution of this policy area (see Figure 6.1 for a schematic representation) as a prelude to discussing the impediments today facing efforts to realize an effective CFSP.

THE EARLY YEARS: ABSENCE OF 'FOREIGN POLICY'

The creation of the European Communities following the end of the Second World War, and in the context of increasing Cold War tensions, reflected both the desirability of cooperating in the construction of a peaceful and

1952	**European Defence Community (EDC):** French proposal for common foreign policy and common system of defence, on supranational basis. Signed on behalf of Belgium, France, Germany, Italy, Luxembourg and Netherlands. Proposal fell when French National Assembly withheld ratification.
1961	**Fouchet Plan:** French proposal for a European Political Union, on intergovernmental principles, to coordinate foreign policy. European Political Commission to be based in Paris. Rejected by majority of Member States as a Gaullist ploy to undermine the EC.
1970	**Luxembourg Report:** Establishment of European Political Cooperation (EPC), as an intergovernmental process with no institutional base. Aimed to provide mechanism for foreign policy cooperation/coordination to give political direction to the EC's external relations.
1987	**Single European Act:** provided treaty basis for EPC, which remained an intergovernmental process between High Contracting Parties. Dedicated EPC Secretariat established in Brussels but not a Community institution – staffed by seconded Member State officials.
1993	**Treaty on European Union:** CFSP established as intergovernmental pillar of the Union (Pillar II). Provision for Joint Actions with QMV to apply at implementation stage (rarely used in practice). CFSP Secretariat incorporated into Council Secretariat. Reference to common defence as aspiration for the future. Commitment of Union to ensure overall consistency of 'external activities'.
1997	**Treaty of Amsterdam signed:** Clarifies and strengthens CFSP provisions. 'Common strategies' to be determined by European Council. Provision for increased use of QMV and 'constructive abstention' procedure to increase flexibility. Secretary-General of Council Secretariat to be High Representative for the CFSP, Policy Planning and Early Warning Unit to be established in Council Secretariat.

Figure 6.1 CFSP: antecedents and development.

prosperous Western Europe and of seeking, collectively, to recover some of the international influence lost by West European states individually. For much of its history, as we have seen, European integration has focused upon economic and social matters. However, in the periods of great uncertainty and potential instability which characterized both the beginning and the end of the Cold War, conventional security concerns were uppermost in the minds of policy makers. So it was with the 1952 European Defence Community Treaty, which we discuss more fully in Chapter 7. The spectacular defeat of this federalist proposal for a fully integrated European Army caused the abandonment of attempts to submit security and defence issues to supranational decision making. Indeed, such was the caution generated by this debacle that discussion of the relatively less sensitive area of foreign policy was avoided for almost a decade.

During this period attention focused upon functional integration, through development of the European Communities. The Treaty of Rome made no reference to orthodox foreign policy issues, still less to defence. Nevertheless the necessity for what became known as EC 'external relations' was acknowledged. The EC was accorded formal legal personality and was thus empowered, in its areas of competence, to undertake negotiations and conclude international agreements on behalf of its members. A further provision of the Rome Treaty empowered the EC to enter into association agreements with third parties. As we have seen from previous chapters, these provisions formed the basis for the EC's evolution as an international actor of some significance – despite the absence of a formal foreign policy role.[4]

By the early 1960s the need to balance the European Community's growing significance in external economic relations with an explicit foreign policy dimension became a subject of often contentious discussion. In Gaullist France there was particular concern at the increasingly significant role played by the European Commission in external relations. Consequently the Gaullist vision of an intergovernmental European construction was very much reflected in the 1961 Fouchet Plan. This draft treaty for a European Political Union provided for a common foreign policy, which was to be formulated in a highly institutionalized yet strictly intergovernmental setting, and a European *Political* Commission based in Paris. In sharp contrast to the federalist provisions of the 1952 European Defence Community (EDC) Treaty, the intention, here, was to curtail supranationalism through undermining the role of the EC institutions, in particular the Commission. This anti-federalist proposal suffered a similar fate to its federalist predecessor, serving only to emphasize the caution required in approaching this policy area.

The controversies of the 1960s essentially centred upon two contrasting approaches to policy making; integrationist (or supranational) and intergovernmental. The focus for these tensions was, and continues to be, the extent to which the European Commission should be involved in the formulation of foreign policy. However the issue was temporarily resolved, following the resignation of President de Gaulle, when the 1969 Luxembourg Report was adopted. This recommended establishment of a system of foreign policy cooperation on an intergovernmental basis, operating entirely outside the EC framework. Moreover, in explicit rejection of the Fouchet proposal to create institutions that would rival the Commission's role in external economic relations, no new institutional structure was envisaged. Thus the ensuing system of European Political Cooperation (EPC) initially lacked even a dedicated secretariat. Since many of the problems arising from the operation of EPC are still evident today, it is worth examining its development.

EUROPEAN POLITICAL COOPERATION

EPC involved regular consultation and formal quarterly meetings between national Foreign Ministers, supported by a Political Committee (PoCo), comprising Political Directors (senior Foreign Ministry officials) representing each Member State and a range of specialist Working Groups composed of Foreign Ministry officials. Cooperation between Member State missions in third countries was also encouraged. Formal external representation was provided by the Presidency, supported, from the mid 1970s, when the onerousness of the responsibility became apparent, by the immediate past and future Presidencies in what became known as the troika. Thus EPC comprised highly formalized, multi-level, intergovernmental cooperation.

Administrative support, in the early years, was provided by the country holding the Presidency, and all meetings took place in the capital of the Presidency country. This placed a heavy burden on national officials and also caused problems of continuity arising from the inability to establish a collective, institutional memory. Consequently, by the late 1970s, the practice had evolved of seconding national officials to assist successive Presidencies. While this afforded useful experience in working cooperatively, on a daily basis, with counterparts from other Member States, the peripatetic nature of the EPC process remained an impediment to its effectiveness. As Simon Nuttall observes 'The fact that EPC archives had to be carried halfway across Europe in a suitcase every six months gave rise to particularly unfavourable comment' (Nuttall 1992:20).

Despite intermittent proposals for enhancement of EPC, it was not until its codification in the 1986 Single European Act that an EPC Secretariat was established in Brussels.[5] However the Secretariat was not a permanent body; it comprised five national diplomats plus administrative staff – all seconded from an expanded, five-member troika. It also remained entirely separate from the General Secretariat of the Council of Ministers, which supports the Council and Presidency in EC policy areas. Reflecting fears, on the part of some Member States, of creeping communitarization of foreign policy, this arrangement ensured that Secretariat staff remained largely dependent for information upon colleagues in their respective national Foreign Ministries, some of whom viewed this new body with suspicion as a potential rival. Consequently, in the early years, the Secretariat 'concentrated on making itself useful and threatening no one' (*ibid*). While becoming recognized, by successive Presidencies, as an invaluable support to the EPC process, the Secretariat lacked the resources necessary to play a proactive policy role.

Despite the formal separation between the EC and EPC, which the SEA maintained, the practical development of policy had, from the outset, impinged upon EC competences – necessitating liaison between EPC personnel and the European Commission. Indeed it is difficult to identify a policy area discussed in EPC which did not impinge upon EC matters. The very first EPC Ministerial Meeting, in November 1970, had as agenda items the Middle East and the Conference on Security and Cooperation in Europe (CSCE). Policy in both these areas impinged upon EC competences and, ultimately, Commission involvement was significant. At this first meeting, however, the Commission delegation was, with reluctance, admitted to the last hour of the day-long meeting.[6]

The EPC/EC relationship was a source of considerable tension in the early years, with Member State diplomats 'at best inclined to treat the Commission with the high courtesy of condescension' (Nuttall 1996a: 130). The Commission, for its part, reacted with considerable defensiveness – taking care not even to comment upon 'non-EC' issues but opposing, vigorously, any perceived encroachment by EPC on EC policy competences.

The first ten years of EPC's operation were characterized by a series of *ad hoc* arrangements to accommodate Commission involvement in those frequent circumstances where EC and EPC matters overlapped and where EC instruments were essential to policy implementation. Finally, in 1981, it was agreed that the Commission should be 'fully associated' with EPC at all levels. This formula, which has persisted, permitted attendance of Commission representatives at all EPC meetings, including those in the Presidency capital. Moreover, in 1983, in recognition of its role in external policy, the Commission's participation in the troika was agreed by Member States – a decision taken somewhat reluctantly, since the Commission thereby gained a permanent place in external representation alongside the rotating six-month Presidencies. There was, thus, a gradual evolution of the EPC/Commission relationship after its inauspicious beginning, although sensitivities remain.[7]

More generally, in the 15 years which separated the Luxembourg Report and the SEA, the EPC process became established and largely accepted practice, its cautious evolution having posed no major threat to the national foreign policies of Member States. Conversely, however, EPC was open to the criticism that, given its highly elaborate and time consuming procedures, its achievements were modest.

The aims of EPC were broad: to increase mutual understanding on foreign policy issues through regularly informing and consulting partners; and to strengthen solidarity through harmonization of views, coordination of policy positions and, where possible or desirable, joint action. The first of these aims was largely achieved. Consultation between Foreign Office ministers and officials of the Member States became routine at all levels, the Coreu telex system which directly linked EC Foreign Ministries facilitating instantaneous communication.[8] While this level of interaction fostered habits of cooperation, the more ambitious aims of policy coordination and joint action produced a mixed record.

The EPC process proved highly successful as a source of declaratory statements deploring/welcoming developments upon which Member States were agreed, but tended to remain silent on areas of disagreement. Nevertheless some policy successes can be claimed, for example in coordinating sanctions against South Africa – albeit with reluctance on the part of the UK government. However it is in the context of the Conference on Security and

Cooperation in Europe[9] that EPC success is most frequently claimed. This process of East/West consultation which commenced in 1973 provided an opportunity to test the new EPC mechanism. From the outset the (then nine) Member States presented joint positions and played a positive role in the ongoing construction of East/West dialogue.

In the United Nations General Assembly and its related organs EPC Ministers again established the practice of caucusing before meetings in order to coordinate positions. In the global context of the UN, however, conflicting policy priorities of Member States have tended to impede this process and it has proved impossible, since the end of the 1970s, to achieve commonality even in 50 per cent of General Assembly votes.[10] This is not an impressive record given the explicit SEA commitment to adopt common positions at international fora; moreover it reflects routine divisions on mundane issues as well as occasional high profile disputes between Member States. Again these problems continue, despite reiteration of the commitment to conformity in the TEU.[11]

The difficulties experienced in coordinating positions at the General Assembly are compounded in the context of the Security Council, partly as a result of the different statuses of EU Member States. There has been little support from Member States for the European Parliament's proposal that, in the context of UN reform, the EU should be granted permanent member status to replace the UK and France. Rather there is a view that Germany should join France and the UK as permanent members. Moreover the French and UK governments' members have felt in no way bound to represent the EU in the Security Council. Indeed they have made proposals, for example establishment of the Contact Group on Yugoslavia, involving France, Russia, the UK and the USA, which 'annoyed and upset' other EU members (Interview, external Mission, January 1996). In addition there is regular, public disagreement between France and the UK – owing, in part, to the tendency of the UK government to support US policy, as has been the case during recurring controversies over renewal of UN sanctions against Iraq following the Gulf War.[12]

Lack of agreement between Member States has clearly been the most significant impediment to the formulation of coherent foreign policy. However the estrangement of the Commission from the policy process has also been of particular significance, given the extent to which policy instruments fall within Community competence. Nevertheless, throughout the Cold War, EPC evolved, albeit in a low-key fashion. While able to claim successes in policy coordination of a routine and largely declaratory nature, there was a tendency to disarray when Member States' interests conflicted or at times of crisis. The end of the Cold War heralded a number of crises which both highlighted the shortcomings of EPC and suggested the need to fashion a more robust foreign policy system which might avoid them.

THE END OF THE COLD WAR AND THE 1990–1 IGC

In 1990 the parallel Intergovernmental Conferences – on Political Union and Economic and Monetary Union – began their deliberations. The Political Union IGC was charged with transforming EPC into a foreign policy system capable of meeting the challenges of the post-Cold War period. In circumstances where US commitment to the Atlantic Alliance was increasingly in question, growing fears of political instability in Eastern Europe and the Balkans created a policy environment dramatically different from that in which EPC had operated. During this period expectations were growing, both within and outside Europe, that the EC would in future play a central role in maintaining peace and stability in Europe as a whole.[13] Throughout the IGC the urgency of its task was constantly demonstrated, whether in the need to forge new relationships with CEE countries or manage the emerging conflict in Yugoslavia. However, the first major crisis of the post-Cold War period occurred, not in Europe, but in the Middle East.

The invasion of Kuwait by Iraq in August 1990 elicited a rapid and unified response from EC members, with agreement on an oil embargo, freezing of Iraqi assets and support for United Nations sanctions. Indeed Italian Foreign Minister, de Michelis, expressed satisfaction that EC members had reacted 'effectively and with clarity of intentions and decisions' (quoted in Salmon 1992:245). Serious divisions arose, however, when decisions had to be taken on more robust action – both because Member States were divided over the use of military force *per se* and because EPC was an essentially political system which lacked military instruments. Ultimately each of the 12 Member States adopted a distinct position.[14] The resulting low point for European cooperation was described by *The Times* (22 August 1990) as 'a babble of different instructions, botched national initiatives and a confused public argument over ends and means'.

Immediately after the Gulf War ended, conflict erupted in Yugoslavia. This provided a second chance to redeem the reputation of EPC, and hence influence the deliberations of the ongoing IGC. There was widespread acceptance that, in this European conflict, the EC should play the role of mediator. The EC, for its part, was anxious to accept the challenge –

> 'This is the hour of Europe.' Jacques Poos, Luxembourg Foreign Minister speaking on 29 June 1991 after leading the EC troika in negotiating the first of many failed ceasefires.
>
> (Buchan 1993:67)

The first year of conflict in former Yugoslavia showed EC officials to be inexperienced mediators, while the usefulness of EC unarmed monitors was increasingly called into question as fighting in Croatia escalated. Some Member State governments called for a military deployment but again the familiar impediments arose – lack of agreement between Member States and lack of appropriate military instruments. By early 1992 EC monitors were relieved to be joined by UN peacekeepers.[15] Meantime, however, there had been a further damaging display of EC disunity initiated by the German government over recognition of Croatia and Slovenia.[16]

Against this background the Political Union IGC concluded in December 1991. The Treaty on European Union, which included provision for a Common Foreign and Security Policy, was signed and, following a difficult ratification process, entered into force on 1 November 1993.

COMMON FOREIGN AND SECURITY POLICY

The events of the 1990–1 period fuelled expectations that the TEU would create the conditions for proactive foreign policy making – that is greater overall policy coherence, increased decision making capacity, and enhanced access to policy instruments, including the ability to enforce policy where necessary.

In the event, while the TEU made reference to these matters, its overall impact was further to consolidate the structural division between foreign policy and other aspects of external policy; and to maintain the relative estrangement of the Commission from foreign policy making. This was a defeat for those, including the Commission, who had argued for incorporation of EPC into the Community. In practice the Union's 'pillar' structure ensured that only Pillar I (the EC) was subject to the Community method of decision making. The two new pillars, CFSP (Pillar II) and Justice and Home Affairs (Pillar III) were intergovernmental and, for the most part, subject to unanimity in the Council.[17] Nevertheless, in a promising allusion to the importance of ensuring overall coordination of external activities, the TEU Common Provisions stipulated that –

> The Union shall in particular ensure the consistency of its external relations, security, economic and development policies. The Council and the Commission shall be responsible for ensuring such consistency.

Accordance of joint responsibility for ensuring cross-pillar consistency in external activities suggested an enhanced role for the Commission in CFSP; indeed TEU provisions marginally strengthened provisions for the Commission's 'association'. Effectively, in the CFSP context, the Commission operates as a sixteenth 'member state', in that its representatives may make policy proposals but have no special right of initiative. While, as we shall see, the Commission has been less than content with this role, a number of institutional changes were made to facilitate increased involvement with CFSP. These are outlined below.

The inter-pillar relationship appeared also to be strengthened through a provision for the European Parliament to question the Council and make

recommendations concerning the operation of CFSP. However a more sceptical reading would suggest that this was necessitated by the TEU provision
(Article J.11) for administrative expenditure to be charged to the budget of
the European Community – whereas, in the case of EPC, all funding had
been provided by the Member States. The potential for controversy arising from the decision that the Community should fund an essentially
intergovernmental process was quickly realized. Thus, according to the
Commission (1996b:13), 'The current procedure for common foreign and
security policy decisions involving expenditure is both opaque and
inefficient; separate negotiations have to be held for each decision'.

A further disappointment for integrationists was the failure of the Treaty
to accord legal personality to the EU; the power to conclude international
agreements on behalf of its members remained solely with the EC, in its
areas of competence. Thus when matters fall under Pillar II (CFSP), as was
the case in establishing the EU administration of the Bosnian city of Mostar,
it is necessary for individual, bi-lateral agreements to be made by all 15
Member States. Each agreement is then subject to separate national ratification procedures. This unwieldy process caused great embarrassment in the
context of the EU's contribution to the Bosnian peace settlement (Interview,
Council Secretariat DGE, February 1997). Ratification by each Member
State is also necessary (as we have seen in previous chapters) on conclusion
of 'mixed' Association Agreements with third countries, which greatly
delays entry into force of such Agreements.

CFSP included few substantive new provisions. Its objectives remained
broadly stated, although the language in which they are couched is generally
stronger than that of EPC. Thus the opening formula of Title V of the TEU
'A common foreign and security policy is hereby established' contrasts
markedly with the EPC undertaking to 'endeavour jointly to formulate and
implement a European foreign policy' (SEA, Title III). The commitment to
and procedures for adopting common positions and joint actions are somewhat elaborated and strengthened in the TEU. There was also provision for
use of QMV in relation to detailed implementation of joint actions agreed
unanimously. While this provision suggested a movement from the unanimity which characterized EPC, it has been little used in practice.

The policy environment of the period was reflected in the TEU's only
significant innovation, which aimed to provide the EU with access to military instruments. Thus, in a provision cautiously worded to accommodate
the reservations of Atlanticist Member States, the TEU referred to 'the eventual framing of a common defence policy, which might in time lead to a
common defence'. In the interest of achieving this aim, the Western European Union was declared to be 'an integral part of the Union' (TEU Art.J.4
[17]). While the inclusion of a defence dimension in the TEU represented an
important departure from the exclusively civilian character of the European
Community and the essentially political nature of EPC, the TEU formula
represented a compromise between divergent Member State positions. In

consequence it was silent on the many complex and sensitive issues which would need to be addressed in order to put the proposal into effect. These issues, which are discussed more fully in Chapter 7, remain largely unresolved.

Giving effect to the TEU: institutional changes

To reflect the formal role in CFSP now accorded to the Council of Ministers (replacing the EPC formula of 'foreign ministers meeting in political cooperation') the EPC Secretariat was, in 1994, incorporated into Directorate-General E (External Relations) of the Council General Secretariat. In an explicit attempt to facilitate cross-pillar coordination, this arrangement brought together CFSP officials with those responsible for external economic relations. Consequently staff of DGE serve both the Pillar II Political Committee, which advises the General Affairs Council on CFSP matters, and the Committee of Permanent Representatives (COREPER) which advises the Council on Pillar I issues.[18] There is considerable tension between PoCo and COREPER, which reflects both broader inter-pillar strains and the nature of the bodies themselves. Thus the Political Directors who comprise PoCo are very senior national officials who tend to resent the influence of the Brussels-based COREPER members. Moreover PoCo deals only with Pillar II matters, whereas COREPER sees all material discussed by the Council 'it is the gatekeeper for everything' (Interview, Council Secretariat DGE, July 1997).[19] Consequently the task of DGE staff charged with liaison between the two is said to be sensitive.

Within DGE itself there remain considerable differences in approach between the Pillar I and II sections, with trade officials largely content to function as a traditional secretariat, while CFSP Unit staff are eager to play a policy advice role. These differences reflect the fact that the Commission has sole right of initiative in most aspects of external economic relations, whereas policy initiation in the CFSP Pillar traditionally lies primarily with the Presidency. Consequently the CFSP Unit is involved in drafting proposals for common positions and joint actions. CFSP Unit desk officers also have responsibility for liaison with each of the approximately 25 CFSP Working Groups. While it was intended, following entry into force of the TEU, that Working Groups would have a cross-pillar focus, in practice most meet separately in Pillar I and Pillar II configurations – a further reminder of the inter-pillar tensions that exist at all levels of the CFSP process.[20]

To reflect its increased responsibility, the CFSP Unit is very different in character from its EPC predecessor. It now comprises permanent officials of the Council Secretariat in addition to 15 diplomats seconded, for a four-year period, from each national Foreign Ministry. This is intended to provide continuity while maintaining the practice of utilizing Member State information sources – and also allowing Foreign Ministry officials to keep a close eye on what transpires in Brussels. Consequently this arrangement tends to raise fears of divided loyalties among the seconded diplomats.[21] Moreover the information provided by Member States is variable in quantity and quality, and this continues to impede the CFSP Unit's efforts in supporting Presidency policy initiatives. Presidencies, themselves, vary in the extent to which they seek or accept policy advice from the Unit, with smaller Member States generally more receptive to this support. Nevertheless the CFSP Unit is in much closer contact with the Presidency than is normal elsewhere in the Secretariat. Here an important aspect of its role is in assisting the Presidency to coordinate policy within the Council. This is facilitated by the access enjoyed by CFSP Unit staff to the policy processes of all 15 Member States. Potentially, the Unit might also contribute to cross-pillar coordination through liaising with CFSP officials in the Commission.[22] At present, however, this relationship is in its infancy and there is a need for greater effort in overcoming mutual misunderstanding and incipient rivalry.

In Pillar I, also, the Commission has made changes to support the upgrading of EPC to CFSP, and its own enhanced role in this policy area – if the Commission was to play a role similar to a Member State in the CFSP process, then it would need the equivalent of a foreign ministry. Consequently the EPC Directorate located in the Secretariat General of the Commission was reorganized and expanded, becoming DGIA, which was originally given responsibility for CFSP and external political relations, including management of the EC's Delegations. DGI and DGVIII were responsible for external economic relations with the developed and developing worlds respectively. However this experiment lasted only two years, after which the political and economic desks were again merged and horizontal responsibilities reallocated. Necessitated in part to accommodate the accession of Austria, Finland and Sweden in 1995, which increased the number of Commissioners requiring portfolios, this change involved the creation of a further Directorate-General for external policy, DGIB.

This brings to five the number of DGs and Commissioners concerned exclusively with external relations (Figure 1.1 sets out the current responsibilities of these 'Relex' DGs). The Relex Commissioners meet on a monthly basis in an attempt to coordinate vertical and horizontal issues, but there is no doubt that the overlaps between their areas of responsibility generate antagonisms; and that these tensions are also evident within the DGs. Indeed it is widely acknowledged in Brussels that the College system is not working; and that particular problems pertain to coordination of external policy. Proposals for reform of the Commission's organization and operation to take effect on appointment of the new Commission in 2000 are discussed below.

Responsibility for CFSP and for the EC Delegations remains with DGIA, whose officials participate in all CFSP Working Groups. However the extent to which Commission representatives play a proactive role in Working Groups is, in practice, variable – as is the effectiveness of the Groups themselves. Some Working Groups are said still to have 'an EPC mentality, they feel under less pressure to get a result' and in these areas Commission input is minimal (Interview, Council Secretariat DGE, July 1997). However the need for greater effectiveness of Working Groups generally, and for a more consistent input from the Commission in particular, is widely acknowledged. This reflects in large part the importance of the Commission's role in policy implementation. As will be evident from our discussion of the CFSP's operation, the major instruments of policy employed in furtherance of CFSP, whether in the administration of aid or the imposition of economic sanctions, fall within EC policy competence.

When the TEU entered into force in November 1993, the Commission had amassed more than 30 years' experience of conducting external economic relations. While jealousy of its prerogatives in this field is understandable, it has undoubtedly contributed to the problems affecting overall coordination of external activities. Nevertheless it is acknowledged that the Commission should be 'more proactive in CFSP and allow ideas to be subsumed within a Presidency paper. There must be a sense of the greater interest of the Union' (Interview, Commission DGI, July 1997).

After little more than two years of the CFSP's operation, it had become clear that it did not represent the major change from EPC anticipated by its proponents; and that greater commitment both from the Commission and from the Member States would be required if CFSP was to be effective. Below we examine the record of CFSP from its inauguration in 1993, as a prelude to discussing the most recent attempt, in the 1997 Amsterdam Treaty, to enhance its effectiveness.

The operation of CFSP

The TEU gave the European Council responsibility for providing the 'general political guidelines' of the Union. The 1993 Brussels European Council, in consequence, set out the following five priority areas for CFSP joint actions:

- Promotion of a stable peace in Europe through reinforcement of the democratic processes in CEE countries.

- The Middle East: support for the peace process through political, economic and financial means.

- South Africa: support for the transition to a multi-racial democracy through assisting with the electoral process and through development cooperation.

- Former Yugoslavia: continued support for conflict resolution efforts and humanitarian action.

- Russia: support for the democratic process through assisting with the monitoring of elections.

Table 6.1 indicates that these broad policy guidelines have been followed, albeit to varying degrees, and that the scope of joint actions has expanded, notably to include arms control and nuclear non-proliferation issues and in response to conflict in the Great Lakes region of Africa. While this may suggest that the CFSP system is capable of defining and pursuing policy goals, the specifically 'political' (Pillar II) aspects of the ensuing joint actions have been relatively modest. Thus, in the priority areas identified by the 1993 European Council, the Community/Commission, as we shall see, has played a major role.

Much effort has focused upon former Yugoslavia, where CFSP initiatives have undoubtedly contributed to the peace process, in support of UN and

Table 6.1 Principal CFSP joint actions under Article J.3, 1993–7.[1]

Area	Event	Date
Ex-Yugoslavia	Support for the convoying of humanitarian aid in Bosnia–Herzegovina	1993
	Support for EU administration of Mostar	1994
	Support for the electoral process in Bosnia–Herzegovina	1995
	Appointment of a Special Envoy for the city of Mostar	1996
	Support for local elections in Bosnia–Herzegovina	1997
Russian Federation	Dispatch of a team of observers to support parliamentary elections	1993
South Africa	Support for the transition towards a democratic and multi-racial South Africa	1993
Stability Pact	Conferences and diplomacy to promote harmonious relations between countries of Central and Eastern Europe	1993
Middle East	Support for the peace process	1994
	Coordination of international operation to support electoral process for Palestinian Council	1995
Great Lakes Region	Appointment of EU Special Envoy to the Great Lakes Region of Africa	1996
	Support for democratic transition in Zaire	1996
Non-proliferation	Preparation for 1995 conference on Non-Proliferation Treaty	1994
	Export controls, dual-use goods	1994
	Participation in Korean Peninsula Energy Development Organization (KEDO)	1996

Note

1 Joint actions which involve modification or extension of ongoing actions are omitted. The majority of these apply to ex-Yugoslavia.

NATO efforts. Thus the EU assumed responsibility, under a UN-appointed mayor, for administration of the city of Mostar in Bosnia–Herzegovina. Here WEU personnel have been utilized in a policing role. Further CFSP commitments included assistance in monitoring the 1996 Bosnian elections and support for the convoying of humanitarian aid. However the humanitarian aid and reconstruction programmes themselves (totalling 187 million ECU in 1996) fall within Pillar I and are the responsibility of the European Community Humanitarian Office (ECHO). Despite this division of responsibility there is said to be a relatively coherent overall strategy, and good cooperation between the Pillars. This reflects, in part, political impetus from Member State governments, themselves under considerable pressure to 'do something' (Interview, Council Secretariat DGE, July 1997).

In the case of CFSP's first priority – relations with the CEE countries – the division of responsibility between the Pillars has very clearly tilted towards the Community. Here the CFSP joint action was the Stability Pact, which involved a series of 'preventive diplomacy' initiatives aimed at preventing border disputes between CEEC.[23] This initiative, which operated between May 1994 and March 1995, appears modest when compared with the EC's major, long-term role in managing the Phare programme, negotiating the Europe Agreements and developing pre-accession strategies in collaboration with candidate countries (see Chapter 5 for discussion of these matters). Nevertheless several of these initiatives include a cross-pillar element – the Europe Agreements, for example, provide for 'political dialogue'; that is discussion of CFSP matters.

Relations with Russia have followed a similar pattern, although here political direction through the CFSP process has been more evident. Support in monitoring the 1993 Russian parliamentary elections was an early CFSP joint action. At the same time the Commission was involved in negotiating the terms of a Partnership and Cooperation Agreement. However the Chechen crisis erupted as these negotiations were reaching conclusion, and the Partnership Agreement then became a 'political' issue. Consequently decisions on whether, and when, the negotiations should be concluded were taken in the CFSP forum (Interview, Council Secretariat DGE, February 1997).

The case of South Africa also provides an interesting example of CFSP in operation, and of the CFSP/EC division of labour. Here the scope of the joint action was a matter of controversy between Member States. The UK government, in particular, was anxious to preserve the traditional separation between political and economic matters, and hence to limit the joint action to electoral observation. In the event, however, the joint action specified both support for the 1994 elections and for the broader processes of political and economic development. The election monitoring exercise, which involved equal representation from each Member State and the Commission, with administrative coordination by DGIA, has been judged 'an almost unqualified success' (Holland 1995:567). However observing elections, as

Holland concedes, is a specific, finite task upon which all Member States can readily agree. Negotiation of the development cooperation aspect of the package, a Commission (DGVIII) responsibility, has proved more controversial. Indeed the Commission's negotiations have been obstructed by the insistence of Member States, led by the German government, that a 'negative list' – comprising 39% of South African agricultural products – be excluded from the Trade and Cooperation Agreement' (Euro-CIDSE March/April 1996:10). Two years later, these negotiations have yet to be concluded. Clearly the inclusive nature of the joint action's wording has not contributed significantly to overall coherence in this policy area.

It is in relation to the Middle East peace process that EU/EC involvement has, arguably, been most significant – and least acknowledged. Reflecting considerable European interests in the region, and long-term EC and EPC involvement,[24] it was inevitable that support for the peace process would be a priority of CFSP. In political terms there has been a consistent effort to adopt a policy position distinct from that of the US; indeed EPC/CFSP declarations have traditionally been more readily critical of Israeli actions and supportive of the Palestinian cause. This has increasingly been accompanied by substantial economic assistance to the Palestinians. The EC is now the principal donor, providing 45 per cent of all assistance in 1996; indeed at 120 million Dollars, the European contribution was almost twice that of the US. In particular the EC has contributed to the 'running costs' – salaries of officials, police, teachers – of the Palestinian Authority (Hollis 1997:21). It has been agreed that financial support will continue after expiry of the current arrangements at the end of 1998.[25]

Given the scale of the EU effort, it is not surprising that EU officials and Member State ministers have been exasperated by the continued domination of the peace process by the US government. Indeed the US has failed even to invite European representatives to summit meetings, thus denying the EU the political role it seeks 'based on its new responsibility for bankrolling that process' (Hollis 1997:21). A very specific example of failure to recognize EU efforts relates to the 1995 elections for the Palestinian Authority, the conduct and monitoring of which (at a cost of 17.5 million ECU) was the subject of a CFSP joint action. Ultimately, however, the EU effort was almost unnoticed, since 'Jimmy Carter arrived on election day and got all the visibility' (Interview, external Mission, January 1996). Thus, it is argued, the peace process might be likened to 'a ship with the US on the bridge and the EU in the engine room, shovelling coal' (Interview, Council Secretariat DGE, July 1997).[26]

While the exasperation of EU officials is understandable, the poor visibility of EU initiatives cannot be attributed only to the ability of US representatives to attract media attention. Considerable responsibility lies with the EU itself. There has been poor coordination between the Pillars in this policy area, and evidence of interinstitutional rivalry. An example, here, is the considerable suspicion with which Commission officials met the appointment of Miguel Moratinos as CFSP Special Envoy to the Middle East. This was reflected at several levels, including reluctance of EC Delegation staff to provide logistical support on the ground (Interview, Council Secretariat DGE, July 1997). On occasion, too, there has also been highly public controversy over the policy of individual Member States[27] – although Robin Cook's visit to the region on behalf of the 1998 UK Presidency took place with the prior knowledge and approval of all Member States.

These examples have highlighted two central weaknesses of CFSP – lack of overall coherence in policy formulation and inadequate articulation between policy making and policy implementation. These weaknesses are reflected in poor visibility and failure to assert the EU's identity as an actor in world politics. However, given that a major contribution of CFSP has been assistance with election monitoring, a task in which the UN and the OSCE are also very much involved, it is not clear that there is a strong will to assert a collective identity in this way. It is tempting, in consequence, to conclude that CFSP has proved little more effective than its predecessor.

Those closely involved with CFSP, both within and outside the EU, nevertheless argue that its effectiveness should not be assessed solely through examining the record of joint actions; but that a number of qualitative, and less tangible, differences distinguish CFSP from EPC. This is attributable, not so much to the discovery of a new will to cooperate, but to the gradual evolution of understandings and practices – in response both to external expectations and incremental changes internally.

Internally, the development of CFSP has been characterized by 'cultural and generational change', the latter assisted by the accession of new Member States in 1995. Thus Working Group meetings under CFSP are not only more frequent but also more meaningful than in the days of EPC, despite the maintenance of an 'EPC mentality' in some Working Groups. In successful Working Groups, however, there is 'tremendous pressure to get a result'. This reflects both external pressure, generated by the expectations of third parties, and the impetus provided by more proactive Community involvement (Interview, Council Secretariat DGE, July 1997).

The evolution of meanings and practices characteristic of the change from EPC to CFSP is exemplified by the developing EU/US relationship. Here, although contacts had become 'steadily more numerous and intense' since the 1990 Transatlantic Declaration initiated a system of regular meetings at political and official levels, the increasing range and depth of the US/EU dialogue following introduction of CFSP necessitated appointment of additional staff at the US Mission to the EU.[28] This occurred during a year (1995) when the US cut over 100 diplomatic posts elsewhere in Europe. A contributory factor, here, was the increasing concentration of CFSP in Brussels rather than in Member State capitals. This has resulted in discontinuation of the system whereby a US official, known as the 'rover', was formally based in Brussels but operated from US Embassies in Presidency capitals, in order to follow the EPC process. Today US Embassies prefer to handle relations with the Presidency themselves; they increasingly see the EU as 'interesting turf'. Consequently a task of the former 'rover' is to support the Embassies by organizing six-monthly 'torch passing' consultations, which mirror the changing composition of the EU troika (Interview, US Mission, January 1996).

Intensification of the EU/US relationship is illustrated by the New Transatlantic Agenda (NTA) and accompanying Joint US/EU Action Plan, adopted in December 1995. Covering the work of all three Pillars of the Union, the NTA is both more comprehensive and more action oriented than its 1990 predecessor. (See Chapter 2 for fuller discussion of the NTA.) The major focus on Pillar II matters leaves no doubt that the US government 'supports the CFSP very strongly' – as a means of enhancing the EU's effectiveness as a global actor capable of burden-sharing with the US in Europe and beyond (Interview, US Mission, January 1996).[29]

Despite the cross-pillar focus of the NTA, in practice conduct of the EU/US dialogue has remained very much the province of the Commission, which is jealous of its well established relationship with the US administration on trade matters (discussed in detail in Chapter 2). Consequently on Pillar II and III matters, where 'constitutionally' there should be a clear lead from the Presidency, the Commission has tended to regard the Presidency as an interloper (Interview, Council Secretariat DGE, July 1997). Thus, despite increased expectations of CFSP, and some evidence of qualitative change since the days of EPC, these enduring tensions provide a major obstacle to the formulation of coherent external policies. They remain central to criticisms of the CFSP's operation and to proposals for further reform.

THE AMSTERDAM TREATY REFORMS: MAKING THE CFSP WORK?

The TEU provided for a further IGC to review its operation, commencing in 1996. In the event, delays in ratification meant that the review process began scarcely two years after entry into force of the Treaty. Nevertheless it was not considered premature, by the Council or the Commission in their respective reports on the TEU's operation, to express disappointment at the failure to progress towards a more proactive, coordinated approach to external policy (Council 1995; Commission 1995b). In consequence it was expected that external policy would be among the major areas of debate at the IGC. The ensuing Amsterdam Treaty provisions indicate that some progress was made in relation to the two central problems affecting external policy –

- **The coordination problem:** affecting policy formulation and implementation within and across Pillars.

- **The visibility problem**: affecting the ability of the EU to assert its identity as an actor in global politics.

The Amsterdam provisions on defence, although clearly impinging upon policy implementation, are dealt with in Chapter 7.

Policy formulation in Pillar II

The Amsterdam Treaty reflects experience with the operation of CFSP since 1993. Most of the provisions in this area had been agreed long before the conclusion of the IGC and are part of an evolutionary process. Thus the intention of the Amsterdam Treaty amendments is to increase the effectiveness of policy formulation in the CFSP process through clarifying and strengthening the provisions of the TEU.

Member State governments had a common intent to provide a strategic direction for policy at the highest level. To this end the European Council has been given an explicit strategic role – to 'decide on common strategies to be implemented by the Union in areas where the Member States have important interests in common'. Furthermore, this new concept of 'common strategies' requires that the European Council 'set out their objectives, duration and the means to be made available by the Union and the Member States' (Art.J.3.2 [13.2]). This may be broadly drawn but it contains real substance when compared with the kind of outputs that have previously emerged from European Councils. The intention is to strengthen the consistency of the CFSP by involving heads of government and the Commission in strategic decision making. The success of this innovation will inevitably depend upon the ability of the European Council to reach agreement. This, in turn, will reflect the quality of preparatory work undertaken by the CFSP Secretariat, the Working Groups, PoCo, the Presidency and the Council in presenting policy options to the European Council.

To give effect to a common strategy, once adopted, the Council is charged with adopting joint actions and common positions. In a further attempt to increase the effectiveness of policy making in this area, joint actions and common positions, which had become a source of confusion, are now more carefully defined. Thus joint actions are intended to address 'specific situations where operational action by the Union is required' (Art.J.4.1 [14.1]). Common positions are seen as broader in nature, hence they 'shall define the approach of the Union to a particular matter of a geographic or thematic nature' (Art.J.5 [15]).

In a potentially significant change from the original TEU provisions, joint actions will normally be implemented by qualified majority voting. The Amsterdam amendment envisages that use of QMV will be automatic once a common strategy has been unanimously agreed by the European Council. Inevitably, in this most sensitive of areas for the susceptibilities of Member State governments, the introduction of majority voting is subject to safeguards. QMV may not be applied to decisions 'having military or defence implications'. This provision may seem to have wide application to any likely CFSP actions but, even if it does not, Member States can still have recourse to the so-called 'emergency brake'. This is a right of veto over the taking of a decision by QMV on the basis of 'important and stated reasons of national policy' (Art.J.13.2 [23.2]). Users of the 'emergency brake' will, however, face problems. The Council, acting by QMV, may refer the matter upwards to the European Council for a unanimous decision, where the Prime Minister of the vetoing Member State would have to justify its use to his or her colleagues.

The provisions on QMV may not have a great deal of immediate practical significance because Member States will usually seek to avoid taking formal votes in the Council – although this is not to deny that the existence of voting procedures will inevitably influence their calculations. In this context, the more important development in the Amsterdam Treaty may be the 'constructive abstention' procedure. This allows the Council to proceed with a decision even though one or more Member States (but no more than the Members whose votes would constitute one-third of the total under QMV procedures) prefer to abstain. An abstaining Member State –

> shall not be obliged to apply the decision, but shall accept that the decision commits the Union. In a spirit of mutual solidarity, the Member State concerned shall refrain from any action likely to conflict with or impede Union action based on that decision and the other Member States shall reflect its position.
>
> (Art.J.13.1 [23.1])

This practical addition to CFSP procedures should allow the Council to circumvent particular national difficulties with a proposed policy.

To assist the Presidency and European Council in formulating policy the Amsterdam Treaty provides, in a Declaration to the Final Act, for a new Policy Planning and Early Warning Unit to be established within the General Secretariat of the Council. The Declaration indicates that its tasks will involve monitoring international developments and providing 'timely assessments and early warning'. But it will also have a more proactive role in assessing the 'Union's foreign and security policy interests and identifying areas where the CFSP could focus in future'. The Unit will consist of personnel drawn from the General Secretariat, the Member States, the Commission and the Western European Union (WEU). While it was clearly envisaged that the unit would make an important contribution to overall policy coordination, much will depend upon the quality of seconded personnel and the willingness of Member State governments to share information.[30]

Policy formulation in Pillar I

As previously noted, the structure of the Commission and the proliferation of DGs dealing with external policy has impeded policy coordination in Pillar I. Proposals to address this problem, in particular through strengthening the role of the Commission President, were included in a *Communication* to the 1996–7 IGC (Commission 1997a). These proposals were reflected in the Amsterdam Treaty through an addition to Article 163 [219] of the TEC, which states 'the Commission shall work under the political guidance of its President'. Additionally a 'Declaration on the organization and functioning of the Commission' accords to the President 'broad discretion' in allocating and reshuffling portfolios. The Declaration also notes with approval the Commission's intention to reorganize its departments – 'in particular the desirability of bringing external relations under the responsibility of a Vice-President'. (Declaration 32, TEC). There is optimism among Commission officials that the reforms, which are intended to be in place when the new Commission takes up office in 2000, 'will definitely change the atmosphere of competition between the DGs' (Interview, Commission DGI, July 1997).[31]

Cross-pillar policy coordination

During negotiation of the Amsterdam Treaty the provisions on CFSP and external economic relations were linked; indeed they appeared in the draft Treaty under a single heading – 'Section III: An effective and coherent external policy' (Conference of the Representatives of the Governments of the Member States 1997:96). This attempt to combine these areas was a negotiating ploy intended to demonstrate the logic of an overall approach to external policy (Interview, Council Secretariat DGE, October 1997). Ultimately, Member State insistence upon maintaining the pillar structure of the Union ensured that the symbolically important notion of 'external policy' was lost. CFSP continues to be a TEU policy area; external economic relations a TEC competence.

In the light of this failure formally to link the pillars, the Amsterdam Treaty merely reiterates the TEU provision that consistency of 'external activities as a whole' shall be ensured by the Council and Commission, adding the stipulation that the two institutions 'shall cooperate to this end' (Article C [3]) This tacit recognition that they have not always acted cooperatively might be read in conjunction with a new clause providing for the Council to 'request the Commission' to submit proposals for implementation of a joint action (Art.J.4.4 [14.4]). This has been variously interpreted as acknowledging the importance of the Commission's role, particularly in policy implementation, and providing a mechanism for requiring the Commission to act in areas where it may be tempted to drag its feet (Interviews: Commission DGIA, July 1997; UK Foreign and Commonwealth Office, September 1997).

In order to facilitate Council/Commission cooperation it is anticipated that a Commission Vice-President with overall responsibility for external relations will become the 'special interlocutor of the Foreign Ministers' (Commission 1997a:9). A further provision which will potentially strengthen the Commission's involvement with CFSP is its participation in the proposed Policy Planning and Analysis Unit. This hardly denotes a significant increase in Community involvement, however, and the Amsterdam provisions fall far short of according to the Commission a role commensurate with its Pillar I policy implementation responsibilities.

The financing for CFSP is the final cross-pillar issue to be addressed by the Amsterdam Treaty. Much more detail than previously is provided in the new Article J.18 [28], and more particularly in the attached Inter Institutional Agreement. The new procedures are designed to speed the disbursement of funds and remove blockages.

Visibility: the political and legal personality of the Union

Problems associated with the ambiguous status of the EC/EU, not least the confusion and exasperation of third parties, have been a recurring theme in preceding chapters. More specifically, the inability of the EU to make legally binding agreements has proved an impediment in the area of CFSP, as the Mostar example demonstrates.

The framers of the Treaty of Amsterdam sought to resolve these difficulties by providing the Union with legal personality. However, explicit legal personality is not granted to the Union in the Treaty – apparently at the insistence of the UK government. Instead there is legal personality 'in all but name' (Interview, Council Secretariat DGE, July 1997). Thus Article J.14 [24] provides a procedure whereby the Union, represented by the Presidency, can negotiate agreements through a unanimous Council authorization – and conclude them, again by a unanimous Council vote. Such agreements, as well as involving Pillar II CFSP matters, can also now involve Pillar III provisions on police and judicial cooperation. However the underlying concerns of Member States are revealed in Declarations attached to the Final Act, which state that these provisions do not imply any transfer of competence.

The incorporation in the Community pillar, as Title IIIa of the TEC, of policy on 'Visas, asylum, immigration and other policies related to free movement of persons' is arguably the most significant innovation of the Amsterdam Treaty. It has important implications for external policy, and in particular for representation in third countries, which Member States remain reluctant to address. After five years of discussion plans are not yet finalized for a common mission in Abuja – to be entitled 'The Common Embassies of the Delegation of the Commission of the European Community and the Member States of the European Union'. In anticipation of the Amsterdam proposals in this area, consular facilities will be common.

Of greater political significance is the response provided by the Amsterdam Treaty to Henry Kissinger's well known jibe about Europe's telephone number. There is to be a permanent High Representative for the CFSP, who will be the Secretary-General to the Council (the administrative duties of the present Secretary-General to be undertaken by a new Deputy Secretary-General).[32] The functions of the Secretary-General of the Council, High Representative for the common foreign and security policy are to:

> assist the Council in matters coming within the scope of the common foreign and security policy, in particular through contributing to the formulation, preparation and implementation of policy decisions, and, when appropriate and acting on behalf of the Council at the request of the Presidency, through conducting political dialogue with third parties.
> (Art.J.13 [23])

The establishment of the new High Representative to assist the Presidency is coupled with the end of the troika arrangements involving past and future Presidencies. Under the Amsterdam provisions assistance 'if need be' will be provided only by the next Member State to hold the Presidency (Art.J.8.8 [18.8]). The implication is that permanence and 'institutional memory' in Union foreign policy will now be provided by the High Representative, supported by the General Secretariat of the Council. The Commission remains 'fully associated' in these tasks and it is anticipated that the Vice-President with responsibility for external relations will represent the Commission in this new troika. Again this arrangement is disappointing for the Commission, which had hoped to see an enhanced role for its President in external representation. Instead the location of the High Representative in the Council Secretariat further consolidates the intergovernmental character of CFSP. Potentially, also, it further enhances the role of the Council Secretariat in this policy area.

The Amsterdam Treaty also provides a formal basis for the practice of appointing 'special representatives' or envoys with a mandate to represent the Union on particular issues (Art.J.8.5 [18.5]). This provision might usefully be read alongside Article J.10 [20], which reiterates the exhortation that overseas Missions of the Member States and the Commission 'shall step up cooperation'. There is acknowledged to be a very patchy record of cooperation in this respect, which has been reflected in misunderstandings about the role of EU special envoys and, in particular, about the support such envoys should expect from EC Delegation staff. However the Commission has recently approved proposals for strengthening its external service, and it is hoped that, in addition to generally enhancing the effectiveness of the service, this will support cross-pillar coordination in third countries. The programme, which was approved in April 1997, focuses upon recruitment, training and the obligation to serve abroad for staff of external relations DGs.

CONCLUSION

We have outlined the slow and often faltering evolution of a foreign policy system for the EC/EU since 1970. In the face of significant divisions between Member States concerning the possibility and desirability of common policy in this area, the EPC system was a compromise which facilitated routine consultation and cooperation, but precluded proactive policy formulation. However in the late 1980s the successful deepening of policy integration internally, combined with the dramatically changed external policy environment of the immediate post-Cold War period, appeared to provide the conditions for significant progress towards a common foreign policy. In the event the CFSP provisions of the TEU, while strengthening the policy making machinery, proved a disappointment to integrationists who had anticipated at least partial communitarization of this policy area. Thus CFSP remained an intergovernmental process, subject almost entirely to unanimous voting procedures. Indeed the TEU, in creating the pillar structure of the Union, further consolidated the separation between external economic relations and foreign policy.

Despite this, CFSP marked an important stage in the evolution of foreign policy. The location of a dedicated CFSP Unit within the Secretariat-General of the Council of Ministers, and the general intensification of the CFSP processes, heralded a perceptible shift towards the basing of EU foreign policy making procedures in Brussels rather than in communication between officials in national capitals. This has undoubtedly placed heavy demands upon national officials who participate in the specialized CFSP Working Groups or in PoCo – which now meets approximately every ten days compared with monthly meetings under EPC arrangements. Our interviews revealed that this shift has also been apparent to third party representatives – evidenced, in particular, by the changed focus of procedures and staffing levels of the US Mission and Embassies.

In outlining these developments we have also identified a number of enduring problems, of which the most significant is lack of commitment, by Member State governments, to the achievement of coherent and effective external policy. This does not simply reflect divisions over the content and direction of policy, which impede foreign policy formulation in other pluralistic political systems, not least the USA. Rather there are, in the EU context, fundamental divisions between Member States over the extent to which common policies are desirable at the EU level. These divisions impinge, in turn, upon the overall coordination of external policy.

Today, as in the past, divisions over policy coordination crystallize around the nature and extent of Commission involvement with CFSP or, more specifically, the extent to which CFSP should be communitarized. Thus, during the 1996–7 IGC six Member States – Denmark, Finland, France, Portugal, Sweden and the UK – remained opposed to any aspect of Pillar II being transferred to the Community; the remainder supported limited communitarization (European Policy Centre 1996). This reflects enduring distrust of the Commission's external activities, which tends to be replicated at all levels in the CFSP system – from the separation of Working Groups into Pillar I and II configurations dealing with the same topic or region, to tensions between Commission Delegations and Member State Missions in third countries. Consequently the problems affecting cross-pillar policy coordination are fundamental. In operational terms, from use of the economic instruments of statecraft to the simple mechanics of providing food, lodging and travel for a Union Special Representative, the two are inextricably linked.

The reforms introduced by the Treaty of Amsterdam largely fail to address this issue. As we have seen, the Amsterdam provisions represent an extension of the existing compromise. CFSP remains firmly in Pillar II but there has been a further attempt to strengthen decision making capacity, including a significant extension of majority voting – albeit subject to safeguards. The introduction of a 'constructive abstention' procedure also suggests an expedient compromise between the requirements for collective action and the national susceptibilities of an individual Member State.

Further evidence of the consolidation of CFSP in Pillar II is the enhanced role of the General Secretariat of the Council – an intergovernmental institution which has the advantage of sitting at the right hand of the Presidency. A reading of the Amsterdam Treaty might suggest that the opportunities thus provided have been adroitly used.[33] At the same time, the creation of a 'Mr or Ms CFSP', as the High Representative is colloquially known, again within the Council Secretariat, will give the Union a focal point for third parties, even if formal legal status has been denied to the Union.

These reforms may assist in strengthening the leadership capacity of the Presidency and the European Council, and hence the ability to provide overall political direction. However a coherent and effective external policy would inevitably require a more proactive input from the Commission at a number of levels, given its role in implementation and the sheer scale of its external relations effort. Ultimately it cannot make sense that the Union operates two external affairs bureaucracies alongside national ministries. Equally, the existence of separate Commission Delegations and national embassies and consulates in third countries appears, to say the least, inefficient in the light of the incorporation of Pillar III immigration and asylum issues into Pillar I at Amsterdam. Moreover the cost of this duplication of effort has become increasingly apparent, not least as Member States have attempted to extend separate representation to the new states created by the disintegration of the Soviet Union.[34]

Although the Amsterdam Treaty does not resolve the central problem of incoherence between the Pillars, it has refined and strengthened the CFSP mechanisms. A striking aspect of the package is the extent of detail included in the CFSP provisions – reflecting the insights of those who have attempted to operate the nascent CFSP. This extends from funding questions to the security clearance of General Secretariat staff.

The institutional machine has been improved – it remains to be seen whether the Member States will be prepared to use it effectively. There are indications of growing awareness, even in large Member States, that it is both desirable and necessary to do so. As we noted at the start of this chapter, the UK government, traditionally among those most sceptical of increased integration, has acknowledged the combined impact, upon its capacity to formulate an independent foreign policy, of EU membership and the changing conditions of interdependence in the international system, (FCO, DTI 1996:17–18). Ultimately Member State governments have an interest in creating a European actor capable of connecting the economic power of the EC to some form of collective political purpose.

In typically low-key, but incremental fashion, this is already occurring. Today, meetings of the General Affairs Council routinely include, alongside traditional 'external relations' items, a wide range of CFSP matters requiring cross-pillar cooperation. Among the numerous items discussed at the 2070th Council meeting (General Affairs) in February 1998, are the following examples –

> The EU will further develop the EU–China cooperation in the field of human rights conducted by the European Commission.
>
> (Council 1998:8)

> The Council called on the authorities in Belgrade and the leadership of the Kosovo Albanian community urgently to begin a full and construc-tive dialogue. It agreed that implementation of the Education Agreement would be an important step, *which the EU would be prepared to support substantially* . . .
>
> (*ibid*:10 emphasis added)

These small steps play their part in constructing, incrementally, the EU's role as an actor in global politics. This process has undoubtedly gained impetus from significantly increased expectations of policy responses from the EU, in combination with new understandings about the nature of foreign and security policy in an interdependent, post-Cold War world.

7 Defence of the Union, security of Europe

In this chapter we move beyond examination of the various sectors of EC/EU external policy, to consider broader issues associated with the EU's role in post-Cold War Europe. Discussion ranges from the aspiration, enshrined in the Treaty on European Union, to construct a common defence for the EU, to the potential for the EU to play a central role in ensuring the stability and security of Europe as a whole. These issues are highly significant. They place the EU at the heart of major contemporary debates concerning European security – in which two very different sets of understandings compete to shape approaches to security issues. They also evoke earlier controversies over the nature of the EC/EU which impinge, in turn, upon its capacity as an actor in global politics.

In the early 1970s, when the EPC system of foreign policy cooperation was initiated, fears were expressed that this would inevitably lead to the development of a predatory, militarized 'European super-state' (Galtung 1973). Alternatively, it was contended, the EC should remain a 'civilian power', playing an important role in the promotion of world peace (Duchêne 1972). In the event, as the previous chapter demonstrated, the achievements of EPC were modest and EC influence, whether benign or malign, failed to meet these early expectations.

Twenty years later, the terms of the renewed debate reflect recent failures, not least the inability to provide an effective response to the outbreak, in 1991, of violent conflict in the Yugoslav Federal Republic.[1] The EU was criticized for its inability to act 'in the manner of a conventional superpower' (Buchan 1993:4). Ultimately, it was contended, 'defence is the key to the development of the Community's place in the world' (Hill 1993:318). This sentiment is frequently echoed in media reporting, where absence of military instruments directly at the disposal of the EU is seen as an impediment to the achievement of external policy aims generally.[2] Thus the EU as an external actor is contrasted with a (militarily strong) state – and found wanting. This appraisal undoubtedly contributed to pressure for the development of an EU defence dimension, provision for which was included, as an aspiration for the future, in Article J.4 [14] of the Treaty on European Union.

As in the 1970s, however, there is an alternative perspective informing contemporary debate. This focuses upon the EU's presence as an 'island of peace' in Europe, serving as a reference point for its relatively unstable neighbours to the East and South (Tunander 1997). From this perspective both the security of the EU itself, and of the region more widely, can best be ensured through extension of the stability and prosperity enjoyed within the EU. Consequently the key security challenge to the EU is not defence of its territory, which is no longer the central issue, but the need to construct a policy towards its 'near abroad' which responds in a sensitive manner to aspirations for inclusion and fears of exclusion. Thus it is important to ensure that access to the communication and support networks provided by the EC/EU is prioritized; and the construction of exclusionary, defensive walls avoided. Thus, in the translation of presence into actorness, the 'soft' security provided by development assistance and humanitarian aid is likely to be more efficacious than the 'hard' security of military defence.[3]

This broad approach to security and stability in Europe clearly emphasizes the significance of the EU's 'civilian' role. There are, nevertheless, limits to the capacity, and will, to pursue policies based upon inclusion, whether through enlargement or various forms of structured support. There are also regions, particularly towards the periphery of Europe, which are evidently unaffected by the EU's supposed stabilizing influence. Here humanitarian concerns, as well as the broader interests of European security, may on occasion demand some form of military intervention. There are many lessons to be learned from the tragic conflicts in ex-Yugoslavia, but one must surely be that a more robust approach to conflict management in the early stages would have been more effective than the EU's exclusively civilian efforts. In recognition of this, the Amsterdam Treaty introduces explicit reference to 'humanitarian and rescue tasks, peacekeeping tasks and tasks of combat forces in crisis management, including peacemaking' (Article J.7.2 [17.2]).

Consideration of European security in the post-Cold War environment suggests, in principle, three potential roles for the EU –

- defence of the Union's territory;
- intervention in conflicts beyond EU borders;
- provision of stability and security for the wider Europe.

In practice, all three of these roles are problematic, in terms of EU capability; and contested, not least by claims that NATO is the more appropriate organization to perform them. Assessment of the EU's potential as an actor in each of the three security dimensions thus necessitates brief consideration of NATO's parallel involvement and, in particular, the extent to which there has been complementarity in the post-Cold War evolution of the two organizations.

In important ways, the EU's potential as a security actor is based upon a fourth security dimension – the role of the EU itself as an 'island of peace'.

Consequently we begin with a brief examination of the genesis of this under-lying dimension of security, which is essentially a reflection of presence rather than purposive action.

EVOLUTION OF THE EC/EU AS A COMMUNITY OF SECURITY

In the aftermath of the Second World War, the desire to maintain peace in Europe was a major concern of policy makers, providing significant impetus for cooperation and integration between the countries of Western Europe. *Agenda 2000* acknowledges the success of these efforts –

> Over the last four decades and in line with the basic intentions of Europe's founders, the Member States have developed between them a real Community of security within which it is inconceivable that there would be the slightest threat of recourse to force as a means of settling disputes.
>
> (Commission 1997c:27)

Today this is a largely taken-for-granted achievement. In the early years, however, this outcome was by no means assured. Despite much rhetoric about the desirability of creating some form of federal Europe it appeared that, as in the past, the construction of defensive walls rather than the for-ging of integrative links would be the most likely approach to security prob-lems in Western Europe. The events of this period, and the policy responses they provoked, are crucial to an understanding of the EU's construction as a 'Community of security'.

The first post-war cooperative ventures between West European countries were rooted in concern to prevent a resurgence of German militarism. Thus the 1947 Treaty of Dunkirk was a mutual defence agreement between the UK and France. This was extended, a year later, to include the Benelux countries, becoming the Brussels Treaty. The members of the Brussels Treaty Organization agreed 'to take such steps as may be held necessary in the event of renewal by Germany of a policy of aggression'. This agreement was reinforced by a generalized collective defence commitment should any of the signatories be 'the object of an armed attack' (Article V).

By mid 1948, however, it had become increasingly clear that peace was threatened not so much by renewed German aggression as by the rapidly deteriorating relations between Western governments and the Soviet Union. In this tense period the protection offered by membership of the Brussels Treaty Organization appeared far from adequate. Consequently, immedi-ately after signature of the Treaty, its members began negotiations with the governments of the USA and Canada for establishment of a transatlantic collective defence arrangement. The ensuing Washington Treaty, which created the North Atlantic Treaty Organization (NATO) and to which Denmark, Iceland, Italy, Norway and Portugal also acceded as founding members, entered into force in August 1949. NATO participation formally committed the USA and Canada to the defence of Western Europe; and, ultimately, to the maintenance of a formidable military presence in Europe throughout the Cold War period.

While this commitment formed the backbone of the West European security architecture, NATO was an exclusively defensive alliance focused upon potential aggression from the Soviet Union. In consequence it did not resolve the internal security problems of Western Europe, of which the most sensitive was the relationship between France and Germany. Nor did it adequately determine the role to be played by the West Europeans in their own defence.

These issues surfaced only a year after the creation of the Atlantic Alliance, when the US's costly involvement in the Korean War convinced American policy makers that West European states should assume greater responsibility for their own defence. To this end the US government pressed for German rearmament and the construction of a European defence force, including ten German divisions, under NATO command. This was vehemently rejected by the French government, which produced an alternative proposal – for establishment of a European Defence Community (EDC). This essentially federalist proposal envisaged a fully integrated European Army 'tied to political institutions of a united Europe' – including a European Minister of Defence (Weigall and Stirk 1992:75). For French policy makers the proposed EDC had the advantage of placing German rearmament under European political control.

The EDC proposal was the subject of intense and prolonged debate, not least in France. In 1952 the Treaty establishing the European Defence Community was opened for signature and was eventually ratified by Belgium, Germany, Luxembourg and the Netherlands, with Italy on the point of ratification. In August, 1954, however, the French National Assembly rejected the proposal by a substantial majority. The significance of these events cannot be overestimated. The measures taken to meet this crisis, as we shall see, were directly responsible for the subsequent evolution of the EC as a civilian power.

In defence terms the difficulties caused by the collapse of the EDC proposals were quickly resolved. On a UK initiative it was agreed that West German rearmament would be achieved, as originally proposed, within the framework of NATO, but via an explicitly European institution, the Western European Union (WEU), created in 1954 by the amended Brussels Treaty, which was extended to include West Germany and Italy.

This compromise solution had the effect of entrenching NATO's position as the principal instrument of European defence.[4] The Western European Union established modest headquarters in London and developed an equally modest role – as a discussion forum for European NATO members when the presence of US representatives was considered undesirable. Both NATO and the WEU, however, were strictly intergovernmental organizations. Following the failure of the EDC, attempts to submit security and defence issues to supranational decision making were abandoned for the foreseeable future, and West European collaborative efforts focused upon less sensitive areas.

From 1949 NATO security guarantees effectively provided a defensive wall behind which West European governments were able to concentrate upon economic reconstruction, assisted by US financial assistance in the form of Marshall Aid. Further impetus for these efforts was provided by the establishment of the Soviet Bloc as an apparently monolithic enemy espousing a non-capitalist economic system and strongly anti-capitalist rhetoric. In these circumstances the successful regeneration of the West European capitalist economies was not only a matter of increasing prosperity and the ability to meet welfare needs – it was perceived also in terms of ensuring the survival and, indeed, demonstrating the superiority, of the capitalist system itself. In the context of the Cold War, despite the considerable emphasis upon military issues, security essentially involved the survival of competing economic and social systems. In Western Europe this was increasingly perceived in terms of economic integration.

The EDC proposals of the early 1950s were formulated alongside an earlier initiative which had both economic and security implications. Thus the European Coal and Steel Community (ECSC), established in 1952, placed the coal and steel production of its members (France, Germany, Italy and the Benelux countries) under the partial control of a supranational High Authority. At its core was the desire to pool the coal and steel resources of France and Germany, hence inextricably linking the economic recovery of these former adversaries – while also facilitating supervision of German industrial production to prevent unauthorized manufacture of armaments. Thus the aims of the ECSC were by no means simply economic; it was intended to address the major security concerns of the early Cold War period. This is made explicit in a Memorandum from Jean Monnet, in which he sets out his vision of the ECSC as the starting point of a broader European integration process[5] –

> Wherever we look in the present world situation we see nothing but deadlock – whether it be the increasing acceptance of a war that is thought to be inevitable, the problem of Germany, the continuation of French recovery, the organization of Europe . . . From such a situation there is only one way of escape: concrete, resolute action on a limited but decisive point, bringing about on this point a fundamental change, and gradually modifying the very terms of all the problems.
>
> (Jean Monnet 1950, quoted in Vaughan 1976:51)

These ideas were shared by a number of prominent Western politicians and intellectuals. They underlay establishment of the ECSC, the first of the European Communities, and they clearly reflect the desire to construct, through a process founded initially upon economic integration, a Community of security in Western Europe. In practice, of course, this construction suffered numerous problems and setbacks. Nevertheless, in the relative stability of the Cold War period, when the major players were evidently the USA and the USSR, West European politicians enjoyed a unique opportunity to construct the EC's 'civilian' role.

COMMON DEFENCE: THE TEU AND ITS AFTERMATH

The failure of the EDC initiative, and the Cold War reality that territorial defence of Western Europe as a whole was realized through NATO, ensured that for more than two decades defence-related issues were discussed outside the EC context. However in the early 1980s, as a result of tensions in the transatlantic relationship, it was proposed that the scope of the EPC process should be extended to include security and defence issues.[6] The defeat of this proposal, because of opposition from the Danish, Greek and Irish governments, led the (then) seven Western European Union members to propose, in 1984, that this organization be reactivated. While little was achieved beyond this broad aspiration, the WEU format was subsequently employed, for the first time, to coordinate naval patrols in the Persian Gulf during the Iran–Iraq war, an 'out-of-area' role which was, at that time, denied to NATO.

In 1987 the agreement by the USA and USSR to withdraw all intermediate nuclear forces (INF) heralded the end of the Cold War. Inevitably, it also initiated debate about the future of NATO – and the potential need for an exclusively European defence capability. Thus, immediately after conclusion of the INF Agreement, proposals were launched for the formation of a joint Franco–German brigade as the first step towards a European military force. Shortly afterwards the WEU adopted a 'Platform on European Security Interests' which declared that 'the construction of an integrated Europe will remain incomplete as long as it does not include security and defence' (Preamble, The Hague Platform 1987). At this time, too, Portugal and Spain were invited to join the WEU. They formally acceded in 1990, bringing the membership to nine, while Greece and Turkey also indicated a desire for WEU membership. (The evolving membership of the EU, WEU and NATO is illustrated by Table 7.1.)

Thus in the closing stages of the Cold War, and in anticipation of the 1990 IGC on Political Union, a number of preliminary steps had been taken towards creation of a European defence dimension. Ultimately these were reflected in the provisions of the Treaty on European Union. Thus Article J.4.1 [17.1] referred, somewhat cautiously, to 'the eventual framing of a common defence policy, which might in time lead to a common defence'. In

Table 7.1 Membership of NATO, WEU and EU compared.

NATO		WEU		EU	
		Full members			
Belgium	(1949)	Belgium	(1954)	Belgium	(1957)
Canada		France		France	
Denmark		Germany		Germany	
France		Italy		Italy	
Iceland		Luxembourg		Luxembourg	
Italy		Netherlands		Netherlands	
Luxembourg		UK			
Netherlands				Denmark	(1973)
Norway		Portugal	(1988)	Ireland	
Portugal		Spain		UK	
UK					
USA		Greece	(1992)	Greece	(1981)
				Portugal	(1986)
Greece	(1952)	*Associate members*		Spain	
Turkey		Iceland	(1992)		
		Norway		Austria	(1995)
Germany	(1955)	Turkey		Finland	
				Sweden	
Spain	(1982)	*Observers*			
		Denmark	(1992)		
		Ireland			
		Austria	(1995)		
		Finland			
		Sweden			
		Associate partners			
		Bulgaria	(1994)		
		Czech Rep.[1]			
		Estonia[2]			
		Hungary[1]			
		Latvia			
		Lithuania			
		Poland[1]			
		Romania			
		Slovakia			

Notes
1 Invited to begin accession negotiations by EU and NATO, June 1997.
2 Invited to begin accession negotiations by EU, June 1997 (Slovenia also invited).

the interest of achieving this aim, the Western European Union was declared to be 'an integral part of the development of the Union' and was requested 'to elaborate and implement decisions and actions of the Union which have defence implications' (Article J.4.2 [17.2]).

In a Declaration attached to the TEU, the role of the WEU was stated to be 'the defence component of the European Union' *and* 'the European pillar of the Atlantic Alliance' (Declaration I). This dual role reflects significant differences among WEU and EU members over the future European security architecture.

A second Declaration attached to the TEU extended membership invitations to EU members not yet members of the WEU – in the interest of strengthening the link with the EU. The other European members of NATO were offered associate membership – at the insistence of the UK government and in the interest of strengthening the European pillar of the Atlantic Alliance. As a consequence Iceland, Norway and Turkey became Associate Members of the WEU, but only Greece acceded to full membership. This established a situation, which seems likely to be maintained, in which all full members of the WEU are also members both of NATO and of the EU.[7] Ireland, as a neutral country, opted only for observer status in the WEU – in which it was joined, after their accession to the EU in 1995, by Austria, Finland and Sweden. Denmark, although a member of NATO, also opted for observer status; indeed the Danish government opted out of the TEU's defence provisions following popular resistance to the Treaty.

The Danish position on defence matters is of interest because of the two sets of ideas by which it is informed; and the interaction of these ideas with broader understandings about the EU's potential security role. First, Danish opinion sees the WEU as 'a bogey institution . . . fully in accordance with chauvinist, interventionist and Euro-nationalist ideas of mainly French provenance' (Heurlin 1996:180). A major factor underlying this perception is that NATO, during the Cold War, could operate only within its defensive area, whereas the WEU could theoretically have been involved in aggressive military activities. The lingering influence of this view was evident from the strong public opposition, in Denmark, to this aspect of the TEU. The second factor affecting Danish policy is a preference, shared to some extent with other Nordic and neutral countries, for a 'soft' security approach to international relations – demonstrated by the fact that Denmark's defence budget is exceeded by its expenditure on development aid and humanitarian assistance.[8]

The complexities surrounding WEU membership reflect the particular sensitivity of this policy area for Member State governments. They reveal three broad positions on European defence and security – the Atlanticists, led by the UK, proponents of an EU defence dimension, led by France, and the neutral countries plus Denmark, which prefer to de-emphasize military defence in favour of soft security. This disunity, and the associated lack of coincidence between EU and WEU membership, have inevitably impeded development of an EU defence dimension. Thus, while inclusion of reference to defence was undoubtedly a major innovation of the TEU, potentially heralding a departure from the exclusively civilian nature of the EU, it provided only a framework for future policy. Building upon this framework has proved difficult.

The TEU makes an explicit distinction between defence policy, which is considered to be prior, and a common defence, which 'might' be realized at some unspecified future date. While accommodating the concerns of those Member States which would prefer to see the EU remain a civilian power, this formula also contributed to the general ambiguity surrounding defence policy. This is due not only to the difficulty of separating policy formulation from the instruments by which policy is to be realized, but also because the Treaty provides no elucidation of what is meant either by defence policy or by a common defence. It is not clear, for example, whether defence policy is intended to subsume military aspects of security policy; nor whether common defence refers to the common organization of forces or simply to cooperation between Member States' armed forces.

The attempt to put flesh on the meagre bones of the TEU provisions has subsequently occupied attention at the WEU, and to a lesser extent at NATO – as part of the process of adapting to the post-Cold War environment.

Adaptations at the WEU

In November 1994 the WEU published its 'Preliminary Conclusions on the formulation of a common European defence policy'. This was 'directed towards the reduction of risks and uncertainties that might threaten the common values, fundamental interests and independence of the Union and its Member States' (WEU Council of Ministers 1994:2). No definition of fundamental interests was attempted, however. As Anne Deighton has observed, the banality of the recommendations shows that formulating a defence policy in the absence of an identifiable threat is 'something of a thankless task' (Deighton 1997:5).

The Maastricht Treaty also required the WEU to consider ways of enhancing its capacity for policy implementation. There was a need to clarify and develop the relationship with the EU, and to develop an operational planning capacity – and, indeed, operational capabilities. Shortly after signature of the TEU, in order to facilitate closer liaison with Brussels-based institutions, the headquarters of the WEU moved from London to Brussels. Subsequently the term of the WEU Presidency was reduced from one year to six months, with the aim of eventually harmonizing the sequence of EU and WEU Presidencies. However this cannot be achieved while membership differences remain; additionally there are concerns that a dual presidency might place excessive burdens on smaller Member States (Interview, WEU Secretariat, January 1996).

It was anticipated that the WEU's role as an 'integral part of the development of the Union' would necessitate close liaison between WEU staff, officials of the CFSP Unit in the Council Secretariat and DGIA officials. However in practice – from the perspective of the EU – the level of contact with the WEU has been disappointing. Additionally, it is claimed, information flows from the EU to the WEU are not reciprocated (Interview, Council Secretariat DGE, July 1997). The reasons for the lack of progress in this area are directly related to the WEU's structural position between the EU and NATO, which requires it to develop relationships with both organizations. In contrast to relations with the EU, the WEU/NATO relationship has been considerably strengthened in recent years. This reflects the fact that there is greater affinity between the organizational cultures, and indeed the personnel, of the two organizations; moreover the WEU has, since its creation, been dependent upon NATO in operational terms. A consequence of the enhanced WEU/NATO relationship is that the WEU is in possession of sensitive NATO information. Since EU officials lack the necessary security clearance there is a reluctance to entrust them with such information.[9]

The Amsterdam Treaty attempts to address the continuing problem of poor EU/WEU liaison through providing for WEU officials to be seconded to the Policy Planning and Early Warning Unit to be located in the Council Secretariat; and for Council Secretariat personnel to undergo security clearance.[10] Nevertheless the organizational separation, and independence of operation of the WEU, are maintained in the TOA. Consequently defence matters remain effectively outside the EU – there is, for example, no suggestion of an EU Council of Defence Ministers.

The second area to be addressed as a consequence of the TEU provisions has been the operational capacity of the WEU. In 1993 a Planning Cell was established, comprising seconded military personnel and civilian officials from WEU Member States and Associate Members.[11] Among its tasks the Planning Cell is responsible for preparation of contingency plans and the design and preparation of military exercises. The first such exercise, WEU CRISEX, took place in 1995–6. The Planning Cell also maintains a list of forces nominated by WEU members as potentially available for use in WEU operations – these Forces Answerable to the WEU are known by the 'unsuccessful acronym' FAWEU (Interview, NATO Secretariat, January 1996). They include a number of multinational forces, notably the Eurocorps, created in 1991 from the existing Franco–German brigade with the addition of contingents from Spain and Belgium. This was explicitly intended to provide the nucleus for the creation of an independent European defence force.[12] This force, and the other multinational configurations subsequently developed, are available both to the WEU and to NATO.[13]

Despite these initiatives the WEU Council of Ministers reported (1995:15) that 'the FAWEU concept has still not been put into practice in a way that would confirm the existence of a WEU capability effectively to generate force packages'. Moreover, unlike NATO, the WEU has no dedicated command and control facilities; nor, of course, does it have access to the substantial US military assets potentially available to NATO. Thus, while there has been some development of its operational capacity, the WEU remains a small and inexperienced organization with limited access to military resources.

NATO adaptations: the European security and defence identity

In the context of considerable uncertainty over NATO's future, the TEU provisions on defence were originally greeted with some suspicion at NATO. The notion of a 'European security identity and defence role' was formally endorsed at the 1991 Rome Summit (Rome Declaration on Peace and Cooperation, November 1991:2). However it was not until the 1994 Brussels Summit that the concept of a European Security and Defence Identity (ESDI) *within NATO* was developed.[14] By this time NATO had successfully expanded its tasks beyond collective defence and seemed assured of a future role.

At the Brussels Summit measures were announced to support the development of the WEU as the 'European pillar' of NATO, through elaboration of the concept of Combined Joint Task Forces (CJTF). Defined as 'a deployable multinational, multi-service formation generated and tailored for specific contingency operations' CJTF would, in principle, enable the WEU to use NATO's collective assets, particularly command centres, in order to carry out operations under WEU command (Cragg 1996:3). While progress in giving concrete form to the CJTF concept was initially slow, its fuller development was announced at the June 1997 Madrid Summit, including 'the necessary practical arrangements for release, monitoring and return of NATO assets' (Madrid Declaration 1997:3).[15] By this time the nuclei of three CJTF headquarters had been established within NATO 'parent headquarters' in Norfolk (Virginia), Naples and Brunssum (Cragg 1997:34).

Although requiring further elaboration, the CJTF concept might in time achieve its aim of enhancing the WEU's operational capability without incurring costly duplication of resources.[16] However NATO assets are not themselves substantial and it is very unclear whether, and in what circumstances, a CJTF might include US assets available to NATO. Moreover, when considered from the perspective of the aspiration to develop a common defence for the EU, the CJTF concept raises further difficulties. In particular it perpetuates WEU dependence upon NATO, since it would be necessary for the WEU to request that a CJTF be made available, with the possibility of refusal should one NATO member exercise its right of veto.[17] Additionally the requirement for 'monitoring' of assets utilized by the WEU suggests close NATO supervision of any WEU-led operation.

Finally, in relation to collective defence issues, while it is maintained that use of a CJTF for Article 5 (territorial defence) operations is 'not excluded', such use is evidently not envisaged (Cragg 1996:3).[18] It is clear that collective defence of its members' territory, albeit a residual category since the end of the Cold War, will remain primarily, if not exclusively, a NATO responsibility for as long as the Alliance persists. Although the Brussels Treaty collective defence provisions remain, on paper, the tasks envisaged for the WEU, for which a CJTF might be employed, relate to peacekeeping and crisis management beyond the territory of its members. It is to these issues that we now turn.

EXTERNAL INTERVENTION AND THE IMPACT OF YUGOSLAVIA

In the Cold War context of bloc-to-bloc confrontation there had been no demand, and hence no structured provision, for peacekeeping activities in Europe. From the perspective of NATO, maintenance of peace had been a matter of forward defence and nuclear deterrence. Consequently NATO appeared to be irrelevant to the crisis which erupted, in June 1991, in the former Yugoslavia. In these circumstances, Yugoslavia became a testing ground for post-Cold War security arrangements; and the subsequent events profoundly influenced the outcome of controversies over the most appropriate arrangements for Europe's security – not least the aspiration that the EU should develop a traditional security role.

Yugoslavia – an early test for CFSP

The initial phase of the conflict occurred during the currency of the 1990–1 IGC on Political Union, where the issues of security and defence were the subject of ongoing controversy between Member States. Consequently the crisis was perceived, by proponents of an EC security and defence dimension, as an opportunity to demonstrate the EC's ability to manage crises on its borders. Shortly after Yugoslav Federal forces entered Slovenia, Foreign Minister Jacques Poos made clear the views of the Luxembourg Presidency –

> if one problem can be solved by the Europeans, it is the Yugoslav problem. This is a European country and it is not up to the Americans. It is not up to anyone else.
>
> (Jacques Poos quoted in Smith 1996:1)

The first six months of the conflict saw considerable EC diplomatic activity as well as use of economic instruments (Salmon 1992; Buchan 1993). However proposals for military intervention, under the auspices of the WEU, were abandoned in the face of opposition, in particular from the UK.[19] Buchan is probably correct in his assessment that this proposal, which reflected IGC debates about a security and defence role for the EC rather than the state of readiness of WEU arrangements, was 'dangerously frivolous' (Buchan 1993:68).

However the EC's extensive involvement in the early stages of the conflict resulted not only from excessive enthusiasm, but also from the absence of alternatives in circumstances where the dangers of superpower confrontation were past but Cold War security arrangements had yet to be replaced.[20]

Thus the EC's role in coordinating the monitoring of ceasefires was undertaken at the request of the CSCE – whose own conciliation mechanisms, agreed only in 1990, were not yet operational.

In the event the presence of unarmed, civilian EC monitors had little effect in preserving the several ceasefires negotiated by the EC troika during 1991; moreover the monitors themselves were in considerable personal danger. In January 1992 five EC monitors were killed when their clearly marked helicopter was shot down. This tragic incident, perhaps more than any other, highlighted the limitations of an exclusively civilian approach to the conflict; and hence the need for access to peacekeeping and peacemaking capabilities. While deployment of UN peacekeeping forces provided the immediate solution, the need, in the longer term, for a European capability in this sphere was a concern for policy makers. At the WEU, in consequence, the organization's potential role in external intervention was under consideration. Similar concerns were also preoccupying NATO policy planners.

'New' security challenges: WEU and NATO adaptations

In June 1992 the WEU declared its willingness to participate in 'conflict-prevention and crisis-management measures, including peacekeeping activities of the CSCE or the United Nations Security Council' (Petersberg Declaration, I,2 1992). Thus, in addition to the common defence provisions of the amended Brussels Treaty, the WEU was to develop a new role, in accordance with Chapter VIII of the UN Charter, as a 'regional arrangement' for the implementation of tasks at the request of the UN.[21] The new tasks envisaged for the WEU – subsequently known as the 'Petersberg Tasks' – were humanitarian and rescue, peacekeeping and peacemaking.

At this stage, NATO adaptations developed in parallel with those at the WEU. Thus in June 1992 NATO Foreign Ministers announced the organization's readiness to become involved in peacekeeping operations in support of the CSCE. Effectively ending the Cold War prohibition on NATO operations 'out of area', this announcement had major implications for NATO's future role.

WEU and NATO operational roles

Following the decisions to extend their roles beyond collective defence, both NATO and the WEU were anxious to demonstrate their usefulness in carrying out the new tasks. Accordingly, both organizations offered their services in monitoring (and subsequently enforcing) UN sanctions against Serbia imposed in May 1992. For almost a year both organizations, independently, operated naval patrols in the Adriatic. This created a situation where, according to one NATO commentator, it was possible 'to walk across the Adriatic on flat-tops'. After much discussion this situation was rationalized by combining the operations under NATO command, but under the overall direction of a joint NATO–WEU Military Committee (Schulte 1997:30). 'Operation Sharpguard' then continued as a joint endeavour until the lifting of sanctions in 1996. The folly of this initial competition between the two organizations was not repeated; indeed there was subsequently considerable divergence between their roles.

In the case of the WEU, Operation Sharpguard was the only explicitly military operation undertaken in relation to ex-Yugoslavia. The two further WEU involvements have been small scale and essentially civilian. The first of these, again in the context of UN sanctions against Serbia, was the Danube Embargo. Here the WEU coordinated a deployment of 260 police officers and customs officials to support Bulgarian, Hungarian, and Romanian enforcement measures. As had been the case with the Adriatic venture, this deployment was an independent WEU initiative undertaken prior to entry into force of the TEU.

In 1995, the EU requested WEU support for the administration of Mostar, undertaken by the EU as its contribution to implementing the 1995 General Framework Agreement for Peace (the Dayton Agreement). In this case the WEU has coordinated a deployment of approximately 180 police officers. This is the only occasion on which the WEU has acted at the request of the EU in pursuance of a CFSP joint action. While the task of establishing a joint Croat–Muslim police force for the important and deeply divided city of Mostar is not without significance, it has to be seen in the wider context of attempts to establish civilian police authorities throughout Bosnia–Herzegovina.[22]

The development of NATO's role in ex-Yugoslavia contrasts markedly with that of the WEU. Shortly after commencement of its naval operation in the Adriatic, NATO became involved in air operations, initially to monitor UN-imposed no-fly zones. A series of UN Security Council resolutions subsequently legitimated the incremental development of NATO's air operations, culminating with Operation Deliberate Force, a three-week bombardment of Bosnian Serb positions around Sarajevo which paved the way for the Dayton peace negotiations to begin.

A further, early NATO contribution is also worth noting because of its potential relevance for future operations. In November 1992 NATO supplied the UN Protection Force in Bosnia (UNPROFOR) with an operational headquarters, comprising approximately 100 staff, plus equipment and supplies. This enabled NATO to support UN ground operations without itself deploying ground forces. Introduced at a time when it seemed unlikely that Congress would approve commitment of US forces, this initiative is the source of the CJTF concept which, as we saw above, has subsequently been developed as a mechanism, potentially, for supporting WEU-led operations. Further experience of the utilization of NATO command centres – in this case for operations involving both NATO and non-NATO members – was gained in the context of peace enforcement operations in Bosnia.

In accordance with the terms of the Dayton peace agreement, and with

UN Security Council legitimation, a NATO-led Implementation Force (IFOR) of 60,000 personnel was deployed in Bosnia to provide a more muscular replacement for UNPROFOR. IFOR was composed of contributions from all 16 NATO members, with the largest contingent of 20,000 from the USA, and 17 non-NATO members, subsequently increasing to 20. The incorporation into IFOR of contingents from a number of 'former adversaries', in particular Russia, was a significant achievement which augured well for the continuance and development of NATO's role.[23] Indeed IFOR has been described by NATO's Secretary-General, not without justification, as 'a turning point not only for the former Yugoslavia but also for the Atlantic Alliance' (Solana 1996:3).

The tasks of IFOR and its successor, SFOR (Stabilization Force),[24] included peace enforcement and support for civilian organizations involved in post-conflict peace building measures – the UN, the OSCE and the EU. To this end IFOR/SFOR has deployed approximately 350 civil–military cooperation specialists (CIMIC), who are primarily US reservists with backgrounds in areas such as law enforcement, education, public transport, engineering, agriculture, public health and communications. As a consequence of experience in Bosnia, civil–military relations, an area previously unfamiliar to NATO, has become the subject of planning and development. This could include a role for the military in supporting civil law and order, involving 'training of more military forces in crowd control . . . and further investigation into the potential of non-lethal weapons' (Schulte 1997:38).

This potential expansion of NATO's role, which would parallel tasks being developed by the WEU, highlights the extent of adaptation accomplished by an organization which, until 1990, embraced a strategic concept involving early first use of nuclear weapons. Consequently there is optimism among NATO officials that 'the Alliance is now well placed to respond fully and effectively to the challenges of the new century' (Cragg 1997:35).[25]

Policy implications of the Yugoslav conflict

During the course of the conflict in ex-Yugoslavia the WEU, and indeed the EU, became increasingly marginalized, while NATO's role expanded considerably. Maintenance of this expanded role is not necessarily assured, however. In the specific context of the Balkan conflict it reflects a political agreement among its membership and beyond, central to which has been the evolving policy position of the US government.

Opinion among US policy makers, following initial reluctance to become involved in a new European war, was influenced not only by the escalation of the conflict but by perceptions of mismanagement on the part of the EC and the UN. These perceptions played a significant role in ensuring US support for the adaptation of NATO. However it is not only US policies which were influenced. In July 1994 the German Constitutional Court ruled that German forces could participate in peacekeeping missions abroad in support of UN, NATO or WEU missions, thus enabling German participation in IFOR. Moreover both the French and Spanish governments indicated their willingness to participate more fully in the Alliance's integrated military structure, thus abandoning their semi-detached status. Given previous French prioritization of EU/WEU links, this suggests a significant policy shift in the case of France. However the *rapprochement* with NATO is dependent upon increased European representation among major NATO commands, a condition which US policy makers are unlikely to concede.[26]

The circumstances which have united NATO members during the Bosnian operation may not easily be replicated; in particular doubts remain about US participation in any future peacekeeping tasks in Europe. Consequently, despite the adaptations achieved, NATO may lack the political impetus to take up its new role. Nevertheless NATO officials and commanders clearly envisage future NATO involvement in peacekeeping and related tasks. Indeed General George A. Joulwan, then Supreme Allied Commander Europe (SACEUR), has stated 'our forces can go anywhere needed to perform missions from the low end to the high end of the conflict spectrum' (Joulwan 1996:7). If political approval for this range of missions was forthcoming, this would leave very little role for the WEU beyond the coordination of policing tasks as undertaken in Bosnia. Even here, as we have seen, there is potential for NATO to expand its role.

Despite NATO adaptation to new tasks, the political impetus to act remains questionable. Here, providing that NATO continues to exist, and to fulfil its primary function of collective defence, the solution to this problem could be the CJTF concept, discussed above. In relation to peacekeeping and related tasks, CJTF command and control facilities would potentially be available, not only to the WEU, but to any 'coalition of the willing' – subject to NATO approval and monitoring. While this aspect of CJTF may prove irksome to the governments of some EU Member States, it is less crucial in relation to peacekeeping tasks than would be the case if territorial defence was at issue. Aspects of the CJTF concept are undoubtedly attractive to EU Member States. The ability to utilize the highly trained multinational personnel and supporting equipment of a CJTF would, in principle, obviate the need for duplication of effort – an advantage given the lack of domestic support for increased defence expenditure.

The notion of a coalition of the willing is itself of considerable interest, since it addresses the problem of inadequate consensus among EU Member States; and, indeed, among WEU members. It would also enable neutral Member States to participate in peacekeeping tasks in support of a CFSP Joint Action. The concept of a 'coalition of the willing' was put into practice in March 1997 when an Italian-led 'Multinational Protection Force' deployed 7000 troops in Albania following the collapse of civil authority in that country.[27] Although in military terms the Albanian intervention was a low level mission which did not require the support of CJTF assets, it nevertheless provides an example of the type of coalition that might, in the future, wish to avail itself of such assets. It also provides a model for the EU peacekeeping role prescribed in the Amsterdam Treaty, as we shall see.

The Albanian intervention aimed to protect the distribution of aid and support the re-establishment of a viable police force. Subsequently the operation was extended, to provide security for the July 1997 parliamentary elections, which were conducted under OSCE supervision. The relevance of the Albanian operation for future EU involvement in humanitarian/ peacekeeping tasks is that it demonstrated the potential for combining EC/EU instruments and the WEU. Thus the Commission coordinated the international aid effort, the 'willing coalition' undertook measures to secure aid routes and the WEU utilized the experience gained in Mostar in coordinating civilian police support.

Shortly before commencement of the operation, Hans van Mierlo, speaking for the Dutch Presidency, provided an EU formula for the future when he announced – 'I judge there is now a coalition of the willing which is now ready to provide forces' (Quoted in *The Guardian*, 25 March 1997). Despite this approval by the Presidency, the intervention was not formalized as a CFSP Joint Action, which would have required unanimity, and the coalition force included contingents from non-EU countries (see note 26). Nevertheless this operation, which was mounted with minimal delay under a UN Security Council mandate and with OSCE support, demonstrates the possibility of constructing a European coalition.

Collective intervention and the Amsterdam Treaty

As was the case with the initial EC involvement in ex-Yugoslavia, the Albanian intervention took place in the context of an ongoing IGC (1996–7), convened to review the provisions of the TEU. Consequently there was, as previously, an incentive to demonstrate the utility of proposals under discussion.[28] The notion of a coalition of the willing, tested in Albania, was clearly reflected in the Amsterdam Treaty – through inclusion of the 'constructive abstention' procedure among the revised CFSP provisions (Article J.13.1 [23.1]).[29]

While this would potentially enable a coalition of the willing to operate on behalf of the EU without availing itself of the WEU, the TOA maintains and marginally strengthens reference to the EU/WEU link. Moreover it specifically refers to the WEU Petersberg Tasks (Article J.7.2 [17.2]). Here a further concession to the notion of 'the willing' is evident. Thus, in order to accommodate non-WEU members wishing to contribute to humanitarian or peacekeeping tasks, it is explicitly stated that 'all Member States are entitled to participate fully in the tasks in question'. The Council is charged with agreeing the 'necessary practical arrangements' with the WEU (Article J.7.3 [17.3]), thus keeping open the option of utilizing WEU mechanisms should this be considered desirable.

In some respects the provisions of the TOA suggest the increased likelihood of a conflict intervention role for the EU. They are more specific in referring to peacekeeping and related tasks while, at the same time, permitting greater flexibility in their execution. In other respects, however, the Treaty provisions in this area are as ambiguous and confused as previously. Thus reference to the 'possibility of the integration of the WEU into the Union' is immediately followed by the caveat that Union policy 'shall not prejudice' the NATO commitments of 'certain Member States' (Article J.4.1 [14.1]). Ultimately there is a conviction, held in particular by the UK government, that any intervention requiring a significant military input should be NATO led. However, in circumstances where NATO involvement may be uncertain, undesirable or unnecessary, UK policy makers would be prepared to 'contemplate the idea of the WEU undertaking (very small) enforcement missions' (Bailes 1997:50). Despite its recent involvement only with civilian policing tasks, the possibility of a future military role for the WEU is consequently not excluded.

The TOA provisions ensure that, should the need arise for low level intervention, the EU is potentially better able to proceed than formerly – with or without the WEU. However care is also taken not to preclude or discourage NATO involvement in such activities. Thus NATO seems assured of a role in the medium term, having successfully added to its fundamental collective defence function the new tasks of peacekeeping and peacemaking.

NATO has also developed a role in the wider sense of projecting stability beyond the NATO area – both in relation to Central and Eastern Europe and the Mediterranean region. Here, while there are some parallels, NATO activities are very much narrower in scope. As we shall see, in the 'soft security' area of projecting stability, the contribution of the EU has not been marginalized.

STABILIZATION OF THE WIDER EUROPE

The EU's potential both to provide a 'security community' model for the wider Europe, and to actively project stability beyond its borders, ensures that it is highly significant both as presence and as actor in the post-Cold War security environment. EU initiatives in this area accord with notions of 'soft security' – in that they reflect understandings about the meaning of security which depart from the traditional emphasis on military capability. This is an important issue for EU actorness – because of the significant role, for Europe as a whole, that the EU is called on to play; and because, as we have seen, the EU is deficient in military capability and is thus precluded from playing a traditional security role. In consequence location of the EU's stabilizing functions within a 'security' discourse requires further consideration.

In recent years there has been considerable debate about the meaning of security, which largely reflects the changed circumstances of the post-Cold

War world.[30] This debate has developed from the argument that there now exists in Europe a 'new' security agenda associated with rapid change, social destabilization and the ensuing challenges to established identities of individuals and societies (Wæver *et al.* 1993). In this perspective the focus of analysis is shifted from the traditional concerns of state security to examination of the various sources of 'societal insecurity'. These can range from the threat of armed violence (from internal or external sources) to economic and/or environmental changes deleterious to social cohesion.[31] In the former Eastern bloc, for example, the rapidity of political, economic and social change has been deeply destabilizing and feelings of insecurity are widely evident – presenting, for the authors of one extensive study, 'a paradox of insecurity among few external threats' (Kramer and Smoke 1996:282).

While the consequences of societal insecurity are unpredictable, two broad trends are discernible in Central and East European countries. First there has been an attempt to identify with ideas and institutions deemed to be representative of 'the West'. Exemplified by the ten formal applications to join the EU from CEEC between 1994 and 1996, this strategy reflects a desire to escape from insecurity by becoming part of the 'secure' West.[32] Second, in regions at the periphery of Europe, where the possibility of inclusion in a Western identity is problematic, there has been a resurgence of ethno-nationalist sentiment. In some cases, notably ex-Yugoslavia and the Caucasus, this has contributed to the outbreak of violent conflict.[33]

In the case of Russia and Ukraine, whose internal stability and external policies are of particular significance to European security, elements of both the above broad trends are discernible. The Chechen war and conflict over the future of Crimea demonstrate the potential for violent conflict in Russia and Ukraine respectively. The governments of both countries have also sought Western aid and developed links with Western institutions. However in both countries, but especially in Russia where a catastrophic loss of world status has greatly exacerbated feelings of insecurity, there is much uncertainty concerning the orientation of external policy. In particular there is ambivalence about the extent to which a Western identification is desirable or achievable.[34]

These uncertainties have been aggravated by a tendency for Western and 'Central European' commentators to construe Russia (and to a lesser extent Ukraine) as Eastern/Asiatic, and hence ineligible for inclusion in the West/Europe. Indeed, the very concept of Central Europe has been assiduously promoted to establish the Western credentials of certain countries, in particular Hungary, Poland and the Czech Republic – to ensure that their claims for Western assistance, and applications to join Western institutions, are prioritized over those of their 'Eastern' neighbours (Neumann 1996b). The 'asymmetric approach' to CEEC on the one hand, and to NIS, including Russia, on the other, has not gone unnoticed in Russia (Borko 1997:205).[35] Clearly it is essential that Western policies toward NIS/CEEC are carefully managed, in order to avoid establishing a dynamic of inclusion and exclusion which undermines the potentially stabilizing effects of closer cooperation.

In addition to policies directed towards CEEC/NIS since the end of the Cold War, both the EU and NATO have attempted to strengthen their relations with the Mediterranean region. This reflects the perception that the Southern Mediterranean is also a potential source of risk associated with 'societal insecurity'. Consequently, in 1995, the EU launched its Euro–Mediterranean Partnership initiative, which includes 12 non-member countries and provides for multilateral dialogue on a range of topics from weapons proliferation to wetlands protection – alongside bilateral Association Agreements and the MEDA financial assistance programme. Central to the Partnership is the aspiration to create a Euro–Med free trade area by 2010 (see Chapter 5). NATO also launched a Mediterranean Initiative in 1995. This involves dialogue and confidence building measures, on a strictly bilateral basis, with six countries – Egypt, Israel, Jordan, Mauritania, Morocco and Tunisia. However, when compared with the Euro–Med Partnership, the NATO initiative is very limited. Indeed it is acknowledged that NATO involvement in the Mediterranean is problematic; and that 'the EU is the Alliance's "first line of defence" in dealing with many of the potential challenges in the region' (Asmus, Larrabee and Lesser 1996:29).[36] This is an important conclusion which might equally be applied to 'soft security' approaches towards Eastern Europe, where EU and NATO strategies are more readily comparable.

Reflecting an appreciation that the integration process which created Western Europe's 'Community of security' was supported by NATO defence guarantees, all CEE applicants for EU membership have also expressed a desire to join NATO. This places great responsibility upon policy makers in the context both of NATO and the EU to ensure that there is complementarity between their policies; and that they avoid creating a mutually reinforcing, exclusionary dynamic. We briefly examine this issue below.

EU relations with CEEC/NIS

As we saw in Chapter 5, despite efforts to prevent the emergence of overt hierarchies of preference, the relationships developed between the EU and CEEC/NIS since 1989 have effectively produced a three-tier 'caste system' (Sperling and Kirchner 1997:155). At the apex are the five CEEC which began accession negotiations in March 1998. Below are the remaining five CEE applicant countries, which are potential EU members but are considered unready to begin accession negotiations. A third group of NIS countries, including Russia and Ukraine, having signed Partnership and Cooperation Agreements, has been 'drawn into the EU trading orbit without any prospect of EU membership' (*ibid*). In relation to the NIS, as we have seen, the EU is attempting to address the potentially destabilizing effects of this hierarchical arrangement by enhancing its relations with Russia and Ukraine through development of its 'Action Plan' initiative.

Concern to address the broader interests of European security and stability is also evident from inclusion of Estonia and Slovenia within the first tranche of potentially acceding countries.[37] Inclusion of Estonia will, it is hoped, give impetus to the transformation processes in Latvia and Lithuania, thus contributing positively to stability in the Baltic region. Moreover Estonia has close links with Finland, good port facilities and geographical proximity to Russia. Consequently Estonian accession, if successfully negotiated, will have political and economic implications far greater than the small size of that country might imply. The case of Slovenia also reflects strategic as well as economic considerations. The accession of Slovenia would effectively extend the EC's 'Community of security' into the Balkan region. As in the case of Estonia, this would signal to neighbouring countries, in particular Croatia, that 'good behaviour' in respect of democratization and respect for human rights is likely to be rewarded.

NATO relations with the former Eastern bloc

On 19 December 1989 the then Soviet Foreign Minister, Eduard Shevardnadze, made an official visit to NATO headquarters in Brussels. Occurring one month after the opening of the Berlin Wall, this historic visit presaged an unexpected stream of visitors from more than 20 CEEC. Such was the influx that, on occasion, the rather unprepossessing facilities of NATO headquarters proved barely adequate (Interview, NATO Secretariat, January 1996).[38] Many of the 'former adversaries' were anxious to forge links with NATO; indeed in 1991, shortly after the formal dissolution of the Warsaw Pact, Poland, Hungary and (then) Czechoslovakia indicated a desire to become NATO members.

NATO responded positively to these overtures, and there has been an incremental development of structured links with CEEC/NIS (who came to be known as 'cooperation partners'). The initial relationship was political, involving CEEC/NIS, collectively, in the North Atlantic Cooperation Council (NACC), established in December 1991. In response to pressure for a fuller relationship, and in order to defer making a decision on the difficult question of enlargement, NATO launched its Partnership for Peace (PfP) initiative, based on bilateral military cooperation, in 1994.[39]

PfP facilitated development of NATO/CEEC/NIS military links, which proved beneficial in the context of NATO's coordination role in Bosnia – 15 PfP members participated in IFOR/SFOR. It also provided anticipatory socialization for aspirant members. It did not, however, solve the difficult problem of whether to admit new members and, if so, how this could be achieved without seriously damaging relations with Russia – where there was strong opposition to an eastern enlargement of NATO.[40]

Between 1993 and 1997 enlargement was the subject of considerable debate, at the centre of which were concerns about its potential impact on the internal stability and external policies of Russia. Proponents of enlargement portrayed Russia as an actual or potential threat to CEEC; in effect proposing NATO expansion as a modified version of Cold War containment (Brzezenski 1994). Opponents argued that it would contribute to the destabilization of Russia, hence provoking the very situation feared by advocates of enlargement. These latter arguments were linked to a 'Russia first' policy, which prioritized development of a special relationship with Russia over strengthening links with CEEC (Harris 1993).[41] Neither side seemed greatly interested in Russia's actual military capabilities – revealed, not least, by the 'humiliating disaster' of Chechnya (Baev 1997:184).

The decision on the precise extent of NATO's first enlargement was eventually announced at the 1997 Madrid Summit, when the governments of the Czech Republic, Hungary and Poland were invited to open negotiations for membership, with a view to accession in 1999. The US government refused to countenance enlargement beyond these three countries, despite intense lobbying by the Romanian government and considerable support for Romanian (and, indeed, Slovenian) membership among European NATO members.[42] The French, Italian and Spanish governments, in particular, made strenuous efforts to achieve a more balanced enlargement to include at least one new member from South-East Europe. This would have averted criticism that NATO was extending its defence guarantees and stabilizing influence only to those countries which needed them least. Interestingly there was no strong lobby for inclusion of the Baltic Republics – despite the fact that some commentators considered them to have greatest need of NATO guarantees. Indeed, in discussing the 'dilemmas' associated with Baltic security, Asmus and Norick argued (1996:134) that the solution lay in *EU* enlargement to 'at least one Baltic country' – a conclusion which supports the proposition that the EU is destined to play the more significant role in extending security across the region.[43]

The outcome of the Madrid Summit clearly raises difficult issues of inclusion and exclusion. These were addressed in two ways, which effectively differentiate between CEEC and NIS. First, disappointed aspirant members were assured that the first enlargement would not be the last. These assurances were accompanied by enhancement of PfP and upgrading of NACC to form the Euro–Atlantic Partnership Council. The EAPC is intended to provide political oversight of PfP activities, and is said to represent NATO commitment to 'carry its cooperation with its partners to a qualitatively new level' (Balanzinos 1997). Thus, like the EU, NATO has developed a form of 'enhanced pre-accession strategy for pre-ins' (see Chapter 5). Second, following intense diplomatic effort, the NATO–Russian relationship was strengthened, prior to the Madrid Summit, through the (May 1997) 'Founding Act on Mutual Relations, Cooperation and Security between NATO and the Russian Federation'.[44] Ukrainian sensitivities about exclusion from Western institutions were also addressed – through a 'Charter on a Distinctive Partnership between NATO and Ukraine'.[45]

In these ways NATO has attempted to accomplish the difficult task of fulfilling political demands for enlargement without generating destabilizing tensions. It remains to be seen whether the measures designed to placate the excluded will be effective. Ultimately NATO enlargement has to be seen, not in terms of extending stability to a wider Europe, but as an exercise in damage limitation.

Impacts of EU and NATO policies

There has been no formal coordination of EU and NATO policy towards the CEE countries. This is 'not accidental'; it reflects US reluctance to involve non-NATO members, even indirectly, in discussions which impinge upon the future of NATO. It also reflects fears that aspirant members might use one set of negotiations to gain leverage in the other (Interview, external Mission, January 1996). In these circumstances the extent to which there has been complementarity between EU and NATO policies has implications for the shared aim of extending stability across Europe. Below we examine the extent of complementarity in two areas – anticipatory socialization and the processes of inclusion/exclusion.

In relation to anticipatory socialization, both organizations have explicitly used the membership aspirations of CEE governments to influence the direction and pace of transformation processes. The focus of NATO efforts has been military restructuring and, more particularly, civil/military relations and democratic control of the armed forces. In the case of the EU, an early focus upon economic transformation was widened to cover, for the ten applicant countries, readiness to implement the entire *acquis communautaire*. Indeed in *Agenda 2000* the Commission makes very clear the aim of closely supervising policy development in CEEC. It recommends that, in future, financial assistance should be conditional upon the success of applicant countries in 'implementing the programmes aimed at preparing them to meet their obligations as future Member States' (Commission 1997d:2).

Clearly, in relation to anticipatory socialization, there has been complementarity between EU and NATO policies. However NATO efforts have been narrowly focused and, according to NATO's Special Advisor for Central and East European Affairs, this has diminished their effectiveness (Donnelly 1997). Conversely, a striking example of the broad focus, and influence, of the EU's role is provided by the Czech/Slovak 'divorce' at the end of 1992. The relatively non-conflictual nature of this process reflected both close supervision of the negotiations by EC officials and the desire, on the part of the Czech and Slovak governments, to ensure that prospects for integration into the EC would not be damaged by a poorly controlled or acrimonious separation (Pehe 1992; Interview, external Mission, June 1996).

Areas of complementarity between the EU and NATO, but also important differences, are also evident in relation to the creation, and management, of processes of exclusion and inclusion. Thus both organizations have implicitly recognized a Central/Eastern Europe distinction – and there is no doubt that the combined impact of EU and NATO policies places the Czech Republic, Hungary and Poland in a particularly privileged position. Nevertheless both organizations have attempted to balance their close relations with 'Central European' countries. Here, however, policy divergences between the EU and NATO are evident. NATO, as we have seen, has prioritized links with Russia; the EU has taken the more radical step of opening accession negotiations with Estonia and Slovenia. This divergence reflects the different character of the two organizations and the related differences in their policy making processes.

In the case of the EU, a strategy for gradual progression towards enlargement is evident from early 1993. While the issue of Eastern enlargement has been difficult for EU Member States, and will continue to be so, there is an understanding that it will require adjustment and accommodation on the part of existing members as well as candidates for membership; and that pre-accession and accession processes must necessarily involve intense and protracted discussion. Decisions in respect of NATO enlargement have been very much more arbitrary.[46] They have been excessively influenced both by residual fears of Russia as a military threat and by the vagaries of US domestic politics.

Ultimately the explanation for the divergences in policy between the EU and NATO lies in the nature of the two organizations. NATO is, essentially, a Cold War intergovernmental organization created for the specific purpose of harnessing US military capacity to the task of maintaining, through deterrence, a stable East/West divide in Europe. Since the end of the Cold War, NATO has undergone considerable adaptation. Nevertheless, the rationale for its continued existence remains in doubt, as is evident from the qualified support for NATO among US politicians.[47] In these circumstances arguments for a limited extension eastward are difficult to sustain.

The EC/EU has had a very different role in relation to Eastern Europe. During the Cold War its purpose was to seduce rather than to deter. Its presence has always been significant in providing a model or reference point – initially to demonstrate the viability of capitalism, latterly also as a 'Community of security'. In consequence the enlargement of the EU does not create the tensions associated with NATO enlargement; the EU by its nature is oriented towards creating links rather than constructing divisions. Nevertheless the propensity of the EU to develop a hierarchy of privileges, demonstrated in relation to CEE and NIS countries as elsewhere, contributes to a potentially destabilizing inclusion/exclusion dynamic. EU policy makers are intensely aware of this potential. The extent to which they are able to develop non-exclusionary relationships across the wider Europe may be decisive for stability and security in the region. However agency in this respect, as elsewhere, will be contextualized and constrained by the inter-action between internal and external factors which shapes the EU's evolving relationship with its neighbours. Thus the internal impact of EMU, or external tensions generated by NATO's proposed enlargement, may deter-mine whether or not the EU is able to play a decisive role in extending 'soft security' across Europe.

CONCLUSION

We have considered three distinct roles potentially available to the EU in the sphere of defence/security in post-Cold War Europe – common defence of the Union's territory, intervention in external conflicts, and projection of stability across the wider Europe. All three of these roles rest, implicitly, upon the EU's presence as a 'Community of security'. However the EU's role as a 'soft security' actor depends, also, upon the construction of shared understandings concerning the meaning of security in contemporary Europe.

Despite the provisions of the TEU, reinforced by the 1997 Amsterdam Treaty, we see little prospect of the EU assuming a role in collective defence, nor of gaining direct access to military instruments. After an initial flurry of activity the EU/WEU relationship has not developed as anticipated by the Treaties, and NATO remains, for the foreseeable future, the ultimate defence guarantor of its members. Here, of course, a number of problems remain – not least the lack of coincidence between EU and NATO membership and recurring doubts about the future viability of NATO as an organization. Since EU Member States remain fundamentally divided over these matters, and territorial defence today is largely a residual category, there has been little incentive to address them.

While the significance of common defence has clearly diminished, that of collective intervention has increased. EU aspirations in this respect are expressed in the Amsterdam Treaty, which provides sufficient flexibility to enable limited interventions in the absence of Member State unanimity. In principle this could allow the EU to play a role in this respect. However adaptations at NATO since the end of the Cold War, and experience in ex-Yugoslavia, suggest that any large-scale military interventions, at least in the medium term, are likely to be NATO led. While NATO's recent foray into civil/military relations suggests an ambition further to expand its role, it is far from clear that NATO is the most appropriate organization to perform such tasks. Thus a future role for the EU could be involvement in low level interventions, where it is well suited to employ its 'soft security' instruments alongside limited military and/or policing tasks in association with the WEU or an *ad hoc* coalition of the willing.

It is in the final area discussed above, which is in our view the most significant for European security in the future, that the role of the EU is decisive. The insecurities affecting Europe are increasingly non-military, and the notion of societal security captures the growing significance of the EU's civilian, 'soft security' instruments. This implies not only the importance of the EU's presence as an 'island of peace' but also the development of shared understandings concerning the EU's central role as a security actor. As the Austrian Foreign Minister, Alois Mock (1995:17), has argued –

> Particularly with regard to the non-military security threats of today's Europe . . . the Union alone has the cohesion, the know-how and the resources to tackle these problems with any chance of success. It alone has the capacity to approach risks to stability in a comprehensive manner, taking into account their political, economic and social dimensions.

8   Identity, legitimacy, eligibility
Delimiting EU actorness?

On ne tombe pas amoureux d'un grand marché.
> (Jacques Delors quoted in Martiniello 1995:39)

The Turkish issue quite overshadowed the grand historical drama of the old
Warsaw Pact satellites being formally embraced by the EU yesterday ...
Turkey's anger drowned out a Lithuanian choir singing 'We love you Europe'
in the rain outside the conference chamber.
> (*The Guardian*, 13 December 1997)

Identity is essentially about belonging. It involves the creation of 'we' groups
of insiders whose identity is defined in terms of values or characteristics
deemed to be common, and with reference to 'they' groups of outsiders
deemed to have different common values or characteristics. In the context of
the EU, identity issues have relevance both in the sense of individual or
group orientation towards the EU, and in the sense of an EU collective
identity in relation to other actors in the global system.[1] These two meanings
of 'an EU identity' relate to actorness in different ways. Identification
towards the Union impinges upon internal legitimation of EU action;
collective identity of the Union is an important aspect of the EU's presence,
which shapes perceptions of and behaviour towards 'outsiders'.

The first sense in which we consider identity is internal to the EU. It
involves the attempt to 'deepen European citizens' sense of belonging to the
European Union' (Commission 1996b:21). This reflects concern that, given
its frequently proclaimed commitment to democratic values and principles,
action by the EU should be legitimized by popular consent, if not popular
support. Here there is a sense that, beyond a certain (undefined) point, lack
of popular consent/support will prove an impediment to actorness. In consequence legitimacy based upon consent is a resource, to be considered, as
was maintained in Chapter 1, among the requisites for actorness.

The second area where identity concerns us has both external and internal
referents. This involves the criteria by which belonging, or eligibility for
membership, is established. Both presence and actorness are important here.

The attractiveness of the EU flows from its position as the relatively affluent, politically stable core of Europe, located at the centre of multiple, overlapping networks of association and influence. In relation to this 'magnetic' presence, actorness is displayed through the ability to determine the criteria governing eligibility – for Union citizenship; for admission of migrants or asylum seekers; for partnership/association with third countries; or for accession to membership.

Below the issues of legitimacy and eligibility are considered separately, prior to assessment of the overall significance of identity for EU actorness.

LEGITIMACY – A REQUISITE FOR ACTORNESS?

As a policy system claiming to be founded upon democratic principles, and seeking actively to promote these principles elsewhere, it is axiomatic that the policies of the European Union require some measure of democratic legitimation. Here it is possible to argue that, since many aspects of external policy lie outside exclusive Community competence, indirect legitimation is derived from the political systems of EU Member States. However we have maintained that, in order to be considered a global actor, the EU must be capable of differentiation from its internal constituents. This demands a focus upon the legitimacy of the EU system itself.

The potential sources of EU legitimacy are threefold, and essentially interrelated – the appropriateness and effectiveness of EU institutions; the legal basis or 'rule of law' upon which the EC/EU is founded and which determines, *inter alia*, the scope of its policy competences; and perceptions (both elite and popular) concerning the 'rightness' of the authority upon which EU policy is based. This last is crucial, in that accordance of legitimacy involves not only the validation of rules and procedures but also 'the acceptance of decisions as something which one should defend, even at personal cost' (Obradovic 1996:194). Legitimate political systems engender a sense of moral obligation which transcends individual self-interest. Thus legitimacy implies more than a utilitarian calculation of benefit, it suggests some degree of affective orientation towards, or identification with, the political system and the values it represents. While this affective dimension of legitimacy is our central concern here, the three factors potentially contributing to EU legitimacy are closely interrelated.

The legal bases of EC/EU actorness have considerable significance for external policy, as has been demonstrated in the preceding chapters. For example, accordance of exclusive legal competence to the EC in relation to trade in goods has legitimized, and hence strengthened, the Commission's role as an international negotiator in that policy area. Conversely, however, the position of EC negotiators, and overall perceptions of EC actorness by third parties, are undermined by reluctance to accept the legitimacy of an expanded external role for the EC. This is particularly evident in areas –

such as 'new' trade issues and global environmental policy – where areas of competence are disputed. The denial of legal personality to the Union, which has the effect of impeding implementation of CFSP decisions, is further evidence of unwillingness to legitimize an expanded external role for the EU. Here, of course, we are essentially dealing with elite opinion. This is important, nevertheless, since European integration was initially seen as an elite project in which the salient actors were 'the leaders of all relevant political groups who habitually participate in the making of public decisions' (Haas 1958:16). From this perspective, if political elites are unwilling to accord legitimacy to aspects of external actorness, then popular support, which is seen as lagging behind elite opinion, is unlikely to be forthcoming. We return to this issue later.

The development of democratic institutions and procedures is an aspect of legitimation which could potentially link elite and popular opinion. Our concern, here, is with the nature and sources of attitudes towards EU institutions, rather than the democratic credentials or inadequacies of the institutions themselves, about which much has been written elsewhere.[2] It should be noted, nevertheless, that institutional and procedural reforms intended to reduce the EU's 'democratic deficit' have not been conspicuously successful in generating active popular involvement with the EU. Thus, for example, increases in the powers of the European Parliament introduced both by the SEA and the TEU did not generate increased public interest in that institution; indeed overall turnout for EP elections has declined gradually but steadily since direct elections were introduced in 1979.[3] Concern over this failure to stimulate public interest in EC matters was greatly exacerbated by the difficult TEU ratification process in 1992 – leading a number of commentators to conclude that the EU was suffering from a 'legitimacy crisis' (García 1993; Laffan 1996; Obradovic 1996).[4]

The apparently negative relationship between institutional reform and public interest/support, which can be observed from the evolution of the EC/EU, indicates the importance of popular sentiments, or feelings of belonging, in providing the ultimate test of the legitimacy of the institutional and legal order – and potentially, also, of the EU's external activities. This, of course, is our central concern. Discussion of these matters begins by examining an important debate, in which protagonists hold competing views on the meaning of identity and its formation – and hence upon the extent to which a sense of belonging to the EU is possible or desirable.

Can we learn to love the European Union?

In complex, contemporary societies, individuals encounter a range of identity sources. This does not suggest that they are free randomly to choose their identities, rather they are more or less knowledgeable agents involved in a creative process of identity construction in which personal preferences interact with those structural factors which govern the availability of various identities. Thus identity is a social construct and is, in part, a function of eligibility. It derives from membership of a social group or organization, or espousal of a set of ideas and values held in common by a number of others. Sources of identity may include gender, sexuality, sporting activity, occupation, social class, ethnicity, religion, a political organization or ideology, a nation state, a region or a city. Potentially, too, individuals may identify with the European Union; indeed the concept of EU citizenship explicitly invites them to do so.

The availability of a range of identity sources is not necessarily experienced as challenging or destabilizing; multi-faceted identities are the norm. Thus it is possible to combine several identities with ease – for example to think of oneself simultaneously as a lesbian woman, a medical practitioner, a Liverpudlian and a Scot. Such an identity would become problematic only in circumstances where major incompatibilities arose between its components. Thus, in the case of our hypothetical identity, tensions might arise if the British Medical Association attempted to discourage involvement in the lesbian/gay movement; or if the Scottish people were urgently called upon to defend themselves against the English. In such circumstances, those attempting to politicize identity would demand that a choice be made and a superordinate loyalty declared – for 'identity politics assumes that one among the many identities we all have is the one that determines, or at least dominates our politics' (Hobsbawm 1996:41).

In the present context, the multi-faceted nature of identity, and the discourses of identity politics, suggest two interrelated questions. First, to what extent and in what circumstances might identification with the EU be considered a facet of individual or collective identity? Second, to what extent would an EU identification be compatible with other aspects of identity? The central issue arising from these questions is undoubtedly the nature of, and the relationship between, an EU identification and national identity. Attempts to address this issue have tended to fall within two broad schools – rationalist approaches, which offer broadly materialist explanations for identification; and primordialist approaches, which emphasize the ties of blood, soil and shared historical experience, real or imagined.[5] Primordial attachments are essentially romantic and, potentially, passionate; rationalism allows for the possibility of wider, transnational or even cosmopolitan dimensions of identity.

In rationalist approaches there is a focus upon the contingent and multi-faceted nature of contemporary identities, in which affect is to a considerable extent replaced by pragmatism, even instrumentality. As we have seen, the major part of the EU's own efforts at identity building reflects rationalist assumptions. For rationalists the EU is an essentially modern, progressive response to the particularism of the past and the globalization of the present. At the same time identification with the EU is generally seen as complementing, rather than replacing, national and local identities. Essentially, in this analysis, the potential exists for development of multi-level identifications which parallel the EU's multi-level policy system. While commentators adopting a broadly rationalist perspective share a measure of optimism that some form of European identification is possible, they tend to differ over its nature and extent.

Some commentators envisage the development, over time, of a relatively encompassing EU identity. Indeed they regard the process of identity formation as already occurring, especially among the young and well educated (Dogan 1994; Howe 1995).[6] Dogan, in particular, emphasizes the significance of generational change, which he finds (from Eurobarometer survey evidence) reflected in the decline of nationalism and the development of 'a supranational consciousness' among young people (Dogan 1994:294).[7]

This generational difference is associated with a broad future orientation which reflects, in part, what might be regarded as the EU's 'legitimating myth'; that is rejection of Europe's warlike past in favour of a peaceful and prosperous common future. The widespread acceptance of this formula – indicated, again, by Eurobarometer survey reports – convinces both Dogan and Howe that identification with the EU will partially replace national identity.[8] Indeed Howe (1995:33) maintains that the political significance of national identification will diminish; and that 'the European loyalty will gain the upper hand'.

The approaches of Howe and Dogan evidently involve an affective dimension echoing, perhaps, the Commission's plea that 'A people's Europe must also exist in our hearts' (Commission 1991b:40). Other commentators, however, envisage the development of a new type of transnational *civic* identity which would complement national or local affective identities (Chryssochoou 1996; Weale 1995). Thus it is envisaged that 'sentiments and affections' will largely remain with the Member States; but that 'a democratic European political system could encourage and bring forth the civic virtues of loyalty, citizen respect and constructive cooperation' necessary to facilitate and legitimate policy making at the EU level (Weale 1995:224). This could develop from a fully elaborated concept of EU citizenship, coupled with the enhancement of democratic procedures; however it does not imply a process of state building. This formulation is useful in suggesting the separation of aspects of identity to reflect the division of tasks between national and EU levels of governance. However it is certainly demanding, and perhaps excessively optimistic, in terms of its insistence upon the need for high levels of civic competence and the emergence of a new form of democratic polity.

Commentators who emphasize the importance of romantic attachments and, in particular, of national identity, reach rather more pessimistic conclusions concerning the potential for an EU identification, although they do not reject the possibility that some form of EU 'civic' identification may coexist with national identity. However these sources of identity are incapable of challenging or replacing national identity. This is because '*national* political identification has become the cultural and political norm, transcending other loyalties in scope and power' (Smith 1992:58, emphasis in original). When compared with national identity, identification with the EU can only be a superficial construct based on a hazy common future rather than a shared, vibrant past. Moreover EU identification is conditional upon the provision of substantive benefits. In consequence, unlike national identification, an orientation towards the EU is unlikely to survive major policy failure (Obradovic 1996:199).

For primordialists the power of the nation to attract and retain allegiance arises from its ability to evoke a deep sense of kinship deriving from shared ancestry and historical experience (Obradovic 1996). It is considered that, in order to attain legitimacy, the EU would require to develop both 'a deep continental cultural identity' (Smith 1996:76) and a powerful legitimating myth which 'represents an account of origin, identity and the prepolitical unity of a community' (Obradovic 1996:215). However this 'cannot be invoked on the European scale' (*ibid*). In short, from this perspective, the EU is incapable of generating the depth of affective identification considered necessary to provide policy legitimation; hence legitimacy is unattainable.

A more nuanced, and optimistic, assessment is provided by Brigid Laffan (1996). In her discussion of the relationship between identity and legitimacy, Laffan argues that *both* civic and affective orientations towards the EU are necessary to the attainment of legitimacy; and that the affective dimension has previously been neglected. In part this is because European integration was, for a considerable period, perceived by the peoples of Europe as compatible with national identity, and hence to complement rather than challenge that identity – although the UK and Denmark have been notable exceptions in this respect (Laffan 1996:86–7).

This issue is also discussed by Paul Taylor, who argues that identification with the EU is considerably stronger among the original six Member States because of the greater compatibility between their national systems and the EC system, which they did, of course, create (Taylor 1996:146). Laffan, however, points to the importance of an EC identification in strengthening and legitimizing programmes of economic and social modernization in Greece, Portugal, Spain and Ireland (Laffan 1996:87). For the new Mediterranean members, EC membership also helped to consolidate recently acquired democratic credentials. In the case of the UK, however, EC membership marked a stage in a difficult adjustment to loss of status in the international system, while for the Danish people EC membership challenged an established Nordic identification. The Norwegian rejection of membership also reflects, in part, the importance of a Nordic identification (Lawler 1997). More recently this has been evidenced by the particularly low level of support for the EU among the Swedish public.[9]

In those countries where compatibility between national and EU identification appears to have been least problematic, however, a number of factors have recently combined to disturb this perception. This is particularly noticeable in the case of Germany, where the aftermath of unification and the prospect of EMU combined to challenge the compatibility of German/ EU identities. Indeed reaction against a European identification is evident, in several Member States, from the growth of right-wing nationalist parties. Thus in France, for example, the *Front National* vigorously opposed the introduction of EU citizenship. However the xenophobic nationalism associated with contemporary right-wing extremism undoubtedly reflects socio-economic factors. The economic benefits of market liberalization have been unevenly distributed and it is unsurprising that, across the EU, a poorly educated underclass of long-term unemployed should perceive European integration as a threat rather than an opportunity.[10] Nevertheless contemporary doubts about the compatibility of EU and national identities have extended beyond extremist groups and a marginalized underclass. Evidence from Eurobarometer surveys indicates that, while still a minority, a growing proportion of respondents is uncertain whether EU membership is beneficial to their country – 37 per cent in 1996, compared with 22 per cent in 1990 (Commission 1996a:9–10).

In the context of the major challenges posed by EMU and the prospective Eastern enlargement, a stronger affective orientation towards the EU may be necessary to policy legitimacy. In Laffan's terms (1996:95) there is a need to strengthen 'the flickering gleam of a transnational political community'. This would not require for its basis, as the primordialists maintain, kinship or adherence to a common culture or myth; nor is 'nostalgia for the past' as significant to identity as has been suggested (Laffan 1996:100). However a sense of shared community would require more than the trappings of civic identity; it would involve a willingness to recognize the intrinsic worth of other citizens of the EU. This would require mutual trust and toleration of diversity.[11] There is a danger, however, that increased toleration of other EU citizens, and a heightened sense of EU membership, could be associated with intolerance of non-citizens. Membership implies exclusiveness, as our discussion of eligibility will show.

It is difficult to imagine that people will speak of love for the EU in the way that love of country is discussed. Evidently national identity will remain salient for many, probably most, EU citizens; although only for a minority will it assume the intensity suggested by primordialists. Legitimation of EU policy does not depend upon a traditional process of nation building, indeed this would be entirely inappropriate; rather it requires a sense of belonging to a heterogeneous transnational community. However this will need to be sufficiently robust to endure occasional policy failures; and to accept some measure of internal redistribution of benefits. Considerable efforts have been made, over the years, to generate support for and identification with the EC/EU; to create from above a community of identity. As a prelude to discussion of the relationship between identity, legitimacy and external policy, the record of these efforts is considered below.

Creating a people's Europe?

From the outset the European integration process was accompanied by a grand rhetoric proclaiming the intention to create a community of interest between peoples. Thus, in founding the European Coal and Steel Community, the signatories of the Treaty of Paris –

> Resolved to substitute for age-old rivalries the merging of their essential interests; to create, by establishing an economic community, the basis for a broader and deeper community among peoples long divided by conflicts; and to lay the foundations for institutions which will give direction to a destiny henceforward shared.
>
> (Preamble, Treaty of Paris, 1951)

In the context of European identity, the principles set out in the Paris Treaty are of enduring interest, for two reasons.

First, the rudiments of a legitimating formula are offered – involving the rejection of Europe's conflictual past in favour of a peaceful and prosperous common future. This somewhat prosaic formulation evidently lacks the capacity to generate that passion which has typified the legitimating myths of national identities. Indeed it was very much hoped that, in matters of loyalty and identification, passion would be replaced by reason. This optimism doubtless underestimates the power of affective identifications. Nevertheless the pessimistic 'return to the future' hypotheses which followed the end of the Cold War served, paradoxically, to demonstrate the enduring potency of the belief that, in Europe, integration provides the only alternative to anarchy.[12] The almost desperate desire, on behalf of applicant countries, to be part of the European project surely attests to this.

Second, the preferred means of achieving 'a broader and deeper community' is indicated in the Paris Treaty preamble – that is, through an incremental process of policy integration, initially in the economic sphere, and an accompanying process of institution building. This approach, which avoided specifying a desired end-state for the European construction, reflected divisions among political elites concerning the scope and destination of the integration process; divisions which were evidenced, in particular, by the disastrous failure of the European Defence Community (see Chapter 7). However it also reflected the view that the peoples of Europe were not yet ready to accept the new destiny offered to them. The chosen method of integration, in consequence, was 'designed to reduce to a minimum the likelihood of an inflammatory public debate on the scheme' (Lindberg and Scheingold 1970:21).

In terms of public involvement, therefore, the early years of institution building reflected the neo-functionalist view, which was influential among Community officials, although rather less so among politicians, that the successful transfer of technical tasks to the European level would gradually engender support for the new policy system. Initially, it was believed, recognition of the material advantages flowing from economic integration would ensure the support of organized interest groups and other representative bodies. This would be followed by the gradual development of popular awareness and, ultimately, support.[13] The belief that an instrumental, rather than an affective, orientation to the EC would provide an adequate basis for policy legitimization clearly reflected the rationalist basis of neo-functionalist thinking, which envisaged the development in the EC of 'a benign social climate in which more and more people will be preoccupied with the satisfaction of material needs' (Lindberg and Scheingold 1970:251).

The acquiescence of a largely uninformed public was considered by Lindberg and Scheingold to denote the existence of a 'permissive consensus' for European integration (*ibid*:277). This notion has proved of enduring interest; indeed, through the use of Eurobarometer public opinion surveys Commission officials have attempted, bi-annually, not only to establish the existence of a permissive consensus but to measure its strength – or, more recently, to chart its apparent erosion (Commission 1996a:8). However, the first major setback to the integration process did not derive from inadequate popular support, but from the absence of elite consensus on the nature and scope of policy integration. Thus the 1965–6 Gaullist boycott of Community institutions not only revealed the fragility of the European project, it also demonstrated the shortcomings of neo-functionalist analyses and methods. In the face of opposition from key elite members, reliance on an essentially elite-driven process was clearly inadequate. Moreover, since elite opinion was divided, it could no longer be assumed that popular support for integration would inevitably emerge in its wake.

For Community officials, an important lesson of the 1965 crisis was the need actively to stimulate support for the European project. This translated, in practical terms, into a campaign for the early introduction of direct elections to the EP, which took place for the first time in 1979. At that time, it was considered that this opportunity for popular participation would stimulate support for, and ultimately identification with, the Community. To encourage this process a new rhetoric was launched, in which 'a people's Europe became an avowed political objective' (Commission 1991b:6).

It was not until the mid 1980s that a serious attempt was made to give substance to the 'people's Europe' concept. In the context of the 'relaunch' of the enlarged Community, Jacques Delors' comment (quoted at the start of this chapter) reflected a belief that the success of the Single Market programme depended upon a level of active public support which had previously been absent. To this end the Adonnino Committee was appointed, in 1985, to consider how the notion of a people's Europe might be realized. The Committee recommended a number of measures, both substantive and symbolic. Of largely symbolic importance were the adoption of the European passport, anthem, and, of course, the logo/banner (which, at UK insistence, is not officially referred to as a flag). The prevalence of the logo on EC assisted construction projects, EC approved beaches and, in some Member States, names of towns and cities, car registration plates and so on, has doubtless raised the profile of the Community/Union.[14] The more substantive measures included in the Adonnino Report related to promotion of the movement of people (particularly young people) between Member States – for example through the popular and successful Socrates/Erasmus student mobility programme.

In addition to these broad measures intended to generate awareness and support, there was at this time a strongly held view, within the Commission and several Member State governments, that the Single Market process should be complemented by a social dimension. Eventually this took the form of the 1989 Community Charter of the Fundamental Social Rights of Workers, which subsequently formed the Social Chapter of the TEU. This was significant in that it was the first formal enshrinement of 'rights' in the Community context. It was particularly important in the UK context, in that debate over this issue, and the then Conservative government's opt-out from social policy measures, stimulated support for the EC within the trades union movement and the Labour Party. Indeed this period witnessed a significant reorientation of interest group activity from national to Community institutions in all Member States (Kohler-Koch 1994). Nevertheless this increasing involvement with the Community remained largely at the elite level. Despite the growing impact of EC policies on individuals' lives there was little evidence of widespread popular identification with the EC.[15]

The TEU marked a further, important phase of community building efforts. Even more than previously there was a need for public acceptance of the ambitious new policy aims introduced at Maastricht in the 'political' areas of Common Foreign and Security Policy, but most particularly in relation to Economic and Monetary Union. The introduction of a common European currency to replace national currencies is hardly likely to escape public attention. Here, for the first time, it was proposed that national symbols would be replaced rather than paralleled or supplemented by European symbols. Moreover introduction of the Euro will involve considerably more than symbolic change. As Sutherland (1997:10) has argued, what is demanded by EMU is no less than 'a secular change in economic policy, economic behaviour and, above all, public opinion'.

In recognition of the need for greater public awareness and support, and a sense of belonging to the newly created European Union, the TEU introduces the concept of Union citizenship. Here, in an explicit attempt to fashion the European Union into a political community, a number of political rights was introduced to complement the socio-economic rights of the Social Chapter. Henceforward the 'people's Europe' was to be referred to as a 'citizen's Europe'. In principle the TEU provisions are significant, in that they create a new form of citizenship, which is complementary to Member State citizenship (TEU Articles 8–8e [TEC 17–22]). In practice, however, the new rights conferred upon Union citizens are modest, and any additional legitimacy they confer is largely formal.[16]

In addition to its general lack of substantive content, two factors in particular limit the usefulness of EU citizenship as a legitimating formula. First, and most important, EU citizenship is not independent; it derives from Member State citizenship. Thus Member State rules on citizenship are prior – they determine eligibility for Union citizenship, which becomes 'a sort of complementary supra-citizenship' (Martiniello 1995:41). Second, Union citizenship confers rights but imposes no specific duties or obligations. There is no requirement to pay taxes, nor is there any expectation of the performance of public service, whether civil or military. Ultimately the content of Union citizenship is simply 'too thin to generate any corresponding sense of public duty' (Welsh 1993:28).[17]

In the period since entry into force of the TEU, the inadequacy of the EU citizenship provisions has been of minor importance when compared with controversies attending EMU. From the outset, the opt-outs obtained by the Danish and UK governments indicated divisions over EMU, and these have persisted.[18] In this policy area, sceptical elites have been able to point not only to the symbolic loss of national currencies but also to the deleterious effects of the neoliberal economic policies necessitated by the convergence criteria. And, indeed, to the uncertain benefits of EMU itself. This combination of elite dissensus and increased economic inequality is clearly associated with the erosion of support for the EU charted by Eurobarometer since 1990 (Commission 1996a).[19]

EMU, and indeed enlargement, are policy areas whose long-term success depends, in part, upon the willingness of EU publics to tolerate economic sacrifices.[20] The processes of deepening and widening associated with these policy areas clearly impinge in important ways upon the actor capability of the EU. Hence in these areas, no less than in traditionally 'sensitive' areas such as CFSP, the extent to which policy success is dependent upon loyalty towards, or identification with, the EU is central to our discussion of actorness.

As we have seen, the issue of identification with the EC/EU became a matter of concern for policy makers as integration deepened. Popular consent/support was increasingly required not only for purposes of legitimation but also to ensure successful policy implementation. Thus far the focus has been upon the overall legitimacy of the policy making process, which is an essential requirement for actorness in any democratic political system. Below we examine the significance of the identity/legitimacy relationship for external policy more specifically.

Legitimacy and external policy

Legitimacy, it has been maintained, is a resource to be considered among the requisites for actorness. In discussions of external policy and, more particularly, of interstate relations, the legitimacy of the political system *per se* is not generally a major concern; the EU is a special case in this respect, as in others. Nevertheless policy legitimacy, in the sense of public support for particular foreign policy decisions or orientations, has, in recent years, greatly preoccupied US scholars in particular.[21] In the context of the EU these aspects of legitimacy are linked. Thus public support for the EU's external role implies acceptance of the EU as a policy system.

There has been, since the outset, a close relationship between European integration, European security and Europe's place in the world more generally. We have already noted that opinion surveys consistently indicate the high priority accorded to the EU's role in the preservation and promotion of peace. Originally, of course, this reflected the desire to maintain peace among the Member States. Echoes of this concern are evident today from the tendency to frame the integration process itself in security terms, so that any faltering of that process appears to threaten a return to the past.[22]

Contemporary perceptions of the EU's security functions, as we saw in Chapter 7, also extend outwards, to the wider Europe and beyond. Moreover the EU's role in extending security and stability beyond its borders is broadly conceived – in social, economic and environmental terms in addition to traditional military conceptions of security. In this respect, too, despite the evident failure of EU policies in ex-Yugoslavia, strong public support has been evident since 1990 for the development of an EU common foreign and security policy and, to a lesser extent, an EU defence dimension. Similarly, high levels of support have consistently been recorded for other aspects of EU external policy (Taylor 1996; Leonard 1997).[23]

Basing his analysis on Eurobarometer material, Taylor (1996:159) found it 'striking that overall the publics were generally happy to see some functions managed at the European level, especially foreign policy and defence'. Overseas development and global environmental issues are further areas where there was strong support for policy management at the EU level. Conversely there was general hostility to an EU role in areas directly affecting personal or family well-being. Thus, for example, 'European Union citizens were deeply convinced that other EU national doctors and medical practice were not to be relied upon!' (*ibid*). It is interesting to note the extent to which these opinions resonate both with subsidiarity as an organizing principle of the Union[24] and with the notion, suggested above, that multi-level identifications might parallel multi-level policy systems.

The conclusions reached by Leonard, whose analysis is based primarily upon UK data, support this proposition. Leonard found that –

> Poll after poll reveals that the public expects the European Union to step in where national political systems are failing: maintaining peace and security, tackling unemployment, fighting international crime, terrorism and drugs and protecting the environment.

> (Leonard 1997:47)

Leonard reports high levels of support for transfer of these policy areas to the EU – 72 per cent in relation to environmental policy and terrorism, 61 per cent in respect of foreign policy and 60 per cent favouring an EU defence dimension (*ibid*). In identifying these areas of external policy as priorities for the EU, respondents (not only in the UK) also consistently placed EMU and the Common Agricultural Policy 'towards the bottom of Euro wish lists' (Leonard 1997:47).

These analyses indicate a widely held perception that, after its most highly approved function of maintaining an 'island of peace' within its own borders, the EU's most important role is perceived as protecting and promoting European interests in the wider world. This suggests public support for the Union's aim 'to assert its identity on the international scene' (TEU Art.B [2]).[25] While these conclusions must be treated with caution, they suggest a broad perception of compatibility between national and 'European' interests in relation to external policy. As noted above, this contrasts with growing doubts about the compatibility of aspects of internal policy. These differing assessments of the benefits of EU membership reflect the complexity of contemporary identities. Thus it is possible to conceptualize various levels or contexts where interests, and identities, are protected from external threats – from the 'outsiders' whose existence confirms the identity of those who belong. This is an important aspect of identity formation, as we argue below. Thus, the Commission informs us darkly, should integration fail –

> Europe, a mere geographical entity, will come under the influence of outside powers which will extort the price of its dependence and its need for protection.
>
> (Commission 1990b:5)

This notion of the EU as protecting rather than challenging identity suggests that, in the case of external policy, there is a sense in which national identities have come to *incorporate* an EU identity. While areas of incompatibility clearly remain, and are revealed in contestation over the direction of specific policies, at a deep level relationships with outsiders are increasingly mediated through identities in which the national and European dimensions are mutually constituted. We do not imply by this the development of a single 'EU identification', but rather a French notion of the EU, which interacts with and has become part of French identity, and so on. This process of structuration derives strength from the perception that European integration is both irreversible and unstoppable (Reif 1993:146);[26] and that disruption of the integration process could prove calamitous. Thus even in the case of Denmark, it is argued, identity has increasingly come to accommodate an EU dimension. This reflects an understanding that Denmark's 'comfortable situation depends upon the current European order being upheld' (Wæver 1996:119–20).

The relationship between identity and legitimacy is both complex and dynamic. While approval of a broad but ill-defined external role for the EU appears to be widespread, public resistance to further policy integration internally, particularly in the case of EMU, demonstrates the continuing potential for national identification to act as a brake upon the integration process. Nevertheless, the framing of integration *per se* as the guarantor of stability and security in Europe increasingly involves the use of external referents to legitimize policy. Here national identities both interact with and contribute to the EU's externally oriented collective identity. At the same time internal deepening, whether through completion of the Single Market or introduction of a single currency, necessitates an enhanced external role for the EU. Thus European integration is, itself, both a continually evolving product of interaction and 'a powerful form of interaction that shapes identity' (Wæver 1995:422). This has particular relevance for collective identity formation and the associated dynamics of exclusion and inclusion. It is to these issues that we now turn.

IDENTITY AND ELIGIBILITY

The notion of eligibility has considerable significance for our discussion of the EU's role as a global actor. It provides a further demonstration of the manner in which actorness is constructed through the interaction of external and internal needs and demands. And it illustrates with particular clarity the relationship between presence and actorness. Thus the attractiveness of the EU, which generates a desire to belong, is a function of its presence. The response, in restricting and controlling access through the establishment of criteria for membership, is an important manifestation of actorness which, in turn, enhances presence – in that difficulty in obtaining access has the effect of increasing its perceived value. Moreover, the establishment of eligibility criteria initiates a process of delineating political and cultural boundaries between the excluded and the included which serves to reinforce the collective identity of the EU.

Thus far identity has been discussed primarily from the perspective of the individual, and in the sense of orientation towards the EU. However the processes of identity formation, and in particular the construction of collective identities, also involve a negative, exclusionary dimension. Identification implies belonging or membership which, in turn, implies the exclusion of non-members. Hence we are concerned with the extent to which construction of an EU collective identity is based on a negative relationship with those who are defined as outsiders. This would involve intolerance of difference and be reflected in a lack of openness to new members, whether as citizens or Member States. As Iver Neumann has observed (1996c:168) 'If it is proposed to achieve integration at the price of active othering, that price seems to be too high to pay'.

For some commentators it is axiomatic that collective identities are defined negatively. Thus for Hobsbawm (1996:40) 'Without Outsiders there are no Insiders . . . collective identities are based not on what their members have in common – they may have very little in common except not being the "Others" '. This uni-dimensional interpretation is clearly inadequate as a basis for understanding the complex relationship between identity and difference.[27] Nevertheless Hobsbawm's formulation has some resonance in the context of the EU's undoubted heterogeneity; and given the difficulties experienced in attempting to project an EU collective identity in a more positive sense (as we saw from our discussion of CFSP in Chapter 6). Certainly for primordialists the inability to conjure shared kinship and pre-history would suggest the necessity for a process of 'active othering'.[28] Below this aspect of collective identity formation is examined in relation to the criteria which determine eligibility for membership in/of the European Union.

Eligibility and the individual

For the individual, eligibility to belong is determined by two sets of criteria – the rules governing entry to the EU of migrants and asylum seekers, and the criteria which establish eligibility for citizenship of EU residents.

Immigration and asylum

In the case of entry to the EU, patterns of migration have been associated, historically, with individual Member States; and rules concerning admission of migrants and asylum seekers have been a Member State responsibility.[29] Since the mid 1980s, however, there has been a gradual Europeanization of immigration and asylum policy. The original impetus, here, came from the SEA provisions on (internal) free movement of persons, which convinced several Member State governments of the need for policy coordination on matters pertaining to external borders. This led to the 1985 Schengen Agreement (originally between Belgium, France, Germany, Luxembourg and the Netherlands but subsequently extended) and, in 1986, the establishment of the intergovernmental Ad Hoc Group on Immigration. Discussion in these groups tended, from the outset, to frame migration as a problem, and hence to focus upon restriction and control of migrant flows. Moreover issues of immigration and asylum were consistently juxtaposed with measures to combat international drug trafficking and organized crime. This juxtaposition was maintained in the TEU, where these policy areas are included in a single Article (K1) of the Justice and Home Affairs (JHA) Pillar.[30]

In the early period of their 'Europeanization' these matters were rarely the subject of public debate. However the ending of the Cold War, and the accompanying relaxation of internal controls on population movement within and from Eastern Europe, were followed by a new climate of anxiety concerning immigration. This was largely generated by alarmist predictions, on the part of Western politicians and media, of an imminent 'invasion' of up to 50 million migrants from the East (Thränhardt 1996:227–9). For Thränhardt this represented an explicit attempt to construct a new enemy. 'The end of the Cold War had banished traditional fears and dangers, and this new evil was, it seemed, to take their place' (*ibid*:228).

While, in practice, the Eastern invasion has not materialized, occasional large-scale arrivals – Albanians in Italy and Greece in 1991, Kurds also in Italy in January 1998 – rekindled fears of migrant 'invasions' carrying into the EU the instabilities affecting its neighbours.[31] Thus, in addition to the depiction of migrants as potential criminals, since the end of the Cold War migration from the East (and also from the Southern Mediterranean) has been constructed as a threat to the prosperity and stability of Western Europe; and to the identity of its peoples.

Responses to this 'threat' have occurred both at the Member State level and, increasingly, the EU level. In a bizarre reversal of Cold War practice, several Member States – Austria, Germany, Finland and Sweden – have deployed armed forces along their Eastern borders (Münz 1996:220). This concrete manifestation of 'fortress Europe' has been accompanied by increasingly restrictive Member State immigration and asylum policies; and by an effort to ensure that policies coordinated at the EU level conform with the most restrictive of Member State practices. Thus the resultant 'plethora of resolutions, recommendations and conclusions' emerging from JHA fora has focused almost entirely upon restrictive measures (Baldwin-Edwards 1997:500). In the case of asylum seekers, for example, the thrust of recent EU measures has been to discourage or impede potential applicants from reaching the EU; or, should they arrive, to return them as quickly as possible to their last destination before entering the EU.[32]

This treatment of immigration and asylum issues, involving negative stereotyping of migrants and increasingly restrictive eligibility criteria, appears to support the notion that a process of negative identification, or 'active othering' is contributing to the construction of an EU collective identity. It should be noted, however, that the Amsterdam Treaty makes some attempt to redress this negative approach to immigration and asylum issues.[33] The most significant change is the removal of these matters from the JHA Pillar. The TOA places policy on visas, asylum and immigration within Community competence, alongside policies on free movement of persons – under a new Title [IV] of the TEC.[34] Pillar III will, in future, be restricted to 'Police and Judicial Cooperation in Criminal Matters', including 'combating racism and xenophobia' [Art.29, TEU]. In addition a new TEC provision [Art.13] establishes a Treaty basis for Community action to combat discrimination on the grounds, *inter alia*, of racial or ethnic origin.

The more positive tenor of these TOA provisions suggests that attention may, in future, be given to an issue almost completely neglected at the EU level; that is the status of third country nationals resident in the EU.[35] Here the TOA makes reference to the adoption of 'measures defining the rights and conditions under which nationals of third countries who are legally resident in a Member State may reside in other Member States' [Art.63.4 TEC]. No specific proposals are included, however; and this sub-article is explicitly excluded from the five-year time limit for the adoption of measures elsewhere in Title IV.

Citizenship

The failure, to date, to extend rights to third country nationals is clearly demonstrated by the manner in which EU citizenship is presently formulated. Indeed the dependent and derivative nature of EU citizenship, with its prior requirement for Member State nationality, establishes a hierarchy of rights in which persons resident in the EU effectively fall into four categories:

- EU citizens resident in the Member State of which they are nationals. This is the only category enjoying full rights in the EU context.
- EU citizens resident in another Member State, who are excluded from participation in national elections in their country of residence.
- Third country nationals who are permanently and legally resident in an EU Member State and have access to the formal labour market, and associated workers' rights, but do not enjoy full 'freedom of movement' rights and are ineligible for EU citizenship.
- Third country nationals who are resident illegally in an EU Member State, do not have access to the formal economy and have access only to the most minimal civil and political rights.

While the position of non-legal residents is inevitably more precarious than that of legally resident third country nationals, their status in relation to the EU is largely similar. Thus, for all third country nationals, the ability to obtain EU citizenship and associated rights is entirely a function of Member State regularization and naturalization policies, which differ considerably.[36] This is clearly inconsistent with the principal right conferred by EU citizenship – that is participation in local and EU elections on the basis of residence rather than nationality. As Welsh has pointed out (1993:29):

> If it is at the local level that decisions taken by governments most directly affect individuals, why should immigrants from non-EC states be treated any differently than immigrants from states within the Community?

Clearly EU citizenship, as presently formulated, is both incoherent and exclusionary. In consequence its implications for actorness are mixed. The insistence on prior Member State nationality highlights the continuing dominance of national eligibility criteria. This reflects, in turn, the significance of national identity – and the determination of Member State governments to retain influence in policy areas considered sensitive. Nevertheless the overall impact of exclusionary practices in terms of entry and membership reinforces the construction of a negatively defined collective identity which, in turn, contributes to the presence of the EU. The increasing Europeanization of immigration and asylum policy represents an active response to this phenomenon. This process clearly demonstrates the relationship between deepening integration and the construction of an EU collective identity, on the one hand, and external actorness on the other.

Eligibility for accession

While our discussion of eligibility and the individual revealed only a limited and hesitant Europeanization of these matters, there is nevertheless evidence of an exclusionary dynamic which contributes to the collective identity of the EU. In the case of accession by applicant states, however, the formal and informal processes involved in establishing eligibility provide a very clear demonstration of collective identity formation at the EU level.

The Rome Treaty simply states that 'any European State may apply to become a member' (Art.237). No formal definition of 'European' has yet been offered; indeed this politically sensitive task has been deliberately avoided.[37] Thus, it is contended –

> The term European . . . combines geographical, historical and cultural elements which all contribute to the European identity. The shared experience of proximity, ideas, values and historical interaction cannot be condensed into a simple formula, and is subject to review by each succeeding generation . . . it is neither possible nor opportune to establish now the frontiers of the European Union, whose contours will be shaped over many years to come.
>
> (Commission 1992b:11)

In so far as the requisite 'shared ideas' and 'values' have been defined, these are 'the principles of liberty, democracy, respect for human rights and fundamental freedoms, and the rule of law' (TEU Art.6.1 [new]); that is Western, liberal principles concerning the relationship between the individual and society. The TEU, and more particularly the Amsterdam Treaty, place considerable emphasis upon these matters; indeed the TOA provides for suspension of membership rights of Member States found to be in 'serious and persistent breach' of Article 6.1 principles (TEU Art.7). This new provision evidently targets potential rather than existing members; thus its aim, in part, is to contribute to their anticipatory socialization.

In addition to the broad requirement that liberal principles be espoused, the post-Cold War proliferation of membership applications has produced a strong emphasis upon willingness and ability to take on all the obligations of membership – including the policy areas (EMU, CFSP and JHA) introduced by the Maastricht Treaty, where existing Member States have various opt-out arrangements. Indeed, as we saw in Chapter 5, aspirant members are contemporarily required to undergo an 'apprenticeship', during which they must prepare themselves for accession by approximating as closely as possible the full range of principles and practices which characterize the European Union. This suggests an intolerance of difference in marked contrast with the proclaimed reluctance to establish 'the frontiers' of the Union.

Given this overarching criterion of close approximation, all the current applications for EU membership are problematic – albeit to varying degrees – as *Agenda 2000* makes clear (Commission 1997c). In all cases, however, it has been affirmed that applicants are *eligible* for membership; that is they are considered, in principle, to qualify as European countries. In practice, however, important distinctions have become evident between the membership candidates. These centre around an implicit division between countries considered to belong to 'Central' Europe and those constructed as 'Eastern' or 'Asiatic'. This reflects a complex, post-Cold War political dynamic in which 'Eastern' has retained its meaning, in that it continues to denote alien others, who do not espouse liberal values and principles and are potentially dangerous. However the actual membership of the category 'Eastern' has been redefined in a process which, despite the appearance of delineating geographical regions, has been based, primarily, upon cultural criteria. Thus it is in constructions (and reconstructions) of collective identity that a 'European vocation', is claimed, rejected or denied.

There are three areas where these issues impinge significantly upon prospects for accession to the Union, that is –

- The construction of a division between Central Europe and Eastern Europe so as to privilege the candidacy of the Czech Republic, Hungary and Poland.
- The reconstruction of the Baltic Republics as 'CEE countries', rather than New Independent States, following dissolution of the Soviet Union.
- The treatment of Turkey's long-standing application for membership.

It is in this last case that the intrusion of identity politics has been most evident. Turkey's eligibility for membership was confirmed, in principle, in the 1964 Ankara (Association) Agreement. At that time it was considered that, before accession negotiations could begin, it would be necessary to complete the phased harmonization of Turkish–EC economic policies envisaged by the Ankara Agreement. Turkey's eligibility has twice been formally reconfirmed – in the Commission's (negative) Opinion on Turkey's membership application (Commission 1989) and, most recently, in *Agenda 2000*. In this document Turkey was treated differently from all other applicant countries – ten CEEC and Cyprus – in that no recommendation was made for accession or pre-accession strategies. On primarily political grounds Turkey, alone of the 12, qualified only for 'deepening relations' with the EU (Commission 1997a:51–2).[38]

Whereas the principal reasons for delaying Turkish accession in 1964 were stated to be economic, references to political and cultural factors have been increasingly explicit in recent years.[39] Thus, it is argued –

> nowadays, the objectors have stopped concentrating on economics, pre-ferring to dwell on the Turks' unsuitability on various other grounds; they are insufficiently democratic, they are unkind to terrorists, they were beastly to minorities, they invaded Cyprus in 1974, they are turn-ing to fundamentalism just like the Persians and they do not share the culture of true Europeans. Of all these arguments, the last two are the current favourites.
>
> (G.L. Lewis quoted in Müftüler-Bac 1997:13)

Political and cultural factors have undoubtedly always been a major source of reservations, within the EC/EU, about Turkish accession. Never-theless there has been, since the end of the Cold War, a greatly increased willingness to make these reservations explicit. This does not simply reflect Turkey's diminished strategic importance; indeed (as we argued in Chapter 5) Turkey continues to play a role in relation to Western security.[40] In the civilian context of the EU, however, the end of the Cold War has facilitated a reconceptualization of Turkish–EU relations. There are important reasons for this, which impinge upon the collective identity of the EU. First, the loss of the Soviet Union as a unifying external threat is potentially undermining to the integration process itself (as 'back to the future' prognoses suggest). And, second, the loss of its Eastern boundary, through the development of close relations with CEE 'accession partners', blurs perceptions of an East-ern 'other', in relation to which the fragile collective identity of the EU has been, in part, defined. In these circumstances, Turkey is the most obvious candidate for a process of 'active othering'.[41]

Immediately following the end of the Cold War a search began for new patterns of conflict and new 'others' to unify the West. The eastern boundary of Western Christianity in 1500 was found to have enduring significance (Wallace 1990). Samuel Huntington, in a plea for continued Western soli-darity, developed a 'West versus the rest' scenario in which, he argued, 'the Velvet Curtain of culture has replaced the Iron Curtain of ideology' (Huntington 1993:31). In particular, he notes, 'Conflict along the fault line between Western and Islamic civilizations has been going on for 1300 years (*ibid*). For the immediate future, therefore, Islam will be a central focus of threat to the West (*ibid*:48).

Islamic values/states have been widely identified as the 'new' threat to Western values and societies. In the context of the EU, Islam – personified as 'the Turk' – has several advantages as the alien other. First, there is a strong resonance with ancient fears and prejudices; indeed debates about the

European credentials of 'the Turk' date back at least to the seventeenth century (Neumann and Welsh 1991:340). Second, as in the case of Communism, it is possible to find evidence of the 'enemy' within. Indeed Turkish residents are much more readily identifiable, since they have tended to cluster together, both from choice and necessity, and to maintain their religious and other customs. This has served to emphasize cultural differences and, in particular, the 'strangeness' of the newcomers. Thus, in effect –

> There is a self-fulfilling vicious circle of the separateness of Turkish workers in Europe. With hindsight, it was a cultural and social disaster to introduce a million Anatolian peasants into the self-satisfied and conformist society of West Germany.
>
> (Sir Bernard Burrows, quoted in Müftüler-Bac 1997:31)

Thus have aspects of historical tradition and contemporary experience lent themselves to processes of 'active othering', in which there is a focus upon Turkey as different; as 'the non-European barbarian', whose presence at the gate reinforces a sense of what 'Europe' is – by constantly demonstrating what it is not (Neumann and Welsh 1991:329).

In the context of Turkish–EU relations, the processes which construct Turkey as 'other', and which emanate from within the EU, interact with and are reinforced by Turkish constructions and practices. There is considerable ambivalence, within Turkey, about the relationship with 'Europe'. This is not reducible to a simple dichotomy between secular and Islamicist forces. Despite the use of polarized images of Turkish–EU relations in their political rhetoric, both groups are deeply influenced both by Islam and by centuries of interaction with the West (Helvacioglu 1996). Thus there is an important element of Turkish identity in which nationalism and Islam overlap; and which causes Turks, also, to raise the issue of cultural compatibility in their relations with the EU. This tendency has been exacerbated by the perception that 'Within the European Union, issues of cultural compatibility and cultural integration have recently been emphasized to the point of obsession' (Müftüler-Bac 1997:11).

The growing estrangement between Turkey and the EU can thus be seen as resulting from a social process in which the collective identity of each is reinforced through mutual, active 'othering'. The EU, however, is the instigator and more powerful player in this process – as indicated by the quotation at the start of this chapter. As Neumann and Welsh observe (1991:345) 'the attitude of furious surprise by which Constantinople met European cultural demands is still very much with us'.

In the case of CEEC–EU relations, the involvement of the EU in the processes of inclusion and exclusion has been less overt than in the case of Turkey; indeed official EU sources deny the use of cultural criteria in determining priorities for accession. Even following identification of the chosen five in *Agenda 2000* (this matter is discussed further below) there has been an effort to maintain the appearance of parity of treatment of all ten 'candidates'. Within CEE countries, too, divisions over policy towards the EU have been relatively minor when compared with the Turkish case. In CEEC the notion of a 'return to Europe' has been a common theme, intended to establish that each belongs to a pan-European cultural community.

Despite this, the construction of cultural divisions between applicant countries has been clearly evident – not least from the identity forming processes within CEEC themselves. At the core of these processes has been the creation of a division between the countries (and peoples) of 'East *Central* Europe', which are construed as truly European, and the Slavic, Orthodox 'Asiatic' peoples of the East. Of great influence, here, has been the construction of 'Central Europe' (originally Czechoslovakia, Hungary and Poland) as 'A kidnapped land of the West' (Milan Kundera 1983, quoted in Tunander 1997:17). This notion, which suggests moral, cultural and geographical arguments for prioritization of these countries, has been enthusiastically adopted by intellectuals and politicians in all three 'Central' European countries, and by their supporters in the West.[42] It has also been subject to refinement in several cases. Thus the Czech Republic now includes Slovakia among its 'alien others', and the European/Asiatic dichotomy 'is routinely invoked to demarcate the border between the two' (Neumann 1996b:14). Similarly, Hungarians represent Romanians as 'Asiatic', while Romanians speak likewise of Ukrainians, and the latter of Russians.[43] A similar process of constructing a culturally defined hierarchy of approximation to the West has also been evident in the Balkans. Here, for example, Slovenian claims to a 'Central' European identity are constructed, in part, with reference to the 'Balkan' character of neighbouring countries (*ibid*:15).

While active participation in these competitive processes of identity formation has largely been avoided, they are nevertheless indicative of the EU's significant presence in the region.[44] In the case of the Baltic republics, however, the EC/EU has contributed actively to the construction of these countries' 'return to Europe'.[45] From the outset, when according formal recognition to the new states, the EC celebrated the resumption of 'their rightful place among the nations of Europe' (*EPC Bulletin*, 27 August 1991). Subsequently the EC/EU maintained and reinforced its inclusionary policies towards the Baltic republics. In a move which had important symbolic and substantive impacts, at the end of 1991 the Community transferred – and in a real sense *promoted* – the Baltic republics from the Tacis programme (of financial cooperation with NIS) to the CEEC oriented Phare programme.[46] Effectively, from this time, the Baltic republics have participated, in common with other CEEC, in the incremental processes leading towards accession. The proactive role played by the EC/EU in the inclusion of the Baltic republics created a dynamic that has also served to exclude NIS, such as Ukraine, which claim membership of 'the kidnapped West' (see note 46). Thus the CEEC/NIS division established an early, and important, inclusion/exclusion dynamic which has been reinforced, *inter alia*, by the differing aims and impacts of the Phare and Tacis programmes.

The EU has also contributed to the dynamics of inclusion/exclusion between CEEC. Through imposing stringent criteria for eligibility, and subsequently according roughly equal treatment to applicants, the EC effectively established an apprenticeship scheme which made little provision for participants with 'special needs'. It is only since publication of *Agenda 2000* that the notion of 'catch-up strategies' has been introduced. In this way EC/EU policies privileged those countries most able to establish cultural compatibility with the West at an early stage. Selection of the Czech Republic, Hungary, Poland and Slovenia for early accession (and exclusion of 'Slavic' Bulgaria, Romania and Slovakia) fit this argument. The case of Estonia is different, in that the EC (and the Nordic countries) had actively encouraged cooperation between the Baltic republics and processes of cultural differentiation were less evident here. Nevertheless Estonia was deemed by the Commission to have 'advanced' more quickly than its neighbours. Consequently the decision to open negotiations only with Estonia would appear to create a new inclusion/exclusion dynamic within this sub-region.

In the post-Cold War period the EU's magnetic presence has attracted numerous applications for membership or other close forms of close association. This, in turn, has presented the need/opportunity for fuller elucidation, and more partial application, of eligibility criteria. A consequence of this has been the construction of Turkey as an ineligible 'other', and the EU's contribution to processes of active othering within Central/Eastern Europe. Through participating in these processes of identity formation, the EU's collective identity has, in turn, been reinforced.

CONCLUSION

This chapter has surveyed a range of issues which impinge, in varying ways, both upon the presence and the actor capability of the EU. Our central focus has been upon identity. This is seen as potentially contributing, through feelings of belonging, to legitimization of EU policy; and in terms of eligibility, or establishing the criteria for belonging. The common thread which links these themes is that each contributes, ultimately, to the collective identity, and hence the presence, of the EU.

Legitimacy, it is maintained, is a requirement for actorness. Following an early period when legitimacy was not considered an important issue for the EC, a number of substantive measures were introduced – from direct elections to the European Parliament to EU citizenship – to promote public awareness and participation. Other, symbolic measures (anthem, logo, etc.) intended to promote identification with the EU were also suggestive of state-like processes of collective identity formation. None of these measures has been successful in promoting a strong sense of belonging or loyalty to the

EU, indeed popular support appears to have waned rather than increased in the period since their introduction. This has led some commentators to conclude that the EU is suffering a legitimacy crisis.

There are important implications, here, for our consideration of external actorness, not least because declining support for the EC/EU has been evident only since the early 1990s. Consequently the decline in support/legitimacy might appear to result from the combined effect of two factors – loss of the unifying effect of the Cold War external enemy and the over-ambitious aims of the TEU, several of which were explicitly oriented towards external action by the Union. On closer examination, however, this hypothesis is unconvincing, for two reasons. First, survey evidence suggests that it is in areas of external policy that public approval of the EU's role is highest. Second, there has been, since the end of the Cold War, a strong and persuasive rhetoric which promotes the integration process itself as necessary, not only to the security and prosperity of the peoples of its Member States, but to the stability of Europe as a whole. Here there is evidence of a process of social construction which provides European integration with new meaning, and potentially legitimizes an expanded external role for the EU. While this is a fragile formula when compared with the claims of national identity, there is a sense in which, in relation to external policy, national identities encompass an EU dimension. It is here that we find the intersection between individual and collective identities.

In discussing the construction of an EU collective identity, we have focused upon the concept of eligibility, and in particular the establishment of rules and criteria which determine the right to belong. This concept provides useful links between presence and actorness, in that the need to establish eligibility criteria reflects presence, while the ability to do so is a function of actorness.

In relation to the individual, eligibility refers to the right to enter the EU, as an immigrant or asylum seeker, and the right to citizenship of persons who are already resident. Here the role of Member States has remained dominant in establishing the rules governing eligibility. Thus, for example, EU citizenship can derive only from prior citizenship of a Member State. There has nevertheless been an incremental Europeanization of this policy area, which has reflected an increasingly exclusionary dynamic and a process of constructing 'outsiders', whether resident within the EU or seeking entry, as alien others. This has been construed as a process of 'active othering', in which the collective identity of the EU is reinforced by reference to the otherness of those considered ineligible to belong.

These processes are strongly evident in relation to applicants for accession to the EU. Here, in the face of unprecedented external demands, the ability to determine eligibility has increasingly come to mean that candidates for membership are required to undergo a pre-accession apprenticeship. During this time, under the tutelage of the Commission, they must attempt to transform themselves into an approximation of the Community model. As we have seen, the selection procedures associated with this process have produced a dynamic of inclusion/exclusion which has reinforced perceptions of cultural difference. Nowhere is this more evident than in the case of Turkey, where even the dubious privilege of a pre-accession apprenticeship has been denied.

The negative processes of active othering, which can be observed in relation both to individual and collective 'alien others', undoubtedly contribute to the collective identity, and to the presence, of the EU. Their significance is increased by the absence of a stronger, positive identification, in the sense of feelings of belonging to the European Union. This gives urgency to Brigid Laffan's (1996) plea for a sense of shared community, based on mutual trust and tolerance of diversity, as the most appropriate basis for legitimacy and identity at the EU level.

Conclusion

> To the post-modernist, the polymorphic structure of the EU is simply the reflection of the post-modern condition, and quite likely permanent ... that the study of European integration is in its post-ontological phase is a refreshing development. Endless debate about 'what the EU is' cannot be productive unless tied to detailed, though theoretically informed, empirical studies. Similarly these empirical studies are unlikely to acquire their full significance unless integrated with broad conceptualisations of the nature and significance of the evolving European Union. Hopefully, the decade ahead will harmonise these up till now somewhat unconnected projects.
>
> (Caporaso 1996:49)

James Caporaso's words were published when this study was already under way, but they articulate our own view of what is required. It is for the reader to judge how far we have moved along the road that he has charted.

It was clear, even in the first years of its existence, that the EC could be regarded as one of the 'new actors' in international politics (Cosgrove and Twitchett 1970). The Community was distinguishable both legally and behaviourally from the sum of its Member State parts. Yet much the same could be said for a range of international organizations enjoying a separate institutional existence and run by secretariats exhibiting a degree of autonomy from their political masters. The real question for students of the EC/EU is the extent and weight of actor capability – which we refer to as 'actorness'. As we have argued throughout there is an intimate relationship between presence and actorness. To say that the presence of the EU has grown substantially on a number of dimensions – especially since the mid 1980s – is uncontroversial. This in itself has significant consequences for the global system and particularly for those countries constituting the EU's 'near abroad'. While presence provides a basis for and stimulus to the development of actorness it does not predetermine the latter. With the possible exception of relations with the CEEC, in none of the external policy areas that we have surveyed has the potential suggested by the scale of EU presence been fully realized in terms of actorness.

Towards the end of Chapter 1 we proposed five requirements for actorness:

1 Shared commitment to a set of overarching values and principles.
2 The ability to identify policy priorities and to formulate coherent policies.
3 The ability to negotiate effectively with other actors in the international system.
4 The availability of, and capacity to utilize, policy instruments.
5 Domestic legitimation of decision processes, and priorities, relating to external policy.

We regarded the first of these requirements as unproblematic. The 'mission statement' of the Union has been revised and developed over the years and is formally embedded in the treaties along with provisions in the 1997 Amsterdam Treaty to punish deviant Members. Analysis of the specifics of EU external relations and in particular the content of the latest Association agreements and CFSP *démarche*, reveals a consistent pursuit of a number of normative objectives – an actor with an agenda that goes beyond trade promotion, market opening and orthodox economic development. Very notable is an increasing insistence on democratic values, free elections and human rights. The benefits of association and aid to third parties are made conditional upon performance in these areas and one of the few external policy roles allowed to the European Parliament is as watchdog and publicist of the failings both of EU institutions and their potential or actual foreign partners. Another preoccupation – in line with aspirations to global environmental leadership – is sustainability. This requirement appears alongside human rights provisions in Association agreements and is a key element in the EU's regional activities. On a wider stage the EC has championed the introduction of environmental considerations into the international trade regime at the WTO Committee on Trade and Environment. Finally, although it may not be a formal treaty objective, it is impossible to avoid noticing a propensity of the Community to reproduce itself. Thus, it has long advocated its own form of regional integration and encouraged and favoured attempts in Latin America, Africa and South-East Asia to do likewise.

One is struck immediately by the scope of EU policies. They cover, to a greater or lesser extent, all the significant issue areas of contemporary global politics, except for strictly military and strategic relations. Even here, the Union adopted CFSP joint actions on non-proliferation and was involved in 1996 with the US in KEDO, designed to manage the danger of North Korean acquisition of a nuclear weapons capability. There are no actors with a comparable range of interests, policies and relationships in the contemporary system. The United States is the obvious rival but, as was pointed out to us by a Commission official, 'the US often cannot define a credible negotiating platform – they cannot think of all the North–South ramifications as the Community can' (Interview, DGXI, June 1996). Nevertheless, it has become apparent in reviewing the Union's external policies that breadth of policy coverage may not always be matched by clarity, consistency and coherence.

Trade must be the starting point for any consideration of extent of the Community's ability to identify policy priorities and formulate coherent policies. Exclusive Community competence for the Common Commercial Policy has meant that trade policy priorities have been articulated by the Commission, and that inconsistencies between Member State policies have been resolved into a single external policy (for example in the automobile sector with regard to Japanese imports). The distinctive approach of the EC and especially its predilection for preferential agreements is a relatively permanent feature of international trade discourse. This is not to disregard the influence of national commercial interests in the Council and 113 Committee, which remain substantial and frequently give rise to mean-spirited and protectionist outcomes. Similar comments can be made about other common policy areas, such as agriculture and fisheries, despite the fact that they sometimes provide grounds for incoherence in overall trade policy.

Beyond the Common Commercial Policy there have been difficulties over the extension of competence to services and intellectual property and there is no unified approach between Member States when investment or trade and labour standards appear on the agenda. Although the finance ministers in ECOFIN have long attempted to coordinate their position and to exert influence in international monetary affairs as a group – actorness remains problematic. The most dramatic and significant change in actor capability is likely to be occasioned by establishment of Economic and Monetary Union – which could well place the EU on a par with its principal economic adversary and partner, the United States.

In the case of environmental issues, mixed competence has the potential to cause problems in the formulation of external policy. Yet they have generally been overcome, and differences between Member States have not meant that EU policy has been immobile or reduced to the lowest common denominator. Some incoherence in terms of defining the overall objectives of the Union is inherent because of the intersectoral character of environmental policy. Development policy is a somewhat different case. Here the Community has its own long established and well defined approach to development cooperation but this is ranged against the competing national policies of Member States, often resulting in serious inconsistency 'on the ground'. In relations with CEE countries where competence is shared, the exigencies of ensuring the transfer of the *acquis* have meant that the Commission has been allowed to dominate the setting of targets and requirements for the aspirant members.

It is, of course, in the area of the CFSP that EU actor capability has been most publicly found wanting. The intergovernmental arrangements within

Pillar II do not demand the community discipline that is required within Pillar I, but accentuate the need for collective political will on the part of Member State governments. The sorry chapter of inconsistency, from the German recognition of Croatia through to the divergent paths taken by Member States over Iraq and at the UN, needs no further recounting. Nonetheless there are signs that in smaller and less dramatic ways common policy positions on a wide range of 'political' topics have been formulated through the EPC and then the CFSP mechanism; articulated by the Presidency and then adhered to by Member State governments.

This pattern of achievement and underachievement would not be entirely predictable on the basis of competence. That is to say the lack of a formal initiating role for the Commission and QMV in the Council does not necessarily mean that EU policy will be inconsistent and directionless. There are areas of environmental policy, for example, where – despite shared or very limited Community competence – the EU has taken a strong and distinctive position. Here there will still be reliance upon substantial input from the Commission and very often upon an activist group of 'lead' Member States.

Capability in policy formation is closely related to our third requirement which highlights the importance of negotiation for international actors. In formal terms involvement in diplomacy and access to international organizations and conferences of the parties require recognition and usually full legal personality (although international organizations and NGOs are increasingly granted observer rights). Although enjoying legal personality, the EC's status in international organizations varies widely between full member in the absence of Member States, REIO alongside the Member States and mere observer (the EU has no strict legal personality but is increasingly recognized nonetheless). The Commission is engaged in a campaign to maintain and extend its competence and representational role and is tireless in pushing the claims of the Community as opposed to the Member States in international fora. 'Turf conflicts' with Member States inevitably result, especially within a UN context.

Commission officials can point to the undoubted negotiating efficiency that derives from Art.113 type procedures, but in many areas a shifting bicephalous arrangement pertains with all the extra burdens of daily coordination meetings. In the CFSP the responsibility of representing and negotiating for the Union falls upon the rotating Presidency assisted by the troika. Given the variation in size and diplomatic capability amongst the 15 presidents there are bound to be disparities in performance, and the problems of maintaining such an intergovernmental approach are widely recognized. Whether the Amsterdam revisions to the CFSP will give it more permanence and focus remains to be seen.

One generalization, that may hold across the wide range of EU negotiating activity, is that it tends to be slow to take up positions and, once taken, they are difficult to amend. This is a structural consequence of the Union's internal decision making procedures which in effect adds an extra layer of political complexity (even when there is Community competence). The negotiator has no single constituency but 15, along with the normal special interests and, indeed, the Commission itself. It is, in the circumstances, not surprising that the EU/EC can be a ponderous negotiating partner deficient in the flexibility that may be required to arrive at a speedy conclusion.

The complex and unique nature of the EU system need not always be a source of negotiating disadvantage. Commission negotiators can and do exploit, as a commitment tactic, the potential for long delay should there be a need to refer matters back to the Council. Similarly, as was evident in the discussion of environmental negotiations, competence and coordination problems during a negotiation can also be turned to the tactical advantage of the EC. However, it is also the case that, despite the requirements of Community discipline, Member States are continuously involved in parallel diplomacy and third countries will often be able to operate on two fronts. As we heard on a number of occasions, Member State representatives are not averse to blaming the Commission and privately assuring interlocutors that their government, of course, does not really approve of this EC or EU position.

Overall the European actor has been a surprisingly effective negotiator. This might be expected in many of its bilateral dealings with small trading partners or with the CEEC applicants. These relationships often hardly constitute negotiations at all in that third parties have to take what has been agreed by the Council or accept the totality of the *acquis* – 'opt-outs are not for them'. The real test is provided by relations with large trading partners or within a multilateral context. Here, to its credit, the EC has ensured that its Southern ACP partners are organized within a structure that does allow them to argue collectively with the Community. As was observed in Chapter 2, the GATT Uruguay Round posed an extended and severe test for the EC. Despite delays and dissensions and actions by the Commission which continue to sow suspicion with the Member States, it eventually managed to pass the test. The Common Commercial Policy and its relationship to the GATT/WTO almost ordains that the EC find a solution to its negotiating problems.

The fourth requirement for actorness was the availability of instruments, providing amongst other things the underlying bargaining leverage upon which successful negotiation depends. In many ways this dimension of actorness constitutes the mobilization of presence. Here it may be worth distinguishing between specific instruments of relational power and the EC's structural power position at the apex of its pyramid of preferences. Despite the long-run significance of the latter, most attention has been directed to relational power capabilities. In this respect the EU remains a 'civilian power'. As we saw in Chapter 7, aspirations towards the acquisition of a dedicated military capability through the WEU have not been fulfilled. Thus in the exercise of relational power the EU remains exclusively reliant upon economic instruments across the spectrum of its policies. These include denial of access to the Single Market – and ultimately denial of association/ membership. Coupled with this is the granting and withdrawal of aid. A range of instruments exist in the trade field allowing for contingent protection and countervailing action – with anti-dumping action as the weapon of choice. The use of such instruments is strictly limited to trade disputes, with the General Affairs Council solemnly approving punitive duties against South Korean exports of underpriced zip-fasteners and personal fax machines. However, there has also been an increasing articulation of economic instruments to broadly defined political objectives – particularly human rights. This is why coordination between Pillars I and II is so critical for a successful CFSP. The actor's 'muscle', for the foreseeable future, resides within Pillar I.

Our final requirement for actorness, legitimacy of decision processes and priorities, has increasingly become a problem with the expansion of the EU's internal and external activities. The difficulties encountered in ratifying the Maastricht Treaty attest to this. Indeed there have subsequently been concerns that the EU is suffering a legitimacy crisis. We do not fully share this concern, however. While there is little evidence of a shift of affective identification from the national to the EU level, there are clear indications of acceptance that the external roles played by the EU are complementary, in important ways, to Member State policies. This suggests a broader acceptance of the EU's external roles than would be the case where policies impact directly on everyday lives.

As we have frequently observed, the EU is not a state; and attempts during the 1980s to equip it with the symbols of statehood may have been misguided. However the substantial change involved in replacement of national currencies may yet provide a significant challenge to legitimacy which could impact more generally, including upon external policy. On the other hand, Economic and Monetary Union offers the prospect of completing the economic dimension of actorness and creating a new monetary entity of primary importance in the global political economy.

Having established that, today, the EU is a global actor of some significance, we now turn to examine the contribution that it makes to global politics; that is to identify and assess its external roles. A central concern, here, is with the interaction between presence, opportunity and the capacity and willingness both to respond to external demands and to initiate action. The complex interaction between these factors produces patterns of actorness, and associated roles, which fall broadly into three categories –

- Areas where the Treaty of Rome accords legal responsibility to act.
- Areas where action has been necessitated by economic presence.
- Areas where there is a distinctive EU policy agenda.

The Rome Treaty provides for an EC role in trade policy and lays the foundations for its involvement in development cooperation. This provides a firm legal basis for actorness, and establishes Community competence in these areas. However a reading of the TEC provides little guidance to the subsequent development of actorness in these policy areas. This reflects, to a significant extent, the growth of the EC's presence as its policy scope became wider and its membership expanded. Presence, based in particular upon economic strength, is undoubtedly the major source of the EU's influence in the world. Much has been said about the importance of the Single Market, and its magnet effect has been very evident throughout our discussion. Similarly, the external impacts of internal policies, in particular the Common Agricultural Policy, have been amply demonstrated.

Action by the EC/EU has been necessitated by the impact of its economic presence in several areas. A particular example, here, is the development of its 'gatekeeper' role. Whether in governing access to the Single Market, or determining the eligibility criteria for membership or accession, the relationship between presence and actorness can readily be demonstrated. This relationship is mutually reinforcing, in that the ability to determine access reinforces the collective identity of the EU, and hence its presence. Moreover, in circumstances where there is an element of dependency upon the EU, the opportunity has been afforded for the development of unprecedented actorness – through the role of patron/mentor. This is most clearly evident in relation to the countries of Central and East Europe, which have been subjected to a lengthy pre-accession apprenticeship involving 'the most peremptory and intrusive terms imposed on Western countries not defeated in war (*The Guardian*, 20 April 1998). In the area of development cooperation, too, the EC plays a dominant role as patron/mentor, particularly in relation to the ACP Group. Here, however, the relationship between presence and actorness is such that action is constrained rather than promoted by presence; in that the dependency of ACP 'partners', whose weakness is so apparent, engenders a responsibility to maintain the Lomé relationship.

Environmental policy is a further area where presence has necessitated action by the EC/EU. This is particularly the case in relation to regional environmental matters, where the EC has played an important role, in cooperation with its neighbours, in environmental management. The EC's broader presence, for example in relation to its fishing effort or its position as major producer and exporter of CFCs, has also necessitated involvement in global environmental diplomacy. Indeed, it was in this area that EC involvement at the transcontinental level led to the creation of the UN category of REIO. This provides one rather legalistic example of how actorness can be socially constructed through the development of shared understandings concerning the EC's role. However, in some areas such understandings remain tenuous. For example, the relationship between presence and actorness in global environmental change issue areas is weaker than in those trade and aid relationships where economic presence is central. Hence, although here, as elsewhere, presence preceded actorness, the aspiration to a leadership role in environmental diplomacy could not entirely have been predicted on this basis.

The role of environmental leader falls within those areas where there is evidence of a distinctive EU policy agenda. These would also include the aspiration to exercise leadership in aspects of 'new' trade issues (on the basis of the EC's own internal experiences of commercial liberalization) and the EC's embryonic market opening strategies. In these areas there continues to be a relationship between presence and actorness; but presence, here, serves to facilitate rather than promote action. Indeed, in areas where there is both opportunity and will to act, presence can be a source of influence and an instrument of policy. However the ability to respond proactively to new policy areas associated with trade and global environmental change is constrained by internal divisions – which are reflected in disputes over competence. Thus the areas where there is an aspiration to leadership are also areas where the role of the EC/EU is problematic.

This applies equally to those policy areas entrusted explicitly to the EU. Here the Common Foreign and Security Policy was intended to be the principal means through which a political direction for the Union as a whole could be established and expressed. Indeed the creation of the Union itself, and the statement of broad external policy objectives and guiding principles which accompanied it, was intended to provide an overall framework for external policy. However a more effective articulation between political will and economic presence has been slow to materialize in practice. For the Commission it has been 'a supreme frustration' that the full potential of economic presence has not been realized. This is seen as reflecting a lack of confidence, internally, in the Union's capability as an actor, which is based upon a tendency to 'look at external policy in terms of what is lacking . . . 95 per cent of foreign policy has nothing to do with military hardware but we allow the 5 per cent to colour our view of ourselves' (Interview, DGI, June 1996). Nevertheless, there is now a realization that the Commission must take a more proactive role in 'political' or 'trade plus' matters and that it must, 'in the greater interest of the Union', be prepared to allow ideas generated within the Commission to be subsumed within a Presidency paper (Interview, DGI, July 1997). In Chapter 6 we noted the routine use of the EC's economic presence in the furtherance of political objectives. This can also be observed from high profile initiatives such as the burgeoning policy towards China, which has been drafted by Commissioner Sir Leon Brittan and is intended to 'promote the EU as a global partner and diplomatic power' (*The Guardian*, 3 February 1998).

Nowhere is the increasingly effective articulation between presence and actorness more evident than in policy towards the 'near abroad'. Of particular interest is the relationship with countries where accession is not currently an issue. For example policy towards Russia is viewed, externally, as having been relatively successful; the EC is seen as 'more helpful to Russia than the Americans' (Interview, external Mission, June 1996). The

Euro–Mediterranean Partnership Initiative also provides an excellent example of an area where wide ranging political and security-related policy objectives have been linked to the EC's economic presence; and where the EU's quiet diplomacy is seen as particularly appropriate (Asmus, Larrabee and Lesser 1996).

Relations with the CEE and Mediterranean countries are again indicative of the EU's distinctive policy agenda; and of a further role which we have identified for our actor – as deliberate exporter of its own 'model', its policy preferences and its methods. Here presence denotes more than the clearly observable effects of economic strength; indeed an important source of the EU's influence has been as a model – of regional economic integration in the face of globalizing forces, or as 'community of security' in post-Cold War Europe. Again, presence has been linked to actorness. The EC/EU has actively promoted the 'export' of its economic model – to Africa and South America as well as to the near abroad – and attempted to project stability beyond its borders.

The development of the Union's role as a purveyor of 'soft security' is not only a reflection of the relationship between presence and actorness, however. Here the opportunities afforded by the changing external environment of the post-Cold War period have been associated with new understandings about the meaning of security, to generate increased expectations, both internally and externally, that the EU can and should play a security role. The rapid growth of the European Community Humanitarian Office is a notable outcome of this process. Evolving understandings about the meaning of security also have significance, internally, for the processes of legitimation. In this case there has been an active attempt, primarily on the part of the Commission, to 'securitize' the integration process itself – through promoting the understanding that the consequences of failure would be disastrous (Commission 1990b; Wæver 1996).

Such understandings, we have argued, contribute to the construction of intersubjective structures which provide distinct patterns of opportunity and constraint within which actorness is shaped and displayed. It is thus through the evolving, cyclical relationship between presence and actorness that new meanings and practices are constructed. Here, because of its peculiar characteristics, the very existence of the EU has influenced the development of the contemporary international system. The changing practices of third parties interacting with the EU, attest to this. The very substantial number of external Missions accredited to the EC is significant; but perhaps even more important has been the perceptible shift of US diplomatic effort from the Member States to the EU. These subtly changing practices reveal the processes involved in responding to the EU's growing presence; and in constructing understandings about EU actorness. They are also evident internally. With varying degrees of enthusiasm Member State governments have shifted both their conceptions of foreign policy and their practices:

The role of the Foreign Office [FCO] has radically changed as the EU has grown in importance. Ninety per cent of London based FCO staff now deal with EU matters. As one former FCO civil servant said, 'There is a feeling in the foreign office that nothing moves without first going through a European filter – there is almost no area of policy that does not have a European dimension.

(Leonard 1997:26)

Elsewhere the evolution of new understandings has been, perhaps, less subtle. Thus, for example, the understanding that an Eastern enlargement of the EU is inevitable has generated a dynamic of inclusion and exclusion, and associated processes of 'active othering', with which the EU has been complicit through the elaboration and application of eligibility criteria (Neumann 1996c). Particularly noticeable, here, has been the recently increased willingness of prominent politicians to state publicly that Turkey is ineligible. These processes of active self-definition have, in turn, contributed significantly to the collective identity, and hence the presence, of the EU.

Clearly presence is central to an understanding of the construction of actorness. Here a generalization would be that presence denotes latent actorness. However the relationship between presence and actorness is not direct. It is mediated by the patterns of constraint and opportunity afforded by the external environment in which the EU operates; and by the capacity to respond. This last is central to the complex and uncertain relationship between presence and actorness. It denotes the political will to create a European actor capable not only of responding to external expectations but of actively contributing to the construction of understandings and practices which in turn shape the expectations of others.

Patterns of opportunity, and the ability to respond effectively, are central to an appreciation of the outcome of these complex processes of structuration. Since the end of the Cold War the EU has been confronted by an external environment which is perhaps uniquely conducive to EU actorness. Following initial concerns that violent upheaval across much of Eastern Europe would present an unsurmountable military challenge to the EU, there has been a significant development of shared understandings that economic and environmental interdependence give pre-eminence to economic instruments of policy. The EU's response to these new opportunities has been highly ambitious. Externally it has attempted to seize a leadership role in environmental diplomacy; embarked upon an unprecedented programme of pre-accession relations with 11 countries; developed an important initiative in the Mediterranean region and entered into a new 'great power' relationship with China. Internally a significant and highly controversial process of deepening is under way as the final stages of Economic and Monetary Union are reached and the single currency launched.

Our study builds up a picture of the European actor during the mid 1990s. The full implications of EMU and enlargement cannot be predicted and it is quite possible that, in retrospect, the current period may come to be regarded as the zenith of actorness. It is perhaps more probable, but by no means certain, that current developments are laying the foundations of extended presence and enhanced actor capability.

It has been our contention that an attempt to view the EU through the conceptual lenses of statehood will result in an image that obscures its fundamental characteristics as an international actor. In a purely chronological sense the contemporary EU is a postmodern political entity reflecting the inadequacies of the European nation state, the special opportunities and expectations attending the end of the Cold War and the development of an increasingly globalized economy. In the other sense of the word, the EU's 'polymorphic' nature is in equal measure intriguing and annoying – especially for those outsiders who have to interact with it. Ruggie's view that the EU may represent the first postmodern political form need not imply (and by definition probably could not imply) that it represents the first of a new class of global actors arising from the ashes of the Westphalian order. Although the EU assiduously propagates aspects of its own model there are, in practice, no contemporary comparators. It remains, as the International Lawyers say, *sui generis*. Instead, it holds up a mirror to some of the profound changes that have occurred in the late twentieth century global system. For political and diplomatic practitioners in that system and for its academic students, whatever their specialisms, an understanding of the peculiarities of the European actor is indispensable.

Notes

Introduction

1 See Authors' Note for an explanation of our utilization of the titles European Community and European Union.

2 At the suggestion of one Political Counsellor, we interviewed her a second time six months after her transfer to London. On this occasion, however, she plied *us* with questions about the outcome and implications of the impending UK General Election!

3 This approach is exemplified by the work of Simon Hix (1994), and is increasingly employed in analysis of EU 'domestic' policy. See, for example, Peterson (1995); Marks, Hooghe and Blank (1996); Kohler-Koch (1996).

4 At the time of writing, the Treaty of Amsterdam (TOA) had been signed but had not yet entered into force. Since the TOA will have the effect of altering the numbering of all Articles, both in the TEC and the TEU, we have included the new numbering in square brackets immediately following the existing numbering. Non-Euro anoraks may choose to ignore this exciting refinement.

5 In EC terminology Maghreb refers to Algeria, Morocco and Tunisia. See also Chapter 5, note 47.

6 The European Court of Justice (ECJ) also plays an important role, particularly in circumstances where competence is unclear. Thus it has continuously adjudicated the extent of the Common Commercial Policy (CCP) and has contributed to the evolution of Community competence in the 'new' area of environmental diplomacy. See Chapters 2 and 3.

7 In the interest of accuracy we should note that Pillar I actually comprises the European Communities – that is the EC, Euratom and the ECSC. The original Treaty of Rome appellation European Economic Community was replaced, in the TEU, by the title European Community.

8 For discussion of the role of Permanent Representatives see Hayes-Renshaw, Lequesne and Lopez (1989). The operation of the Council system is fully described in Hayes-Renshaw and Wallace (1997).

9 In such circumstances Member States are effectively invoking the Luxembourg Compromise – an agreement instituted in 1966 to accommodate fears of creeping supranationalism on the part of the French government. Although the Single European Act introduced Qualified Majority Voting in specified policy areas, and use of this procedure was subsequently extended by the TEU, Member State pleas concerning 'national interest' continue to intrude in areas of external policy considered 'sensitive'. See, for example, the Portuguese government's position on textiles referred to in Chapter 2.

10 In relation to external policy, the new emphasis on sound, efficient management has resulted in a proposal to separate policy initiation from the management of

EC programmes. This has attracted considerable criticism and, indeed, resistance – to the extent that implementation of the proposal (planned for April 1998) has been difficult to achieve.

1 Actors and actorness in global politics

1 The draft Treaty produced at the end of the Irish Presidency in December 1996 explicitly accords legal personality to the Union (Conference of the Representatives of the Member States 1996). However the text finally agreed at Amsterdam the following June merely establishes a procedure whereby the Union can negotiate agreements through a unanimous Council authorization of the Presidency. A further, unanimous Council vote will be required to authorize the conclusion of agreements, which may still be subject to domestic ratification procedures in the case of some Member States (TEU Art.J.14 [24]).

2 Although we do not underestimate the importance of their influence, we would question whether social categories can legitimately be considered as actors – as will be apparent from the criteria of actorness we have adopted.

3 These figures are taken from a European Commission report (1995a). However the precise number of procedures is the subject of disagreement between the institutions. The Treaty of Amsterdam, on entry into force, will both simplify and reduce the number of decision making procedures, at least in the EC Pillar.

4 For a discussion of the challenges facing structural realism in the 1990s see Vogler (1996).

5 The EC research framework programme 1990–4 allocated 5700 million ECU, more than two-thirds of which targeted the areas of communications and information technology and biotechnology (Commission 1991c:11).

6 This issue is at the centre of Cox's concerns, and in 1993 he saw the possibility that social democratic ideas might prosper in Central and Eastern Europe; and that this might increase the influence of these ideas in Western Europe. The case of Sweden is instructive, in that the Swedish government has used EU membership to legitimize domestic policy change. Public disapproval of the gradual dismantling of the Swedish social model, however, has focused on the 'undemocratic' EU. Thus, in Sweden, public support for EU membership fell from a slim majority in favour in January 1995 to 27 per cent in favour in the autumn of 1996 (Commission 1996a).

7 The 'structuration theory' of Anthony Giddens provides a starting point for much work in the constructivist vein, although the strategic-relational approach of Bob Jessop provides a more structurally oriented alternative. See Giddens (1984) and Jessop (1990) for examples of this literature. For a criticism of constructivist approaches, which rejects the validity of attempts to overcome the agency/structure dichotomy, see Hollis and Smith (1991).

8 There are currently 164 Missions accredited to the EC. There has been a steady increase in accreditations since the mid 1980s, reflecting both the importance to third parties of the Single Market programme and, of course, the creation of new states following the disintegration of the Soviet Union.

9 Notions of shared sovereignty have frequently been employed by politicians. For example Geoffrey Howe, when UK Foreign Secretary, visualized the 'shared sovereignties' of the Member States as the intertwined strands in a skein of wool.

10 Notions of post-territoriality primarily refer to the transcendence or blurring of boundaries within the EU. In relation to the EU's *external* boundaries, contemporary debates about enlargement to the East and South are creating a dynamic of inclusion and exclusion which essentially involves the *delineation* of borders. While these are based primarily upon political and cultural criteria,

they also have an important territorial dimension. These matters re-emerge in Chapters 5, 7 and 8.

11 Today, the EU is maintaining this distinctive stance through, for example, its support for the Palestinian Authority and strengthening its relations with Cuba.

12 A particularly nice, but by no means untypical, example is provided by a 1997 headline – 'Germans urge Europe to rescue Bulgaria' (*The Guardian*, 28 February 1997).

13 A more recent scheme, proposed by Hill (1993:317), sets out the requirements for an EC 'single foreign policy'. If the EC were to meet these requirements, which range from democratic accountability and judicial scrutiny to a single cultural policy and common armed forces, it would attain 'the external quality of a state (and *ipso facto* superpower status)' (*ibid*:316).

14 In addition, of course, the Environment Directorate-General (DGXI), and others, also have significant external involvement.

15 In the case of development policy, for example, the difficulties in developing a coherent approach are demonstrated by the involvement, to a greater or lesser extent, of all five Relex DGs.

16 These articles were introduced into the TEC only after entry into force of the TEU in 1993. For discussion of their operation, and the *ad hoc* arrangements for sanctions which pertained prior to 1993, see MacLeod, Hendry and Hyett (1996).

2 The EU as an economic power and trade actor

1 This represents a precipitate relative decline since the 1950s, when the present 15 members of the Union represented 11.8 per cent of world population (and the US 6.1 per cent). Such a demographic trend will continue into the twenty-first century when, by 2025, the two late twentieth century economic giants will each comprise no more than around 4 per cent of world population (Commission 1996a). By that time most estimates agree that on current rates of growth, and assuming that it survives as a single entity, the scale of the Chinese economy will have surpassed that of both the EU and USA.

2 The initial average level of tariff protection for goods, set by the 'six' in 1960 at 8.2 per cent, was actually lower than the average of their existing national tariffs – 9.3 per cent (Swann 1975:238). Under GATT 1947, Art.XXIV (6), compensation must be paid to countries whose exports are damaged by such a change, where a higher tariff than existed before for a particular national market is imposed. It was this issue that provided the basis for the first of many challenges by the US, using the GATT disputes procedure. In the so-called 'chicken war' the US objected to the level of compensation paid in relation to its poultry exports to Germany.

3 For the non-specialist, Heidensohn (1995:50–73) provides a guide to the main rules and policy instruments.

4 The relationship between the Agriculture and GAC formations of the Council became of political interest during the Uruguay Round negotiations, when special 'Jumbo Councils' containing the relevant ministers had to be constructed. Also during that period informal councils of trade ministers were held in order 'to counterbalance the excessive influence of the ministers of agriculture' (Woolcock and Hodges 1996:315).

5 These informal procedures, which include agreements under Art.113 [133], are detailed in Macleod, Hendry and Hyatt (1996:98–100). They conclude that, 'The practical effect of these various procedures and declarations should not be underestimated. They are observed closely in the day-to-day conduct of the business of the Council and Commission in external relations.'

6 ECJ Opinion 1/75 established that the Community's right to make commercial policy was exclusive and not concurrent with that of Member States. In case 45/86 relating to the Generalized System of Preferences a basis in Art.113, rather than in the development clauses of the TEU, was established. In Opinion 1/92 it was ruled that, when the Community entered into international agreements on competition, these could not be based on Art.113. The most significant recent ruling has been Opinion 1/94, which adjudicated the scope of the Common Commercial Policy and the respective rights and responsibilities of the Council and Commission in the wake of the Uruguay Round.

7 The relevant Treaty Article is TEC 40 [34](2), which refers to a common organization of agricultural markets including a 'common machinery for stabilizing imports and exports'.

8 The original negotiations for the ITO were based on a much more ambitious definition of the scope of an international trade regime, covering such issues as employment and social conditions but also commodity markets, investment and business practices. The more limited GATT that emerged as acceptable to the US Senate was part of what Ruggie (1983) has described as the 'embedded liberalism compromise'. It is interesting to speculate about the possible shape and competences of the EC as a trade actor had the original ITO design come to fruition.

9 The significance of the GATT/WTO for the Community is also underlined by the fact that the only external representation of the Council General Secretariat is also in Geneva, where it services meetings of the 113 Committee and coordination meetings before specific WTO sessions (Interview). In the GATT/WTO context the Commission speaks on every issue and the Member State representatives speak only upon budgetary questions. Furthermore, it was the Commission acting for the Community that signed the accession agreements of new GATT members and in the Tokyo Round was the sole party (excluding the individual Member States) to most of the agreements made (Macleod, Hendry and Hyett 1996:289). During the period of the Uruguay Round the Commission's incumbent in Geneva was Paul Tran Van Trinh, described by one commentator as the 'undisputed overlord of the *Maison de l'Europe*' and the only EC Head of Delegation who admitted to getting 'a fair margin of manoeuvre' from the Member State Ambassadors (Buchan 1993:60).

10 Although the practice under the GATT has been decision making by consensus, and this is continued by the Ministerial Conference and General Council of the WTO, a resort to majority voting is envisaged. Under such circumstances the number of votes cast by the EC shall not exceed the number of its Member States (WTO, Art.IX). One minor, but telling, indication of how the organization actually constructs the European Community is that it is explicitly treated as a 'government' in WTO documentation. For example, the EC response to the recent WTO Trade Policy Review appears in the WTO Secretariat's report as 'Report by the Government' (WTO 1997a:11).

11 *The Economist* defined services as 'things which can be bought and sold but which you cannot drop on your foot' (12 October 1985, cited in Ruggie 1993:142).

12 The import of the ECJ's ruling is to require unanimity rather than QMV voting in the Council for many service and intellectual property questions. The initiative for attempting a settlement of the issue came from Commissioner Brittan, who pursued it despite the willingness of major Member States to accept 'mixed agreements' and the drawing up within the Commission of an acceptable 'code of conduct' for future WTO negotiations (Interview, DGI, July 1997).

13 See The Irish Draft (Conference of the Representatives of the Governments of the Member States 1996:86).

14 The Commission's view is that there is no '*domaine réservé*' for Member States in services and TRIPS (WTO 1997b:3).

15 In the 1997 WTO Trade Policy Review, 'Members noted with satisfaction, that in a growing number of areas, the Single Market and external liberalization had been mutually supportive, resulting in improved market access for external suppliers and increased exposure of the EU economy to competition. For example, aspects of the EU's participation in recent multilateral services negotiations drew on internal reforms' (WTO 1997b:2).

16 FDI grew five-fold from 1982 to 1990, the EC accounting for 47 per cent of the total (*Financial Times*, 2 June 1992).

17 Gordon Brown, Treasury News Release 11/98, 23 January 1998. Brown was writing as President of ECOFIN to the Managing Director of the IMF.

18 The reference here is to the Multilateral Agreement on Investment (MAI) negotiations within OECD which collapsed in 1998 after sustained opposition from NGOs and from the French government. Their object was to devise an investment regime which would comprise GATT-like safeguards for investors against action by national governments. The Commission argued strongly that negotiations should be handled within the WTO, where Community rights were well established (Interview, July 1997). The Member States failed to agree and in the 'absence of a common view in the EU, the US preference for negotiations in OECD prevailed' (Woolcock 1996:30). The EC is not a full member of the OECD despite the fact that its participation is mentioned in the Treaty of Rome (TEC Art.229 [302] and 231 [304]). It has speaking but not voting rights on all except budgetary issues. Morever, although the Commission is present, the Member States can represent both their own and Community interests.

19 The operative article is TEC Art.109 [111] in which, by way of a series of derogations from Art.228 [300] which governs the making of agreements between the Community and states and international organizations, the decision making procedures for establishing the EC as a fully fledged international monetary actor are provided. These include: (1) the power for the Council acting unanimously to make exchange rate agreements for the single currency in relation to other currencies; (2) acting by QMV to formulate 'general orientations' for exchange rate policy in relation to other currencies; (3) acting by QMV to decide the arrangements for international monetary negotiations and the conclusion of agreements ensuring that the Community expresses a single position and that the 'Commission shall be fully associated with the negotiations'; (4) acting by QMV to decide the 'position' of the Community on international economic and monetary issues and acting unanimously to decide its representation. The right of initiative is given to both the Commission and the ECB for (1) and (2) and to the Commission alone 'after consulting the ECB' for (3) and (4). The European Parliament is only to be consulted in relation to (1).

20 This aims to achieve better access to third country markets through a 'more focused, systematic and coordinated use of available trade instruments'. So far this has involved the gathering of information on trade 'obstacles' but the Commission intention is to target particular countries (WTO 1997a:18).

21 In this the EC is not alone. In the period 1988–92 the EC initiated 15 per cent of the world total of anti-dumping investigations, while Australia and the United States were responsible for 27 per cent and 29 per cent respectively (Hoekman and Kostecki 1995:172).

22 A related and politically significant point is that although, under Art.228 [300] on the conclusion of agreements exclusively concerned with trade (within the scope of Art.113 [133]), QMV applies and there is no requirement for Parliamentary assent; the Council must decide Association Agreements by unanimity and an assenting majority vote in the European Parliament is required (Art.228

[300](3)). The ACP countries were originally associated under separate articles 131–6 [182–5] of the TEC, which cover the 'association of overseas countries and territories'.

23 As defined in GATT Art.XXIV(8), a customs union means the substitution of a single customs territory for two or more customs territories. As with the setting up of the EEC 'restrictive regulations of commerce' are removed within the union, while 'substantially the same duties and regulations' are applied by each member of the union towards outsiders (as in the Common External Tariff). A Free Trade Area means 'a group of two or more customs territories in which duties and other restrictive regulations of commerce . . . are eliminated on substantially all trade between the constituent territories in products originating in such territories'. The Lomé Convention enjoys its own GATT waiver.

24 This point was made by Galtung (1973). Here he argued that the EC pursued a strategy of equality towards the US and Japan but one of divide and conquer elsewhere. This involved the exploitation, fragmentation and penetration of other economies. 'The general picture, in other words, is one of highly differentiated policy pursued by the EC in various directions of the political compass. In one formula: equality at the top, towards the US and Japan, efforts to dominate in all other directions' (*ibid*:63). Writing in the early 1970s Galtung's main target was the ACP relationship. In fact the EC made strenuous efforts to multilateralize this relationship, in an attempt to avoid the structural fragmentation that Galtung predicted.

25 An example would be the claim by New Zealand for GATT Art.XXIV(6) compensation for the loss of its bilaterally negotiated trade concessions when Finland, Austria and Sweden joined the Union. DGI and VI had long experience with the US over compensation cases and settled the matter decisively in the face of some Member State opposition, thus avoiding a prolonged GATT disputes procedure (Interview).

26 Frequent reference was made to the difficulty of finding out where blockages had occurred in the EC system and to the influence of individual Commission officials who could single-handedly impose major costs on outsiders dealing with the EC. This occurs in the realm of technical detail and the implementation of the Common Commercial Policy, for which the Commission is exclusively responsible. A change in the number of digits of customs code required for sheepmeat imports, for example, can cause problems and extra expense for exporters which may be burdensome, but which are not the basis upon which to launch a campaign generating sufficient 'political heat' to obtain a reference back to the Council. Instead, it becomes vitally important for the representatives of third countries to know their way around the Commission, and sometimes the Council Secretariat as well, and to be able to target key officials. There was a consensus amongst members of the Brussels Missions interviewed that a critical difference between dealing with the EU and dealing with a state, as far as bilateral trade policy was concerned, was the absence of clear lines of accountability. When they had been in other postings it had usually been possible to resolve technical problems by seeking a political decision from the relevant minister, but in Brussels this was not possible. The case of the eight digits of customs code for meat was resolved by 'finding a reasonable Irish Commission official'. Most of the Missions staff interviewed stressed the significance of their contacts in the Commission and the importance of the nationality of individual *fonctionnaires*, and indeed the 'national' characteristics of whole DGs.

27 An example quoted by more than one interviewee was that of Namibian seedless grapes. Their production had been developed with German assistance but attempts to negotiate an annual export quota of 1000 tonnes into the Single Market for the period December to February met with furious resistance in the

Council from Italy, France and Spain. Eventually, at Italian insistence, the quota allowed was reduced to 350 tonnes – far less than the amount of grapes consumed in Rome in a single day (Interviews, January and June 1996).

28 The first summit of the Asia-Pacific Economic Conference (APEC) convened in Seattle in 1993, pointedly served this purpose and excluded the Europeans, as have subsequent *démarches* (M. Walker, 'Clinton Plots his New World Order' *The Observer*, 17 November 1996).

29 In 1994 the US exported $108 billion worth of goods to the EU and imported $119 billion. Trade in services was of the order of $50 billion in each direction. According to a US estimate even a 1 per cent increase in the over $150 billion annual exports to the EU would create 20,000 new American jobs (United States Mission to the European Union 1996:63).

30 The US corporate sector in Europe is organized for the purposes of monitoring Union policies and lobbying Union institutions by the EU Committee of the American Chamber of Commerce in Belgium (AMCHAM). There is a useful discussion of different US business approaches and activities towards the Single Market in Hocking and Smith (1997:123–47).

31 At a late stage in the negotiations, and because of the significance of agriculture, Canada was for a time replaced by Australia (Paemen and Bensch 1995:128, 194–5). For a detailed account of Quad meetings at several locations and in several formations at the culmination of the Uruguay Round in mid 1993 see *ibid*:227–9.

32 Blair House is a US Government residence across the street from the White House. The substance of the agreement was the settlement of a long-running bilateral dispute over oilseed (soya) and EC agreement to accept cuts in agricultural subsidies as part of the Round. The American concession was the so-called 'peace clause' in which it was promised not to instigate any new challenges to EC agriculture over a six-year period.

33 There were also long-standing questions of market access and tariff reduction across a range of goods. In previous rounds an overall tariff cutting formula had been used, as opposed to a case by case 'offer and response' procedure. In the Uruguay Round the US, because of the structure of its overseas trade, demanded the latter while the EC championed the former. In this area, as in services, the EC line was in part a reflection of its own 'across the board' liberalization experience with the creation of the Single Market. Tariff disagreements with the USA, along with French objections to the cultural implications of liberalization in audio-visual markets were issues that remained unsolved even after the Blair House deal on agriculture. In the event, the impact of the complex of agreements was to double from 20 to 44 per cent the proportion of industrial products with duty free access to developed markets, and to increase the number of 'bound' tariff lines to 99 per cent.

34 It was of particular importance to the EC because of the apparent incentives for the US side – stemming from Congressional demands in support of particular commercial interests – to abandon a strictly multilateral approach and opt for specific deals and an 'early harvest' from the Round. EC negotiators regarded themselves as champions of multilateralism and were prominent in discussions of general functioning of the GATT and the creation of the new WTO structure which involved, amongst other things, a strengthened disputes procedure.

35 At the end of the summer of 1993 the EC was concerned with 'multilateralizing' the Tokyo scheme. 'In September alone its tariff team met more than twenty countries, some of them more than once, solely for this purpose (Paemen and Bensch 1995:233).

36 For the French Ambassador to the GATT, who penned a 'fable' on the subject, it was not that the EC was an elephant confronting another (US) elephant, rather

that its ambassador thought he was an elephant whereas in reality he was an ape representing 12 monkeys –

> And seated in a corner behold! twelve apes
> Shouting, quarrelling, jacknapes
> The one ever ready to slight the rest.
>
> (From 'L'éléphant, le singe et le chat')

The French text of this fable is reproduced with a translation in Paemen and Bensch (1995:199–202). GATT Director General Arthur Dunkel was represented by the sagacious cat.

37 At the end of the mid-term review in the spring of 1989 a painstakingly constructed compromise (with the developing countries) was held up because Member States, despite consultation with the 113 Committee, refused to agree, and Portugal invoked the Luxembourg compromise. There were accusations of Commission irresponsibility and 'lack of transparency'. Subsequently Commissioner De Clerq had to fend off Italian demands that in future the Council Presidency should sit beside the Commission during negotiations (Woolcock and Hodges 1996:311; Paemen and Bensch 1995:142–3). Another area of intra-EC difference related to 'rules and disciplines', and in particular to the reform of anti-dumping measures. The national trading interests of Member States were split along roughly the same lines as for textiles, with a 'free-trading' North and a 'protectionist' South. 'Once again, the Community negotiator found himself ducking and weaving in the multilateral discussions simply in order to avoid a split in the Community ranks' (Paemen and Bensch 1995:157).

38 The ultimate solution of the EC's agricultural difficulties was actually assisted by the regular change of Presidency. In 1989–90 Spain, France and Italy held the office, but as Woolcock and Hodges (1996:315) argue, subsequent more disinterested Presidents in Office were able to provide greater coherence and negotiating flexibility for the Commission by utilizing informal trade councils and restraining the Agricultural Council (Blair House occurred under the British Presidency).

39 This was all the more impressive because a relatively reluctant EC had begun the negotiations at Punte del Este with a 25-word mandate, fully aware that while all the new agenda items in this radically different Round posed difficulties for all the players, they raised potentially acute problems of competence for the Community. In the event, most of these were solved pragmatically during negotiations – a process assisted by internal application of Art.100A [95] in the completion of the Single Market. This was facilitated by an understanding that the Commission should be allowed to take the lead and apply Art.113 [133] procedures 'without prejudice' to ultimate competence for the duration of the Round. The real difficulties only occurred subsequently, with the implementation of the results of the Round. Post-Uruguay distrust and denial of competence, the fragmentation of the Commission, and evident differences between DGI, IA and IB and their Commissioners, have led to fears that external trade policy is losing coherence and credibility. There are certainly difficult questions surrounding the 'new trade issues' on the WTO agenda, such as the incorporation of labour standards into the trade regime, which have divided Member States. It is also true that if there is no global round in progress there is little incentive to address such problems (Interview, DGI, July 1997). Nonetheless, the WTO Secretariat describes the EC as 'a driving force behind recent GATS negotiations, making substantial offers or commitments and devoting considerable energy to the encouragement of other participants to do likewise' (WTO 1997a:10).

40 Before entry into force of the TEU, economic sanctions were deployed by a

Council regulation under Art.113, severing or reducing economic links. This caused a number of problems, including reference to the vexed issue of the scope of the Common Commercial Policy in relation to transport services, a normal target for economic sanctions. Under Maastricht two dedicated amendments to the TEC are provided to clarify matters in relation to the CFSP, Art.228a [301] and 73g [60]. The former reads as follows:

> Where it is provided, in a common position or in a joint action adopted according to the provisions of the Treaty on European Union relating to the common foreign and security policy, for an action by the Community to interrupt or reduce, in part or completely, economic relations with one or more third countries, the Council shall take the necessary urgent measures. The Council shall act by qualified majority on a proposal from the Commission.

The other relevant new article, 73g [60], covers CFSP measures involving movements of capital and payments. It permits a Member State to take immediate unilateral action in cases of urgency. For a review of the law and practice of the EU's economic sanctions see Macleod, Hendry and Hyett (1996:352–66).

3 International environmental diplomacy

1 Since 1987 more than 50 per cent of fish consumed within the Single Market have been sourced from beyond European fishing grounds. The EC has signed 13 bilateral fisheries agreements with African states, paying compensation in return for the right of EU registered vessels to fish within their exclusive economic zones. In the case of Senegal this compensation amounts to more than the total of their Lomé IV development assistance. With global fish stocks under severe strain, this extension of EU fishing 'effort' raises controversial questions of sustainability (Eurostep, undated, *The Fight for Fish: Towards Fair Fisheries Agreements*, Brussels).

2 Bailey (1972), for example, reviews the European Community's 'place in the world' in its first decade of existence and, while devoting a whole chapter to the 'world energy problem', makes no mention of environmental degradation.

3 An important initiative in this regard is the IPPC or Integrated Pollution and Prevention Control, which provides for a system of controls and impact assessment covering the whole range of pollutants; and is scheduled to come into force for new industrial installations in 1999.

4 The legal basis for the former was TEC Art.100 [94] and, for the latter, TEC Art.235 [308].

5 There is now, under Amsterdam, a Treaty provision that 'Environmental protection requirements must be integrated into the definition and implementation of Community policies and activities ... in particular with a view to promoting sustainable development' (TEC Art.3c [6]).

6 The Commission interservice group on carbon taxation included DGXXI (Taxation), DGIV (Competition), DGXVII (Energy), DGXVI (Regional Policy), DGXII (Science and Research), DGXV (Financial Institutions) in addition to DGXI.

7 The EC case followed the Mexican one in 1994 and was based upon dissatisfaction that Mexico had not pushed its 1991 panel decision to adoption by the GATT Council. For details see Esty (1994:268–9).

8 One legal commentator notes that key articles were 'drafted by diplomats rather than lawyers', resulting in a judicial opinion that they were 'less than crystal clear' (Somsen 1996:190). Article 130r [174] (4) provided for the operation of

the subsidiarity principle, which effectively removes decision making from the Community level wherever possible, while Article 130s [175] required unanimity in the Council of Ministers with 'consultation' of the Parliament. This inter-governmental approach to specifically environmental issues contrasts markedly with the provisions of Article 100a [95], which established qualified majority voting in the Council for matters relating to the completion of the Single Market. The question of competence in international environmental negotiations and the preservation of Member States' rights was covered specifically for the first time in Article 130r [174] (5); while the right of individual state members to 'exceed' the conditions of Community protective measures formed the substance of Article 130t [176].

9 The circumstances of the 1970 ERTA Case 22/70 Commission v. Council were as follows. Since 1962 there had been negotiations for a European Road Transport Agreement involving EEC and non-EEC Member States, which were renewed in 1967. In 1969 the EC adopted Regulation 543/69 concerning the harmonization of social provisions for drivers, which provided the basis for the Commission's (rather than the Member States') assertion of its right to pursue external nego-tiations on the ERTA. The ECJ found in favour of the Commission in what, at the time, was seen as a very extensive interpretation of Community competence – that 'as and when such common rules come into being, the Community alone is in a position to assume and carry out contractual obligations towards third countries affecting the whole sphere of application of the Community legal system'.

10 The involvement of the Community alongside Member States in external environmental policy is explicitly recognized in TEU Article 130r [174] (4) – 'Within their respective spheres of competence, the Community and the Member States shall co-operate with third countries and international organizations'.

11 ECJ Opinion 1/76 (Rhine Navigation Case). This involved the negotiation of an agreement on a 'laying up fund' to deal with overcapacity in barges on certain waterways which necessarily involved Switzerland, a non-member. The Court ruled that, although there were no internal rules, the Commission nevertheless had implied external competence to negotiate because this was necessary to achieve EC Treaty objectives on transport. The law was further developed in the important context of the new trade issues included in the Uruguay Round, in ECJ Opinion 1/94 (WTO).

12 This pattern is also evident in FAO sponsored negotiations on the 1995 Code of Conduct for Responsible Fisheries (where the Commission described itself to be 'major actor') and the 1993 Agreement to Promote Compliance with Inter-national Fishing and Management Measures by Fishing Vessels on the High Seas (Commission 1996b:67–8).

13 The UK resisted these attempts and the outcome of the Amsterdam deliberations was TEU Article 24 which, in relation to the CFSP and police and judicial cooperation, allows the Council to conclude agreements acting unanimously on a recommendation of the Presidency.

14 The relevant provisions are Articles 6, 4(2b), 18 and 22 of the *United Nations Framework Convention on Climate Change*, UN Doc.A/AC.237/18 (Part II) Add.1, 15 May 1992. Also, Articles 2, 31 and 35 of the *Convention on Biodiversity*, UNEP, Na.92–7807, 5 June 1992.

15 Resolution 3208 (XXIX), 11 October 1974.

16 In 1996 the scheduled UNCED review conference (in the form of a UNGA Spe-cial Session 9–13 June 1997) was under consideration – with a view to ensuring that Commission President Santer would be afforded proper status if the Session is at head of state level; and that mention of the EC duly occurs in the final declaration.

17 The lead states mentioned in terms of climate change were UK, Netherlands, Germany and Denmark. With the very notable exception of the UK, these are the three advanced environmental modernizers often mentioned in the EC environmental policy literature. See Sbragia (1996:241).

18 DGI of the Council General Secretariat covers environmental protection, foodstuffs and health and is staffed by ten administrators. It has a logistical and drafting function and assists the Presidency in the preparation of negotiations.

19 This 'special relationship' exists even with the Climate Change Secretariat in Bonn (Interview, Council Secretariat DGI, July 1997).

20 During the Basel Convention negotiations in Geneva there was a parallel Council meeting in Luxembourg which allowed constant reference back. Another example, here, is provided by the fortnight-long negotiations held in Jakarta in 1995 on the biosafety protocol to the Biodiversity Convention. Here Member States felt that the Commission was 'going too far' and matters were put on hold, while other delegations were left in ignorance of the EC position. Officials saw positive advantages in the impact that this had in 'producing a favourable outcome' (Interview, Council Secretariat DGI, July 1997).

21 Phare and Tacis funding for environment and nuclear projects between 1991 and 1995 totalled 912.4 million ECU, while 515 million ECU of this was devoted to action on nuclear safety. This includes the 62.5 million ECU specifically devoted to the closure of Chernobyl under an EU/G7 action plan (Commission 1997k:109, 149–50).

22 Approximation as a concept in EC law is very far from the commonplace meaning of the word. 'It means the complete alignment of national legislation so that it complies 100% with requirements of EU legislation. And not just on paper, but – of course – also in fact' (*Enlarging the Environment*, 6 September 1997:3).

23 Some similar comments, particularly about the interest of the Commission in 'expanding its turf', and the lack of a constructive and flexible mandate from the Council, are to be found in an article by a European commentator – and are quoted with approval by Benedick. See Jachtenfuchs (1990).

24 Report of the Ninth Meeting of the Parties, Montreal, September 1997. UNEP Information Unit for Conventions www.unep.ch/iuc/, 17 September 1997.

25 EC 1990 figures and projections for CO_2 emissions are given in Table 1, Vellinga and Grubb (1993:7).

26 He described the UNCED as this 'parade of vanity and hypocrisy . . . We are not only not saving the earth we are not even saving our own consciences' (*The Guardian*, 30 May 1992). Commission President, Jacques Delors, did attend but was not allowed to address the Conference and, in what may be a significant indicator of actor capability, he was forced to hitch a ride home in Mitterand's presidential Concorde.

27 One way in which the EC has responded directly to the requirements of its accession to the FCCC is in the establishment of a 'monitoring mechanism' – by Council Decision 93/389 which allows the Commission to collect, consolidate, and evaluate national emissions data required for 'implementation review' of FCCC commitments.

28 Framework Convention on Climate Change, Conference of the Parties Third Session, Kyoto, 1–10 December 1997, Kyoto Protocol to the United Nations Framework Convention on Climate Change, FCCC/CP/1997L.7/Add.1, 10 December 1997.

29 In relation to the Montreal Protocol there have been some worrying problems. In the early 1990s, when some Member States did not submit data on CFC production and consumption the Commission refused to disaggregate EU-wide data on grounds of commercial confidentiality (Greene 1992:14–15). Compliance with existing FCCC requirements has also been patchy across the EU with only nine

of the 15 having reported by mid 1997 (J. Lanchbery, verbal evidence, ESRC Climate Convention Seminar, London, 5 September 1997).

4 Development cooperation

1 As we saw in Chapter 2, the CAP also had the effect of driving down world prices of temperate food products, thereby reducing export earnings of countries such as Argentina and Brazil.

2 In the 1980s food aid accounted for almost 50 per cent of all EC aid. However, despite an increase in its volume (from 3.2 billion ECU in the 1980s to 4.2 billion ECU in the 1990s), the proportion of food aid has now fallen to approximately 10 per cent of total EC aid (Cox and Koning 1997:xv).

3 We have no wish to imply that we subscribe to a model of development as a linear process. For a persuasive, alternative approach to 'human development' see UNDP (1996; 1997) and for a highly accessible 'Critical Introduction' to the subject see Dickson (1997).

4 Scholarly interest has tended to reflect periods of intense North/South dialogue. In the late 1970s, following UK accession to the EC in 1973 and signature of the first Lomé Convention in 1975, there was a growth of interest in the English language literature which suggested to one commentator (Kahler 1982:200) that 'Writing on the Lomé Accords may be the most successful cottage industry to emerge from the agreements'.

5 In 1957, in addition to the African colonies, France retained a number of small dependencies in the Pacific and Caribbean. Belgium also retained colonies in Africa (at that time Congo Brazzaville and Ruanda–Urundi). While the Netherlands retained a colonial presence in South-East Asia, and Italy had a UN mandate over Somaliland, they did not have major colonial interests. Germany had no remaining colonial attachments.

6 For a critical discussion of Eurafricanism as ideology, and its influence on EC development policy, see Shaw (1979) and Martin (1982). Fuller treatment of the concept of association, its antecedents and contemporary implications, is provided by Grilli (1993).

7 The French government has recently de-emphasized the relationship with Africa. Nevertheless it was only in early 1998 that the 'cooperation' ministry was absorbed into the foreign ministry, while President Chirac continues to maintain a separate 'African office' (*The Guardian*, 5 February 1998).

8 The difficulties over bananas during the GATT Uruguay Round are discussed by Stevens (1996).

9 French colonies in North Africa were, and have remained, the subject of separate arrangements. These are discussed in our treatment of the Mediterranean region in Chapter 5.

10 See, for example, a joint communiqué issued in 1961 by Presidents Nkrumah of Ghana and Brezhnev of the Soviet Union, which denounced EC associationism as:

> a European scheme designed to attach African countries to European imperialism, to prevent the African countries from pursuing an independent neutral policy, to prevent the establishment of mutually beneficial economic ties among these countries, and to keep the African countries in a position of suppliers of raw materials for imperialist powers.
>
> (Quoted in Martin 1982:229)

11 The AASM countries were among the poorest in the world. Between 1961 and 1968 the economies of EC Member States grew at an annual rate of over 4 per

cent while those of the majority of AASM stagnated. Only Mauritania and Ivory Coast enjoyed economic growth rates comparable with those in the EC; in four cases – Senegal, Niger, Chad and the Central African Republic – there was negative growth during this period. Consequently, by the end of Yaoundé II, the economic gap between EC countries and the AASM had widened (Erridge 1981:12–14).

12 There was, in particular, a need to accommodate UK arrangements with Commonwealth countries. However this was a source of controversy between the UK and French governments. Eventually, 20 African, Caribbean and Pacific countries were invited to participate in the new Convention. At French insistence, the UK's former colonies in Asia were excluded on the grounds that inclusion of these large countries would detract from the 'Eurafrica' relationship.

13 The extent to which Lomé is compatible with NIEO principles was subsequently the subject of considerable debate. A useful synopsis of the arguments is provided by Shaw (1979).

14 There has been much criticism of Stabex, which is complicated to administer and provides disproportionate benefits to ACP countries with substantial export sectors. For an assessment of the operation of Stabex under Lomé I and II see Hewitt (1984). A more recent assessment is provided by Mahler (1994).

15 The Sugar Protocol was intended to provide some measure of protection for the cane sugar exports of UK Commonwealth countries in a situation where the EC was producing large quantities of beet sugar. It was deeply resented by beet sugar producers and ultimately resulted in the EC dumping sugar on the world market, thus depressing sugar prices. For a critical discussion of the principles of the Sugar Protocol see Erridge (1981). A more recent, and more positive, evaluation is provided by Hermann and Weiss (1995). The Rum Protocol has been deemed the most beneficial for producers (Cosgrove 1994). Separate Protocols for beef and veal were introduced only in 1990.

16 Despite their innovative features and apparent generosity, the operation of the Lomé trade provisions has revealed a number of flaws. First, preferences tend to perpetuate existing trade patterns, thus maintaining dependence both on EC markets and on a limited range of export commodities. The Stabex system reinforces this tendency. Diversification of production is also discouraged by use of quota restrictions and application of anti-dumping measures and rules of origin regulations. Chapter 2 discusses these matters more fully.

17 While it was a new provision, the inclusion in Lomé II of the System for the Promotion of Mineral Production and Exports (Sysmin) represented a defeat for the ACP negotiators, who had urged that Stabex be extended to include mineral exports. Sysmin involves the financing of projects to enhance mineral output rather than compensation for falling prices, and hence is geared towards ensuring continuity of supply for EU importers. Sysmin funds have been consistently underutilized, by as much as 40 per cent (ACP–EC 1997:10–11).

18 ACP debt doubled between 1981 and 1986, when it amounted to $130 billion, of which $102 billion was owed by sub-Saharan African countries. At the end of 1986 the overall ACP debt service ratio stood at approximately 34 per cent (Ravenhill 1993:42).

19 In practice, since ACP negotiators have insisted that all the Titles of the Convention be renegotiated on every occasion, it is evident that the Commission wished to delay the recurrence of these onerous and protracted negotiations.

20 This has led to suspension or partial suspension of assistance to a number of ACP countries. For a discussion of the implications of Article 5 see *The Courier*, July/Aug 1991, Special Edition, 'Human Rights, democracy and development'.

21 These measures were supported by the Development and Cooperation Committee of the European Parliament. The EP, which had previously taken considerable

interest in development cooperation, increased its ability to influence the outcome of negotiations as a result of the SEA requirement for parliamentary ratification of the new Convention.

22 Understanding of the decisive role played by women in development processes has grown over the past 20 years. See Kabeer (1994) for a useful introduction to this area. The EC's *Fourth Medium-Term Community Action Programme on Equal Opportunities for Women and Men (1996–2000)* includes commitment to mainstream gender issues in all policy areas (Commission 1996d). In relation to development policy, the Council has issued two resolutions on the integration of gender. Nevertheless the Commission's Green Paper on the future of development cooperation (Commission 1997a) includes few references to gender issues. Incorporation of gender implies a more fundamental reformulation of development thinking than simply 'adding women' and is, in consequence, notoriously problematic (Bretherton 1998).

23 In response to ACP concerns in this regard, it was agreed that suspensions under Article 5 would not be unilaterally imposed, as had occurred under the first period of Lomé IV, but would be subject to formal agreement between the parties (Article 366a, Lomé IV *bis*).

24 ACP negotiators also achieved some success in the area of trade. Here a highly effective ACP team focused attention upon broad issues associated with trade promotion; a departure from the previous, narrow focus on EC preferences. In consequence the principles of the Convention now recognize 'the fundamental importance of trade in energizing the development process' (Art.6a). This is significant in the context of the Commission's 1992 report 'Development cooperation policy in the run-up to 2000' which focused almost exclusively upon aid – a matter of concern for NGDO and ACP representatives alike (Interviews: Euro–CIDSE, June 1996; external Mission June 1996).

25 The position of the French government reflected, in part, a desire to compensate for the effects of the 1994 devaluation of the African Financial Community franc.

26 The German government sought only a modest reduction, to reflect the financial burden of unification. The UK government, in a stance consistent with its neoliberal ideological orientation and its recalcitrant attitude toward EU membership generally, sought a 30 per cent reduction in its EDF contribution.

27 In the past the Community was prepared to deal with socialist regimes attempting various forms of central planning, or dictatorships which failed to plan at all. This insistence on maintaining links with governments of all complexions throughout the Cold War period was described by one Member State official as 'the Commission's proclivity to give comfort to international pariahs' (Quoted in Nuttall 1996a:140).

28 ACP preferences have, in any event, been subject to erosion in recent years – as a result of trade liberalization generally and the GATT Uruguay Round in particular.

29 Cosgrove (1994:229) identifies a modest range of products where preferences have been successful in stimulating exports, most notably Caribbean rum.

30 For a fascinating discussion of 'banana politics', see Cynthia Enloe's (1989) *Bananas, Beaches, and Bases*.

31 The ACP Finance Working Group, which manages the EDF, approves the contribution for the following year. General oversight is provided by joint ACP–EC bodies (the ACP–EC Development Finance Cooperation Committee, which reports to the ACP–EC Council of Ministers). The EP is involved on a consultative basis only, but is required to approve the discharge procedure which releases EDF funding from the Council to the Commission. While there is a temptation for the EP to withhold approval, in protest at its lack of involvement in EDF processes, this is seen as 'not constructive' (Interview, Council Secretariat, DGE,

July 1997). The EP has, since 1973, called for budgetization of the EDF, that is, incorporation of the EDF into the Community budget – a position supported by the Commission. However the Member States are resistant to this, since it would reduce their ability to control EDF expenditure. In consequence, when reference to development policy was included in the TEU, a Declaration on the European Development Fund proclaimed 'the European Development Fund will continue to be financed by national contributions in accordance with the current provisions' (Declaration 12, TEU).

32 There is some form of EC representation in all ACP Member States. Many have full EC Delegations although in some cases these cover more than one ACP member. Where there is no Delegation there are EC offices staffed by advisory or support staff. Heads of Delegation are authorized to agree contracts for smaller projects or technical assistance up to specified amounts.

33 Despite this provision a disproportionate number of contracts is awarded to European companies, particularly in the area of services. Nevertheless, the system provides ACP members with a much wider choice than is normally available in the case of bilateral programmes. Award of contracts to enterprises, by origin, for the seventh EDF was as follows (figures are percentages and only major beneficiaries are shown) –

- **Supplies:** UK 20.92; ACP 19.79; France 19.03; Italy 14.09; Netherlands 11.95

- **Services:** France 18.47; UK 13.53; Belgium 11.81; Germany 10.55; ACP 9.73
  (Source ACP–EC 1997:16)

34 DGVIII has a substantially lower staff/expenditure ratio than the overseas aid departments of most EU Member States, while at the same time serving a larger geographical area (van Reisen 1997a:168).

35 A recent example of the effect of ACP political divisions was the inability to agree on the appointment of a new Secretary-General to replace Ghebray Berhane. This impasse, which reflected tensions between Francophone and Anglophone members of the ACP, lasted for more than a year, ending with the appointment of Peter Magande in 1996.

36 Negotiations over South Africa's relationship with the EC have been complex and difficult, largely as a result of the dual nature of the South African economy. In terms of aid, there has been a ready acceptance of projects which target the rural poor, such as water and sanitation upgrading. However difficulties have arisen in other areas. The refusal to support the construction of a steel plant near Cape Town reflected fears for European steel production and, more broadly, a view that, 'South Africa does not qualify as a developing country' (*The Guardian*, 21 September 1996). Trade negotiations have been even more difficult and protracted. South Africa exports both industrial products and temperate agricultural products which are potentially in competition with EC exports. Consequently EC negotiators, at the insistence of various Member State governments, have excluded more than 40 per cent of South African products from any trade agreement. 'Even the Dutch government has objected to inclusion of cut flowers' (Interview, DGVIII, July 1997).

37 In this respect a recent comparative study of Southern coalitions – which covered OPEC, G77, the Latin American Debt Coalition, the ACP and ASEAN – identified only the ACP and ASEAN as successful. The criteria for success were membership expansion and achievement of long- and short-term economic and political gains. In respect of these latter it was argued that, while the performance of ACP economies had been disappointing, gains had nevertheless been made by ACP negotiators. Hence a typical response from a Pacific

negotiator – 'Just think what would have happened without Lomé!' (Quoted in Sandberg and Shambaugh 1993:162).

38 The non-Lomé LLDCs are all in Asia – Afghanistan, Bangladesh, Bhutan, Burma, Cambodia, Laos, Maldives, Nepal, Yemen. The EC has some form of special relationship with all of these countries except Burma. In this case EC privileges have been suspended due to the use of forced labour in that country (van Reisen 1997a:177).

39 Itself a regional grouping, the EU claims to be 'a natural supporter of regional cooperation initiatives'. Financial support for such initiatives has increased from 339 million ECU under Lomé I to 1300 million ECU under Lomé IV *bis* (ACP–EC 1997:23).

40 Certainly President Chirac chose Africa as the venue for the first official foreign tour of his Presidency; and proclaimed his continued commitment to maintaining 'intense cooperation' (*The Guardian*, 31 May 1996). Indeed for the foreseeable future it would be impossible for Member State governments, in particular the French government, to ignore the political and economic crises affecting so much of sub-Saharan Africa.

41 The major emphasis of the proposals on trade is the need to reconcile future EC–LDC relationships with WTO principles. Here the ACP Group is 'deeply disturbed by the prospect of disruption in our fragile and vulnerable economies . . . which would arise from the insensitive application of WTO rules and obligations' (Interview, external Mission, June 1996). In the case of aid, the proposals imply an overall simplification of the system, including abolition of Stabex and Sysmin and a shift from project-related grants to direct budget support – to be targeted, primarily, toward institutional and socio-economic reform. In recognition of the fact that ability to manage EDF programmes of this nature would itself be a function of institutional capacity, the Green Paper proposes that –

> A phased and individualized approach should be adopted in which the degree of responsibility for administrative and financial management of the aid grows as good governance improves in the recipient state.
>
> (Commission 1997a:47)

42 In addition to the ALA programmes there are also, of course, substantial EC commitments to Central and Eastern European countries and the Mediterranean region, which are the subject of the next chapter.

43 Since the EC was, and remains, Latin America's second largest export market (after North America), concerns over the operation of the Community's common external tariff were well founded. In addition, as a consequence of the introduction of the Common Agricultural Policy in the 1960s, the market access of Latin American temperate products was severely restricted. Thus it is unsurprising that Latin American policy makers have evinced suspicion, even antipathy, towards the Community.

44 New GSP treaties, commencing in January 1995 for industrial products and January 1996 for agricultural products, have been negotiated with all non-Lomé LLDCs except Burma. Each has a duration of four years (van Reisen 1997a:163).

45 At this time the US government was openly 'advising' and covertly supporting the Contra rebel forces attempting to overthrow the Nicaraguan regime.

46 More recently, the decision by the ACP Group to accord observer status to Cuba did not evoke strenuous objections from EU sources, although the UK Presidency reassured the US government that human rights conditionalities would be stringently applied in relations with Cuba (*The Guardian*, 7 April 1998).

47 This divergence is reflected, in turn, in the separation of responsibility for Asia between DGI and DGIB.

48 Recently, however, problems have arisen over Burmese accession to ASEAN in 1997 – in that there has been tension between EU policy on human rights, in the context of the Common Foreign and Security Policy, and the economic priorities of DGI. See Chapters 2 and 6 for further discussion of the EU–ASEAN relationship.

49 Chapter 6 considers these provisions in greater detail.

50 Examples include CFSP positions on Rwanda, Niger and Burma where, for varying reasons, the Commission has been unhappy with positions adopted. The Commission has traditionally been reluctant to impose penalties which will interrupt or sever links with third parties, arguing that the maintenance of relations provides an important lever through which policy can be influenced.

51 Here the operation of the EC's Common Agricultural Policy (by DGVI) is a particular problem area, in that it has the effect of artificially depressing world market prices, and hence undermining Southern producers and the development assistance provided to support them. A recent example is the dumping of subsidized beef in Southern Africa, a region where DGVIII supports the development of communal cattle farming (Curtis 1997:11). The fisheries issue, which is discussed in Chapter 3, is a further area where inadequate policy coherence has negative impacts in the South.

52 In practice, of course, this formula is not accurate, since neither Greece nor Luxembourg operates development policies.

53 This is evident from the example, above, of EC activity in Central America. A further example is Community policy towards South Africa during apartheid. In the context of a special programme to assist the victims of apartheid, and in the face of sustained UK opposition, the Commission maintained a flow of assistance to an organization deemed, by the UK government, to be a cover for the ANC (Nuttall 1996a:140).

54 According to the European Parliament (1993:17) 'the EC has a favourable image in the Third World . . . and is not burdened by the stigma of a colonial past'. It was evident from our interviews that this view is shared, to a large extent, by third country representatives.

5 Ever closer association?

1 Aspects of relations with the 'near abroad' are also dealt with in Chapter 6, which discusses foreign policy, Chapter 7, which deals with security matters, and Chapter 8, which discusses identity.

2 Our concern is specifically with EC/EU relations with Eastern Europe. Consequently we do not discuss Member State initiatives, such as those associated with the Federal Republic of Germany's *Östpolitik*, nor the East/West dialogue initiated in the context of the Conference on Security and Cooperation in Europe (CSCE). However this latter did provide a forum for EC contacts with Eastern Europe, and the EC contributed positively to the CSCE process (see Chapter 6).

3 This TEC article will be repealed upon ratification of the Amsterdam Treaty. It is superseded by TEU Art.O [49]. This revised Article [49] includes the provision that acceding states must 'respect the principles set out in Article 6(1)' – which refers to 'the principles of liberty, democracy, respect for human rights and fundamental freedoms, and the rule of law'. These principles are given great prominence in the Amsterdam Treaty.

4 This point is perhaps missed by Piening (1997:47) when he comments that the EC 'unashamedly appropriated the name of the entire European continent in describing itself and its institutions'. The meaning of 'European' is not defined in the Treaty and particular problems have arisen in relation to Turkey's application for membership. These matters are discussed further in Chapter 8.

5 The CMEA was the Soviet-dominated East European regional economic organization. Also known as Comecon, it was disbanded in 1991.

6 Soviet refusal to recognize the EC unless the CMEA was also accorded recognition impinged upon the ability of the EC to participate in international organizations. See Chapter 3 for discussion of Soviet acceptance, in 1979, of EC participation in global environmental negotiations as a Regional Economic Integration Organization (REIO).

7 As a result of this initiative a limited agreement was eventually concluded with Romania in 1980.

8 Trade and cooperation agreements were concluded with Hungary in September 1988, Czechoslovakia in December 1988, Poland in September 1989, the Soviet Union in December 1989 and the German Democratic Republic and Bulgaria in May 1990. Negotiations for a similar arrangement with Romania, to replace the more restricted 1980 agreement, were suspended in April 1989 because of that country's abuse of human rights but resumed the following year.

9 According to Nuttall (1996a:142) the decision to give this responsibility to the Commission resulted from its attendance at G7 summits over the previous 15 years. This matter is also discussed in Chapter 2.

10 Phare funding, in some form, currently extends to all countries shown shaded in Figure 5.1, with the exception of Serbia and Croatia.

11 Elites in a number of East European countries were actively engaged in this process, as were various Western commentators. Essentially at issue was the attempt to establish the 'Western' credentials of various countries – as distinct from the alleged 'Eastern' vocation of their neighbours.

12 The Commission (1997h) also applies the label 'Central European Countries (CEC)' to the same 15 countries. No explanation is offered for this intriguing (and potentially significant) difference, but the CEEC appellation is more usual.

13 A number of commentators have been explicit in providing definitions and analyses which clearly advance the candidacy for membership of Western institutions, including the EU, of a particular group of states. One of many such examples is Adrian Hyde-Price's definition of East Central Europe – comprising the Czech Republic, Hungary, Poland and the Slovak Republic. These countries are said to form –

> a distinct group by virtue of their unique culture and history; their relatively advanced economic and political reforms; their particularly close relations with the West; and the degree of regional cooperation they have forged within the Visegrad framework.
>
> (Hyde-Price 1996:7)

14 According to the Commission's euphemistic formula (1997h:13) these five countries relate to the EU 'in quite different contexts and circumstances'.

15 The process of reconstructing the identity of the Baltic Republics is one in which Scandinavian politicians and commentators have been much involved. It has also been strongly advocated by US policy makers, who have tended to support the Baltic Republics' candidacy for EU membership to compensate for their exclusion from NATO (Interview, external Mission, February 1997).

16 This semantic digression is intended to convey a sense of the complex and highly sensitive political issues associated with the EU's evolving relations with its Eastern neighbours.

17 For these two countries the EU has developed Action Plans designed to 'focus and prioritize EU policy . . . in all the main areas of cooperation' – economic transformation, democratization, security, foreign affairs and justice and home affairs (Commission 1997i:5).

18 The EBRD, which became operational in 1991, was intended to channel resources emanating from G24 sources in order to promote private sector developments in countries undergoing economic transformation. For a brief discussion of EBRD's aims and somewhat chequered early history see Sedelmeier and Wallace (1996:362–4).

19 In the event a number of unforeseen events also occupied the attention of EC and Member State policy makers during this period – not least the Gulf crisis which began in August 1990 and the worsening political situation in Yugoslavia during the same year.

20 The designation of the association agreements as 'Europe Agreements' in July 1991, mid-way through negotiation of the first set of agreements, was intended to symbolize the EC's particular commitment (short of membership guarantees) to CEEC undergoing transition.

21 The full text of the Europe Agreements is to be found in the *Official Journal* – see, for example, *OJ* L348, 31 December 1996 (Poland–EU). Useful summaries are provided by Sedelmeier and Wallace (1996:368–9) and Piening (1997:57–60).

22 The Czechoslovak agreement was renegotiated upon the separation of the Czech and Slovak Republics, when the rights and obligations of the original agreement were split between the two countries.

23 Between 1989 and 1995 the EU's share of CEEC trade almost doubled, accounting for over 60 per cent of those countries' exports and imports. Consequently the EU is by far their most important trading partner (Commission 1997h).

24 It had become evident by this time that the social and human costs of transformation would be high. Political and economic change in the CEEC has led to increased economic deprivation, lower health standards and reduced life expectancy (UNDP 1996:19). Detailed discussion of the internal impacts of transformation is beyond the scope of this discussion. For a useful, general source see Bryant and Mokrzycki (1994) and for a discussion which focuses upon the particular impacts of transformation upon women, see Einhorn (1993).

25 These concerns were reflected in the launch of the 'Pact on Stability in Europe' as one of the first initiatives of the Common Foreign and Security Policy (CFSP) following entry into force of the TEU in November 1993. This attempt to address boundary disputes and minorities issues in CEEC is briefly discussed in Chapter 6.

26 These concerns were also reflected in strong EC support for the establishment in 1992 of the Central European Free Trade Area (CEFTA) following the Visegrad Declaration by Czechoslovakia, Hungary and Poland in 1991. CEFTA's inauguration generated little enthusiasm on the part of CEEC politicians and officials (it was dismissed within a month by the Czech Prime Minister, Vaclav Klaus, as 'an artificial creation of the West'). Nevertheless its membership has expanded to include Slovenia, and intra-CEFTA trade has grown considerably since 1993, passing 1989 levels of intra-CMEA trade by 1995 (Commission 1997g:10–11). There is some evidence of a revival of interest in CEFTA, particularly in Hungary and Poland, as a result of disillusionment with the CEEC–EC relationship (Dangerfield 1995).

27 The structured dialogue was a multi-level as well as a multilateral process. At the highest level it involved 'end-on' Councils (sometimes inaccurately referred to as joint Councils) with a timetabled programme of meetings across two Presidencies. At DG level the 'dialogue' involved up to 80 committees comprising Commission officials and their CEE counterparts. Sadly, we are unable to report any positive assessments of this process. For Ministers it involved 'get-togethers – not sexy, boring'; 'not even decision shaping'; it was, in the frequently quoted words of Netherlands Foreign Minister, Wim Kok, 'neither structured nor a dialogue' (Interviews, DGIA, DGII, external Missions, 1996). In the case of CEE

participants, multilateral cooperation was evidently tolerated only in the interest of furthering bilateral discussions. There was strong awareness that any meaningful negotiations would, in accordance with the EU tradition, be on a bilateral basis; moreover this bilateral approach was welcomed by CEE representatives (Interview, DGII, September 1996).

28 To assist with this huge task the Commission issued detailed questionnaires to each candidate country. The responses, which comprised 3000 pages on average, related to the work of all 24 DGs. This exercise was greatly resented by CEEC officials, although the Commission found it 'useful and educative'. One purpose of the questionnaire was 'to assess the ability of CEEC to provide the type of information routinely required by the Commission' (Interview, DGIA, September 1996).

29 In addition to the three volumes referred to in this discussion, *Agenda 2000* also contains fairly lengthy Opinions upon each of the ten applicant CEEC. For an extensive treatment of the implications of *Agenda 2000* for CEE countries, see Mannin (1999).

30 The Commission's Opinions were based upon assessment of ability to meet the accession criteria in the medium term (five years). While none of the CEEC10 presently satisfy the criteria, the 'chosen' five are considered to approximate them most closely. A 'line could have been drawn' after Hungary, the Czech Republic and Poland but there was a further gap between Slovenia and Estonia and the five 'pre-ins'. (Interview, DGIA, February 1998). Only the Slovak Republic was rejected specifically on the grounds of lack of progress towards democratic reform, although concern was expressed regarding the treatment of minorities in Estonia, where there is a substantial Russian population.

31 There has been considerable criticism of the management and operation of the Phare programme, which has greatly expanded in size (from two countries to 13) and policy scope since 1989, without commensurate increases in Commission staff. It is considered that the previous demand driven approach, and associated decentralization of administration to CEEC, have been responsible for a lack of strategic vision which should be remedied with the reorientation of the programme towards accession (Commission 1997h:58).

32 A precedent, here, is provided by the Greek accession, which was agreed by the Member States, following particular urging from the French government, despite a negative Opinion from the Commission.

33 Between 1990 and 1996 the EU and the Member States combined provided 70 per cent of Western aid to CEEC; more than 70 per cent of emergency non-food aid and more than 60 per cent of FDI (Commission 1997g).

34 There are numerous examples of the EU's presence as a point of reference – thus 'One of the first responses to the unceremonious dumping of 129 journalists from Hungarian radio consisted of how "Europe" would view this' (Kolankiewicz 1994:481).

35 A contrast can be noted with development cooperation policy, discussed in Chapter 4. Thus, for example, it is only in the case of Austria that a major proportion of bilateral aid (29.6 per cent) is oriented towards CEEC. The next highest *proportion* is that provided by Germany (11.4 per cent). Most Member State governments direct only a tiny proportion of aid towards CEEC – Portugal, for example, directs 98 per cent of bilateral aid towards sub-Saharan Africa and 0.4 per cent towards CEEC.

36 Enlargement to the East, in particular to include the original 'Visegrad countries' of 'Central' Europe, has been strongly advocated by a number of academic commentators who, it is claimed, 'played an important role in ... providing the forces in favour of a more open policy with important arguments' (Sedelmeier and Wallace 1996:374). For further examples of 'engaged' academic

discussion of these matters, see Ash, Mertes and Moïsi (1991) and Hyde-Price (1996).

37 UK reservations on Hungarian raspberries were particularly resented, given the Thatcher government's outspoken support for enlargement. The German government's position on steel imports was more easily understood by CEE negotiators than its strenuous objections to Polish potatoes (Interview, external Mission, June 1996).

38 Similar problems have affected the trade negotiations with South Africa, as we saw in Chapter 4.

39 This pattern was to be repeated, in 1993, during the final stages of the GATT Uruguay Round negotiations (see Chapter 2).

40 By March 1998 this was evident from the legislative proposals emanating from the Commission in the context of *Agenda 2000*; in that proposals for reform of the CAP and structural funds were very much less radical than had been antici-pated and considered necessary. When seen alongside the failure of the 1996–7 IGC to agree the institutional reforms necessary for enlargement, this suggests both a hesitant and a divided approach on the part of the EU.

41 Today the MNC are considered to be Morocco, Algeria, Tunisia, Libya (with which the EC currently has no formal relations); Egypt, Israel, Jordan (despite its lack of a Mediterranean coastline), Lebanon, Syria and the Palestinian Authority; Turkey, Cyprus and Malta. Before their accession in the 1980s Greece, Spain and Portugal were also included in this category.

42 The sensitivity of EC–Algerian relations is demonstrated in a number of ways, not least the almost complete absence of policy statements on Algerian internal affairs in the context of European political cooperation (EPC) or CFSP (see Chapter 6). When the UK Presidency did initiate an EU troika *démarche* to Algeria, following a period of considerable internal violence early in 1998, this was firmly rebuffed, indicating that there was, at that time, no role for the EU in Algeria's internal problems.

43 By that time the political regime in Libya was no longer acceptable to the EC. Algeria, although by then independent, had maintained its privileged position in relation to the EC. Consequently the Algerian government was not interested in negotiating a similar arrangement at that time. Subsequently, however, it was decided that Algeria, Tunisia and Morocco should be treated similarly (Siotis 1974:75–6).

44 Contemporarily the countries of former Yugoslavia, together with Albania, are considered by the EU as CEEC rather than MNC.

45 In 1992 the EC obtained 27 per cent of its oil imports and 32 per cent of natural gas from the Mediterranean region, despite a considerable effort to reduce energy dependency over the previous 20 years.

46 In addition to economic recession, a number of factors combined to influence the EC position in its negotiations with MNC governments. Thus the accession of the UK increased the emphasis on the Middle East, and the Euro–Arab Dialogue, at the expense of Maghreb countries in particular. Moreover the revolution in Portugal in 1974, the application for membership by Greece in 1975 and the death of Franco the same year raised the prospect of early expansion of the EC's Mediterranean membership.

47 In EC terminology Maghreb effectively refers to Algeria, Morocco and Tunisia (since the EC has no formal ties with Libya, and Mauritania is a member of the ACP Group). The Mashreq countries are Egypt, Jordan, Lebanon and Syria.

48 The Arab Maghreb Union (AMU) comprises Algeria, Morocco, Tunisia, Libya and Mauritania. The AMU was intended to emulate the EC – 'to turn the Arab Maghreb into one country, with one passport, one identity and a single currency' (King Hassan II of Morocco quoted in Pomfret 1992:86). However trade

between the five AMU members accounted for only 3 per cent of their total trade in 1992 and there is little complementarity between their economies – they are essentially in competition for markets.

49 The horizontal cooperation programme involves establishment of EC–MED networks, and in the 1992–5 period a considerable number was established in each of the areas below (Cox and Koning 1997:74).

- **MED-URB:** cooperation between local authorities. Focus on quality of urban life and local democracy.
- **MED-CAMPUS:** inter-university collaboration.
- **MED-MEDIA:** collaboration between media professionals and organizations.
- **MED-INVEST:** support for small and medium enterprises in MNCs.
- **MED-TECHNO:** application of efficient technologies in MNCs.
- **MED-MIGRATION:** cooperation between NGOs and local communities on migration related issues.

The MED-URB, MED-CAMPUS and MED-MEDIA programmes have been frozen since 1996 because of misuse of subsidies (see Court of Auditors 'Special Report No. 1/96 on the MED Programme', *Official Journal* 240, 39, 19 August 1996). They are to be relaunched 'as soon as a satisfactory management system has been set up' (Council of the European Union 1997c:9).

50 The Maltese political elite has long been deeply divided over relations with the EC/EU. The Labour Party, which is opposed to EU membership for Malta, returned to office in 1996 after several years in opposition, during which the 1990 application was made. A further change of government led to reactivation of the Maltese application in 1998.

51 Relations with Morocco had been further complicated by the decision of the European Parliament (in January 1992) to withhold assent to renewal of Morocco's financial protocol, on human rights grounds. The Spanish government used this impasse as an opportunity to propose a general strengthening of EC–Maghreb relations. However the viability of this proposal was very much in question from the outset, since two members of the Maghreb Arab Union were excluded (albeit for different reasons) while the internal situation in Algeria made EC–Algerian relations increasingly difficult. Moreover the Moroccan government was increasingly disposed to revert to its earlier emphasis upon bilateral relations with the EC.

52 The EC is Israel's largest trading partner, accounting for approximately 35 per cent of exports and 50 per cent of imports. In 1994 more than 85 per cent of Israel's trade deficit was with the EC.

53 Since entry into force of the TEU, the EU has played an important role in supporting the Palestinian Authority (see Chapter 6).

54 Annual funding to the region will double during this period, from 550 million ECU in 1995 to 1143 million ECU in 1999. Nevertheless the agreed sum for the five-year period falls short of the 5500 million ECU recommended by the Commission in the interest of 'geographical equity' (Commission 1995g:41). This reflects controversy between Southern and Northern Member States, in particular the UK and Germany, concerning the most appropriate East/South balance of financial support. The Cannes Summit also approved five-year funding proposals for CEEC (6693 million ECU) and NIS (2224 million ECU).

55 In practice implementation was delayed until early 1998 owing to an attempt by the UK government, subsequently abandoned, to strengthen human rights conditionality (Interview, DGIB, February 1998).

56 The decision to hold the Conference during the Spanish Presidency reflected, in part, the very active role played by the Spanish government in promoting

Mediterranean initiatives. This can be seen, for example, from its tactics in blocking agreement on the Tacis programme pending assurances of increased funding for the Mediterranean region (Interview, DGIB, February 1998). For a detailed discussion of the Spanish government's role during the preparatory stages of the Barcelona Conference itself, see Barbé (1996).

57 The political and security partnership aims to promote (*inter alia*) development of the rule of law and democracy; respect for human rights and fundamental freedoms; peaceful settlement of disputes. And to prevent (*inter alia*) terrorism; proliferation of nuclear, chemical and biological weapons; excessive accumulation of conventional arms. In one of the most contested areas of the Declaration, reference is made to the right to self-determination of peoples, within the context of international law and UN resolutions. Neither the Israeli nor the Turkish government was comfortable with this element of the Declaration (Barbé 1996:39).

58 The third chapter includes: developing human resources through education and training; health promotion; promoting understanding between cultures and exchanges between civil societies; reduction of migratory pressures; joint action against drug trafficking. MNC governments were unhappy with the EU tendency to conceptualize migration in security terms and, at their insistence, matters relating to racism and xenophobia were added to this section of the Declaration (Barbé 1996:35).

59 There has also been evidence of tension between the French and Spanish governments as a result of Spanish policy activism towards the Maghreb countries, a traditional area of French influence (Barbé 1996:28).

60 As in the case of the Europe Agreements, the Euro–Med Agreements are mixed agreements negotiated with individual MNC by the Commission on behalf of the EC and the Member States.

61 While market opening by the Med partners is to be phased in over a 12-year period, increased competition will inevitably damage local enterprises. It is predicted, for example, that 2000 Tunisian companies will be driven into bankruptcy (Marks 1996:17). There will also be loss of customs receipts and other revenues from imports.

62 The question of Turkey's identity as a European country is discussed in Chapter 8.

63 The increase in EC–Turkish trade since entry into force of the customs union has been almost entirely to the advantage of EC producers. In *Agenda 2000* the trade surplus with Turkey is estimated at 9 billion ECU (Commission 1997a:51). Despite this the Turkish government is said to be 'making a determined effort to meet the terms set by the Community in relation to tariff reductions and standards' (Interview, DGIA, September 1996).

64 Settlement of the Cyprus dispute has traditionally been, and remains, a UN responsibility. However the ramifications of the decision to open negotiations for the accession of Cyprus to the EU could be widespread, including a Turkish veto of NATO enlargement. In an attempt to assist progress in the dispute, the EU appointed Sir David Hannay as special envoy to Cyprus in 1997. The US government has also taken a close interest, deploying Richard Holbrooke (who played a major role in relation to the Bosnian conflict) as a mediator in Cyprus in mid 1997.

6 Towards a common foreign and security policy?

1 Policy towards Algeria is an area where EPC/CFSP pronouncements have been rare, at the insistence of the French government. A more specific example is the British handover of Hong Kong in 1997. In this case the EU remained silent until the issue of monitoring post-handover Chinese behaviour arose (Interview, Council Secretariat DGE, July 1997).

2 The impact of external perceptions and expectations is cumulative. The EU's global reach is evidenced not only by its frequently reported role in Bosnia or the Middle East, or its 'China strategy' (*The Guardian*, 25 March 1998); but by numerous smaller events. For example – a formal rebuke delivered to the EU troika of Ambassadors to the United Arab Emirates following criticism of a public execution in that country by the European Parliament (in October 1997); or Cuba's formal application to join the ACP group in March 1998.

3 See Chapter 8 for discussion of the more negative dimensions of collective identity formation.

4 The provisions of the fourth Lomé Convention, discussed in Chapter 4, reveal the extent to which the EC has been involved in the conduct of foreign policy.

5 The incorporation of EPC in the Single Act was of largely symbolic importance. EPC remained a voluntary process between High Contracting Parties – employing, in this section of the Act only, the distinctive language of intergovernmental relations.

6 The difficult evolution of the Commission's role in EPC is discussed in Nuttall (1996a:130–50).

7 In recent years, for example, there has been a general sense of Commission resentment at the increasing involvement of the Presidency in the EU/US dialogue, a process which has been carefully nurtured by the Commission. A more specific example can be found in the 1994 formal objection by the Commission to a Presidency declaration on Rwanda, on the grounds that it had economic implications. An acrimonious exchange of notes ensued.

8 In the past Coreu transmissions have tended to be confined to relatively insignificant matters, because of Member State concerns about the security of the system. Coreu is no longer a telex system but an X400 computer-based messaging system, a significant upgrading. While officially now called Cortesy, the Coreu name has stuck. The upgrading has been associated with increased use of the system (by approximately 20 per cent annually) and, we are informed, an improvement in the quality of messages, which now represent 'a real sharing of information' (Interview, Council Secretariat DGE, July 1997). Some interviewees from the Commission and the FCO were less enthusiastic about the system, however.

9 Since December 1994 the CSCE has been known as the Organization for Security and Cooperation in Europe (OSCE).

10 This record improves somewhat if the voting behaviour of Greece (after 1981) is excluded, although it remains below 60 per cent, having reached a high point of 66 per cent in 1978. See Regelsberger (1993:270–91).

11 A particularly embarrassing example of disunity occurred in April 1997 when France, Germany and Italy dissociated themselves from an agreed position towards human rights violations in China. The Dutch Presidency made public a letter of rebuke to other EU governments while the Commission, perhaps a little smugly, expressed its 'very great concern' at the 'complete disarray' of EU foreign policy (*The Guardian*, 5 April 1997).

12 Policy towards Iraq caused even greater disarray in February 1998, during the UK Presidency, when the UK and French governments publicly adopted opposing policy positions over US proposals to take military action against Iraq following the ejection of UN weapons inspectors from that country. Both the European Parliament and the Dutch Foreign Minister strongly condemned the UK Presidency for 'keeping European Union colleagues in the dark over policy on Iraq' (Hans van Mierlo quoted in *The Guardian*, 10 February 1998).

13 This is reflected in the 1989 decision of the Western Economic Summit that the EC should be responsible for coordinating Western aid to Central and Eastern Europe. More recently the view that 'European integration supports stability on

the continent' was strongly emphasized by US diplomats (Interview, US Mission, January 1996).

14 For a brief discussion of the policy considerations of each Member State government, see Salmon (1992:237–43).

15 Chapter 7 contains a fuller discussion of the conflict in ex-Yugoslavia.

16 Recognition is an important instrument of diplomacy which had been effectively used as a threat in the early weeks of negotiation with the Federal (Serbian) government. Once accorded, however, its usefulness is spent. Nevertheless the German government, mindful of its historic links with Croatia and under pressure from sections of domestic opinion, advocated early recognition of Croatia and Slovenia. By November 1991 it had persuaded its EC partners to promise recognition by 15 January 1992, providing certain conditions were met. In the event the German government recognized both republics on 16 December, at the close of the IGC. This made full EC recognition the following January inevitable, if acrimonious.

17 The inclusion in the new Pillar III of issues such as immigration and asylum policy, international crime and terrorism added yet a further dimension to external policy; and a further source of perplexity to third parties.

18 For a clear, concise discussion of these matters see Hayes-Renshaw and Wallace (1997).

19 There is evidently a considerable effort to ensure that Pillar I matters are not impinged upon – certain Permanent Representatives are reported to 'react strongly' if PoCo discusses Pillar I issues; moreover such matters may not be transmitted by Coreu. Consequently 'problems arise' (including formal complaints in COREPER) when inexperienced officers in Member State capitals, in writing reports on the situation in Zaire, for example, refer both to human rights issues and to economic development (Interview, Council Secretariat DGE, July 1997).

20 Member State attitudes here are revealing. Pillar I Working Groups are staffed from the Permanent Representations in Brussels, whereas Pillar II Working Groups are staffed from capitals' foreign ministries, typically at Director level. Since 1994 CFSP Counsellors have been appointed at the Permanent Representations to assist in providing continuity to this somewhat fragmented system of Member State representation in CFSP processes.

21 Some of the seconded diplomats have expressed a preference to remain permanently with the Unit, others are anxious to resume their national diplomatic careers. At present it is unclear whether a change to permanent status will be allowed, but some staggering of appointments is already occurring – in part to address the problem that the desired aim of providing continuity would have been somewhat undermined had all secondees departed simultaneously at the end of their four-year term.

22 An example of productive collaboration, here, is a recent joint visit to Helsinki by CFSP officials in the Council Secretariat and the Commission, to advise Finnish officials on the conduct of the Presidency, which Finland will hold for the first time in 1999.

23 The Stability Pact (also referred to as the 'Balladur Plan' since it was an initiative of the French Prime Minister of the time) sought to promote cooperation between CEE countries. It eventually produced numerous declarations on neighbourly relations between them. In many respects the aims of the Stability Pact coincided with those of the OSCE, which was eventually entrusted with overseeing the various agreements. The geographical scope of the Stability Pact was confined to the CEEC and the Baltic States.

24 Aid and trade privileges for the Palestinians commenced in 1986, and in 1989 the Council agreed that the EC should take an active role in the region. One result of this decision was the appointment of an EC representative to the Occupied

Territories, thus – 'in effect the EC had an ambassador to the Palestinians before any of its member states had one' (Marks 1996:9).

25 The EU's contribution to the peace process should be considered alongside the broader Euro–Mediterranean relationship and, in particular, the Barcelona Process. Strenuous efforts are made to separate the peace process from the Barcelona Process, which brings together Maghreb, Mashreq and other Middle Eastern countries (including both Israel and the Palestinian Authority) in regular, technical meetings. See Chapter 5 for discussion of these matters.

26 This incident was frequently referred to in the course of interviews with Brussels officials, with evident outrage. It is of interest to note that Israeli officials whom we interviewed also regarded it as particularly ironic.

27 An example here is Jacques Chirac's visit to the region in 1996 (in his capacity as French President) when he became the first head of state to address the new Palestine Legislative Council, and used the occasion to publicly criticize the Israeli government – thus undermining the rather quieter diplomacy being conducted in the region, simultaneously, by the EU troika.

28 The US, in common with a small number of other countries, renamed its Mission following entry into force of the TEU. On being informed that Missions could not be accredited to the EU, which has no legal personality, US officials replied that Congress had approved the change and the decision of Congress could not be reversed!

29 An example of this 'cooperation' is EU participation in the Korean Peninsula Energy Development Organization (KEDO) in 1996. KEDO was very much a US initiative, involving an agreement to supply North Korea with light water reactors in return for disavowal of nuclear weapons. EU support in funding the agreement was secured following intense pressure from the US government. In other areas, however, notably in the case of relations with Iran and Cuba, the EU has adopted an independent stance, rejecting the US policy of isolating these countries and emphasizing, instead, the importance of dialogue (see Chapter 2 for discussion of the EU response to the US Helms-Burton Act, which provided for US sanctions against foreign firms trading with Iran or Libya).

30 Since establishment of the CFSP unit is the subject of a separate Declaration it need not await ratification of the Amsterdam Treaty, although hopes that it could be established at an early date have not been realized. Inevitably there has been intense speculation among CFSP personnel, both in the Council Secretariat and the Commission, about the nature and operation of the proposed unit. The Commission view was that the unit should involve personnel 'at the highest level' (Interview, DGI, July 1997). The UK government considered that the Planning Unit should be small in size ('not all Member States need be represented') (Interview, UK Permanent Representation, October 1997). Eventually it was decided that the Unit should comprise 20 'A' grade officials, one from each Member State plus Commission and WEU representatives.

31 A major administrative change affecting the Relex DGs has now taken place. This involves separation of policy level staff from those responsible for administration of the Community's various 'cooperation' programmes – known as the *Service Commun Relex* (SCR). Policy staff are now co-located in the refurbished Charlemagne Building. This change is deeply resented by 'non-policy' staff and has been disruptive and demotivating (Interviews, Commission DGIA, December 1998).

32 There is much speculation, also, concerning the identity of the High Representative. Opinion seems to favour appointment of a politician with a fairly high profile, preferably from one of the smaller Member States. The names of Dick Spring and Carl Bildt are frequently mentioned. In the UK there was speculation that Paddy Ashdown might be appointed.

33 Here it is perhaps worthy of note that the integration of the previously separate EPC secretariat into the Council Secretariat in 1994 provided, for the first time, direct access to the IGC preparatory and support processes for CFSP Unit staff with considerable experience of the operation of Pillar II.

34 Even larger Member States have found this a financial burden. The UK, for example, has been obliged, in several countries, to utilize rooms in the German mission. Nevertheless there is a very significant difference in the overall representation of large and smaller Member States (Council of the European Union 1997a).

7 Defence of the Union

1 Criticisms of policy failure reflected not only the fact that Yugoslavia was a European country in close proximity to the EC's borders, but that the EC had maintained links with Yugoslavia through periodically updated trade agreements since 1970. In consequence, the EC might have been expected to have greater influence in resolving the crisis, at least during its early stages.

2 A Press report following the brief detention in Kabul of European Commissioner Emma Bonino is typical in this respect – 'despite being the largest single aid donor to Afghanistan, the EU lacks the political and potential military leverage which back up diplomats of nation states' (*The Guardian*, 30 September 1997).

3 See Chapter 5 for fuller discussion of policy towards the 'near abroad'. Issues of inclusion and exclusion affecting these regions are also considered in Chapter 8.

4 It remained so, despite intermittent complaints from the USA about 'burden-sharing' by the European members and simmering resentment on the part of the French government at US dominance of the Alliance. Ultimately this resulted, in 1969, in French withdrawal from NATO military structures, although France remained a member of the political organization. Following recent changes in French policy towards NATO, French officials resumed participation in aspects of NATO's military planning in December 1995.

5 Monnet was then head of the French Planning Commission. His Memorandum was addressed to the French Foreign Minister, Robert Schuman, who subsequently launched the ECSC proposal (known as the Schuman Plan).

6 These tensions include controversy over the siting of US Cruise and Pershing missiles, particularly in West Germany and the UK, and the announcement by President Reagan in 1983 of the Strategic Defense Initiative. This announcement, without prior consultation of other NATO members, raised serious questions about the sincerity of US defence guarantees to Europe – and hence the future of NATO.

7 While it remains the case that all EU members are invited to accede to WEU membership, in practice this is a sensitive issue in that the close links between WEU and NATO might imply the extension of US commitments to non-NATO members. Consequently the US government, supported by the UK government, opposes fuller involvement of the neutral countries in the affairs of the WEU. A further sensitive issue is the difference in WEU membership status between Greece and Turkey. Under the terms of the Brussels Treaty, WEU members could be drawn into a conflict with Turkey in defence of Greek interests. For this reason the UK government opposed Greek membership of the WEU but conceded this issue as part of a broader compromise on WEU/EU relations. Subsequently the UK government has attempted to ensure that Associate Members, including Turkey, participate as fully as possible in WEU affairs (Bailes 1997).

8 In 1993 the figures were approximately 16 billion Kroner for 'soft security' and 14 billion for defence (Heurlin 1996:180).

9 Paganon (1997) provides a useful discussion of the evolution of the WEU/NATO relationship since 1993. The entry into force in June 1996 of a Security Agreement

between the organizations is evidence of the progress made. It also paved the way for closer cooperation on sensitive issues – thus effectively increasing the distance between the WEU and the EU.

10 This provision is contained in a Declaration annexed to the Amsterdam Treaty, thus allowing arrangements for security clearance to be put into place in advance of ratification.

11 The Planning Cell currently comprises a Director and 55 staff, approximately two-thirds of whom are military officers. Representation from Member States is slightly higher than the quota for Associate Members. Eleven of the 13 eligible countries have seconded personnel, the exceptions being Iceland and Luxembourg. For a fuller discussion of the organization and role of the Planning Cell see Rosengarten (1997).

12 There has subsequently been a proliferation of (modest) multinational con-figurations potentially answerable to the WEU – the Multinational Division, with Belgian, British, German and Dutch brigades, the Anglo–Dutch amphi-bious force, Euroforce and Eurmarfor (respectively land and naval units) comprising French, Italian, Portuguese and Spanish personnel and the Franco–British European Air Group.

13 The WEU has also established a satellite interpretation centre in Torrejon, Spain and an Institute for Security Studies, based in Paris.

14 The formula 'ESDI within NATO' reflects standard usage and, evidently, a determination to make clear that ESDI does not refer to an independent Euro-pean 'identity'. The authors have been unable to locate a single instance where the qualification is omitted.

15 These issues are said to have been greatly troubling NATO commanders, in particular the arrangements for return of NATO assets in the event of an emergency (Interview, NATO secretariat, January 1996). CJTF is essentially a political concept, seen as a panacea for a number of problems facing NATO – including the need to accommodate European defence aspirations and also, potentially, domestic resistance to involvement of US ground forces in conflict situations. Military planners were subsequently confronted with the challenge of operationalizing the concept.

16 Early indications suggest, however, that the cost of operationalizing the CJTF concept may be more substantial than politicians had supposed. For example, the concept involves the need for high levels of readiness and also for rotation of headquarters staff.

17 It was proposed, early in 1997, that decisions to make CJTF assets available to the WEU should be taken by majority voting. However this proposal was vetoed by the Turkish government.

18 As a point of clarification, the collective defence clauses of the WEU Brussels Treaty and the NATO Washington Treaty are labelled Article V and Article 5 respectively!

19 Proposals for military intervention were also influenced by popular and media pressure to 'do something'. They received strong support from the German gov-ernment, although German forces were at that time constitutionally prevented from becoming involved, and were endorsed by the WEU assembly. UK oppos-ition was led by Douglas Hurd, then Foreign Secretary, who made much of British experience in Northern Ireland, claiming that Yugoslavia was 'a new Ulster'.

20 The dissolution of the Warsaw Pact (July 1991) and the disintegration of the Soviet Union (December 1991) removed any residual risk that a regional conflict might provoke superpower confrontation. In these circumstances the US government, which during the Cold War would have taken a close interest in the evolving conflict, concurred with the EC view that this was an essentially European issue.

21 This accords with the UN Secretary-General's report *Agenda for Peace: Preventative Diplomacy, Peace-making and Peace-keeping*, also published in June 1992, which aimed to enhance the UN's capacity to respond to the security challenges of the post-Cold War environment. Among its recommendations, *Agenda for Peace* proposed an increased role for regional arrangements in support of the UN (Boutros-Ghali 1992).

22 The UN recruited approximately 1700 personnel to create an International Police Task Force for this purpose. Policing issues have been one of the most difficult areas of the peace implementation process.

23 See *NATO Review* (1997, March) for a discussion by Colonel General L. P. Shevtsov of the conduct of NATO–Russian relations in IFOR/SFOR.

24 Largely owing to US fears of becoming involved in a long-term commitment in Bosnia, the duration of IFOR was specified as one year, although it was evident from the outset that this would be insufficient for the completion of its tasks. After much uncertainty about the continuance of US involvement, a UN mandate was obtained for the creation of SFOR. Approximately half the size of IFOR, SFOR nevertheless includes all 36 IFOR participating countries. In an attempt to prevent similar problems at the end of SFOR's mandate in mid 1998, the US government indicated commitment to maintaining troops in Bosnia, albeit at a further reduced level. However this did not prevent the US government from using the threat of withdrawal from Bosnia to influence the policy of its European 'allies'.

25 At the time of writing Anthony Cragg is NATO Assistant Secretary General for Defence Planning and Operations.

26 For a discussion of recent French policy toward NATO, and broader proposals for modernization of the French military, see Le Gloannec (1997).

27 The Albanian intervention, known as Operation Alba, was authorized by the UN Security Council (Resolution 1101, 28 March 1997). The force comprised troops from Italy (approximately half), France, Denmark, Austria, the Netherlands, Spain, Portugal and Greece. Troops from non-EU countries also participated, including Turkey, Hungary and Romania.

28 We do not suggest that this was a deciding factor in the Albanian case. There are substantial Italian interests in Albania and the Italian government was greatly concerned by the deteriorating internal situation and by the large number of Albanian refugees attempting to enter Italy.

29 This procedure, and the related 'emergency brake' procedure, is discussed more fully in Chapter 6.

30 These debates are not in themselves new; although they are certainly a novel, post-Cold War concern for traditional security analysts. However, during the Cold War peace researchers were fundamentally concerned with the meaning of and conditions for peace. See, for example, Johan Galtung's (1969) seminal discussion in the *Journal of Peace Research*.

31 The concept of societal security has been developed by the Copenhagen Research Group over a number of years. It is intended to complement, rather than replace, analysis of state security and has consequently attracted criticism both for departing too radically from, and for not moving sufficiently far beyond, traditional approaches. For debates about the validity and usefulness of the concept see Huysmans (1995), McSweeney (1996), Buzan and Wæver (1997).

32 The ten applicant countries were Bulgaria, Estonia, Hungary, Latvia, Lithuania, Poland, Czech Republic, Romania, Slovenia and Slovakia.

33 For a brief survey of the actual and potential sources of interethnic conflict in the Caucasus, and elsewhere in the former Soviet bloc, see Ponton (1996).

34 For a fascinating discussion of these issues (which are considered further in

Chapter 8) see Iver Neumann (1996a) *Russia and the Idea of Europe*. See, also, several contributions to Tunander, Baev and Einagel 1997.

35 As we saw in Chapter 6, the meaning of CEEC in EU usage has evolved since 1989. It now includes the Baltic republics and the former Yugoslav republics. Russia, Ukraine and all other former Soviet republics are currently referred to as New Independent States (NIS).

36 There are numerous impediments to increased NATO involvement in the Mediterranean, both internal and external. Internally, NATO members are divided on this issue. The US government is jealous of its central role in the Middle East; the French government is primarily concerned with the Maghreb, where it opposes NATO involvement; Greece and Turkey engage in competitive vetoes of NATO activity in the region. An example of the external problems, here, is the threat by Colonel Quadifi of Libya to 'launch a jihad' if NATO attempts to expand its influence in the region (Winrow 1996:54).

37 The decision to include Estonia and Slovenia was, nevertheless, the subject of controversy – not least because a 'line could have been drawn', in terms of preparedness for accession, after Hungary, the Czech Republic and Poland (Interview, DGIA, February 1998). However this would have suggested a potentially destabilizing distinction between 'Central' and 'Eastern' European countries which the Union has been careful to avoid in public discussion. Conversely the European Parliament and the Nordic Member States (which have a particular interest in the Baltic region) favoured opening accession negotiations with all ten applicants in the first instance, on the understanding that some would move forward to membership more quickly than others. This was rejected on the grounds that it might create false expectations which would ultimately exacerbate feelings of exclusion.

38 Some delegations, we were informed, caused considerable disarray by arriving by bus, unannounced.

39 PfP relationships vary in scope and intensity, ranging from exchange of information to joint training exercises. Initially PfP was greeted with suspicion. Aspirant NATO members were unimpressed by this delaying tactic; and, from the perspective of Russia, the prospect of encirclement by NATO's 'partners' was unattractive, although greatly preferable to NATO enlargement. Nevertheless 29 countries eventually joined PfP – including Austria, Finland, Sweden and Switzerland and, with some reluctance, Russia. For Russian politicians, participation in PfP alongside numerous relatively insignificant countries appeared inappropriate, if not demeaning.

40 Thus Russian President Boris Yeltsin spoke of a Cold Peace – 'When NATO approaches the borders of the Russian Federation, you can say there will be two military blocs, and this will be a restoration of what we already had' (quoted in *International Herald Tribune*, 9–10 September 1995.

41 The references to Harris and Brzezenski are illustrative of the major positions in a debate which has occupied much space in the International Relations journals, in particular *Foreign Affairs*, *International Affairs* and *Survival*. More recently these issues have been aired in the *Review of International Studies*, see MccGwire (1998); Ball (1998).

42 It was considered that only this limited enlargement would be acceptable to Congress. There is opposition to the principle of NATO enlargement in the US – encapsulated in the words of opposition campaign coordinator Karina Wood – 'Why does Clinton seek to burden American taxpayers and soldiers with costs and obligations that the eastern Europeans are not able to pay, to defend them from enemies which exist only in their memories . . .?' (Quoted in *The Guardian*, 23 February 1998).

43 In February 1998 President Clinton signed a 'charter' promising US support for

the NATO membership applications of the three Baltic republics. However it was immediately stressed by US officials that it was not in the administration's power to guarantee NATO membership to these countries.

44 Among other provisions, this established a NATO–Russia Permanent Joint Council, which meets regularly at a number of levels, thus ensuring exchange of views and information. However the success of this initiative depends both upon domestic political circumstances in Russia and upon the extent to which Russian policy makers are convinced that NATO's internal adaptations denote genuine change in the nature and purpose of the organization.

45 Signed at the Madrid Summit, two months after the NATO–Russia Founding Act, this 'Charter' contains only a general commitment to cooperation and consultation without the formal arrangements provided for in the Founding Act. Ukrainian officials had sought a 'special' relationship; however the meaning of distinctive and special overlaps in the Ukrainian language, so the wording of the Charter is apparently satisfactory for domestic purposes in Ukraine (Interview, NATO secretariat, October 1997).

46 Here Alison Bailes (1996:28) asks the intriguing question, 'If NATO were to re-examine itself conceptually as the EU is doing, what might – and what should – be the result?'

47 An example here is the strong warning from US Senator John Werner in the face of reluctance by European NATO members to support a US proposal to launch air strikes against Iraq – 'Make no mistake, there is a direct relationship between decisions taken on Iraq in the next few weeks and US support for NATO' (quoted in *The Guardian*, 10 February 1998).

8 Identity, legitimacy, eligibility

1 The Treaty on European Union, which marked an important stage in attempts to forge an EU identity, makes reference to both senses in which identity is discussed. Thus the Common Provisions refer to the EU as 'an ever closer Union among the peoples of Europe, in which decisions are taken as closely as possible to the citizen' (Art.A [1]). Also included among these Provisions is the intention of the Union 'to assert its identity on the international scene' (Art.B [2]).

2 There is an extensive literature dealing with the 'democratic deficit' of the EC, much of which focuses upon the role of the European Parliament. See, for example, Lodge (1991), Duff (1994), Neunreither (1994).

3 The EC average turnout was 63 per cent in 1979, 61 per cent in 1984, 58.5 per cent in 1989 and 55.6 per cent in 1994. These figures are affected by the fact that attendance at the polling station is compulsory in Belgium, Greece, Italy and Luxembourg. The average figures also disguise differing trends – for example turnout in the UK has gradually increased, from 31.6 per cent in 1979 to 36.2 per cent in 1994.

4 There has been considerable debate about the implications of the TEU ratification process, in particular the original rejection of the Treaty in the 1992 Danish referendum. However not all commentators were persuaded of the existence of a legitimacy crisis. Franklin, Marsh and McLaren (1994) conclude that the Danish result reflected the unpopularity of the, then, Danish government rather more than dissatisfaction with the terms of the TEU. Hedetoft (1994) accords rather more salience to TEU issues in the Danish debate, but concludes that the controversy over the TEU had the effect of increasing public awareness of EU issues; thus serving to 'Europeanize' Danish opinion (*ibid*:41).

5 Benedict Anderson (1991, 2nd edn) provides, in 'Memory and Forgetting' (the final chapter of *Imagined Communities*), a fascinating account of the processes by which nations imagine themselves to be old.

6 Although there are common elements in their thinking, the approaches of these analysts are quite distinct. Thus Dogan (1994), whose central concern is the decline of nationalism, makes extensive use of survey material from the Eurobarometer publications. Howe's (1995) focus is primarily socio-psychological, in that he seeks to identify the values and beliefs which may contribute to the development of a sense of community among EU citizens.

7 Here it is of interest to note, given the relatively high levels of scepticism recorded in the UK, that during the TEU ratification process the generational difference in attitudes towards the EU was significantly higher in the UK than in any of the other Member States (Cohen 1994:32–3).

8 The consistency with which respondents identify the preservation of peace in Europe as the most important role of the EC/EU has regularly been noted in Eurobarometer reports – see, for example, Commission (1994).

9 In 1996 only 18 per cent of the Swedish population considered EU membership to have been beneficial (Commission 1996a:9–10).

10 In the Länder of the former East Germany there is evidently a special problem in this respect, for a variety of reasons. Nevertheless the headline 'Neo-Nazi tide sweeps through east Germany' is clearly alarmist (*The Guardian*, 21 January 1998).

11 In an attempt to gauge changes in popular attitudes over time, Paul Taylor has analysed the evolution of Franco–German relations between 1947 and 1994. In 1954, during the early phase of community building, there was considerable mutual suspicion. However by 1994 levels of mutual trust were high; indeed the French had come to trust the Germans more than any other European people (Taylor 1996:166–77).

12 'Back to the future' prognoses emphasized the importance of the Cold War, and in particular the existence of a common external 'enemy', in promoting and supporting integration in Western Europe. Thus the end of the Cold War was seen as potentially, also, heralding disintegration and renewed conflict in Western Europe. For a strongly argued example of this position, see John J. Mearsheimer (1990).

13 Neo-functionalist theorists, among whom Ernst Haas and Lindberg and Scheingold were prominent, dominated the early study of European integration. They were almost exclusively American and espoused a strongly normative, rationalist view of the progress and desirability of integration in Europe. Moreover their views closely mirrored the opinions and practices of Commission officials. For a succinct discussion of the relationship between neofunctionalist theorists and Commission officials in the early years of European integration see Wallace and Smith (1995).

14 The effectiveness of such symbols in promoting public awareness/support must be questioned, however. For example, Merseyside's designation as the only Objective One region in England has brought large amounts of EC structural funding, and numerous high profile projects adorned with the EU logo. Despite this, a by-election for the European Parliament in December 1996 produced a turnout of only 11.4 per cent. Journalists covering the by-election claimed to have found only minimal public awareness of the EC's role in the region (*The Guardian*, 12 December 1996).

15 Thus, for example, extensive research among women's organizations in the UK found that, despite the increasing significance of EC equality legislation, awareness of EC matters was largely confined to women occupying leadership positions in national organizations (Bretherton and Sperling 1996).

16 In addition to reiteration of the rights to freedom of movement and of residence within the Union, the rights of EU citizens are: to stand for election and to vote in local and European elections (but not national elections) in the Member State of

residence; the right to petition the European Parliament and to appeal to the European Ombudsman; and the right to diplomatic protection, in third countries, by the representatives of any of the Member States.

17 Following rejection of the TEU in the 1992 referendum, the Danish government negotiated an opt-out from the citizenship provisions. This demonstrates that symbols which denote belonging can be highly sensitive.

18 There was a resurgence of controversy over EMU early in 1998, prior to the decision, taken that June, on eligiblity to proceed to the final stage of monetary union on 1 January 1999. Thus, in January 1998, EMU was challenged as unconstitutional in the German Constitutional Court (the challenge was rejected). At the same time splits were revealed in the French governing coalition, with the Communist Party publicly demanding a referendum on EMU.

19 In Germany, for example, widespread fears that the single currency would prove weaker than the Mark were considered, by early 1998, to have generated 'mass resistance' (*The Guardian*, 8 January 1998).

20 As we saw in Chapter 5, there is clearly a determination, on the part of the Member States and the Commission, to minimize the cost of enlargement. Nevertheless the proposed funding of enlargement through reductions of expenditure on the Common Agricultural Policy and, more particularly, on structural and cohesion funding, will undoubtedly be noticed. So, too, will the eventual phase-out of the UK budget rebate.

21 A cursory reading of the International Relations journals published in the USA will reveal the extent of this preoccupation. Recently much attention has focused upon public attitudes to NATO enlargement; indeed NATO sponsors a Project on Attitudes Towards the Atlantic Community, which is studying this issue among others (see *NATO Review*, January 1997).

22 The framing of the integration process in security terms is frequently found in EC information material. Thus, for example, warnings about 'the danger of failure' pervade a booklet ostensibly celebrating 40 years of successful integration (Commission 1990b:7).

23 The broad coincidence between the conclusions of these authors is of interest, not least because they are based upon substantially different sets of data. Taylor draws upon EU-wide Eurobarometer surveys conducted between 1991 and 1994, which allows him to make national comparisons – pointing, for example, to the relatively low level of support in Greece for a CFSP. Leonard makes some use of published data, including Eurobarometer material and British Social Attitudes surveys. However he draws heavily upon unpublished data on UK attitudes to the EU, collected by MORI in 1996 and Opinion Research Business in 1997.

24 The principle of subsidiarity, as introduced by the TEU, requires that 'the Community shall take action . . . only if and in so far as the objectives of the proposed action cannot be sufficiently achieved by the Member States and can therefore, by reason of the scale or effects of the proposed action, be better achieved by the Community' (Art.3b [TEC Art 5]).

25 Clearly such notions must be treated with caution. Survey material tends to produce both a caricature and a 'snapshot' of public opinion and, in particular, to obscure the substantial differences in orientation towards the EU between social groups – on the basis of age, sex, ethnicity and social class – within Member States. Moreover attitudes toward the EU need to be considered in the context of generally low levels of public interest in EU matters. Finally, survey material based upon individual responses cannot provide a reliable guide to collective attitudes/behaviour, which has the potential to be considerably more volatile than individual responses might suggest.

26 Reif's conclusion is based upon survey evidence which indicated that the great majority of respondents, including those who were personally opposed to further

policy integration, expected (and accepted) that the EU would gain additional responsibilities in the future.

27 Bhikhu Parekh explicitly rejects the contention that collective identities are formed through emphasizing difference. He maintains that 'Identity is logically and ontologically prior to difference, and the latter cannot be its basis or criterion' (Parekh 1996:256). For discussion of a range of approaches to the relationship between self and other in the formation of collective identity, see Neumann (1996c).

28 Anthony Smith (1992:75–6) has warned that an EU collective identity is likely to be 'forged through opposition to the identities of significant others' and to involve, in particular, 'cultural and racial exclusion'.

29 For a discussion of historical and contemporary patterns of migration in Europe, and Member State responses thereto, see *New Community*, special edition, 22,2 (April 1996) in particular the contribution by Rainer Münz (1996:201–26).

30 The TEU provided only that Member States should regard these areas as 'matters of common interest' (Art.K1). This fell short of measures agreed between Schengen members – including, by the time of TEU implementation, Italy, Spain, Portugal and Greece. For a concise discussion of the development of the Schengen Agreements see den Boer (1996); and for their broader, contemporary implications see Baldwin-Edwards (1997).

31 The arrival in Dover, in October 1997, of a few hundred Roma from the Czech Republic was greeted with hysteria by sections of the British press and public. According to a spokesperson for the Joint Council for the Welfare of Immigrants, the incident attracted an unprecedented number of hostile telephone calls from the public (*The Guardian*, 22 October 1997). A similar reaction occurred in Ireland, in the summer of 1998, following an influx of Romanians.

32 Such measures range from the policy of returning applicants to 'safe third countries', through which they have travelled prior to attempting to enter the EU, to the provision of so-called safe havens both in Bosnia and Iraq. Thus the influx of Kurdish asylum seekers in January 1998 prompted a JHA proposal on this matter – reported as 'EU revives "safe haven" plan to keep out Kurds' (*The Guardian*, 30 January 1998).

33 The extensive revisions to this policy area introduced by the Amsterdam Treaty make it impossible and/or meaningless to provide equivalent references to the revised TEC and TEU. Consequently, to maintain consistency with practice in other chapters, we employ square bracketed references in referring to new Treaty articles.

34 The Amsterdam Treaty allows a period of up to five years after entry into force for adoption of most measures under Title IV. However no time limit is applied to the three most sensitive provisions: on burden-sharing between Member States on asylum issues [Art.63.2.b]; on standard entry conditions and procedures for the issue of long-term visas and residence permits [Art.63.3.a]; and on the extension of residence rights of third country nationals across the EU [Art.63.4].

35 Of the Resolutions, Recommendations and Conclusions of JHA in relation to immigration up to the end of 1996, only one (on third country nationals with long-term residence) fell within this category. However, despite support from the Commission, this failed to establish rights of movement for resident third country nationals (1995d).

36 Eligibility criteria for citizenship applied by Member States range from established residence to ethnicity. For a recent, concise discussion of these matters see Seifert (1997).

37 Despite this, the application for membership from the Kingdom of Morocco in 1987 was summarily rejected, without recourse to the usual formality of a Commission Opinion, on the grounds that Morocco is not a European country. Since

Morocco, when a French colony, was considered to be an integral part of France, the issue could be considered as at least open to debate.

38 In the light of progress with the customs union between the EC and Turkey since 1996, the Commission's comments in *Agenda 2000* focused upon issues of democracy, Turkey's dispute with Greece and the Cyprus conflict.

39 We referred, in Chapter 5, to informal comments by senior Christian Democrat politicians, including Chancellor Kohl, concerning Turkey's eligibility to join a predominantly Christian Europe. However in a more formal context the Dutch Foreign Minister, Hans van Mierlo (speaking for the Presidency) told an EP Committee –

> There is a problem of a large Muslim state. Do we want that in Europe? It is time for us in Europe to be honest. On the one hand Turkey does not fulfil the yardsticks that we have set in Europe. On the other it is a neighbour. We want to keep close.
>
> (Quoted in *The European*, 6–12 February 1997)

40 Turkey's continuing importance to Western strategic interests is a major theme addressed by the contributors to Mastny and Craig Nation (1996) *Turkey Between East and West: New Challenges for a Rising Regional Power*.

41 There is also a sense in which, despite the end of the Cold War, Russia continues to be cast as West Europe's 'other' – in particular in CEEC anxious to establish their credentials as belonging, culturally, to Central Europe. However EU-based politicians have been considerably more wary in their criticisms of Russian policy than in pronouncements about Turkey.

42 This aspect of the cultural division of Europe is also a feature of the arguments of Wallace (1990) and Huntington (1993) referred to above. Further discussion of the issue of 'engaged' academics can be found in Chapter 5.

43 An example is worth quoting to indicate the flavour of these representations. Thus the chairman of the Foreign Affairs Committee of the Ukrainian Parliament declared (in 1992) –

> The integration into the general European structures will move us to Europe, where we were born and grew up as a nation. But we were torn away from there and forced into Asiatic imprisonment. They dressed us in a Muscovite cloak and trained us in the Slavic–Russian language like the grandchildren of Genghis Khan.
>
> (Quoted in Neumann 1996b:15)

44 As indicated in the previous chapter the role of NATO has also been important although, in our view, less crucial. Here the decision to include only the Czech Republic, Hungary and Poland in NATO's present enlargement is indicative of the success of the 'East Central' European lobby.

45 Even before their independence, public pronouncements, for example by then UK Foreign Secretary Douglas Hurd (in April 1991) provided reassurance that the Baltic republics would receive special treatment from the West (Mayall 1991:425).

46 See Chapter 5 for discussion of the practical implications of this transfer.

Bibliography

ACP–EC Development Finance Cooperation Committee (1997) *Report and Resolution of the ACP–EC Finance Cooperation Committee*, Brussels: ACP–CE 2144/97.

ACTIONAID (1995) *The Reality of Aid 1995*, London: Earthscan.

Aho, C.M. (1993) 'America and the Pacific century: trade conflict and cooperation', *International Affairs*, 69,1: 19–38.

Allen, D. (1978) 'Foreign policy at the European level: beyond the nation-state?', in W. Wallace and W.E. Paterson (eds) *Foreign Policy Making in Western Europe*, Farnborough, Saxon House: 135–54.

Allen, D. and Smith, M. (1990) 'Western Europe's presence in the contemporary international arena', *Review of International Studies*, 16,1: 19–37.

Andersen, M.S. and Liefferink, D. (eds) (1997) *European Environmental Policy: the Pioneers*, Manchester: Manchester University Press.

Anderson, B. (1991) *Imagined Communities: Reflections on the Origins and Spread of Nationalism*, London: Verso.

Arter, D. (1993) *The Politics of European Integration in the Twentieth Century*, Aldershot: Dartmouth.

Ash, T.G., Mertes, M. and Moïsi, D. (1991) 'Let the East Europeans in!', *The New York Review of Books*, 24 October.

Asmus, R.D., Larrabee, F.S. and Lesser, I.O. (1996) 'Mediterranean security: new challenges, new tasks', *NATO Review*, May: 25–31.

Asmus, R.D. and Norick, R.C. (1996) 'NATO enlargement and the Baltic States', *Survival*, 38,2: 121–42.

Baev, P. (1997) 'Russia's departure from Empire: self-assertiveness and a new retreat', in O. Tunander, P. Baev and I.V. Einagel (eds) *Geopolitics in Post-Wall Europe: Security, Territory and Identity*, London, Sage: 17–44.

Bailes, A. (1996) 'NATO: towards a new synthesis', *Survival*, 38,3: 27–40.

— — (1997) 'WEU: a British perspective', in A. Deighton (ed.) *Western European Union 1954–1997: Defence, Security, Integration*, Oxford, European Integration Research Unit: 47–62.

Bailey, R. (1972) *The European Community in the World*, London: Hutchinson.

Balanzinos, S. (1997) 'Deepening partnership: the key to long-term stability in Europe', *NATO Review*, July–August: 10–17.

Baldwin-Edwards, M. (1997) 'The emerging European immigration regime: some reflections on implications for Southern Europe', *Journal of Common Market Studies*, 35,4: 497–520.

Ball, C.L. (1998) 'Nattering NATO negativism', *Review of International Studies*, 24,1: 43–68.

Barbé, E. (1996) 'The Barcelona Conference: launching pad of a process', *Mediterranean Politics*, 1,1: 25–42.

Benedick, R.E. (1991) *Ozone Diplomacy: New Directions in Safeguarding the Planet*, Cambridge MA: Harvard University Press.

Boehmer-Christiansen, S. and Skea, J. (1991) *Acid Politics: Environmental and Energy Policies in Britain and Germany*, London: Belhaven Press.

Boer, M. den (1996) 'Justice and home affairs', in H. Wallace and W. Wallace (eds) *Policy-Making in the European Union*, Oxford, Oxford University Press: 389–409.

Borko, Y. (1997) 'Possible scenarios for geopolitical shifts in Russian–European relations', in O. Tunander, P. Baev and V.I. Einagel (eds) *Geopolitics in Post-Wall Europe: Security, Territory and Identity*, London, Sage: 196–216.

Boutros-Ghali, B. (1992) *An Agenda for Peace: Preventative Diplomacy, Peace-making and Peace-keeping*, New York: United Nations.

Bretherton, C. (1998) 'Global environmental politics: putting gender on the agenda?', *Review of International Studies*, 24,1: 85–100.

Bretherton, C. and Ponton, G. (eds) (1996) *Global Politics: an Introduction*, Oxford: Blackwell.

Bretherton, C. and Sperling, L. (1996) 'Women's networks and the European Union: towards an inclusive approach?', *Journal of Common Market Studies*, 34,4: 487–508.

Brinkhorst, P. (1994) 'The European Community at UNCED: lessons to be drawn for the future', in D. Curtin and T. Heukels (eds) *Essays in Honour of H.G. Schermers*, Vol. II, Dordnecht, Niijhoff: 609–17.

Bryant, G.A. and Mokrzycki, E. (eds) (1994) *The New Great Transformation? Change and Continuity in East–Central Europe*, London: Routledge.

Brzezenski, Z. (1994) 'The premature partnership', *Foreign Affairs*, 73,2: 67–82.

Buchan, D. (1993) *Europe: the Strange Superpower*, Aldershot: Dartmouth.

Bull, H. (1983) 'Civilian power Europe: a contradiction in terms?', in R. Tsoukalis (ed.) *The European Community: Past, Present and Future*, London, Blackwell: 149–70.

Bulmer, S. and Scott, A. (eds) (1994) *Economic and Political Integration in Europe: Internal Dynamics and Global Context*, Oxford: Blackwell.

Burton, J.W. (1972) *World Society*, Cambridge: Cambridge University Press.

Buzan, B. and Wæver, O. (1997) 'Slippery? Contradictory? Sociologically untenable? The Copenhagen school replies', *Review of International Studies*, 23,2: 241–50.

Cameron, J., Nerksman, J. and Roderick, P. (eds) (1996) *Improving Compliance with International Environmental Law*, London: Earthscan.

Campbell, B. and Parfitt, T. (1995) 'Virtual adjustment: whose reality?', *Review of African Political Economy*, 63: 3–8.

Caporaso, J. (1996) 'The European Union and forms of state: Westphalian, regulatory or post-modern?', *Journal of Common Market Studies* 34,1: 29–52.

Carlsnaes, W. (1992) 'The agency-structure problem in foreign policy analysis', *International Studies Quarterly*, 34: 245–70.

Carlsnaes, W. and Smith, S. (eds) (1994) *European Foreign Policy: the EC and Changing Perspectives in Europe*, London: Sage.

Carr, E.H. (1947) *Nationalism and After*, London: Macmillan.

Cecchini, P., Catinat, M. and Jacquemin, A. (1988) *The European Challenge, 1992*, London: Wildwood Press.

Chryssochoou, D. (1996) 'Europe's could-be demos: recasting the debate', *West European Politics*, 19,4: 787–801.

Claude, I.L. (1965) *Swords into Ploughshares: the Problems and Progress of International Organization*, London: University of London Press.

Cohen, R. (1994) *Frontiers of Identity: the British and the Others*, Harlow, Essex: Longman.

Collier, U. (1996) 'The European Union's climate change policy: limiting emissions or limiting power?', *Journal of European Public Policy*, 3,1: 122–38.

Commission (1982) 'Memorandum on the Community's development policy', *Bulletin of the European Communities*, Supplement 5(82).

— — (1989) *Commission Opinion on Turkey's request for accession to the Community*, SEC(89), 2290, final.

— — (1990a) *Environmental Policy in the European Community*, Luxembourg: Office for Official Publications of the European Communities.

— — (1990b) *Europe – A Fresh Start: the Schuman Declaration 1950–90*, Luxembourg: Office for Official Publications of the European Communities.

— — (1990c) *The European Community and its Eastern Neighbours*, Luxembourg: Office for Official Publications of the European Communities.

— — (1990d) *Redirecting the Community's Mediterranean Policy*, SEC(90), 812.

— — (1991a) *The European Community: 1992 and Beyond*, Luxembourg: Office for Official Publications of the European Communities.

— — (1991b) *A Citizen's Europe*, Luxembourg: Office for Official Publications of the European Communities.

— — (1991c) *Opening up the Internal Market*, Luxembourg: Office for Official Publications of the European Communities.

— — (1992a) *Development Cooperation Policy in the Run-up to 2000*, SEC(92), 915, final.

— — (1992b) 'Europe and the challenge of enlargement', *Bulletin of the European Communities*, Supplement 3(92), Luxembourg: Office for Official Publications of the European Communities.

— — (1993) 'Commission opinion on the application by the Republic of Cyprus for membership', *Bulletin of the European Communities*, Supplement 5(93).

— — (1994) *Eurobarometer: Public Opinion in the European Union*, 42: Autumn.

— — (1995a) *Intergovernmental Conference 1996: Commission Report for the Reflection Group*, Brussels: May.

— — (1995b) *Report on the Operation of the Treaty on European Union*, Brussels.

— — (1995c) *The European Union and Latin America: the present situation and prospects for closer partnership 1996–2000*, Brussels: COM(95), 495.

— — (1995d) *Proposal for a directive on the right of third-country nationals to travel in the Community*, Brussels: COM(95), 0346, final.

— — (1995e) *Preparation of the Associated Countries of Central and Eastern Europe for Integration into the Internal Market of the Union*, Brussels: COM(95), 163, final.

— — (1995f) 'Strengthening the Mediterranean policy of the European Union: establishing a Euro–Mediterranean partnership', *Bulletin*, Supplement 2/95, Luxembourg: Office for Official Publications of the European Communities.

— — (1995g) *Barcelona Euro–Mediterranean Conference (27–28 November 1995) – Declaration and Work Programme*, DOC(95), 7.

— — (1995h) *Europe and Japan: the Next Steps*, COM(95), 73, final.

— — (1996a) *Eurobarometer: Public Opinion in the European Union*, 46: Autumn.

— — (1996b) *Report from the European Commission to the UN Commission on Sustainable Development on the European Community's Progress Towards Sustainability*, prepared for the Fourth Session, Brussels: April.

— — (1996c) 'Reinforcing political union and preparing for enlargement', *Commission Opinion for the IGC*, Brussels.

— — (1996d) *Fourth Medium-Term Community Action Programme on Equal Opportunities for Women and Men (1996–2000)*, Brussels: V/231b(96).

— — (1997a) 'For a stronger and wider Union', *Agenda 2000*, Volume I, Strasbourg: DOC(97), 6.

— — (1997b) 'Reinforcing the pre-accession strategy', *Agenda 2000*, Volume II, Strasbourg: DOC(97), 7.

— — (1997c) 'Summary and conclusions of the Opinion of the Commission concerning the Applications for Membership to the European Union presented by the candidate countries', *Agenda 2000*, Strasbourg: DOC(97), 8.

— — (1997d) *Green Paper on Relations between the European Union and the ACP countries on the eve of the 21st Century: Challenges and Options for a New Partnership*, Luxembourg: Office for Official Publications of the European Communities.

— — (1997e) 'Composition, organization and operation of the Commission', *Communication from the Commission*, CEECAN500486SG, Brussels: 5 March.

— — (1997f) *InfoFinance 1996*, Brussels, DE 91: June.

— — (1997g) *Towards greater economic integration: the European Union's financial assistance, trade policy and investments for central and eastern Europe*, Brussels: DGIA Evaluation Unit.

— — (1997h) *Phare: an interim evaluation*, Brussels: DGIA.

— — (1997i) *The Tacis Programme Annual Report 1996*, Brussels: COM(97), 400, final.

— — (1997j) *Trade Policy Review of the European Union, 25–26 November 1997: Opening Statement by Mr Hervé Jouanjean*, http://europe.eu.int/en/comm/dg01.

— — (1997k) *Agenda 21, the First Five Years: European Community Progress on the Implementation of Agenda 21: 1992–97*: Brussels.

— — (1997l) *Climate Change: the EU Approach to Kyoto*, COM(97), 481.

— — (1998a) *Euro–Mediterranean Partnership Short and Medium Term Priority Environmental Action Programme (SMAP)*, Brussels.

— — (1998b) *Euro–Mediterranean Partnership: Monthly Information Note*, Brussels: February.

Conference of the Representatives of the Governments of the Member States (1996) *The European Union Today and Tomorrow: Adapting the European Union for the Benefit of its Peoples and Preparing it for the Future*, Dublin II, CONF/2500(96), Brussels: 5 December.

Conference of the Representatives of the Governments of the Member States (1997) *Draft Treaty of Amsterdam*, CONF/4002(97), Brussels: 8 July.

Coplin, W. (1965) 'International law and assumptions about the state system', in J.N. Rosenau (ed.) (1969) *International Politics and Foreign Policy: A Reader in Research and Theory*, (2nd edn), New York, Free Press: 142–52.

Cosgrove, C. (1994) 'Has the Lomé Convention failed ACP Trade?', *Journal of International Affairs*, 48,1: 223–49.

Cosgrove, C.A. and Twitchett, K.J. (eds) (1970) *The New International Actors: the UN and the EEC*, London: Macmillan.

Council of the European Union (1995) *Report on the Functioning of the Treaty on European Union*, Brussels.

— — (1997a) *Représentation diplomatique de la Présidence dans les pays tiers – premier semestre 1997*, Brussels: 6581/97.

— — (1997b) *Coherence of the EC's Development Cooperation with its Other Policies*, Luxembourg, 8631/97: June.

— — (1997c) *Second Euro–Mediterranean Ministerial Conference, Malta, 15 and 16 April 1997: Conclusions*, Euro–Med 5(97).

— — (1998) *Communiqué*: 2070 – General Affairs – 20/02/98.

The Courier (1975) *Special Edition*, No. 31: March.

— — (1990) No. 212: March–April.

— — (1991) *Special Edition: Human Rights, Democracy and Development*, No. 128: July–August.

— — (1994) No. 132: March–April.

— — (1995) No. 145: May–June.

— — (1996) *Lomé IV Convention as Revised by the Agreement Signed in Mauritius on 4 November 1995*, No. 155: January–February.

Cox, A. and Koning, A. (1997) *Understanding European Community Aid: Aid Policies, Management and Distribution Explained*, London: Overseas Development Institute

Cox, R. (1986) 'Social forces, states and world orders: beyond international relations theory', in R.O. Keohane (ed.) *Neorealism and its Critics*, New York, Columbia University Press: 204–54.

— — (1993) 'Structural issues of global governance: implications for Europe', in S. Gill (ed.) *Gramsci, Historical Materialism and International Relations*, Cambridge, Cambridge University Press: 259–89.

Cragg, A. (1996) 'The Combined Joint Task Force concept: a key component of the Alliance's adaptations', *NATO Review*, July: 3–6.

— — (1997) 'Internal adaptation: reshaping NATO for the challenges of tomorrow', *NATO Review*, July–August: 30–5.

Craig Nation, R. (1996) 'The Turkic and other Muslim peoples of Central Asia, the Caucasus, and the Balkans', in V. Mastny and R. Craig Nation (eds) *Turkey Between East and West: New Challenges for a Rising Regional Power*, Boulder CO, Westview Press: 97–130.

Cram, L. (1994) 'The European Commission as a multi-organization: social policy and IT policy in the EU', *Journal of European Public Policy*, 1,2: 195–217.

Currie, D. and Vines, D. (1992) 'A global economic policy agenda for the 1990s', *International Affairs*, 68,4: 585–602.

Curtis, M. (1997) 'Development cooperation in a changing world', in J. Randel and T. German (eds) *The Reality of Aid 1997/8*, London, Earthscan: 4–20.

Dangerfield, M. (1995) 'The economic opening of East and Central Europe: continuity and change in foreign economic relations', *Journal of European Integration*, XIX,1: 16–35.

Davenport, M. (1992) 'Africa and the unimportance of being preferred', *Journal of Common Market Studies*, 30,2: 233–51.

Deighton, A. (1997) *Western European Union 1954–1997: Defence, Security, Integration*, Oxford: European Interdependence Research Unit.

Dessler, D. (1989) 'What's at stake in the Agency-Structure Debate?', *International Organization*, 43,3: 441–73.

Dickson, A. K. (1997) *Development and International Relations: a Critical Introduction*, Cambridge: Polity Press.

Dogan, M. (1994) 'The decline of nationalism within Western Europe', *Comparative Politics*, 261,3: 281–306.

Donnelly, C. (1997) 'Defence transformation in the new deomcracies: a framework for tackling the problem', *NATO Review*, January: 15–19.

Duchêne, F. (1972) 'Europe's role in world peace', in R. Mayne (ed.) *Europe Tomorrow: Sixteen Europeans Look Ahead*, London, Fontana: 32–47.

Duff, A. (1994) 'Building a parliamentary Europe', *Government and Opposition*, 29,2: 147–65.

Duigan, P. and Gann, L.H. (1994) *The United States and the New Europe 1945–1993*, Oxford: Blackwell.

Eatwell, R. (ed.) (1997) *European Political Culture: Conflict or Convergence?*, London: Routledge.

Einhorn, B. (1993) *Cinderella Goes to Market: Citizenship, Gender and Women's Movements in East Central Europe*, London: Verso.

Enloe, C. (1989) *Bananas, Beaches and Bases: Making Feminist Sense of International Politics*, London: Pandora.

EPC Bulletin (1991) *Statement by an Extraordinary EPC Ministerial Meeting Concerning the Baltic States*, 91/251: 27 August.

Erridge, A. (1981) 'The Lomé Convention: a case study', *World Politics*, Paper 12, D233, Milton Keynes: The Open University Press.

Esty, D.C. (1994) *Greening the GATT: Trade, Environment and the Future*, Washington: Institute for International Economics.

Euro-CIDSE (1995) *News Bulletin*, July–August.

—— (1995) *News Bulletin*, November–December.

—— (1996) *News Bulletin*, January–February.

—— (1996) *News Bulletin*, March–April.

European Community Humanitarian Office (1996) *1996 ECHO Annual Review*: Brussels.

European Parliament (1993) *Report of the Committee on Development and Cooperation on development cooperation in the run-up to 2000*, PE 204.967/fin: 15 September.

—— (1994) 'Prospects for a Common Foreign and Security Policy: preliminary review', *Working Papers*, W7, Luxembourg: Directorate General for Research.

European Policy Centre (1996) *Challenge 96*, IGC Intelligence Service, Issue 11, Brussels: November/December.

Eurostep (undated) *The Fight for Fish: Towards Fair Fisheries Agreements*, Brussels: Eurostep.

Featherstone, F. and Ginsberg, R.H. (2nd edn) (1996) *The United States and the European Union in the 1990s: Partners in Transition*, Basingstoke: Macmillan.

Feldman, D.L. (1992) 'Institutions for managing global environmental change', *Global Environmental Change*, March: 42–58.

Foreign and Commonwealth Office, Department of Trade and Industry (1996) *Free Trade and Foreign Policy: a Global Vision*, London: 29 November.

Franklin, M., Marsh, M. and McLaren, L. (1994) 'Uncorking the bottle: popular opposition to European unification in the wake of Maastricht', *Journal of Common Market Studies*, 32,4: 455–72.

Galtung, J. (1969) 'Violence, peace and peace research', *Journal of Peace Research*, 3: 167–89.

— — (1973) *The European Community: a Superpower in the Making*, London: George Allen and Unwin.

García, S. (1993) (ed.) *European Identity and the Search for Legitimacy*, London: Pinter.

Giddens, A. (1984) *The Constitution of Society: Outline of the Theory of Structuration*, Basingstoke: Macmillan.

Greene, O. (1992) 'Implementation Review: the Framework Convention on Climate Change and the Montreal Protocol', Paper to British International Studies Association Annual Conference: December.

— — (1996) 'Environmental regimes: effectiveness and implementation review', in J. Vogler and M.F. Imber (eds) *The Environment and International Relations*, London, Routledge: 196–214.

Grilli, E.R. (1993) *The European Community and the Developing Countries*, Cambridge: Cambridge University Press.

Grosser, A. (1978) *The Western Alliance: European–American Relations since 1945*, London: Macmillan.

Grubb, M. (1995) *The Berlin Climate Conference: Outcome and Implications*, Briefing Paper No. 21, London: RIIA.

Grubb, M. and Anderson, D. (eds) (1995) *The Emerging International Regime for Climate Change: Structures and Options after Berlin*, London: RIIA

Gouldner, A. (1971) *The Coming Crisis of Western Sociology*, New York: Heinemann.

Haas, E. (1958) *The Uniting of Europe*, Stanford: Stanford University Press.

Haigh, N. (1996) 'Climate change policies and politics in the European Community', in T. O'Riordan and J. Jäger (eds) *Politics of Climate Change: a European Perspective*, London, Routledge: 155–84.

Hamilton, K.A. (ed.) (1994) *Migration and the New Europe*, Washington DC: Centre for Strategic and International Studies.

Harris, O. (1993) 'The collapse of the West', *Foreign Affairs*, 72,4: 41–53.

Hay, C. (1995) 'Structure and agency', in D. Marsh and G. Stoker (eds) *Theory and Method in Political Science*, Basingstoke, Macmillan: 189–206.

Hayes-Renshaw, F., Lequesne, C. and Lopez, P.M. (1989) 'The Permanent Representations of the Member States to the European Communities', *Journal of Common Market Studies*, XXVII,2: 119–37.

Hayes-Renshaw, F. and Wallace, H. (1997) *The Council of Ministers*, Basingstoke: Macmillan.

Hedetoft, U. (1994) 'The state of sovereignty in Europe: political concept or cultural self-image?', in S. Zetterholm (ed.) *National Cultures and European Integration*, Oxford, Berg.

Heidensohn, K. (1995) *Europe and World Trade*, London: Pinter.

Helvacioglu, B. (1996) ' "*Allahu Ekber*", We are Turks: yearning for a different homecoming at the periphery of Europe', *Third World Quarterly*, 17,3: 503–23.

Hermann, R. and Weiss, D. (1995) 'A welfare analysis of the EC–ACP Sugar Protocol', *Journal of Development Studies*, 31,6: 918–41.

Hession, M. (1996) 'The role of the EC in implementing international environmental law', in J. Cameron, J. Nerksman and P. Roderick (eds) *Improving Compliance with International Environmental Law*, London, Earthscan: 177–84.

Heurlin, B. (1996) 'Denmark: a new activism in foreign and security policy', in C. Hill (ed.) *The Actors in Europe's Foreign Policy*, London, Routledge: 166–87.

Hewitt, A. (1984) 'The Lomé Conventions: entering a second decade', *Journal of Common Market Studies*, XXIII,2: 95–115.

Hill, C. (1993) 'The capability–expectations cap, or conceptualising Europe's international role', *Journal of Common Market Studies*, 31,3: 305–25.

— — (ed.) (1996) *The Actors in Europe's Foreign Policy*, London: Routledge.

Hindley, B. (1992) 'Trade policy of the European Community', in P. Minford (ed.) *The Cost of Europe*, Manchester, Manchester University Press: 84–101.

Hix, S. (1994) 'The Study of the EC: The challenge to comparative politics', *West European Politics*, 17,1: 1–30.

Hobsbawm, E. (1996) 'Identity politics and the left', *New Left Review*, 217: 38–47.

Hocking, B. and Smith, M. (1990) *World Politics: An Introduction to International Relations*, Hemel Hempstead: Harvester Wheatsheaf.

— — (1997) *Beyond Foreign Economic Policy: the United States, the Single European Market and the Changing World Economy*, London: Pinter.

Hoekman, B. and Kostecki, M. (1995) *The Political Economy of the World Trading System: from GATT to WTO*, Oxford: Oxford University Press.

Hoffman, S. (1994) 'Europe's identity crisis revisited', *Daedalus*, 123,2: 1–23.

Holland, M. (1987) 'Three approaches for understanding European political co-operation: a case study of EC–South Africa policy', *Journal of Common Market Studies*, XXV,4: 295–313.

— — (1995) 'Bridging the capability–expectations gap: a case study of the CFSP joint action in South Africa', *Journal of Common Market Studies*, 33,4: 555–72.

Hollis, M. and Smith, S. (1991) 'Beware of gurus: structure and action in international relations', *Review of International Studies*, 17,4: 393–410.

Hollis, R. (1997) 'Europe and the Middle East: power by stealth?', *International Affairs*, 73,1: 15–29.

Hopkins, R.E. and Mansbach, R.W. (1973) *Structure and Process in International Politics*, New York: Harper and Row.

Howe, P. (1995) 'A Community of Europeans: the requisite underpinnings', *Journal of Common Market Studies*, 33,1: 27–46

Huntington, S. (1993) 'The clash of civilizations', *Foreign Affairs*, Summer: 22–49.

Huysmans, J. (1995) 'Migrants as a security problem: dangers of "securitizing" societal issues', in R. Miles and D. Thränhardt (eds) *Migration and European Integration: the Dynamics of Inclusion and Exclusion*, London, Pinter: 53–72.

Hyde-Price, A. (1996) *The International Politics of East Central Europe*, Manchester: Manchester University Press.

Jachtenfuchs, M. (1990) 'The European Community and the protection of the ozone layer', *Journal of Common Market Studies*, XXVII,3: 261–77.

Jervis, R. (1991/2) 'The future of world politics: will it resemble the past?', *International Security*, 16,3: 39–73.

Jessop, B. (1990) *State Theory: Putting Capitalist States in Their Place*, Cambridge: Polity.

Jordan, A. (1995) 'Implementation Failure or Policy Making? How do we Theorise the Implementation of European Union (EU) Environmental Legislation?', *CSERGE Working Paper* GEC 95–18.

Joulwan, G.A. (1996) 'SHAPE and IFOR: adapting to the needs of tomorrow', *NATO Review*, March: 6–9.

Kabeer, N. (1994) *Reversed Realities: Gender Hierarchies in Development Thought*, London: Verso.

Kahler, M. (1982) 'Europe and its "Privileged Partners" in Africa and the Middle East', *Journal of Common Market Studies*, XXI, 1 and 2: 199–218.

Keeler, J.T.S. (1996) 'Agricultural power in the European Community: explaining the fate of the CAP and GATT negotiations', *Comparative Politics*, January: 127–49.

Keohane, R.O. and Hoffman, S. (1991) *The New European Community: Decision-Making and Institutional Change*, Boulder CO: Westview.

Keohane, R.O. and Nye, J.S. (eds) (1973) *Transnational Relations and World Politics*, Cambridge MA: Harvard University Press.

— — (1977) *Power and Interdependence: World Politics in Transition*, Boston MA: Little, Brown and Company.

Kibble, S., Goodison, P. and Balefi, T. (1995) 'The uneasy triangle – South Africa, Southern Africa and Europe in the post-apartheid era', *International Relations*, XII,4: 41–61.

Kissinger, H.A. (1966) *The Troubled Partnership*, Garden City NY: Doubleday.

— — (1982) *Years of Upheaval*, London: Weidenfeld and Nicolson.

Kohler-Koch, B. (1994) 'Changing patterns of interest intermediation in the European Union', *Government and Opposition*, 29,2: 166–80.

— — (1996) 'Catching up with change: the transformation of governance in the European Union', *Journal of European Public Policy*, 3,3: 359–80.

Kolankiewicz, G. (1994) 'Consensus and competition in the eastern enlargement of the European Union', *International Affairs*, 70,3: 477–95.

Kramer, H. (1996a) 'The EU–Turkey customs union: economic integration amidst political turmoil', *Mediterranean Politics*, 1,1: 60–75.

— — (1996b) 'Turkey and the European Union: a multi-dimensional relationship with hazy perspectives', in V. Mastny and R. Craig Nation (eds) *Turkey Between East and West: New Challenges for a Rising Regional Power*, Boulder CO, Westview: 203–32.

Kramer, M. and Smoke, S. (1996) 'Concluding observations', in R. Smoke (ed.) *Perceptions of Security: Public Opinion and Expert Assessment in Europe's New Democracies*, Manchester, Manchester University Press.

Krasner, S.D. (1985) *Structural Conflict: the Third World Against Global Liberalism*, Berkeley: University of California Press.

La Serre, F. de (1996) 'France: the impact of François Mitterrand', in C. Hill (ed.) *The Actors in Europe's Foreign Policy*, London, Routledge: 19–39.

Laffan, B. (1996) 'The politics of identity and political order in Europe', *Journal of Common Market Studies*, 34,1: 81–102.

— — (1997) 'From policy entrepreneur to policy manager: the challenge facing the European Commission', *Journal of European Public Policy*, 4,3: 422–38.

Lawler, P. (1997) 'Scandinavian exceptionalism and European Union', *Journal of Common Market Studies*, 35,4: 565–94.

Le Gloannec, A. (1997) 'Europe by other means?', *International Affairs*, 73,1: 83–98.

Lehmann, J.P. (1992) 'France, Japan, Europe and industrial competition: the automotive case', *International Affairs*, 68,1: 37–53.

Leonard, M. (1997) *Politics without Frontiers: the Role of Political Parties in Europe's Future*, London: Demos.

Levy, M.A. (1993) 'European acid rain: the power of tote-board diplomacy', in P.M. Haas, R.O. Keohane and M.A. Levy (eds) *Institutions for the Earth: Sources of Effective International Environmental Legislation*, Cambridge MA, MIT Press: 75–132.

Liberatore, A. (1997) 'The European Union: bridging domestic and international environmental policy-making', in M.A. Schreurs and E.C. Economy (eds) *The Internationalization of Environmental Protection*, Cambridge, Cambridge University Press: 188–212.

Lindberg, L. and Scheingold, S. (1970) *Europe's Would-Be Polity*, Englewood Cliffs NJ: Prentice Hall.

Lodge, J. (1991) 'Democratic legitimacy and European Union', *Public Policy and Administration*, 6,1: 21–29.

MccGwire, M. (1998) 'A policy error of historic importance', *Review of International Studies*, 21,1: 23–42.

McConnell, F. (1991) Review of 'Ozone diplomacy', *International Environmental Affairs*, 3,4: 318–20.

McGoldrick, D. (1997) *International Relations Law of the European Union*, London: Longman.

McGrew, A., Lewis, P. *et al.* (1992) *Global Politics*, Oxford: Polity.

Macleod, I., Hendry, T. and Hyett, S. (1996) *The External Relations of the European Communities: a Manual of Law and Practice*, Oxford: Oxford University Press.

Macrory, R. and Hession, M. (1996) 'The European Community and climate change: the role of law and legal competence', in T. O'Riordan and J. Jäger (eds) *Politics of Climate Change: a European Perspective*, London, Routledge: 106–54.

McSweeney, B. (1996) 'Identity and security: Buzan and the Copenhagen School', *Review of International Studies*, 22,1: 81–90.

Mahler, V.A. (1994) 'The Lomé Convention: assessing a North–South institutional relationship', *Review of International Political Economy*, 1,2: 233–56.

Mannin, M.L. (ed.) (1999) *Pushing Back the Boundaries: the European Union's Relations with Central and Eastern Europe*, Manchester: Manchester University Press.

Maresceau, M. (1992) 'The European Community, Eastern Europe and the USSR', in J. Redmond (ed.) *The External Relations of the European Community: the International Response to 1992*, London, Macmillan: 93–119.

Marks, G., Hooghe, L. and Blank, K. (1996) 'European integration from the 1980s: state-centric v. multi-level governance', *Journal of Common Market Studies*, 34, 3: 341–78.

Marks, J. (1996) 'High hopes and low motives: the new Euro–Mediterranean partnership initiative', *Mediterranean Politics*, 1,1: 1–24.

Marquand, D. (1989) 'The irresistible tide of Europeanisation', in S. Hall and M. Jacques (eds) *New Times*, London, Lawrence and Wishart: 205–21.

Marquina, A. (1995) *The European Union Negotiations on Partnership-building Agreements with Morocco and Tunisia*, paper to Second Pan-European Conference on International Relations, Paris: 13–16 September.

Martin, G. (1982) 'Africa and the ideology of Eurafrica: neo-colonialism or pan-Africanism?', *Journal of Modern African Studies*, 20,2: 221–38.

Martiniello, M. (1995) 'European citizenship, European identity and migrants:

towards the post-national state?', in R. Miles and D. Thränhardt (eds) *Migration and European Integration: the Dynamics of Inclusion and Exclusion*, London, Pinter: 37–52.

Mason, T.D. and Turay, A.M. (eds) (1994) *Japan, NAFTA and Europe: Trilateral Cooperation or Confrontation?*, New York: St. Martins Press.

Mastny, V. and Craig Nation, R. (eds) (1996) *Turkey Between East and West: New Challenges for a Rising Regional Power*, Boulder CO, Westview.

Mayall, J. (1991) 'Non-intervention, self-determination and the "new world order"', *International Affairs*, 67,3: 421–9.

Mearsheimer, J.J. (1990) 'Back to the future: instability in Europe after the Cold War', *International Security*, 15,1: 5–56.

Meehan, E. (1993) 'Citizenship and the European Community', *The Political Quarterly*, 64,2: 172–97.

Menon, A. (1995) 'From independence to cooperation: France, NATO and European security', *International Affairs*, 71,1: 19–34.

Mensah, C. (1996) 'The United Nations Commission on Sustainable Development', in J. Werksman (ed.) *Greening International Institutions*, London, Earthscan: 21–37.

Merle, M. (1987) *The Sociology of International Relations*, Leamington Spa: Berg.

Milward, A. (1992) *The European Rescue of the Nation-State*, London: Routledge.

Mintzer, I.M. and Leonard, J.A. (eds) (1994) *Negotiating Climate Change: the Inside Story of the Rio Convention*, Cambridge: Cambridge University Press.

Mock, A. (1995) 'Austria's role in the new Europe', *NATO Review*, March: 15–19.

Moltke, K. von and Rahman, A. (1996) 'External perspectives on climate change: a view from the United States and the Third World', in T. O'Riordan and J. Jäger (eds) *Politics of Climate Change: a European Perspective*, London, Routledge: 330–45.

Muftüler-Bac, M. (1997) *Turkey's Relations with a Changing Europe*, Manchester: Manchester University Press.

Münz, R. (1996) 'A continent of migration: European mass migration in the twentieth century', *New Community*, 22,2: 201–26.

Neumann, I.B. (1996a) *Russia and the Idea of Europe*, London: Routledge.

—— (1996b) *European Identity, EU Expansion and the Integration/Exclusion Nexus*, Working Paper No. 551, Norwegian Institute for International Affairs: June.

—— (1996c) 'Self and other in international relations', *European Journal of International Relations*, 2,2: 139–74.

Neumann, I.B. and Welsh, J.M. (1991) 'The other in European self-definition: an addendum to the literature on international society', *Review of International Studies*, 17,4: 327–48.

Neunreither, K. (1994) 'The democratic deficit of the European Union: towards closer cooperation between the European Parliament and the national parliaments', *Government and Opposition*, 29,3: 299–314.

Nilsson, S. and Pitt, D. (1994) *Protecting the Atmosphere: the Climate Change Convention and its Context*, London: Earthscan.

Nitze, W. (1990) *The Greenhouse Effect: Formulating a Convention*, London: RIIA.

Nugent, N. (1995) 'The leadership capacity of the European Commission', *Journal of European Public Policy*, 2,4: 603–23.

Nuttall, S.J. (1992) *European Political Co-operation*, Oxford: Oxford University Press.

— — (1996a) 'The Commission: the struggle for legitimacy', in C. Hill (ed.) *The Actors in Europe's Foreign Policy*, London, Routledge: 130–50.

— — (1996b) 'Japan and the European Union: reluctant partners', *Survival*, 38,2: 104–20.

Obradovic, D. (1996) 'Political legitimacy and the European Union', *Journal of Common Market Studies*, 34,2: 191–222.

Ockenden, O. and Franklin, M. (1995) *European Agriculture: Making the CAP Fit the Future*, London: Pinter.

O'Riordan, T. and Jäger, J. (eds) (1996) *Politics of Climate Change: a European Perspective*, London: Routledge.

Paemen, H. and Bensch, A. (1995) *From the GATT to the WTO: the European Community in the Uruguay Round*, Leuven: Leuven University Press.

Paganon, J. (1997) 'Western European Union's pivotal position between the Atlantic Alliance and the European Union', in A. Deighton (ed.) *Western European Union 1954–1997: Defence, Security, Integration*, Oxford, European Interdependence Research Unit: 93–102.

Parekh, B. (1996) 'The concept of national identity', *New Community*, 21, 2: 255–68.

Paterson, M. (1996) *Global Warming and Global Politics*, London: Routledge.

Pehe, J. (1992) 'Czechs and Slovaks define postdivorce relations', *RFE/RL Report*, 1,45: 7–11.

Peterson, J. (1995) 'Policy networks and European policy making', *West European Politics*, 18,2: 389–407.

— — (1996) *Europe and America: the Prospects for Partnership*, London: Routledge.

Piening, R. (1997) *Global Europe*, Boulder CO: Lynne Reiner.

Pomfret, R. (1992) 'The European Community's relations with the Mediterranean countries', in J. Redmond (ed.) *The External Relations of the European Community: the International Response to 1992*, London, Macmillan: 77–92.

Ponton, G. (1996) 'The end of the Soviet era', in C. Bretherton and G. Ponton (eds) *Global Politics: an Introduction*, Oxford, Blackwell: 74–99.

Rajana, C. (1982) 'The Lomé Convention: an evaluation of EEC economic assistance to the ACP states', *Journal of Modern African Studies*, 20,2: 179–220.

Randel, J. and German, T. (eds) (1997) *The Reality of Aid 1997/8: an Independent Review of Development Cooperation*, London: Earthscan.

Ravenhill, J. (1985) *Collective Clientelism: the Lomé Conventions and North/South Relations*, New York: Columbia University Press.

— — (1993) 'when Weakness is strength: the Lomé IV negotiations', in I. W. Zartman (ed.) *Europe and Africa: the New Phase*, Boulder CO, Lynne Reiner: 41–61.

Redmond, J. (ed.) (1992) *The External Relations of the European Community: the External Consequences of 1992*, London: Macmillan.

Regelsberger, E. (1993) 'European political cooperation', in J. Story (ed.) *The New Europe: Politics, Government and Economy since 1945*, Oxford, Blackwell: 270–91.

Reif, K. (1993) 'Cultural convergence and cultural diversity as factors in European identity', in S. García (ed.) *European Identity and the Search for Legitimacy*, London, Pinter: 131–53.

Risse-Kappen, T. (1996) 'Exploring the nature of the beast: International relations theory and comparative policy analysis meet the European Union', *Journal of Common Market Studies*, 34,1: 53–80.

Rosenau, J.N. (1990) *Turbulence in World Politics: a Theory of Change and Continuity*, New York: Harvester and Wheatsheaf.

Rosengarten, B. (1997) 'The WEU planning cell', in A. Deighton (ed.) *Western European Union 1954–1997: Defence, Security, Integration*, Oxford, European Interdependence Research Unit: 157–68.

Ruggie, J.G. (1983) 'International regimes, transactions and change: embedded liberalism in the post-war economic order', in S.D. Krasner (ed.) *International Regimes*, Ithaca, Cornell University Press: 195–232.

— — (1993) 'Territoriality and beyond: problematizing modernity in international relations', *International Organization*, 47,1: 139–74.

Salmon, T.C. (1992) 'Testing times for European political cooperation: the Gulf and Yugoslavia, 1990–1992', *International Affairs*, 68,2: 233–53.

Sandberg, E.N. and Shambaugh, G.E. (1993) 'Prospects for North–South negotiations in a changing international political economy', in I.W. Zartman (ed.) *Europe and Africa: The New Phase*, Boulder CO, Lynne Reiner: 159–78.

Sbragia, A. (1996) 'Environmental policy: the "push-pull" of policy making', in H. Wallace and W. Wallace (eds) *Policy Making in the European Union*, Oxford, Oxford University Press: 235–55.

Schulte, G.L. (1997) 'Former Yugoslavia and the new NATO', *Survival*, 39,1: 19–42.

Seddon, D. (1995) 'European aid or trade for South African development?', *Review of African Political Economy*, 66, December: 585–8.

Sedelmeier, U. (1994) 'The European Union's association policy towards Central and Eastern Europe: political and economic rationales in conflict', *Working Papers in Contemporary European Studies*, 7, University of Sussex: Sussex European Institute.

Sedelmeier, U. and Wallace, H. (1996) 'Policies towards Central and Eastern Europe', in H. Wallace and W. Wallace (eds) *Policy-Making in the European Union*, Oxford, Oxford University Press: 353–88.

Seifert, W. (1997) 'Admission policy, patterns of migration and integration: the German and French case compared', *New Community*, 23,4: 441–60.

Shaw, T.M. (1979) 'EEC–ACP interaction and images as redefinitions of Eurafrica: exemplary, exclusive and/or exploitative?', *Journal of Common Market Studies*, XVIII: 135–58.

Shevstov, L.P. (1997) 'Russian–NATO military cooperation in Bosnia: a basis for the future?', *NATO Review*, March: 17–21.

Sibeon, R. (1997) *Contemporary Sociology and Policy Analysis: the New Sociology of Public Policy*, Eastham, Wirral: Tudor Business Publishing.

Siotis, J. (1974) 'The European Economic Community and its emerging Mediterranean policy', in F.A.M. Alting von Geusau (ed.) *The External Relations of the European Community: Perspectives, Policies and Responses*, Westmead, Saxon House: 69–83.

Singer, J.D. (1961) 'The level of analysis problem in international relations', in K. Knorr and S. Verby (eds) *The International System: Theoretical Essays*, Princeton, Princeton University Press: 77–92.

Sjöstedt, G. (1977) *The External Role of the European Community*, Farnborough: Saxon House.

Skjaerseth, J.B. (1994) 'The climate policy of the EC: too hot to handle?', *Journal of Common Market Studies*, 32,1: 25–45.

Smith, A. (1992) 'National identity and the idea of European unity', *International Affairs*, 68,1: 55–76.

Smith, A., Holmes, P., Sedelmeier, U., Smith, E., Wallace, H., Young, A., (1996) 'The European Union and Central and Eastern Europe: pre-accession strategies', *Working Papers in Contemporary European Studies*, 15, University of Sussex: Sussex European Institute.

Smith, C.J. (1996) 'Conflict in the Balkans and the possibility of a European Union common foreign and security policy', *International Relations*, XIII,2: 1–21.

Smoke, R. (ed.) (1996) *Perceptions of Security: Public opinion and expert assessment in Europe's new democracies*, Manchester: Manchester University Press.

Solana, J. (1996) 'NATO's role in Bosnia: charting a new course for the Alliance', *NATO Review*, March: 3–6.

Somsen, H. (1996) 'The European Union and the Organization for Economic Cooperation and Development', in J. Werksman (ed.) *Greening International Institutions*, London, Earthscan: 181–204.

Sondermann, F.A. (1961) 'The linkage between foreign policy and international politics', in J.N. Rosenau (ed.) *International Politics and Foreign Policy: a Reader in Research and Theory* (1st edn), New York, Free Press: 8–17.

Sperling, J. and Kirchner, E. (1997) *Recasting the European Order: Security Architectures and Economic Cooperation*, Manchester: Manchester University Press.

Stanovnik, P. and Svetličič, M. (1996) 'Slovenia and the European Union' Paper presented at Experts Meeting on the Economic Aspects of Slovenia's Integration into the European Union, Bled: 12–13 April.

Stevens, C. (1996) 'EU policy for the banana market: the external impact of internal policies', in H. Wallace and W. Wallace (eds) *Policy-Making in the European Union*, Oxford, Oxford University Press: 325–52.

— — (1997) 'How substantial is EU tariff discrimination?', *GEI Working Paper*, 31, ESRC.

Story, J. (ed.) (1993) *The New Europe: Politics, Government and Economy Since 1945*, Oxford: Blackwell.

Sutherland, P. (1997) 'The case for EMU', *Foreign Affairs*, 76,1: 9–14.

Swann, D. (1975) *The Economics of the Common Market*, Harmondsworth: Penguin.

Szajkowski, B. (1997) 'Poland', in R. Eatwell (ed.) *European Political Culture: Conflict or Convergence?*, London, Routledge: 157–71.

Taylor, P. (1996) *The European Union in the 1990s*, Oxford: Oxford University Press.

Thagesen, R. and Matthews, A. (1997) 'The EU's common banana regime: an initial evaluation', *Journal of Common Market Studies*, 35,4: 615–27.

Thränhardt, D. (1996) 'European migration from East to West: present patterns and future directions', *New Community*, 22,2: 227–42.

Töre, N. (1990) 'Relations between the European Community and Turkey', *European Access*, 3: 8–11.

Tunander, O. (1997) 'Post-Cold War Europe: synthesis of a bipolar friend-foe structure and a hierarchic cosmos-chaos structure', in O. Tunander, P. Baev and V.I. Einagel (eds) *Geopolitics in Post-Wall Europe: Security, Territory and Identity*, London, Sage: 17–44.

United Nations Development Programme (1994) *Human Development Report 1994*, Oxford: Oxford University Press.

— — (1995) *Human Development Report 1995*, Oxford: Oxford University Press.

— — (1996) *Human Development Report 1996*, Oxford: Oxford University Press.

— — (1997) *Human Development Report 1997*, Oxford: Oxford University Press.

United States Mission to the European Union (1996) *US–EU: the New Transatlantic Agenda*, Brussels: Public Affairs Office.

Urwin, D.W. (1991) *The Community of Europe: a History of European Integration since 1945*, Harlow: Longman.

van Reisen, M. (1997a) 'European Union', in J. Randel and T. German (eds) *The Reality of Aid*, London, Earthscan: 160–78.

— — (1997b) 'The EU and Africa', in J. Randel and T. German (eds) *The Reality of Aid*, London, Earthscan: 179–90.

Vaughan, R. (1976) *Post-War Integration in Europe*, London: Edward Arnold.

Vellinga, P. and Grubb, M. (eds) (1993) *Climate Change Policy in the European Community*, London: RIIA.

Vogler, J.F. (1995) *The Global Commons: a Regime Analysis*, Chichester: John Wiley.

— — (1996) 'The structures of global politics', in C. Bretherton and G. Ponton (eds) *Global Politics: an Introduction*, Oxford, Blackwell: 23–48.

— — (1997) 'Environment and natural resources', in W. White, R. Little and M. Smith (eds) *Issues in World Politics*, London, Macmillan: 222–42.

Wæver, O. (1995) 'Identity, integration and security: solving the sovereignty puzzle in E.U. studies', *Journal of International Affairs*, 48,2: 399–439.

— — (1996) 'European security identities', *Journal of Common Market Studies*, 34,1: 103–32.

Wæver, O., Buzan, B., Kelstrup, M. and Lemaitre, P. (1993) *Identity, Migration and the New Security Agenda in Europe*, London: Pinter.

Wallace, H. and Wallace, W. (eds) (1996) (3rd edn) *Policy-Making in the European Union*, Oxford: Oxford Univerity Press.

Wallace, W. (1990) *The Transformation of Western Europe*, London: Pinter.

Wallace, W. and Smith, J. (1995) 'Democracy or technocracy? European integration and the problem of popular consent', *West European Politics*, 18,3: 138–57.

Wallerstein, I. (1984) *The Politics of the World–Economy*, Cambridge: Cambridge University Press.

— — (1991) *Geopolitics and Geoculture: Essays on the Changing world-system*, Cambridge: Cambridge University Press.

Waltz, K.N. (1979) *The Theory of International Politics*, Reading MA: Addison-Wesley.

Weale, A. (1992) *The New Politics of Pollution*, Manchester: Manchester University Press.

— — (1995) 'From little England to democratic Europe?', *New Community*, 21,2: 215–25.

Weigall, D. and Stirk, P. (1992) *The Origins and Development of the European Community*, Leicester: Leicester University Press.

Weiner, A. and Della Sala, V. (1997) 'Constitution-making and citizenship practice – bridging the democracy gap in the EU?', *Journal of Common Market Studies*, 35,4: 595–614.

Welsh, J.M. (1993) 'A people's Europe? European citizenship and European identity', *Politics*, 13,2: 25–31.

Wendt, A. (1994) 'Collective identity formation and the international state', *American Political Science Review*, 88,2: 384–96.

Werksman, J. (ed.) (1996) *Greening International Institutions*, London: Earthscan.

Western European Union Council of Ministers (1994) *Preliminary Conclusions on the Formulation of a Common European Defence Policy*, Noordwijk: 14 November.

—— (1995) *WEU Contribution to the European Union Intergovernmental Conference of 1996*, Madrid: 14 November.

Whitney, C.R. (1994) 'US and Europe of two minds on security needs', *International Herald Tribune*, 3 December.

Winrow, G.M. (1996) 'A threat from the South? NATO and the Mediterranean', *Mediterranean Politics*, 1,1: 43–59.

Winters, L.A. (1994) 'The EC and world protectionism: dimensions of the political economy', *Discussion Paper*, 897, London: CEPR.

Woolcock, S. (1996) 'An agenda for the WTO: strengthening or overburdening the system?', *GEI Working Paper*, 17, ESRC.

Woolcock, S. and Hodges, M. (1996) 'EU policy in the Uruguay Round', in H. Wallace and W. Wallace (eds) *Policy-Making in the European Union*, Oxford, Oxford University Press: 301–24.

WTO Trade Policy Review Body (1997a) *European Union: Report by the Secretariat*, http://www.wto.org/wto/reviews.

—— (1997b) *Review of the European Union's TPRB Evaluation*, http://www.wto.org/wto/reviews.

Wurzel, R.K.W. (1996) 'The role of the EU Presidency in the environmental field: does it make a difference which state runs the Presidency?', *Journal of European Public Policy*, 3,2: 272–91.

Young, O.R. (1972) 'The actors in world politics', in J.N. Rosenau, V. Davies and M.A. East (eds) *The Analysis of International Politics*, New York, Free Press: 125–44.

—— (1989) *International Cooperation: Building Regimes for Natural Resources and Environment*, Ithaca and London: Cornell University Press.

Zartman, I.W. (ed.) (1993) *Europe and Africa: The New Phase*, Boulder CO: Lynne Reiner.

Zetterholm, S. (ed.) (1994) *National Cultures and European Integration: Exploratory Essays on Cultural Diversity and Common Policies*, Oxford: Berg.

Index